Moonpaths

Moonpaths

Ethics and Emptiness

THE COWHERDS

OXFORD
UNIVERSITY PRESS

OXFORD
UNIVERSITY PRESS

Oxford University Press is a department of the University of Oxford. It furthers the University's objective of excellence in research, scholarship, and education by publishing worldwide.

Oxford New York
Auckland Cape Town Dar es Salaam Hong Kong Karachi
Kuala Lumpur Madrid Melbourne Mexico City Nairobi
New Delhi Shanghai Taipei Toronto

With offices in
Argentina Austria Brazil Chile Czech Republic France Greece
Guatemala Hungary Italy Japan Poland Portugal Singapore
South Korea Switzerland Thailand Turkey Ukraine Vietnam

Oxford is a registered trademark of Oxford University Press in the UK and certain other countries.

Published in the United States of America by
Oxford University Press
198 Madison Avenue, New York, NY 10016

Cataloging-in-Publication data is on file at the Library of Congress
ISBN 978–0–19–026050–7 (hbk.); 978–0–19–026051–4 (pbk.)

9 8 7 6 5 4 3 2 1
Printed in the United States of America
on acid-free paper

Contents

Acknowledgments

We thank the College of Humanities and Social and Behavioral Sciences of Central Michigan University for generous financial and logistical support for the conclave that launched this project and the Central Michigan Department of Philosophy and Religion for hosting us. Thanks also to Yale-NUS College for research support, and to Ling Xi Min and Rocco Hu for research assistance in the preparation of this volume.

List of Contributors

AMBER CARPENTER is Associate Professor at Yale-NUS, and Senior Lecturer in Philosophy at the University of York. Her Ph.D. (London) focused on Greek philosophy; her publications in international specialist journals concern primarily Plato's metaphysical ethics, and related epistemological issues—including the intelligence of plants. She is a co-founder of the Yorkshire Ancient Philosophy Network. Her book, *Indian Buddhist Philosophy*, appeared in 2014; her study in the *pudgalavādins* can be found in *The Moon Points Back* (2015). A recent discussion of Greeks and Indians together came out in the *Proceedings of the Aristotelian Society*, Supplementary Volume 2014. She coordinates, with Rachael Wiseman, the Integrity Project (integrityproject.org).

JAY L. GARFIELD is Kwan Im Thong Hood Cho Temple Professor of Humanities and Head of Studies in Philosophy at Yale-NUS College, Professor of Philosophy at the National University of Singapore, Recurrent Visiting Professor of Philosophy at Yale University, Doris Silbert Professor in the Humanities and Professor of Philosophy at Smith College, Professor of Philosophy at Melbourne University, and Adjunct Professor of Philosophy at the Central University of Tibetan Studies. Garfield's most recent books include *Engaging Buddhism: Why it Matters to Philosophy* (2015), *Madhyamaka and Yogācāra: Allies or Rivals?* (edited, with Jan Westerhoff, 2015), *The Moon Points Back: Buddhism, Logic and Analytic Philosophy* (edited, with Yasuo Deguchi, Graham Priest and Koji Tanaka, 2015), *Indian Philosophy in English from Renaissance to Independence* (with Nalini Bhushan, 2011), and *Contrary Thinking: Selected Papers of Daya Krishna* (edited with Nalini Bhushan and Daniel Raveh, 2011) and, with the Cowherds, *Moonshadows: Conventional Truth in Buddhist Philosophy* (2010). *Investigation of the Percept* (with Douglas Duckworth, M David Eckel, John Powers, Yeshes Thabkhas and Sonam Thakchöe, as well as *Minds Without Fear: Philosophy in the Indian Renaissance* (with Nalini Bhushan) are forthcoming (2016 and 2017, respectively).

CHARLES GOODMAN earned his Ph.D. in Philosophy from the University of Michigan. He is Associate Professor in the Philosophy Department and the Department of Asian and Asian-American Studies at Binghamton University. Goodman is the author of several articles on Buddhist philosophy, ethics, and applied ethics, and of *Consequences of Compassion: An Interpretation and Defense of Buddhist Ethics* (2009). His second book, *The Training Anthology of Śāntideva: A Translation of the Śikṣā-samuccaya*, is forthcoming (2015).

STEPHEN JENKINS is Professor of Religious Studies at Humboldt State University. Beginning with his doctoral work at Harvard University, his research has focused on Buddhist concepts of compassion, their philosophical grounding, and their use in the rationalization of warfare and other forms of violence.

GUY NEWLAND received a Ph.D. in the History of Religions from the University of Virginia in 1988. He is Professor of Religion at Central Michigan University where he has taught since 1988. He collaborated in translating Tsongkhapa's *Great Treatise on Stages of the Path to Enlightenment* (2015) and he translated the Dalai Lama's commentary thereon, *From Here to Enlightenment* (2014), and, with the Cowherds, *Moonshadows: Conventional Truth in Buddhist Philosophy* (2010). His other books include *Introduction to Emptiness* (2008), *Appearance and Reality* (1999), *Changing Minds* (ed., 2001), and *The Two Truths* (1992).

GRAHAM PRIEST is Distinguished Professor of Philosophy at the Graduate Center, City University of New York, and Boyce Gibson Professor Emeritus at the University of Melbourne. He is known for his work on non-classical logic, particularly in connection with dialetheism, on the history of philosophy, and on Buddhist philosophy. He has published articles in nearly every major philosophy and logic journal. His books include: *In Contradiction: A Study of the Transconsistent*, Martinus Nijhoff 1987 (2nd ed., 2006); *Beyond the Limits of Thought*, 1995 (2nd ed., 2002); *Towards Non-Being: the Semantics and Metaphysics of Intentionality* (2005); *Doubt Truth to be a Liar* (2006); *Introduction to Non-Classical Logic From If to Is* (2008); *One* (2014).

MARK SIDERITS has recently retired from the Philosophy Department of Seoul National University, where he taught Asian and comparative philosophy. His research interests lie in the intersection between classical Indian philosophy on the one hand, and analytic metaphysics and philosophy of language on the other. Among his more recent publications are *Buddhism As Philosophy* (2007), with the Cowherds, *Moonshadows: Conventional Truth in Buddhist Philosophy* (2011), *Personal Identity and Buddhist Philosophy: Empty Persons* (2nd ed., 2015), and, together with Shōryū Katsura, *Nāgārjuna's Middle Way: Mūlamadhyamakakārikā* (2013). He has also edited several collections of work on Indian/analytic philosophy including *Apoha: Buddhist Nominalism and Human Cognition* (with Tom Tillemans, 2011) and *Self, No-Self: Perspectives from Buddhist, Analytic and Phenomenological Traditions* (with Evan Thompson, 2013). A collection of his papers on Buddhist philosophy is forthcoming.

KOJI TANAKA is Lecturer in the School of Philosophy, Research School of Social Sciences, at the Australian National University. He works on paraconsistent logic, the philosophy of logic, Buddhist philosophy, and Chinese philosophy. He is co-editor of *Paraconsistency: Logic and Applications* (2012) and is a co-author, with the Cowherds of *Moonshadows: Conventional Truth in Buddhist Philosophy* (2011) as well as numerous papers in logic and Buddhist philosophy.

SONAM THAKCHÖE is Senior Lecturer in Philosophy in the School of Humanities at the University of Tasmania and Director of the University of Tasmania Buddhist Studies in India Program. He holds an Acharya degree from the Central University of Tibetan Studies and a Ph.D. in Philosophy from the University of Tasmania. He is the author of *The Two Truths Debate: Tsongkhapa and Gorampa on the Middle Way* (2007), and with the Cowherds, *Moonshadows: Conventional Truth in Buddhist Philosophy* (2011). His has also published several peer reviewed academic articles.

JAN WESTERHOFF is Associate Professor of Religious Ethics at the University of Oxford, a Fellow and Tutor in Theology and Religion at Lady Margaret Hall, University of Oxford, and a Research Associate at the School of Oriental and African Studies, University of London. His publications include *Nāgarjuna's Madhyamaka* (2009), *The Dispeller of Disputes: Nāgārjuna's Vigrahavyāvartanī* (2010), and *Reality: A Very Short Introduction* (2011). His research concentrates on systematic aspects of ancient Indian Philosophy, especially on Madhyamaka.

Moonpaths

Introduction

Why Ask about Madhyamaka and Ethics?

Jay L. Garfield and Graham Priest

This volume is a successor to our previous polygraph, *Moonshadows: Conventional Truth in Buddhist Philosophy* (Cowherds 2011). Just as that volume was our collective attempt to understand what it is to take truth seriously in the context of the Madhyamaka doctrine of emptiness, this volume is our collective attempt to understand how to take ethics seriously in that metaphysical context. (Some interpret Madhyamaka as a *rejection* of metaphysics. Arguably, this is itself a metaphysical attitude. But at any rate, in what follows, when we refer to metaphysics, this is to be understood as including this possibility.) It is one thing to take the doctrine of the two truths seriously as providing an account of how the world *is*, and to assent to the claim that nothing is more than conventionally real. It is another to understand its consequences for an understanding of ethics and morality. The Cowherds have set themselves the tasks of working out those consequences in a way that does justice to the Madhyamaka tradition in the contemporary philosophical context.

Although Buddhism is manifestly concerned with ethics—with the character of a morally commendable life—it has become almost a commonplace to note how thin the canonical Buddhist literature is on explicit articulation of ethical *theory* or *metaethics*. Indeed, the scarcity of literature attending to the kind of ethical questions so often asked in the Western philosophical tradition in part explains the large and contentious literature attempting to reconstruct the structure of Buddhist ethical theory (Clayton 2001, 2006; Finnigan 2011, 2015; Garfield 2010/2011, 2012, 2015; Gethin 1998; Gómez 1973; Goodman 2002, 2009; Hallisey 1996; Keown 2001, 2005; Siderits 2006, 2007, to name but a few). Nonetheless, despite the scarcity of *theory*, there is a lot of ethical discourse in the Buddhist canon, scattered among *sutta* and *sūtra*, *vinaya*, and *śāstra*. The richness and variety of that discourse both inform Buddhist moral thought and confound those who would easily systematize it.

Buddhist ethical thought begins in what is canonically regarded as the originary Buddhist teaching, the *Dhammacakkapavattana-sutta*, the first discourse given by Siddhārtha Gautama after attaining awakening, at the Deer Park in Sarnath. This *sutta* presents an analysis of the human condition as profoundly unsatisfactory, together with a prescription for escaping that unsatisfactory state. The bad news is that life is characterized by *dukkha* (suffering, pain, discontent, unsatisfactoriness, unhappiness, sorrow, affliction, anxiety, dissatisfaction, discomfort, anguish, stress, misery, and frustration). This is caused by *tṛṣṇā*, or powerful desire—also called *rāga*, an attitude of attachment, and *dveśa*, an attitude of aversion—based in turn on a primal confusion, or delusion, regarding the way that things are (*avidyā*), and especially the illusion that there is a real self.

The good news is that one can get rid of this network of dysfunctional psychological attitudes, and hence of the *dukkha*. This is not easy, however, as it involves a fundamental transformation of our orientation to the world. The route to this solution is the noble eightfold path (*āryāṣṭāṅgamārga*): right view, right intention, right speech, right action, right livelihood, right effort, right mindfulness, right concentration. Following this path, and all the things this entails, is therefore the correct way to live. Of course, this is only an outline of an ethics, and a vast and scattered literature, including narratives, monastic codes, and some systematic moral texts, articulate the details in a variety of ways. Buddhaghosa's *Visuddhimagga* (*Path of Purification*), for instance, develops a sophisticated Theravāda moral psychology (see Heim 2013).

Now, as we can already see in the four noble truths, Buddhist ethics—however it is to be understood—is closely connected to metaphysics as well as to psychology; and the Buddhist world has produced a variety of metaphysical theories, some resolutely realist and reductionist, some idealist, and some that are neither of these. Madhyamaka is of the last of these kinds. It was initiated by Nāgārjuna, and delivered one of the most sophisticated Buddhist metaphysical programs. While many previous Buddhist scholars provided candidate analyses of the fundamental nature of reality, Nāgārjuna argued that there is no fundamental nature of reality. Instead, everything, he argues, in virtue of being dependently arisen, is empty (*śūnya*) of intrinsic nature (*svabhāva*). This analysis in terms of emptiness, or *śūnyavāda,* leads to a reconceptualization of the familiar Buddhist hermeneutical device of the two truths: in the hands of Nāgārjuna and his Mādhyamika followers, it becomes not only ontological (or perhaps meta-ontological), but apparently paradoxical: the ultimate truth is emptiness; nothing exists ultimately, even emptiness itself. Therefore everything exists only conventionally. This immediately raises the question of what kind of truth conventional truth is, and the question of what kind of existence conventional existence is. These are the questions we addressed in *Moonshadows*.

In this volume, we turn our attention from the implications of Madhyamaka for metaphysics and epistemology to its implications for ethics. The connection between ethics and metaphysics is not an innocent one, nor is it one that Nāgārjuna and his followers ignored. After all, just as we can ask whether to be conventionally real or conventionally true is good enough to ground real ontology and real epistemology, or whether it degenerates into cheap relativism in those domains, we can ask whether an ethical doctrine expressed merely in the register of convention can be taken seriously as a genuine theory of value, or whether it inevitably degenerates into either moral anti-realism or relativism.

Indian Mādhyamikas (and their Tibetan followers) took these problems seriously. Nāgārjuna himself takes up the problem of the implications of emptiness for the four noble truths in the 24th chapter of his *magnum opus, Mūlamadhyamakakārikā* (*Fundamental Verses on the Middle Way*), arguing that, while it might appear that the Madhyamaka analysis undermines the force of the truths, in fact it is the only way to make sense of them. In *Ratnāvalī* (*Garland of Jewels*) he addresses ethical concerns directly, providing moral advice to a king that, he claims, is grounded squarely in a Madhyamaka analysis of reality. Nāgārjuna's direct disciple, Āryadeva, develops his ethical theory directly on the basis of the doctrine of emptiness in his *Catuḥśataka* (*Four Hundred Verses*). Candrakīrti's commentary on that text is a fascinating example of the development of ethical ideas in the medium of narrative (Lang 2003), following the tradition of *avadāna* stories (explored in detail in Rotman 2008). And Śāntideva, in perhaps the most extensive treatment of Mahāyāna ethics by any Indian scholar, explicitly connects metaphysics, psychology, and ethics in great detail in his *Bodhicāryāvatāra* (*Engaging in the Bodhisattva's Way of Life,* or *How to Lead an Awakened Life*).

Nāgārjuna, Candrakīrti, and Śāntideva figure prominently in this volume, whose task is the examination of Buddhist ethics in the context of Madhyamaka metaphysics. Our exploration is explicitly philosophical: that is, we are concerned primarily to answer questions about the structure and cogency of

Madhyamaka ethical theory, and the degree to which it is grounded in, or undermined by, the doctrine of emptiness. So, for instance, one question we address concerns the status of the attitude of *karuṇā* or "care" (sometimes translated as "compassion"). Some have argued that the centrality of care to Mahāyāna ethics rests directly on Madhyamaka metaphysics; others (particularly Williams 1998, 2000) have argued that Madhyamaka metaphysics makes it unintelligible. We are also concerned with whether Madhyamaka ethics inevitably degenerates into relativism, given its inescapably conventional status.

We begin our investigations in Chapter 1 with a survey of the multiple approaches to ethics in the Buddhist tradition, in an effort to situate the tradition with which we are most concerned—the Madhyamaka—not only in the general landscape of Buddhism, but in the more specific context of Buddhist (and Western) ethical reflection. This sets the context for addressing some of the foundational texts on their own terms. In Chapter 2, we consider how to read Nāgārjuna's ethical theory as it is articulated in *Ratnāvalī,* using Greek ethical thought as an entrée. Then, in Chapter 3, we turn directly to the problem of relativism that arises from at least one plausible reading of Candrakīrti's understanding of conventional truth, building on the analysis of this problem in *Moonshadows.* Considering the ethical implication of relativism that arises from one plausible reading of Candrakīrti draws our attention to the danger of degenerating into moral relativism, as we argued in the last chapter of *Moonshadows.* Whether emptiness really forces us to fall into the relativistic pit or not, it is important to recall the argument advanced in that volume and to remind ourselves that an articulation of Madhyamaka ethics is not a straightforward matter.

Chapter 4 continues to develop this historical foundation, addressing the problematic but inescapably important passage from the eighth chapter of *Bodhicaryāvatāra,* introducing and explaining each of the three readings represented in canonical and modern literature, each of which will play a role in later chapters in the volume. Śantideva's *Bodhicaryāvatāra* is among the most influential and important Indian texts on Mahāyāna Buddhist ethics. It virtually defines the Tibetan ethical landscape. One of the central philosophical discussions of *karuṇā* occurs in Chapter VIII (roughly, vv. 90–103), where Śāntideva defends the importance of this moral attitude. But this argument is susceptible to multiple readings; and how one reads it inflects the way one reads the remainder of this text. So, part of understanding the content of Madhyamaka ethics, as articulated in this important philosophical source, requires us to engage with the important passage. In Chapter 4 we articulate the three most common readings of this passage. A fourth reading emerges in Chapter 7.

Chapters 5 and 6 address the Śāntideva passage directly. In the fifth chapter we consider one of the three principal readings of the passage—the rationality reading—and connect it directly with Buddhist ethical thought grounded in the eightfold path, and to the early Madhyamaka ethics of Nāgārjuna and Āryadeva. Chapter 6 builds on that analysis, investigating the *ālambana*, or intentional object, of *karuṇā*. This question arises naturally, once one takes seriously the framework of emptiness and of the two truths: how are bodhisattvas, or ethical agents more generally, to regard themselves and others in the context of an attitude of care? As conventional persons? As instances of emptiness? This chapter also serves as a pivot in our dialectic, initiating a move from more historically grounded to more explicitly systematic reflections.

The seventh and eighth chapters move to metaethical ground. In Chapter 7, we ask to what extent it makes sense to systematize Buddhist ethical thought, and into what kind of system it might be systematized. The chapter also considers the charge that the Śāntideva passage, as read by Prajñākaramati, is inconsistent with the Madhyamaka doctrine of emptiness. Chapter 8 articulates one way that Buddhist ethics might be systematized as a coherent metaethical framework—as a family of consequentialist theories.

Chapters 9 and 10 address the connections between metaphysical accounts of the structure of action in Indian and Tibetan Madhyamaka and ethical thought. Karma—the theory of action and its results—has always played an important role in Buddhist ethical reflection. But the Buddhist doctrine of radical momentariness and the doctrine of selflessness raise puzzles regarding the mechanisms by which karma is transmitted both within and between lives, and regarding the attribution of moral responsibility over time. In the ninth chapter, we consider the often-neglected, but critical role of the metaphysics of momentariness in Prāsaṅgika-Madhyamaka for thinking about the relation between action and its consequences, and so for the account of karma so central to much Buddhist ethical thought. Chapter 10 continues this discussion, investigating the ways in which Tibetan scholars understood this account of karma in the context of conventional truth.

The final two chapters of the book are more general philosophical investigations of the relationship between metaphysics and ethics in Madhyamaka. They are less textually grounded, and more concerned with rational reconstruction. The eleventh chapter develops an account that meets the challenge we considered in the Chapter 3, re-reading Candrakīrti in light of the results of the intervening chapters so as to provide a non-relativistic foundation for the ethical project, and arguing that that is precisely the foundation which Śāntideva employs. We conclude in Chapter 12 with an argument that a metaphor from the *Avataṃsaka* or *Huayan (Flower Ornament) Sūtra* which became popular in China as an illustration of the phenomenon of interdependence—that of the net of Indra—may provide the best underpinning of all for the attitude of *karuṇā* central to Mahāyāna moral thought.

An appendix provides a new, and we hope authoritative, translation of *Bodhicaryāvatāra* VIII.90–103 with the commentary by Prajñākaramati. Since this passage plays a central role in many of our discussions, it will be useful to the reader to consult this influential Indian commentary.

The reader will note that individuals or sets of individuals are associated as authors with each chapter. We do take individual and joint responsibility for each chapter, though we do not claim unanimity on all points. This historical material is far from univocal, and reasonable cowherds can disagree about how certain texts and doctrines are to be interpreted, even while agreeing about the broad framework of the two truths and about the fundamental commitments of Buddhist ethics. But we do present what we take to be a cogent, sustained, and collegial examination of the issues raised in Madhyamaka ethics. We have commented extensively on one another's work, have responded to comments, and have often revised our views in light of our fellow cowherds' critique. While individual chapters may reflect the views of their authors to a greater degree than they do the views of the collective, the volume as a whole is our joint product, and we offer it to you in that spirit: a spirit in which insight emerges best from productive interchange among scholars.

1

The Many Voices of Buddhist Ethics

Charles Goodman and Sonam Thakchöe

Buddhist texts frequently extol the value of developing extraordinary generosity, self-sacrifice, and forbearance, and they glorify legendary figures who manifest these virtues. Nonetheless, these texts consistently assert that neither the agents nor the beneficiaries of these actions ultimately exist. According to all schools of Buddhist philosophy, the misconception of the self as substantial, unchanging, and eternal lies at the root of the psychological patterns that lead to immoral behavior. As a result, in order to develop ethical virtues to the extraordinary degree that Buddhism claims is possible, the practitioner must recognize the absence of any real self and the impermanence of the aggregates, the various changing factors that make up the empirical personality. The destruction of self-centered desires, then, necessarily depends on the realization that the elements of our experience arise and cease in each moment. Buddhist ethics is intimately connected, at various depths and to various degrees, with the commitment to non-self and impermanence.

These joint commitments often give rise to seemingly paradoxical statements. For example, in the *Diamond Sūtra*, the Buddha discusses the insight of a spiritual practitioner engaged in the labor of saving all beings from suffering, who yet knows: "Though I thus liberate countless beings, not a single being is liberated" (Red Pine 2001, p. 3). Nevertheless, many Buddhist philosophers insist that their views are consistent, and offer subtle explanations of how these commitments can be reconciled within an impeccably logical understanding of how things are.

It is obvious that doctrines about karma are closely relevant to Buddhist ethics, although the exact role of karma in Buddhist normative thinking is a subject of discussion among scholars. According to many Buddhist doctrines of karma, actions or intentions that harm others set in motion a causal process that eventually leads to suffering for the actor, often in future lives. Indeed, the nature of those future lives is itself determined by this same karmic process. Meanwhile, when an agent intentionally acts to benefit others, consequences will result. These can take the form either of worldly happiness, or of the kind of favorable conditions that make possible the pursuit of spiritual practice and the path toward liberation from bondage to cyclic existence.

These ideas are shared in common among many Buddhist traditions. But there is not just one Buddhist ethical view. The Buddhist tradition is rich and complex, and contains many voices. This is true quite generally, whether the topic is metaphysics, epistemology, meditation, ritual, or other aspects of philosophy and doctrine. It applies, in particular, to Buddhist reflections about what to do and how to live, which we may call "ethics." Indeed, as a very large number of authors, from a wide range of geographical regions and over a long period of time, have contributed to Buddhist discussions of how to live, it would be surprising if they all agreed on the full range of normative issues that they consider.

Fortunately for those trying to make sense of Buddhism, when we restrict our attention to ethics, we can bring some order to this diversity, for the significant differences in this area are mainly between the Mahāyāna (Greater Vehicle, or Great Way), on the one hand, and, on the other hand, non-Mahāyāna traditions, which include a collection of diverse schools from Buddhism's earliest time, as well as the Theravāda now current in, for instance, Sri Lanka and Thailand. The Mahāyāna distinguishes itself by its central commitment to the Bodhisattva vow. This vow commits the Mahāyāna practitioner to remain in cyclic existence for as long as there are suffering beings, acting continually to save and benefit others.

It is (at least in the eyes of the Mahāyāna) an aim markedly different from the aspiration of most Theravādins to attain *nirvāṇa* directly, which will involve the cultivation of loving-kindness and compassion, but will not therefore commit the accomplished person (the ārhat) to remaining in the world after the life in which liberation is attained. Many ethical differences among Buddhists can be traced back to this central difference. But the Mahāyāna itself is not a univocal position, for there were many ways of developing the nature and implications of the Bodhisattva vow, as well as the complicated metaphysics and epistemology of the Buddhist view itself. In India, the Mahāyāna split into two schools: the Yogācāra (masters of practice, also called Cittamātra or

Mind-Only), and the Madhyamaka (or Middle Way School), with which this volume will be primarily concerned.

According to many Mahāyāna Buddhists, the diversity of views within Buddhism is both largely explained and further complicated by the workings of *upāya-kauśalya*, or skill in means. Both the historical Buddha and his more advanced followers are seen as having the ability to know what kind of teaching would be best suited to help each individual student. As a result, they often make statements that do not express their highest or final understanding of how things are, but rather are adapted to the level of understanding of those to whom they are addressed. According to Book X of the *Avataṃsaka Sūtra*,

> Of the past, present
> And future guides,
> None expounds just one method
> To become enlightened.
>
> Buddhas know beings' mind;
> Their natures each different;
> According to what they need to be freed,
> Thus do the Buddhas teach.
>
> To the stingy they praise giving,
> To the immoral they praise ethics;
> To the angry they praise tolerance,
> To the lazy they praise effort.
>
> To those with scattered minds they praise meditative concentration,
> To the ignorant, they praise wisdom;
> To the inhuman, they praise kindness and sympathy,
> To the malicious, compassion.
>
> To the troubled they praise joy,
> To the devious they praise equanimity.
> Thus practicing step-by-step,
> One gradually fulfills all Buddha teachings. (Cleary 1993, pp. 307–308)

This kind of rhetoric is quite typical of the Mahāyāna *sūtras*. It allows Buddhists to explain the existence of forms of Buddhism other than their own as expressions of the Buddha's compassionate concern for those not ready to hear the supreme teaching. It also suggests that, just as there is no single method for awakening, so there may be a variety of ethical norms and practices that are suitable for individuals at different stages of their journeys to awakening. This is an important aspect of multivocality within Buddhism: individual texts are addressed to particular audiences at particular times; not every text is even expected to speak to everyone.

Does it follow that Buddhist ethical teachings cannot be brought under any one single ethical theory? Some Cowherds would say yes. They would draw, for example, on Vasubandhu's and Asaṅga's assessments of the speech of awakened beings. A given act of speech of an awakened person, for Asaṅga, can be evaluated as ethical on many levels. Such an act is rooted in empathy, renunciation, and wisdom, which are, according to Asaṅga, (1) *ethical by nature.* Chapters 2 and 5 of this volume develop this argument.

As Asaṅga goes on to explain, mental consciousness as well as all other accompanying ethically variable mental factors (such as feeling, volition, perception, etc.) associated with the wholesome roots of noble speech, are (2) *ethical by association.* Noble speech as a vocal activity is (3) *ethical by the original cause* for it is motivated by empathy, renunciation, and wisdom, which are its good roots.

The virtuous marks or wholesome impressions left by the activity of noble speech, or the dispositions cultivated in the mental continuum of the speaker due to noble speech, including the joy and happiness it produces in the minds of its listeners, are (4) *ethical by the subsequent relation,* for they act as triggers of future virtuous actions. And the ultimate beatitude of *nirvāṇa*, which is a total freedom from afflictive defilements, of which a noble speech is a necessary causal condition, is (5) *ethically ultimate,* for it is the fulfillment of the ultimate goal of noble speech.

For these reasons, these Cowherds think that Buddhist ethics is multivocal in a further way: it includes considerations we would see as belonging to many different forms of ethical theory, without making any effort to bring these considerations together into one theoretical framework whose structure we can express in the terms of Western normative discourse. Indeed, some claim that the lack of ethical theory in Buddhist texts reflects the valuable insight that no general ethical theory is even possible.

Other Cowherds disagree, and this view is explored in Chapter 8. For example, the *sūtra* quote above does in fact say something quite general about how Buddhas behave: "according to what they need to be freed, thus do the Buddhas teach." It could be argued that this common element should be understood in terms of what we in the West call consequentialism. Consequentialism has itself had many forms. While act-consequentialists evaluate our actions in terms of the value of their consequences, there are indirect forms of consequentialism that evaluate rules or states of character according to the consequences they produce indirectly. Moreover, historically the most important forms of consequentialism, as in the utilitarianism advocated by Mill and Sidgwick, have been welfarist—assessing states of affairs according to how well the lives of sentient beings go. A welfarist consequentialist interpretation of Mahāyāna ethics can draw support from numerous textual passages that describe accomplishing the welfare of all sentient beings as the central goal of the bodhisattva.

However, the likeness is not straightforward. Notoriously, utilitarians and other Western consequentialist ethicists hold that it can often be morally permissible, or even morally required, to kill some people in order to save others from death. But Buddhist texts have often been extremely reluctant to endorse killing under any but the most extreme and unlikely circumstances. Buddhism's very strong rejection of violent means, even to achieve apparently beneficial ends, may depend, at least in part, on the idea that if the agent's motives are not completely pure, severe consequences for the agent's character and psychology may result, together with the view that no ordinary agent's motivations have the purity requisite to kill without karmic consequences. The position of non-ordinary agents is different; thus, notable *Jātaka* stories contain instances of killing by previous bodhisattva instances of the Buddha.

Several influential scholars, most notably Damien Keown (2001), have proposed that Buddhism should be understood as endorsing a form of virtue ethics. The fact that Buddhist texts often devote considerable effort to listing and analyzing various valuable states of character counts in favor of this proposal. Inspired largely by Aristotle's *Nicomachean Ethics*, contemporary virtue ethics moves the focus of ethical evaluation away from actions and toward the character traits that lead to action. The virtues are those character traits in virtue of which human beings flourish, or can be said to be faring well overall—or to be *eudaimon*. Such *eudaimonia* is comprehensive, not distinguishing "morality" from "self-interest" in the first place, so it is no surprise that virtue and happiness typically coincide, or at least that there is no true well-being separate from virtue. Contemporary writers such as Philippa Foot (2001), Rosalind Hursthouse (1999), Christine Swanton (2003), and Lisa Tessman (2005) have developed the basic framework of virtue ethics in quite different ways from Aristotle.

Once again, the analogies between Buddhist and Western views could not be taken to be straightforward. For instance, the centrality of the Buddhist metaphysics of no-self in ethical understanding may seem difficult to reconcile with a person-centred account of the ethical, such as virtue ethics aims to offer. The broader intellectual commitments of the Buddhist tradition affect how its ethical views can be understood. For example, in Buddhism, agent causation, to the extent that it exists at all, is wholly reducible to event causation. There is no agency at the ultimate level. These claims place any Buddhist ethical view in serious tension with any picture that depends on irreducible agent causation based on a real self. If some Western forms of virtue ethics depend on conceiving of agency as metaphysically fundamental, then in that respect they will differ from Buddhist understandings of virtue.

Particularist philosophers, such as Jonathan Dancy (2006), deny the very possibility of a general ethical theory. They see the difficulties and objections faced by utilitarian and Kantian views as evidence that one cannot give universal criteria for how to behave. Instead, each situation requires particular judgments about the set of relevant reasons that can neither be codified nor unified under any overarching framework. We should aspire to train ourselves to be subtle and perceptive in moral situations, and should abandon the aspiration to know systematic differences between right and wrong. Particularism can naturally be combined with some forms of virtue ethics. The emphasis that many Buddhist texts place on the uniqueness of situations and the inconceivable nature of the skillful means of the buddhas can be seen as evidence for this interpretation.

Given that there are these disagreements and difficulties about how to understand the overall structure of Buddhist ethical reflection, how is it possible to work toward a better understanding of normative teachings in this tradition? We can begin to get a grip on the distinctive shape of Buddhist ethical thought by considering the central terms appealed to in Buddhist discussions of how we ought to be and act. One of these is the Sanskrit word *śīla*, translated into Tibetan as *tshul khrims*. In older English translations, this term has often been rendered as "ethics." But such a translation misses the fact that *śīla* has an especially close connection to a particular set of vows or commitments that a practitioner takes on, a resonance that is missing from English "ethics." Thus, for example, the fundamental Buddhist commitments usually are called the Five Precepts (*pañca-śīla*). This problem creates serious pitfalls for translators. Mark Tatz renders a passage from the *Bodhisattva-bhūmi* as follows:

> What is the essence of ethics? Briefly, to possess four qualities constitutes the essence of the ethics of the bodhisattva. What are the four? To correctly receive it from someone else, to have a quite purified intention, to make correction after failure, and to avoid failure by generating respect and remaining mindful of that. (Tatz 1986, p. 47)

To a reader trained in Western philosophy but uninformed about Buddhism, this passage is difficult to understand, because it focuses on a portion of the semantic range of *śīla* not shared with English "ethics."

To correct this problem, we could choose to translate *śīla* as "moral discipline." Such a translation captures the fact that to possess *śīla* is understood as having taken certain morally significant vows, and then actually possessing the capacity to fulfill those vows. However, some of the sets of vows that help to constitute *śīla*, such as the *prātimokṣa* commitments of Buddhist monks and nuns, also include numerous non-moral matters having to do with courteous and dignified behavior. For example, Śāntideva writes:

> One should not eat with a mouth overfull, noisily, nor with mouth wide open. One should not sit with one leg hanging down, likewise one should not rub both arms at the same time. (*BCA* V.92, Crosby and Skilton 1995, p. 42)

Śāntideva would regard the matters discussed in this verse as aspects of *śīla*, but they are not included in the obvious meaning of English "moral discipline." Nor could we render *śīla* simply as "discipline." Buddhists would not wish to dignify the rules of behavior of an army fighting an unjust war with a positive term such as *śīla*, but such an army could be highly disciplined.

We could try to solve this problem, in turn, by adopting a translation like "proper conduct." This phrase includes both etiquette and morality, thereby capturing the entire outward expression of *śīla*. What "proper conduct" is unable to capture is the fact that *śīla* also includes the inner states and habits of mind that make it possible to follow one's vows and commitments. These states could be seen as aspects of "moral discipline," but "proper conduct" cannot stretch to cover them. It seems that none of these proposals exactly matches the semantic range of the original. The reader should keep in mind this discussion when encountering the term *śīla* in the rest of this book.

The Sanskrit word *kuśala* (Tibetan *dge ba*) raises translation issues nearly as serious as those related to *śīla*. Etymologically, the word seems to mean "skillful," and some Buddhist uses of it are appropriately rendered in this way, such as the compound *upāya-kauśalya*, often translated as "skill in means," and the like. But elsewhere, *kuśala* is used to indicate positive evaluation so generally that it frequently seems appropriate to translate it as "good." There is also much to be said for "wholesome," adopted by prominent translators of Theravāda texts. Meanwhile, the equivalent term *dge ba* is routinely rendered as "virtue" or "virtuous" by specialists in Tibetan Buddhism, and the awkward neologism "non-virtue" is used for its opposite, *mi dge ba*. This common choice at least avoids the word "vice," which is also often used, although its contemporary connotations may mislead the unwary reader.

In some Buddhist presentations of this topic, the different aspects of *kuśala* are remarkably diverse. Aristotle argued that there could not be a single form of the good, such as Plato had postulated, because the term "good" could be applied in so many different ways to entities in so many different ontological categories (*EN* 1.6). A similar argument might be made about *kuśala*, if we follow Asaṅga's account in his *Abhidharma-samuccaya*. In an appendix to this chapter, we describe in full detail the thirteen categories of *kuśala* and twelve categories of *akuśala* that Asaṅga presents in that text.

According to Vasubandhu, in the *Abhidharmakoṣabhāṣya* (IV.8) the three roots of *kuśala*—non-attraction (*alobha*), non-aversion (*adveṣa*), non-ignorance (*amoha*)—as well as self-respect (*hrī*) and consideration for others (*apatrapya*), independent of their associations and of their causes, are *kuśala* by nature, in and of themselves (*svabhāvataḥ kuśalam*). This *kuśalam* is compared to a salutary medicine. The three roots of *akuśala*—attraction (*lobha*), aversion (*dveṣa*), ignorance (*moha*)—the absence of self-respect (*ahrī*), and the lack of consideration for others (*patrapya*) are *akuśala* in themselves (*svabhāvataḥ 'kuśalam*). This *akuśala* is compared to harmful drugs and the like (Vasubandhu AKB IV.8cd-9c, *mNgon* pa Ku 174a).

The ethically variable mental states (dharmas) such as volitions, which are associated with the three roots of *akuśala*, self-respect, and consideration for others, are *kuśala* by *association* (*samprayogataḥ kaśalam*). When associated with *kuśala* mental states, they are *kuśala*; when they are not associated with any of these mental states, they are either ethically *akuśala* or neutral (Vasubandhu AKB IV.9bc, *mNgon* pa Ku 174a).

Vasubandhu's and Asaṅga's articulations of the *kuśala/akuśala* distinction make it abundantly clear that Buddhist ethics is multidimensional, and that the domain of ethics comprises both overt actions and states of mind.

A term that stands in a close and complicated relationship to *kuśala* is Sanskrit *puṇya* (P. *puñña*, Tib. *bsod nams*). The core sense of *puṇya* is of an action that, through the causal process of karma, gives rise to happiness or otherwise favorable conditions in the future. By far the most common translation of this term in the past has been "merit." Recently some scholars have objected that this choice of English conveys a sense of desert that, they say, is not foregrounded in the Asian sources; whereas others continue to defend this translation, arguing that karmic causation was indeed intended to serve as a mechanism of cosmic justice. As an alternative, phrases such as "karmic fruitfulness" have been proposed. Now that "good karma" has become a common English expression, we could use it to translate *puṇya* and thereby communicate the meaning quite clearly. We also need to translate *pāpa*, the opposite of *puṇya*, which refers to action that gives rise to suffering and unfavorable conditions in the future. Neither "merit" nor "karmic fruitfulness" has an obvious opposite, but "bad karma" is available. Note, however, that some passages use *pāpa* to refer to the underlying wrong action that generated the bad karma. In using these translations, we should be aware that whereas the English loanword "karma" refers to a certain kind of result that is said to develop from an action, the underlying Sanskrit word *karman* refers primarily to the action itself.

Accounts of the relationship between *puṇya* and *kuśala* in Buddhist literature are not entirely univocal, and there may be no single account that perfectly reconciles all the available evidence. Roughly, though, as we saw above, *kuśala* pertains to awakening and that which is conducive to awakening. Since favorable circumstances in cyclic existence make it easier to come into contact with the teachings and practices that lead to awakening, most or all *puṇya* is included in the category of *kuśala*. However, from the perspective of non-Mahāyāna traditions, there are some states and qualities that lead to *nirvāṇa*, the cessation of cyclic existence, and hence do not project happiness in future lives; instead, they stop the series of future lives. On this kind of view, such states are *kuśala* but not *puṇya*. As Damien Keown has shown, this is what Theravādin texts such as the *Dhammapada* mean when they say that the Arhat is beyond *puṇya* and *pāpa* (see Keown 2001, ch. 4).

At the heart of the ethical cultivation that is central to Buddhism are four virtuous emotions: in Sanskrit: *maitrī* (P. *metta*,) *karuṇā*, *muditā*, and *upekṣā* (P. *upekkhā*). These qualities are as important in the Theravāda as they are in the bodhisattva path of the Mahāyāna. They are referred to either as the Four Immeasurables (P. *appamañña*, Tib. *tshad med bzhi*) or as the Four Divine States (P. *brahma-vihāra*.)

Maitrī is traditionally defined as the sincere wish for others to be happy. The term is etymologically related to the Sanskrit word for "friend," so that we could see *maitrī* as an attitude of friendliness toward all sentient beings. The most common translation of this term is "lovingkindness." "Benevolence" is fairly close to the meaning; some scholars argue for translating this term simply as "love." Of course, "love" has a very wide range of meanings in English, only some of which fit *maitrī*. Śāntideva writes:

> Here wishing for, aiming at, being committed to, and rejoicing in the happiness of others is lovingkindness. This is a form of love (*sneha*) that is not defiled by sexual attraction or by expecting something in return.[1] (*Śikṣā-samuccaya* 212, Vaidya 1999, p. 117)

Karuṇā is traditionally defined as the sincere wish for others to be free from suffering. By far the most common translation of *karuṇā* is "compassion." Although firmly entrenched, the translation is, at least in one respect, ill-fitting: the "passion" in "compassion" comes from the Greek *paschein*, "to

1. *Tatra para-sukhasya-āśaṃsā prārthanā tṛṣṇā-abhinandanaṃ maitrī/kāma-rāga-pratyupakāra-hetubhyām-akliṣṭaḥ sneha ity-arthaḥ.*

suffer," and so is cognate with such English words as "passive," and expresses the venerable European conception of emotions as *passions* (things that befall us). *Karuṇā*, by contrast, has as its root *kṛ*, "to do"—the same root from which "*karma*" comes. In many chapters of this text we use the term "care" to reflect this more active sense.

Muditā is traditionally defined as the ability to take delight in the happiness and good qualities of others. It is opposed to attitudes of jealousy, envy, or shame aroused by contemplating the good fortune or success of others; these negative emotions result from a confused sense of personal inadequacy, which, in turn, depends on a false sense of self. *Muditā* can be rendered simply as "joy," but many scholars would argue that the precise traditional meaning is better conveyed by a phrase such as "appreciative joy" or "sympathetic joy."

Of the four immeasurables, *upekṣā* is by far the most complex concept. One aspect of *upekṣā* is a kind of emotional stability, in which the practitioner is neither exhilarated by success nor depressed by failure. It also includes the ability to accept what arises in experience without grasping it or pushing it away. From an ethical point of view, the most directly relevant aspect of *upekṣā* is the ability to extend the other three immeasurables to all sentient beings equally, without preference or prejudice, and without making any exceptions. The best translation of the term overall is clearly "equanimity," but this third, ethical sense of *upekṣā* is close to the English word "impartiality."

In his *Abhidharma-samuccaya* I.III.2, Asaṅga tells us that all of the four immeasurables share a common element: "stable attention (*samādhi*) and wisdom (*prajñā*), and the mind and mental activities associated with them (*tat-samprayukta citta-caitasika*)" (Asaṅga, AbSI.III.2 Skt. ed. Pradhan; *mNgon pa Kun btus* Sems tsam Ri, 111b). Without wisdom, the mind will remain preoccupied by self-centered thoughts distracted by biased conceptions of self, being, life, or soul, and cannot develop pure, open, and all-inclusive wishes that embrace all beings. For example, loving-kindness functions to remove resentment, whereas self-centered thought functions to create more resentment through narrow prejudices.

Finally, perhaps the most crucial ethical concept distinctive to the Mahāyāna is *bodhicitta*, variously rendered as "Awakening Mind," "mind of enlightenment," "altruistic intention," and so on. *Bodhicitta* is a commitment to attain full awakening for the benefit of all sentient beings. It is an altruistic aspiration to attain the skill necessary to bring others to awakening. This quality in its fully developed form is usually presented as an embodiment of great care (*mahā-karuṇā*) and wisdom (*prajñā*), displaying them in unison as skill in means (*upāya-kauśalya*). The wisdom aspect of *bodhicitta* eliminates attachment, aversion, and confusion, whereas the caring aspect of *bodhicitta* leads the bodhisattva never to desist from activities that benefit others. *Bodhicitta* as wisdom enables the bodhisattva to understand the suffering of others; as an expression of boundless care, it leads the bodhisattva to strive to alleviate their suffering. Wisdom makes the bodhisattva disenchanted with saṃsāric life and confers upon her the freedom of *nirvāṇa*, while her care for others leads her courageously to return over and over again to *saṃsāra*, helping sentient beings through skill in means.

In these contexts, we can see that it is a common claim of many forms of Buddhism that moral development and the recognition of no-self work together, as the common metaphor has it, like two wings of a bird. The rest of our book will explore, in the context of the Madhyamaka form of Buddhist philosophy, how metaphysical teachings and ethical values that might at first seem inconsistent can, in fact, support each other, enabling the practitioner to work for the benefit of all sentient beings.

APPENDIX

Asaṅga on the Meanings of *kuśala* and *akuśala*

We have reproduced here the entire list of Asaṅga's thirteen categories of *kuśala* and twelve categories of *akuśala*, presented at AbS I.I.1,[2] to allow the reader to gain a wider perspective on the complex landscape and multivocality of Buddhist ethics.

(1) The eleven mental states of confidence (*śraddha*), humility (*apramāda*), suppleness (*praśrabdhi*), equanimity (*upekṣa*), self-respect (*hrī*), consideration-for-others (*apatrapya*), non-greed (*alobha*), non-hatred (*adveṣa*), non-ignorance (*amoha*), harmlessness (*avihiṃsa*), and vigor (*vīrya*) are *kuśala by virtue of their nature* (*svabhāvataḥ kuśalaṃ/ngo bo nyid kyi dge ba*) because they are *kuśala* in their own right, not due the force of intention, nor by consequence, etc. (Asaṅga, AbhS I.I.1. Skt. ed. Pradhan; Cf. *mNgon pa kun btus, Sems tsam* Ri 61b) Vasubandhu's *Abhidharmakośakārikā* (*AbhKK*)[3] describes these mental states as the

2. Asanga, *Abhidharmsamuccay*, Skt. ed. Pradhan, Prahlad (Santiniketan, India: Visvabharati, 1950). The Sanskrit manuscript does not come with the numbering of sections. We have appropriated the numberings and the translations of the relevant sections of the text from Sara Boin-Webb's excellent English translation of the text, published as *Abhidharmasamuccay: The Compendium of the Higher Teaching (Philosophy) by Asaṅga* (Fremont, CA: Asian Humanities Press, 2001): 45–49.

3. Vasubandhu, *Abhidharmakoṣakārikā*, Skt. ed. Pradhan, Prahlad (Patna, India: K. P. Jayaswal Research Institute, 1975).

wholesome "sphere" or "roots" *(kuśalamahābhūmikas)* of the *kuśala* states, because these mental states "are found only in a good mind and are found in all good minds." (*AbhKK* II.25 Skt. ed. Pradhan)[4]

(2) The six primary cognitive capacities—from the eye-consciousness to mental consciousness—and the ten ethically variable mental factors—feeling/sensation (*vedanā*), volition or motivation (*cetanā*), perceptual notion (*samjñā/samjñāna*), will or desire for action (*chanda*), and contact (*sparśa*), knowledge/intelligence (*mati*), memory (*smṛti*), the act of attention (*manaskāra*), approval (*adhimukti*), and concentration (*samādhi*)—that are said to always and necessarily accompany every single primary mind are *kuśala by virtue of their association* (*sambandhataḥ kuśalaṃ*).

These mental states, Asaṅga argues, are by themselves ethically neutral. Therefore, the ethical contents of these mental states are contextually determined by the psychological processes that they each accompany. If they are accompanied by the *kuśala* psychological processes, they become *kuśala*, whereas they become *akuśala* if they accompany the *akuśala* psychological roots (Asaṅga, AbhS I.I.1. Skt. ed. Pradhan; Cf. *mNgon pa kun btus, Sems tsam* Ri 61b–62a). Therefore volition, or motivation (*cetanā/sems pa*), for instance, since it is ethically neutral, accompanies all primary mental states, and thus derives its ethical content from the cognitive or psychological processes it accompanies.

(3) The impressions or dispositions (*vāsanā*) left by the eleven wholesome roots are *kuśala in virtue of their consequences* (*anubandhataḥ kuśalaṃ*). The dispositions or impressions (*vāsanā*) of the defiled states left by the major and minor defilements are *akuśala by virtue of their consequences* (*anubandhataḥ kuśalaṃ*).

4. The mental states that are *akuśala (mi dge ba) by nature (svabhāvato 'kuśalaṃ/ngo bo nyid kyis mi dge ba)* consists of the six major defilements (*kleśa/rtsa myon*)—lust (*raga*), anger (*krodha*), ignorance (*avidyā*), pride (*māna*), deluded scepticism (*vicikitsā*), and deluded view (*dṛṣṭiparāmśa*)—which are the unwholesome roots of all defiled minds (*kleśamahābhūmikas/mnyon mongs pa'i sa mang po pa*) and the minor defilements (*upkleśa*) derived from those roots. The six major defilements accompany all defiled minds. All these mental states are *akuśala* by nature since they are non-virtuous by their very identity and their destructive nature does not depend on a non-virtuous motivation (Asaṅga, AbhS I.I.1. Skt. ed. Pradhan; Cf. *mNgon pa kun btus, Sems tsam* Ri 62a). The minor delusions include aggression/anger (krodha), resentment/rancor (*upanāha*), spite/malice (*pradāśa*), jealousy/envy (*īrṣyā*), miserliness/avarice (*mātsarya*), hypocrisy (*mrakṣa*), pretense/illusion (*māyā/sgyu ma*), denial dissimulation (*śāṭhya/gyo*), selfishness (*mada*), violence (*vihiṃsā*), lack of self-respect/inconsiderateness (*āhrīkya*), lack of modesty (*anapatrāpya*), dullness/idleness (*kausīdya*), inertia (*styāna*), mental restlessness (*auddhatya*), inconfidence (*āśraddhya*), laziness/indolence (*pramāda*), distraction (*vikṣepa*), confused memory/forgetfulness (*muṣitasmṛtitā*), and non-alertness/inattention (*asamprajanya*).

(Asaṅga, AbhS I.I.1. Skt. ed. Pradhan; *mNgon pa kun btus, Sems tsam* Ri 61b–62a)

(4) The physical or vocal actions motivated by the eleven wholesome roots are *kuśala* as *emerging* (*utthanataḥ kuśalaṃ*) whereas physical or vocal actions which are motivated by the major and minor defilements are *akuśala* as *emerging* (*utthānato 'kuśalaṃ*) since they emerge from either pure or defiled motivation. (Asaṅga, Ibid.; Cf. *Sems tsam* Ri 61b–62a)

(5) Reality as it is (*tathātā*) is *kuśala* as *ultimate truth* (*paramārthataḥ kuśalaṃ*) whereas saṃsāra is *akuśala* as ultimate truth (*paramārthataḥ 'kuśalaṃ*). (Asaṅga, Ibid.; Cf. *Sems tsam* Ri 61b–62a)

(6) The production of results which are appropriated due to the former habitual practices of those same wholesome roots whereby the tendency (*ruci*) towards them remains naturally and unconsciously is *kuśala in virtue of attaining birth* (*upapattilābhataḥ kuśalaṃ*); the habit of the unfavorable and the corresponding result which arises and consequent to which there remains a tendency only towards the unfavorable *is akuśala in virtue of attaining birth* (*upapattilābhataḥ 'kuśalaṃ*) is. (Asaṅga, Ibid.; Cf. *Sems tsam* Ri 61b–62ab)

(7) The cultivation of what is *kuśala* (*kuśalasya bhāvanā*) due to association with good people to listening to the good dharma, to wise attention (*yoniśo manaskāra*) and the practice of major and minor rules *is kuśala by virtue of application* (*prayogataḥ kuśalaṃ*); misconduct (*duścarita*) that one pursues in one's body, speech and mind, consequent to association with bad people, by listening to wrong teachings and by superficial attention is *akuśala by virtue of application* (*prayogataḥ 'kuśalaṃ*) is (*ayoniśo manaskāra*). (Asaṅga, Ibid.; Cf. *Sems tsam* Ri 61b–62b)

(8) An act of veneration (*pūjākrama*) in respect of a monument (*caitya*), statue (*pustagata*) or a painting (*citragata*), bearing in mind the Tathāgata as object, or of a book (*pustaka*) which is a repository of the Dharma (*dharmādhiṣṭhāna*) bearing in mind the teaching (dharma) as object is *kuśala in virtue of veneration* (*puskārataḥ kuśalaṃ*). Erecting a monument (*caitya*) while seeking the support of certain deities with the idea of causing harm to living beings (*hiṃsāpūrvako*) or with perverse ideas (*kudṛṣṭupūrvaka*), or performing acts of veneration such as offerings (*pūjākrama*) while crowds are devoted to demeritorious (*apuṇya*) practices is *akuśala through veneration* (*puskārataḥ 'kuśalaṃ*). (Asaṅga, Ibid.; Cf. *Sems tsam* Ri 61b–62b)

(9) Helping beings by means of the four kinds of aid—giving, agreeable speech, altruistic service and equality—is *kuśala in virtue of granting*

a favor (*anugrahataḥ kuśalaṃ*). Misbehaving (*mithyā pratipadyate*) towards beings with one's body, speech or mind is *akuśala as offending* (*upaghātato 'kuśalaṃ*). (Asaṅga, Ibid.; Cf. *Sems tsam* Ri 61b–62b)

(10) Obtaining birth in the heavens or in a prosperous and high caste family or obtaining of a state favorable to purification, through good acts of giving and morality is *kuśala in virtue of receiving* (*parigrahataḥ kuśalaṃ*). A good or bad destiny in which one experiences unpleasant results, projected (*ākṣepaka*) or completed (*paripūraka*) due to physical, vocal or mental misconduct, is akuśala *by virtue of receiving* (*parigrahato 'kuśalaṃ*). (Asaṅga, Ibid.; Cf. *Sems tsam* Ri 61b–62b)

(11) Repenting (*vidūṣaṇa*), abandonment (*prahāṇa*), aiding (*ādhāra*), distancing (*dūrībhāva*), suppression (*viṣkambhaṇā*), disassociation (*visaṃyoga*), impediments to the defilements (*kleśāvaraṇa*) and impediment to inappropriate objects of knowledge (*jñeyāvaraṇa*) are *kuśala in virtue of counteracting* (*pratipakṣataḥ kuśalaṃ*). That which is opposed to these counteractions and antidotes *is akuśala* (*pratipakṣavipakṣa*). (Asaṅga, Ibid.; Cf. *Sems tsam* Ri 61b–62b)

(12) The complete abandonment (*paryādāya prahāṇa*) of attraction (*rāga*), aversion (*dveṣa*), delusion (*moha*) and all the defilements (*sarvakleśa*), the cessation of perception and feeling (*saṃjñāvedayitanirodha*), the element of nirvāṇa (*nirvāṇadhātu*) with remainder (*sopadhiśeṣa*) and without remainder (*nirupadhiśeṣa*) and unestablished *nirvāṇa* (*apratiṣṭhitanirvāṇa*) are *kuśala as tranquility* (*upaśamataḥ kuśalaṃ*). That which undermines the favorable (*kuśalāntarāyika*) is *akuśala* in virtue of being an obstruction (*paripantha akuśalaṃ*). (Asaṅga, Ibid.; Cf. *Sems tsam* Ri 61b–62a)

Finally, (13) special qualities such as superknowledge (*abhijñā*), worldly and transcendent (*laukikalokottara*), common and exceptional (*sādhāraṇāsādhāraṇa*) in a person who has attained tranquility (*upaśamaprāpta*) by means of that supremacy (*tadādhipatya*) are *kuśala as natural result* (*niṣyanda*). (Asaṅga, Ibid.; Cf. *Sems tsam* Ri 62a)

2

Aiming at Happiness, Aiming at Ultimate Truth—In Practice

Amber Carpenter

If there is a distinctively Madhyamaka ethics to be found—or a distinctive set of ethical difficulties and responses arising from Madhyamaka metaphysics (or eschewal of metaphysics)—the first place to look for it is in Nāgārjuna, author of the foundational Madhyamaka text, the *Mūlamadhyamakakārikā*.

But this is more easily said than done. Impossibly many diverse texts are traditionally ascribed to Nāgārjuna; and there was more than one author answering to that name. The historical record offers us very little in the way of corroborating evidence about the person of our Nāgārjuna, or about what else he might have written. What we want is an ethical treatise by Nāgārjuna-author-of-the-*Mūlamadhyamakakārikā*; and we want, if possible, an ethical treatise in which he is explicitly writing *as* the author of the *Mūlamadhyamakakārikā*. If there is no such text—if, for instance, our only candidate were the *Suhṛllekha*[1]—then we might conclude that Nāgārjuna at least saw his own revolutionary presentation of the Buddha-*dharma* as having no particular ethical implications whatsoever.

1. The *Suhṛllekha* (*Letter to a Friend*) is traditionally attributed to Nāgārjuna. It is, for the most part, a sort of exhortation to live decently such as one might find indistinguishably in any moralist of any time, proceeding without anything distinctively Buddhist in its exhortations to, or conception of, virtue. There is a great deal of cajoling by graphic images of unfortunate rebirths. At v. 48, however, "right view" is specified as knowing we are suffering, impermanent and without self (and impure); and subsequent verses declare the aggregates empty of self (v. 49) and caused by ignorant action and craving (v. 50).

We do, however, have a much better candidate source for a distinctively Madhyamaka ethics than the *Suhṛllekha*. The much-beloved and widely disseminated *Ratnāvalī* (*Garland of Jewels*) is explicitly ethical—it presents itself as advice to a prince—and it explicitly incorporates some distinctively Madhyamaka commitments, familiar from the *Mūlamadhyamakakārikā*, into its moral advice. It is largely on this basis, in fact, that scholars have concluded that the *Ratnāvalī* is indeed written by Nāgārjuna, founder of Madhyamaka thought.[2] So before presuming what sort of difficulties or innovations a Madhyamaka ethics *ought* to have, we will turn attention here to what Nāgārjuna's ethics actually looks like.

The Old Bait-and-Switch

Since the *Ratnāvalī* is explicit about its moralist ambitions, a few observations will be useful as background to our discussion. Moralists of any kind tend to be slippery customers. But some ancient moralists, both in Greece and in India, were slippery in a very specific respect. First, they accept that we all want to be happy, and promise that we can have this if we just follow their guide to living. Then, as we embark on their regimen of self-transformation as directed, they set about reforming our conception of happiness, so that what we end up aiming at (and attaining, if we do well) is not quite the thing that we originally sought when we set out on the journey. Such reformation in our concept of the final end usually involves shaking us out of a widespread and default presumption that enjoying whatever we desire is what makes us happy, or is what doing well and being well off consists in. Happiness, *truly* doing well or being well off, says the ancient moralist, is something else entirely—usually virtuous living, or else a good attained only through virtuous living. Only this gets us the pleasure or contentment worth striving for.

Such bait-and-switch tactics in a moralist are familiar. But some ancient moralists switch up again: having now promised us the *real* version of what we want (*real* happiness), they then attempt to detach us altogether from aiming at happiness, even reconceived. There is, it turns out, some ultimate good—state, activity, object, way of life—which is what we should really be aiming at. This two-step structure is found in Plato, and even in certain readings

2. See Walser 2002 for a recent consolidation of the state of the argument. Tilmann Vetter (1992) casts some minor doubt on Nāgārjuna's authorship of the *Ratnāvalī*. In his view, stylistic considerations tell both ways; he rests his eventual endorsement of the traditional view on his somewhat idiosyncratic (though not absurd) association of Nāgārjuna's view of the person with the ancient Buddhist "personalists," *pudgalavādins*—which he finds in the *MMK*, and possibly in the *Ratnāvalī* at I.92 (but only in the Chinese and Tibetan), and I.29–35.

of Aristotle—though not in the neo-Aristotle of the Virtue Ethicists. It can also be found, we shall see, in Nāgārjuna's Madhyamaka.[3] In such cases, one thing we will want to know is: What is supposed to be the relationship between the familiar goal (some version of happiness) and the new one (the good, or the right, or the true)? Does attaining this ultimate good require happiness (reconceived as virtue-involving) first; does it promise such reconceived happiness in its wake? Or perhaps both; or indeed, neither?

Let us consider the case of Plato. In the *Republic*, for instance, Socrates clearly wants Glaucon and Adeimantus to give up the widely shared notion that power to gratify desires is what happiness consists in; he offers a well-structured soul, appropriately gratifying those desires that serve the interests of the unity of the person as an alternative conception in Book IV. But the proper aim and focus of our attention should not be happiness at all, but rather the good itself—understanding and enacting this in whatever ways are available to us.[4] Similarly, if one takes Book X of his *Nicomachean Ethics* seriously, Aristotle quite explicitly calls the life of familiar civic virtue "the second best," compared to the life that is organized around enabling the one exceptional and divine activity of contemplation. This activity is more than human, so that the truly highest good is quite different from merely being the best human being one can be.[5]

At the same time, for Aristotle and also (in a different way) for Plato, what will count as happiness-related virtuous activity is (in a way) determined by how it is necessary for human beings to live, given what we are, if the divine activity—or ultimate good—is ever to be open to any of us for however brief a spell. So the two ends are not disconnected. The particular interest—both for the moralist and for the moral theorist—is in the connections, as well as the difference, between these two steps, and in the movement between them.

Turning to Buddhist discourse, the distinction between these two stages and two ends might be likened to the Buddhist distinction between

3. Whether Nāgārjuna in this respect captures a feature already available in the Buddhist ethical thought that he inherited is a topic for another occasion.

4. *Republic* 419e–420b, and 466a emphasize the reconception of happiness, but also its displacement from the center of our concerns; at *Rep.* 421b–c, we are explicitly told to leave happiness to nature, aiming rather at good order instead. And of course *Republic* 505e tells us that all desire is for the good, not happiness at all, nor the pleasant, fine, and just things in which happiness is thought to consist. Vaisiliiou (2011) offers elaboration of this view of Plato's ethics. Although Vasiliou (perplexingly) makes virtue, rather than the good, the ultimate aim, his virtue is not one that plays the role of *constituting* happiness, as some neo-Aristotelians and some contemporary *eudaimonist* interpretations of Socratic ethics would have it.

5. Of course it is complicated here. One might say that, unlike all other species in Aristotle's biology, completely perfecting one's human nature requires aiming at, and partially succeeding in transcending one's human nature. As observed in Chapter 7 of this volume, there must necessarily be significant difference between any version of Aristotelianism characterized as fulfilling our human nature, or becoming an excellent thing of our kind, and Buddhist ethics, which resolutely eschews taking "self" as normative.

conventional and ultimate truth, or reality. On the one hand, there are everyday notions of value and conduct, and the moralist's first task is to remind us that these are liable to standards of consistency and coherence, violated on pain of foreclosing the results we take ourselves to be seeking. Of course we all want to be happy; but if we do not wise up about what that really is, our conduct and desires will be counterproductive, and happiness on any definition elusive. When it is concerned with generosity, conduct and forbearance as personal qualities, or with right livelihood, right speech, and right conduct in our social lives, Buddhist ethics addresses itself to conventional reality. But ultimate reality exerts, on the other hand, a distinct claim on us, offers a good somehow independent of conventional happiness, even as reconceived. Right view of ultimate reality promises liberation even from the positive aspects of a happy life. Ultimately, the Buddhist aims not at a better rebirth, but at no rebirth at all. And yet aiming at this does not relieve one of ordinary commitments to the activities constitutive of a well-lived life, conventionally conceived.

Nāgārjuna's Madhyamaka is famous for claiming that ultimate reality is empty, just as is conventional reality—where emptiness is dependent origination (*MMK* XXIV.18). Arising dependently is the only way to be (*MMK* XXIV.19), and there is no further and independent ultimate reality on which this depends. This may seem to make the distinction between ultimate and conventional reality difficult to sustain, and likewise the distinction between happiness as a conventional end and cessation or enlightenment as an ultimate end. Indeed, Nāgārjuna even more notoriously claims, "There is no distinction whatsoever between *saṃsāra* and *nirvāṇa*; there is no distinction whatsoever between *nirvāṇa* and *saṃsāra*" (*MMK* XXV.19). And yet realizing this very truth is a distinct aim and has transformative effects on one's ordinary outlook. Nāgārjuna's *Ratnāvalī*, or *Garland of Jewels*, takes shape largely within this complicated, sometimes ambiguous terrain. It is neither the extended exposition of the highest truth and ultimate aim, like the *Mūlamadhyamakakārikā*; nor is it, like the *Suhṛllekha*, focused almost exclusively on enjoining the basic decent conduct that will ensure a good rebirth, or happiness. It is as often classified among the wisdom texts as among the compassion texts (Hopkins 1998, p. 26)—which is precisely the way we should expect moral thinking to take shape on any view that seriously maintains that, in some sense, *saṃsāra* is *nirvāṇa*.

Happiness or *Nirvāṇa*? Happiness and *Nirvāṇa*

The *Ratnāvalī* is not, to be sure, the exposition of a systematic moral theory. Indeed, some portions of the *Ratnāvalī* seem to offer straightforward *nīti-śāstra*-type advice about how to govern well. For instance:

> Appoint as your ministers those who know the right politics,
> who are observant of the law, affectionate, pure, faithful, brave,
> of good family, rich in moral virtues, grateful. (IV.23)[6]

This is not Machiavellian astuteness, perhaps, but only because the advice is too bland and generic even for that.[7] The advice occasionally comes with a distinctly partisan air. One should not only "[r]evere the monuments with gold and silver flowers, diamonds, corals, pearls, etc." (III.34), but give such dues only to true teachers, and "not respect, revere, or do homage to others, the Forders" (III.37a–b).[8] The only distinctive character in this advice seems to lie in who should and should not receive flowers.

But this advice is alternated and entangled with advice of a different sort—namely, advice about how to understand the ultimate nature of reality, and why one should do so. If *this* should have anything to do with good governance, that fact itself is a striking one. We can begin to disentangle—and trace the tangles—of these two strands, worldly well-being and liberation, by recognizing Nāgārjuna making the classic two steps of the ancient moralist.

Nāgārjuna, indeed, is plain about this. He sets up the *Ratnavalī* by distinguishing two worthy goals—the good life (*abhyudaya*) and final or settled goodness (*naiḥśreyasa*). He relates them, characterizes each, and correlates each to its respective means of attainment:

> Wherever there is virtuous good living [*dharma-abhyudaya*], final goodness [*naiḥśreyasa*] appears later on.[9] Those who have reached the elevated state of well-being will gradually attain settled goodness. (I.3)

> *abhyudaya* is considered to be *sukham* (happiness, joy, pleasure)
> and *naiśreyasa* to be *mokṣa* (final liberation). The epitome of
> their accomplishment is, briefly, faith and wisdom. (I.4)[10]

6. Translations of the *Ratnāvalī* are from Tucci's edition of the Sanskrit text where it is available, with translations often adapted from his (1934) and (1936). Where the Sanskrit is unavailable, Jeffery Hopkins's (1998) translation from the Tibetan has been used, which in other places also offers useful contrast with or amplification of Tucci's translations. The two approach the numbering of verses differently, Tucci using book and verse numbers (as cited above), Hopkins numbering straight through the entire text. Tucci's IV.23 will therefore be Hopkins's v. 323, and so on. Translations of Book III are taken from Jeffery Hopkins.

7. On a banal and benign note, one should provide "hostels, parks, dikes, ponds, rest-houses, water-vessels, beds, food, hay and wood. Establish rest-houses in all towns, at temples, and in all cities, and provide water-vessels on all arid roadways" (III.42–43). And the detail offered is sometimes positively mundane: "At the sites of the water-vessels, place shoes, umbrellas, water-filters, tweezers for removing thorns, needles, thread and fans" (III.45).

8. One aim of the *Ratnāvalī* seems to have been to persuade local leaders to offer their patronage to the still marginalized Mahāyāna. Gregory Schopen (2005, chapter 1) presents considerable evidence for the "outsider" status of the Mahāyāna during the period when the *Ratnāvalī* was composed, and indeed later; Joseph Walser (2005) takes up the theme in greater, and more tendentious, detail.

9. "In one who first practices high status, definite goodness arises later" (Hopkins 1998).

10. Tucci's (1934) rendering here is wordy, and there is good reason to avoid the language of "salvation": "perfect life [*abhyudaya*] is considered to be happiness [*sukham*] and salvation [*naiśreyasa*] to be final emancipation

Several key terms here will need further scrutiny if we are to understand what is going on in these verses, and in the subsequent exposition that they frame.

But already something of the distinction being made here may seem familiar from more sociological discussions of Buddhism, and particularly of Theravāda Buddhism. It is commonly noted in such contexts that among the laity, it is good *karma*, leading to a good rebirth, which is sought; liberation does not typically figure into their goals. Among monastics, by contrast, *karma* both good and bad is eschewed altogether—the aim is the stilling of all action and fruits, so as to attain cessation.[11] So Nāgārjuna's opening move may be drawing this background; and if it is, we may be tempted to conclude that the *Ratnāvalī* has little to teach us about an ethics informed by a distinctively Madhyamaka account of reality. Its ambition is to tell a prince how to live well enough to secure a favorable rebirth, and besides specifying appropriate donors for patronage, there is likely to be little specifically Madhyamaka in this advice.

But we can see already in these two verses that such an "alternative ends" view—in which one might choose either to go for the good life attained via faith, or to pursue a quite different life of wisdom leading to the quite different end of *nirvāṇa*—is not what is on offer. For verse 3 promises at least that these two ends do indeed meet—whatever the common social arrangements in Buddhist cultures, then or now.[12] There may indeed be two distinguishable goals, and the means of attaining them may be likewise distinguishable. Āryadeva, Nāgārjuna's closest follower, picks this up and repeats it in his *Catuḥśataka*:

> By means of virtuous conduct (*śīla*), one reaches heaven; by means of the [right] view, one attains the highest state of all. (XII.11)[13]

But rather than two alternative tracks, running in parallel and never meeting, the *Ratnāvalī* intermingles the two goals, the respective means to them and the

[*mokṣa*] from contingent life. The concise enunciation of the method of realizing is summarized in faith and wisdom." Compare Hopkins: "High status is considered to be happiness, / Definite goodness is liberation. / The quintessence of their means / Is briefly faith and wisdom."

11. The distinction seems to go back to Spiro (1971), who in fact distinguishes three forms: *nibbanic*, *kammic*, and *apotropaic* Buddhism—the lattermost having to do with protection from harm. In an early review of the book, Richard Gombrich (1972) criticizes the implication that there is tension within the Buddhist view (490–494); but he is friendlier toward the distinction on some version of it in (1975), where he describes "the karma doctrine, for all its power to explain *this* world" as "a fifth wheel in nibbanic soteriology." The distinction between *nibbanic* and *kammic* Buddhism as distinct cognitive and motivational structures is taken up by, among others, Stephen Collins (1982).

12. Indeed, one is tempted to suppose that precisely this promise was the hallmark distinguishing the Mahāyāna from their more established Buddhist opponents; but matters are, as always, murky here.

13. See also *Catuḥśataka* XII.23: "In brief, the Tathāgatas interpret good conduct (*dharma*) as non-violence (*ahiṃsā*), and nirvāṇa as emptiness (*śūnyatā*). For us, there are only these two" (translation from Karen Lang 1986).

reasoning behind them, suggesting a more complicated, dynamic, and unified picture.

What follows will consider how the two ends are defined and related in the opening of the *Ratnāvalī*, in order then to highlight the concrete ways in which the two ends are related throughout the text, both theoretically and practically. Nāgārjuna's distinctive ethical view (or Madhyamaka ethics, at least as presented here) will turn out to be metaphysical not only because metaphysical positions have implications for ethics, but also because reflecting on metaphysics is a constitutive part of ethical practice—not just when aiming directly at enlightenment, but even when aiming at happiness and mundane well-being.

"High Status Is Happiness, Conclusive Goodness Is Liberation"

Nāgārjuna has distinguished two ends; but the distinction is initially drawn using two less familiar terms, both difficult to translate: *abhyudaya* and *naiśreyasa*. Each is immediately correlated with a more familiar *desideratum: abhyudaya* with *sukha, naiśreyasa* with *mokṣa*. These correlations should be illuminating and informative.

Sukha defies translation into a single English word, meaning sometimes pleasure, sometimes delight, happiness, joy, or bliss. A passage from the (Pāli) *Kathāvatthu* gives a sense of its breadth:

> *Th.*: You affirm this [the world is nothing but a cinder-heap]; but is there no such a thing as pleasurable feeling [*sukhā vedanā*], bodily pleasure, mental pleasure, celestial happiness [*sukhaṃ*], human happiness, the *sukhaṃ* of gain, of being honoured, of driving, of resting, the *sukha* of ruling, of administrating, of domestic-and-secular life, of the religious life; *sukha* related to taints [esp. sense-desires] and those of untaintedness; the happiness [of *nirvāṇa*] with remainder and without remainder; worldly happiness, unworldly happiness, with zest and without, *jhāna-sukhaṃ*, liberation-pleasure, pleasures of sense-desire, renunciation-*sukhaṃ*, the *sukha* of solitude, of peace, of awakening [*saṃbodhi-sukhaṃ*]?[14]

14. *Kathāvatthu* II.8.1 translated by Aung and Davids, with modifications. The word used throughout the list is *sukha*; it is perhaps best understood etymologically and by contrast with *duḥkha*. The *su-* prefix in *sukha* is related to the Greek *eu-* prefix—it asserts goodness of that to which it is prefixed, in contrast to the prefix *duḥ*, cognate with the Greek *dys/dus*, which asserts badness. *Sukha* and *duḥkha* are thus direct opposites, indicating good and bad states, respectively, whatever those turn out to be.

Sukha carries a definite affective aspect—so that Naiyāyikas, for instance, could long dispute whether, for that reason, such a thing would be at all possible in a fully liberated state.[15] While it is in this respect unlike colloquial uses of the Greek *eudaimonia* (the keynote of which, through all its elasticity in meaning, seems to be "doing and having whatever one likes"), the functional role each plays in colloquial discourse is the same. There is no doubt that *sukha* is something we want, and in such a way that, as Plato would say, if one were to give this as her reason for action, it would no longer make sense to ask why she wanted that—"That answer is final."[16] But widely agreed though the principle may be, it is just as widely disputed what in fact fits the bill.

Here Nāgārjuna swiftly instructs us: The *sukha* you thought you wanted should be understood exclusively as that of an elevated, perfect life (*abhyudaya*[17]). *Abhyudaya*, the corrected conception of *sukha*, has the rather lovely meaning of "sunrise"—but also, formed from *abhi* and *ut*, the more generic and context-relevant meaning of elevation and increase, particularly prosperity and good result. *Sukha*, that is to say, is properly understood as a "raised-up-ness," a genuinely higher or elevated state, not a mere satisfaction of preferences or accumulation of pleased sensations, though it would undoubtedly include or entail both of these—as the correlation with the more familiar *sukha* suggests. It is the sort of well-being, Nāgārjuna goes on to tell us, that is attained through faithful adherence to virtuous practice in everyday life. (The link between faith and virtuous practice will be expanded on below.) Here Nāgārjuna makes swiftly the classic first move of the ancient moralist: if you want *sukha* (pleasure, joy, happiness), you should understand it to consist in *abhyudaya*, an actual elevated state, or *real* well-being.

But then comes the second move. At the same time that we revise our conception of the thing we already know we want, we have recommended to us a quite distinct ultimate good, the conclusive goodness, *naiḥśreyasa*, of liberation; this is attained through wisdom consisting in insight into the true nature of reality. About *mokṣa*, we learn that it is "settled," "final," "conclusive," or—as Hopkins's translation prefers—"definite" (*niścitaṃ*); and that it is *good: śreyas* indicates excellence, what is splendid, superior, even beautiful. As a noun, it is particularly closely related to welfare, felicity, and fortune[18]—to a life going

15. See Arindam Chakrabarti (1983) for an excellent discussion of the dispute, both its theoretical aspect, as above, and its motivational aspect.

16. *Symposium* 205a; compare Aristotle, *Nicomachean Ethics* I.1, I.4, I.7.

17. The Großes Petersburger has, apart from the generic "aufgehend," "das Emporsteigen, Glück, Heil, Segen" and cites Müller's translation of the word as "Seligkeit." Hopkins translates "high status," which accurately captures the fact that there is nothing to translate here as "life," and although it is rather opaque as a term (if anything, it has rather inappropriate class or sociological connotations), it is not easy to find a better translation. "Elevated state" is perhaps slightly less misleading, but hardly more idiomatic.

18. So, at least, says MMW, 1102.

outstandingly well. While the compound word *naiḥśreyasa* thus points toward living well, its identification with *mokṣa* will force us to ask to what extent this settled, outstanding excellence could have much to do with living a *life*, in any recognizable sense.[19] From the first, then, liberation as the settled superior end is not set antiseptically apart from all worldly concerns, as if it might be contaminated through association. Rather, by the choice of language here, Nāgārjuna draws upon our ordinary concerns—in flourishing, in welfare, in being truly splendid—in order to draw us out of them toward concerns that we do not ordinarily conceive, and for which we may not yet have a language that speaks to us.

About these two goals, Nāgārjuna tells us further (in I.4) that faith is the way to the first; wisdom yields the second. To see a Buddhist advocating, and even requiring, faith may jar. But the faith referred to here, and generally throughout Buddhist moral psychology, is not unreasoned conviction;[20] it is rather something more to do with clarity of mind and ardent trust in the *dharma*.[21] Nāgārjuna is explicit that the faith at issue here is not in god, but in practices; and not even in ritual practices, but in virtuous ones.[22] The relevant elevation in the uplifted, well-lived life is initially introduced as *dharma-abhyudaya* (I.3a), superior regarding *dharma*; and at I.5a, "the one with faith is *dharmaṃ*." This is specified, in I.6, as "He who does not transgress the *dharma* on account of worldly cravings" and so forth. And the opening overview of the position in Book I goes on to spell out such non-transgression not in terms of ritual adherence, but in terms of the virtues (*śuklā*, I.9c):

> Refraining from killing living beings, from theft and from adultery, control over one's own words so as to avoid any false or

19. Arindam Chakrabarti (1983) translates the related *niḥśreyasa* in the Nyāya contexts as "ultimate good." The Großes Petersburger offers for *niḥśreyasa*, "kein Besseres über sich habend, der allerbeste, vorzüglichste; Jemandes Bestes, Heil, Glückseligkeit, Erlösung"; and for *naiśreyasa*: "zum Heile, zur Glückseligkeit führend" supported by several references to the *Mahābhārata*.

20. And since both conviction and confidence can be equally unreasoning, not much is won by translating *śraddha* out of its implicit religious context by force of word choice. (Moreover, Śāntideva at least presents the *Ratna-ulka-dhārani* as citing *śraddha* as responsible for conviction, *adhimukti*, at *Śiṣka-Samuccaya* I.3 (Bendall and Rouse 2006).) We would do better to reconsider the options for what faith might mean, and the role to which *śraddha* is put in the discussion.

21. Vasubandhu, writing somewhat later, puts faith among the "moral faculties," with zeal, memory, absorption, and discernment (*AKBh*. II.4 et alia); and associates faith with a kind of affection (*ad* II.32c) or an ardent trust (IV.37, IV.41) in the Buddha, Dharma, and Saṅgha, or else in the four noble truths (VI.75, although *prasāda* is used here), or in cause and effect (IV.79); he also says faith is a "clarification of mind" (at II.25, which lists all these options).

22. The difference is elaborated in Carpenter (2012) which also considers why such faith as is at issue here might be not only consistent with the Buddha's advice to experience for oneself, but also even particularly appropriate to a Buddhist metaphysical view.

> slandering or cruel or futile speech; complete abstaining from covetousness, hatred and wrong views denying the existence of karma; these virtues constitute the tenfold pure conduct. (I.8–9c)

This is reiterated in Book III, where "eliminating defects and acquiring good qualities are the practices of those seeking high status," and where this is again contrasted with the specific sort of wisdom—"thoroughly extinguishing conceptions"—which is the activity of "those seeking definite goodness" (III.30). In short, the faith which is the means to the true happiness of a genuinely uplifted state is that faith in virtuous practice which enables decent conduct of life in all of its aspects. Such faith is, moreover, necessary for this result.[23]

Our ultimate concern is with the relations between these two sets of correlates: happiness, well-being, faith, and virtue on the one hand; liberation, settled goodness, and wisdom on the other. But we should pause to consider whether, within each set of correlates, "means" is the correct way of describing the relation of faithful practice[24] to well-being, and of wisdom to consummate goodness. Hopkins's translation is unambiguous: "The quintessence of their means is briefly faith and wisdom"—and such language aptly captures the agentive character at issue, and the practical implication that if one wants the latter, in either case, one should undertake to pursue and acquire the former. But "means" omits connotations of completion, perfection, and accomplishment carried by *sādhana*; and it does not distinguish between means that bear no internal relation to their ends, and so are interchangeable—as one may use a hammer to nail a coffin, or a stone if one of suitable size is to hand—and constitutive means, which are neither interchangeable nor distinguishable from their ends—as golfing may be a constitutive means to the end of "having a nice holiday."[25] Aristotelian virtues are often taken to be constitutive means to the end of happiness in this way, and we may well ask whether we should consider faithful good conduct to bear a similar relation to well-being (*abhyudaya*), and likewise wisdom to settled goodness.

What hangs on it is what the attainment of each respective end is like and whether, once the end is achieved, the means to it are no longer present and relevant—just as a hammer is no longer present in nor relevant to the finished

23. Of course declaring "this is the means to that" does not logically exclude the possibility that there are other means; but the ordinary implicature in such a declaration does, and our text gives us no reason to doubt that the ordinary sense is intended here.

24. Choosing "faithful practice" here to convey the importance of the attitude with which good conduct is maintained; according to Śāntideva, writing later (and again on the authority of the *Ratna-ulka-dhāranī*), faith leads not just to "never abandon[ing] moral discipline and training," but specifically gives *joy in* giving and *delight in* the *dharma* (*Śikṣa-Samuccaya* I.3).

25. The example, as the distinction, is owed to Ackrill (1980).

state of the coffin. Is the elevated state of real well-being likewise a finished state, arrived at through faithful adherence to decent conduct, but no longer requiring the continued presence of faith? If so, such faith would be merely instrumental to its end of well-being. If faith were *only* in *karma*—in the connection between action and its result-for-me across multiple lifetimes—we might suppose that faith bears such an external relation to the better life that eventually results.[26] But the scope of faith here seems rather wider than this. We should have faith in practices, in good conduct itself, as well as in certain facts. If it therefore seems unlikely that the elevated state recommended could even in principle exist independently of the continued presence of faith-as-good-practice, then we should consider faith a constitutive means—or perhaps both instrumental and constitutive (as, for instance, the nail in the coffin, which is instrumental in the process of building, but partially constitutes the finished product).

Because of the strong parallels set up in the opening verse, however we see faith related to well-being, we should likewise see wisdom relating to settled-goodness-as-liberation. If we think it unlikely that well-being is separable from faith-as-conduct, we should likewise take settled goodness to be at least partially constituted by the wisdom that is its proper means. This would mean that liberating wisdom is not something one merely engages in along the way, and then abandons in due course. Rather, it would be part of how we should understand the state of settled goodness thus attained. "Insofar as one is possessed of wisdom, one sees things as they are" (I.5b)—where "seeing things as they are" describes liberation, and not just the means to it. Such a settled goodness would not, then, consist in mere feel, but also in whatever cognitive condition wisdom is; indeed, we might suppose that the *settled* or conclusive nature of the goodness attained arises from the insight that allows whatever positive affect that may be involved not to be a passing phenomenon liable to the arising and passing away of other conditioning factors.

Two Orders of Priority

However we may understand the relation of means to end here, our primary concern is with the relation between the two final ends and their respective means. In particular, we might ask which, if either, of the two ends is prior to the other, and in what sense. And we might shed further light by asking what makes the virtues (*śukhā*) of I.9 *good*: Are they good because they give rise to

26. Tucci also notes the recognizable division of virtues here into those of body, speech, and mind, where the lattermost specifically concern abstaining from the "wrong view" of repudiating *karma*.

well-being, as on the instrumentalist account? Or are they good, and *therefore* give rise to well-being, as the constitutive account might suggest? If the latter, we might ask again, what is the *source* of their goodness: Is it *sui generis* and independent, or is it somehow related to the supreme and settled goodness, *naiḥśreyasa*, that is liberation?

In relating the two ends, Nāgārjuna succinctly establishes two orders of priority between them: "Of these two, wisdom is foremost; but faith comes first" (I.5c–d).[27] That is, wisdom is in some unspecified way superior—and so presumably, is its proper good, *naiḥśreyasa*, or liberation. But before this superior good arises, there is faith—and presumably the good it gives rise to, the elevated state of well-being. In fact, faith and well-being are not just incidentally or usually prior in time to settled goodness—they are *invariably* so: it was promised that "those who have reached the elevated state of well-being will gradually attain settled goodness" (I.3c–d).

This is a striking claim. First, it implies that (as Hopkins simply translates) faith is the *prerequisite* to wisdom. Without faith, there is no wisdom—and so without good conduct, there is no settled goodness. There is no shortcut to liberation through wisdom alone; virtue is necessary for conclusive goodness. But these compressed verses tell us more. Not only is there no liberation without virtuous conduct and its elevated state, but as we saw above, "*[w]herever* there is virtuous good living, final goodness appears later on" (I.3a–b)[28]—that is, virtue is *sufficient* for liberation, not perhaps in the sense that this is all one needs, but rather because having this will inevitably bring with it whatever else one may need for settled goodness. We are practically enjoined to pursue happiness, properly conceived, in order to attain awakening—a sense reinforced by the immediate rejection of ascetic practices as wrong conduct, at I.11–13 (discussed further, below). From the first, then, faith will be not only a means to high status but, in another way, to definite goodness as well—and seeking *happiness* thus leads to liberation.[29]

These two contrasting orders of priority thus suggest a distinctive possibility about the relation between these two ends, and the source of virtue's goodness. Virtuous activity may lead to happiness (understood as worthwhile joys of virtuous conduct); it may be what a truly elevated state consists in—and that, of course, is something we all know we want. But it is not, after all, *why*

27. Hopkins offers, "Of these two wisdom is the chief / Faith is its prerequisite" (I.5c–d).

28. "In one who first practices high status, definite goodness arises later" (Hopkins).

29. While virtuous conduct may be constitutive of real well-being, it could at the same time be only instrumental to wisdom and liberation. Hence even this intimate relating of the two ends does not settle the question of whether perfect wisdom casts us outside the whole domain of virtuous conduct, as well as its constraints, as it can seem from verses such as I.45: "When through understanding one has suppressed any notion of existence and non-existence, one is beyond merit and demerit" (see also, for instance, I.44, 57, 60).

virtue is a good thing. What *makes decent conduct good* is rather that it paves the way for the other and truly final end, "conclusive goodness." The elevated state (happiness) consists in just what it does, not because we all happen to want it, or even because it makes us good instances of human beings, but rather because this is the state that best conduces to *wisdom*. As wisdom is the proper means—instrumental or constitutive—to *naiḥśreyasa*, the normative work here is ultimately being done by "conclusive goodness."

This would be why, as Nāgārjuna says, the person of faithful good conduct "is understood as most partaking of splendor or superior excellence [*śreyas*]" (I.6). This means that while our notion of happiness is informed by a corrected understanding of the truly elevated state, the stone against which our conception of true well-being is sharpened is the notion of liberation as the ultimate good. If ascetic practices promoted wisdom, then pursuing them might make us happy—and we would have a rather different conception of what real well-being consisted in. Because, however, they do not make one a superior recipient of perfect goodness, neither will engaging in them elevate our current condition. Real well-being is that which, because it is constituted by (or the result of) the virtues, will give rise to settled goodness; and indeed, the virtues are themselves *virtues* because it is by pursuing and attaining these that we attain just that sort of well-being which *will give rise to* liberation.

If this is the implication of the two orders of priority between well-being and settled goodness, Nāgārjuna will not have to face the objection—readily made to ambitious moral views—of having switched horses in mid-stream. Typically, the ancient moralist gets us on board by our attraction to the first sort of good—some version of happiness—but then, in the second move, substitutes this for some other supposed good we had never conceived of. One is apt to feel tricked. But on Nāgārjuna's view, the settled good that we had never conceived of when we set off down the road of correcting our conception of happiness is not normatively disconnected from the conception of happiness we come to understand as the correct one. And this normative connection does not remain off-stage—it is, as we will see below, brought out in the appeals Nāgārjuna makes throughout the *Ratnāvalī* to views grounded in wisdom—in distinctively Buddhist insight—when enjoining and encouraging virtuous conduct. There is the prospect and the expectation of a certain psychological and motivational transformation: the very process of coming to the correct view of happiness, as virtuous well-being, is what enables us to come to see the settled goodness of liberation as attractive.

If we are not at first attracted by the thought of final liberation, if the prospect of forgoing all pleasures as well as pains does not move us, then we may simply aim at a properly conceived sort of well-being. And we can do this without thereby "missing the point." Because its being the *right* conception is grounded in the fact that it prepares the way for liberation, this will suffice to set us in the right direction—living decently, gradually altering our perspective in such a way that liberation comes into view as worth attaining. Aiming at well-being will in fact bring us closer to enlightenment, even if that is not our aim.

This promise is reiterated at the end of the *Ratnāvalī*:

> *Through faith* in the Great Vehicle, and through practicing what is explained in it, the highest awakening is attained and, along the way, even all pleasures and happiness [*sarvasaukyānī*]. (IV.98)

Wisdom Leading Virtue

So the *Ratnāvalī* opens by presenting us with two distinct ends, invariably associated. They are not two different tines in a forked road between which one must choose, for where the one is, so also eventually is the other. While such association could in principle be purely accidental, and indicative of no deeper normative connection between the two ends, this seems not to be the view of the *Ratnāvalī*. It is not a lucky accident that virtues make goodness arise. Virtues and well-being *just are* that which will enable superior goodness to arise.

But if we are not careful, wisdom—the stated means to highest enlightenment—will drop out of the picture altogether. And if we are to bring the normative order into view, we will need to keep the role of wisdom in sight. For it is wisdom—that which leads to and perhaps partially constitutes liberation—that informs our conception of virtue.

Since the *Ratnāvalī* presents itself as advice to a prince, consider first the political dimension. An extended passage in Book III (verses 30–40, especially) begins by using the *dharma* generally as the reference point for how the community ought to be ordered:

> You should sustain with all endeavor the excellent
> doctrine and the communities of monastics, and decorate
> monuments with gold and jeweled friezes. (III.33)

Sacred monuments should be protected and teachers respected (III.34–37). And teachers should, moreover, be given concrete material support:

> You should make donations of pages and books of the word
> of the King of Subduers and of the treatises they gave rise
> to, along with their prerequisites, pens and ink. (III.38)

We cannot accuse Nāgārjuna of failing to look after his own here. But these teachers with their pens and ink are not, it turns out, just teaching the virtues of self-restraint, generosity, and so on, that Nāgārjuna himself presents as constituting good conduct. Instead of confining themselves to proper practices and faith (so that people may become virtuous and happy), they are teaching wisdom (so that people may become free and good):

> *As ways to increase wisdom, whenever* there is a school
> in the land, provide for the livelihood of teachers and
> give lands to them [for their provision]. (III.39)

That is, it is for the sake of wisdom that one orders the kingdom in just the way that one does, in certain respects. It is the good of *wisdom* that determines what counts as the good ordering of the community—who should be provided with land and resources, and what counts as proper behavior in individuals in the social sphere. Indeed, there is a focus throughout these verses on activities that individuals will be encouraged to perform in their daily lives—"offer[ing] goods and services" (III.35), whether beautifying shrines, or serving teachers and making donations to them.

What makes any particular characteristic or behavior *a virtue*, "to be done," and leading to or composing happiness, is that it ultimately makes the arising of *wisdom*—and so of liberation—possible. So similarly, the correct way to organize society, if that is one's opportunity and responsibility, is in such a way that *wisdom*, and so liberation, is made more rather than less possible. This will be the practical implication—for a prince, as well as for his subjects—of our earlier observation that the normative weight is pulled all along by the ultimate end of settled or final goodness. Worldly matters of correct conduct and the nature of happiness are not settled independently of the goodness of liberation, nor independently of the fact that wisdom is its necessary means—even if motivationally one does not appeal to the goodness of *nirvāṇa* but to the attractions of real well-being.

This might well remind us of the structure of Aristotle's ethics: Ethics is for the sake of politics; politics, however, is not about winning wars, but rather about establishing a lasting and *worthwhile* peace. This requires organizing society in such a way that virtue in general, and the ultimate virtue of contemplation, is best available to as many as might attain it.

Wisdom and the nature of settled goodness determine what counts as virtuous, and so inform our conception of true happiness or well-being, on the personal as well as the political order. To see this at work, let us return to Nāgārjuna's condemnation of ascetic practices, in the *Ratnāvalī*'s first specification of virtuous practices:

> Through penances alone inflicted upon the body one
> cannot get at *dharma*; by that method one is unable either
> to stop doing harm to others or to benefit them. (I.11)

What makes ascetic practices bad is not just that they do not make me happy in the sense of feeling good—that is undisputed and almost definitionally true. Nor is it just that ascetic practices preclude or conflict with virtuous practices—whether they do can only be determined once we know what is virtuous and why. Until then, what virtuous practice consists in is precisely the point under dispute. After all, ascetic practices are not something one indulges in for fun, but rather thinking that they lead to one's ultimate well-being—presumably rejecting any distinction between happiness and goodness, or else denigrating entirely the value of recognizable, everyday well-being. If ascetic practices are supposed to be bad because they conflict with or preclude virtuous behavior, this is a substantial claim about what virtue is, and a claim in need of some justification.

If it is true that "by that method [of austerities] one is unable either to stop doing harm to others or to benefit them" (I.11c–d), this contains a substantial claim about what benefit and harm consist in, and how they are to be valued. One must suppose, contrary to the ascetic, that the practicing of austerities is *harmful*, and that what results are not *benefits*. One must have, then, some alternative account of what harm and benefit *are*, and this begins to stray into the area governed by wisdom. Why, we must ask, are the states of the ascetic—and those he somehow gives rise to in others—counted as harmful and not beneficial? This is not obvious, for ascetics are not obviously failing in ordinary virtues—they do not generally kill, steal, or slander (I.8). It is true that ascetic practices do not generally improve one's material well-being or sensual pleasures, but then neither does a habit of generosity, that central Buddhist virtue. There must, then, be some other reference point according to which the practices of ascetics are harmful to themselves and others.

If we look for some ground for *why* ascetic practices are not themselves virtuous, but rather conflict with true virtue, it seems that the problem with extreme asceticism is that it does not lead toward but rather away from *the kind of* happiness that conduces to wisdom and liberation. We can thus use awareness of wisdom as the means to conclusive goodness to discriminate true well-being from false claimants to that role. Here our ability to recognize a distinction between superior, settled goodness and true happiness—and some minimal grip on what the former is like and what is required for it—form the basis of our being able to judge correctly that the ascetic's so-called happiness is an imposter. Such awareness is asked of, or implicitly attributed to, everyone—that is, to everyone to whom the basic precepts of good behavior described in the opening verses are meant to be intelligible and motivating.

We have thus identified two implications of the structure of the *Ratnāvalī*'s ethics for ordinary morality. First, settled goodness is the normative ground for the virtues constitutive of well-being; any characteristic counts as a virtue because the well-being it leads to will itself precede wisdom and liberation. Second, the very fact that there is a wisdom possible that will give rise to settled goodness operates, even for those who do not have that wisdom, as a standard for clarifying our conception of true happiness. These are two respects in which we can specify the theoretical superiority of *naiśreyasa* over *abhyudaya*. There is, however, a final way in which the *Ratnāvalī* relates its two identified goods, according to which settled goodness—or at least its proper means, wisdom—also has explicit practical force. For, unlike Aristotle's *theoria*, in the *Ratnāvalī* the content of wisdom informs and enables virtuous dispositions.

Thus we find, for instance, appeals to wisdom as explaining and motivating *right conduct* (good practice generally):

> Keep always in your mind that things such as life, good health, and kingship are impermanent; frightened therefore [by impermanence], you will seek for the *dharma* as the only refuge. (II.43)

Impermanence is something it is the business of wisdom to properly understand. It is closely related to the central no-self claim, understanding which leads to liberation. It is not an obvious claim about the nature of things—indeed, it was disputed whether everything was in fact impermanent—and it is still less obvious that this is the observation to be kept in view in order to determine how one should conduct, and value things within, ordinary life. That things are liable to change may, after all, be good reason to devise ways to hold them more securely, or it may be a trivial fact much less relevant than others.

Being motivated by impermanence to take refuge in the *dharma* does not, of course, require that one fully understand impermanence and all of its implications. That would amount to requiring true wisdom for any virtue, and this is decidedly not the view of the *Ratnāvalī*.[30] But some appreciation of impermanence and its relevance is required, and this may in fact be one way to make good the startling claim that virtuous well-being promises wisdom, and settled goodness will follow. For a seed of wisdom here is being planted within one's motivation for virtue. Imperfectly understood, it moves one to practice generosity, patience, and restraint. In the well-being that arises from the practices, the

30. Though it may be Socrates' view in the *Euthydemus*, or Aristotle's in *EN* VI.13.

imperfectness of one's grasp of impermanence becomes evident, and becomes an object of interest and attention in its own right. One begins to seek wisdom, and to value the superior goodness it offers.

Or it may be that the movement from the imperfect grasp of impermanence to the search for wisdom is more directly related to the internal dynamics of practice. It is the appreciation of impermanence, in part, that should change my perspective on my situation in such a way that I am moved to generosity, self-restraint, and patience. But in the particular complex situation, it may not be evident what these virtues require. In attempting to understand better and better in each case what generosity and patience demand *here*, one comes to attend more to what impermanence really is, and how things being impermanent is relevant to one's perspective.

This recourse to impermanence in motivating everyday virtue occurs again in Book IV. While the discussion here is largely direct advice for governing, this is prefaced by foregrounding impermanence (e.g., in verses 13–16) as a justification and motivation for right conduct. Even within discussion of worldly concerns, the inadequacy of material results and pleasures is to be borne in mind (vv. 46–54). So while, in IV.45, the king should be motivated to behave well by the prospect of "enjoy[ing] a long series of royal goods," discussion turns immediately to the nature of the pleasures thus won: "bodily pleasure is a pleasant sensation which merely consists in the removal of pain" (IV.47a); and "in this world *any kind of pleasure* is either a mere removal of pain or a mere imagination" (IV.48a–b).

Thus far, the wisdom invoked may be specifically Buddhist in content; but it is not yet distinctively Mahāyāna, still less particularly Madhyamaka. However, embarking now on a sustained exposition of the moral psychology of pleasure and sensation generally, we are led seamlessly over the next fifteen verses into a consideration of ultimate truth. Being motivated in the ordinary way by pleasure, we examine more closely what this "pleasure" is, and what are the conditions for its arising. We learn that distinct senses have different sorts of objects, and that "the production of consciousness is conditioned by a sense, e.g. the eye and its object" (IV.55c–d). But this only invites closer consideration of the proper objects of perception, which turn out to be in themselves unreal (IV.58). We are, then, no longer considering sage practical advice for the would-be universal monarch. Unfolding that very ambition has led without break to the consideration of the nature of ultimate reality: ". . . constituents like consciousness, sensation, ideas, and forces separately taken are *in se* completely unreal: therefore from the standpoint of the absolute truth [*paramārthataḥ*] there is only unreality [*vaiyarthyaṃ*]" (IV.61). But this "theoretical" meditation should have direct practical implications, particularly for the original motivating desire we thought we were discussing and working toward:

> By [meditation on the principle that] everything is devoid of any essence [*naiḥsvābhāvyāt*] one puts an end to the thirst after association with pleasures and the thirst after dissociation from pain: for those who see (such a truth) there is liberation thence. (IV.63)

Conclusion

On the moral picture presented in the *Ratnāvalī*, we have two distinct and distinguishable ends—each final, in the sense that they can act as an endpoint of explanation of action. We have on the one hand happiness, conceived of as real well-being, a genuinely elevated condition, with respect to which faithful good conduct is the proper means of attaining the pleasure or joy (*sukhā*) we all want. On the other hand, there is the superior settled goodness of liberation, the proper attainment of which requires coming to see the nature of reality aright—specifically the wisdom that grasps emptiness, no-self and dependent arising. The phenomenologies of the two ends differ, and the former can be attained without the latter. They are in this sense independent, and one would not say of the virtuous but unenlightened life that it is not *really* a happy or an elevated one.

But pursuing these respective ends does not, in fact, lead in different directions; nor are we offered two parallel tracks (one better than the other). There is no point at which one hops from pursuing one end to pursuing the other, radically exchanges or abandons one in favor of the other. Improving clarification of what the virtue-based happiness is that one seeks gradually leads one to wisdom itself, and so to pursuing settled goodness directly. This gradual leading from one into the other, as promised in the opening verses of the *Ratnāvalī*, is possible because the normative ground all along—for which pleasures and pains are to be pursued and avoided, and when; for which behaviors are to be encouraged or repudiated; for what *good practice* consists in—is determined from the first by whatever it is that beings situated as we are need to do in order to be led to wisdom, and to a desire for definite goodness itself. In *this* sense, the two ends are not independent, but rather related, and the one dependent upon the other.

And if this is the relation between the two ends, then we see that Madhyamaka ethics has the resources to mount a critique of current practices and concepts, even if there is—in some sense—no difference between *saṃsāra* and *nirvāṇa*.[31] For attaining liberating insight remains the ultimate good by which the goodness of practices and dispositions is measured, even when that liberating insight discovers non-difference between conventional and ultimate reality.

Moreover, at a practical level, introducing considerations pertaining to liberation can motivate one to live a *happy* life, correctly conceived; and conversely, living a properly happy life—seeking, and in a certain measure attaining, the true well-being grounded in ordinary decent conduct—makes one receptive to considerations of liberation, that is, to wisdom. This may well be a concrete manifestation of the *Mūlamadhyamikakārikā*'s claim that without relying on the conventional, there is no understanding the ultimate (*MMK* XXIV.9); and in general, this dynamic interaction between virtue-based happiness (intelligible as such from an everyday perspective) and the ultimate good of wisdom-based liberation may be a distinctive feature of Madhyamaka metaphysics (or subversion of metaphysics) and the distinctive connection it draws between conventional and ultimate reality. While we might worry that this association or assimilation makes ethical progress unintelligible, it may in fact be just this which makes genuine progress possible—first, by enabling the ultimate to act as that which gives order to different conceptions of virtue and well-being; and second, more important, by ensuring that we can use increasing wisdom to improve our conception of well-being, and increasing well-being to improve our motivation for liberation.

The distinctness, yet relatedness between the two final ends is maintained right to the end of the *Ratnāvalī*'s last celebratory synopsis of the advantages of the Mahāyāna, which distinguishes well-being from liberation, but promises both as a single path:

> This Great Vehicle is composed of many virtues. . . . By liberality and morality one realizes the profit of others; by patience and energy one's own profit; meditation & wisdom are conducive to liberation. . . . The teaching of the Buddha is condensed in precepts which are salutary to others as well as to oneself and are conducive to liberation. . . . [It shows] the great path leading to illumination and consisting in acquisition of moral merits and wisdom. . . . (IV.80–83)[32]

31. Chapter 3 of this volume revisits, in the context of Candrakīrti's Madhyamaka, the charge that a Mādhyamika must founder in the dismal slough of conservative relativism, unable to critique whatever the prevailing conventions and conceptions may happen to be.

32. There is actually an argument here, in the verses taken in full, relevant to the *Ratnāvalī*'s status as propaganda for the Mahāyāna: We *ought* to take these words as genuinely "the Buddha's" *because* they encompass the six perfections, and so lead to the welfare of ourselves and others, and to enlightenment.

At least according to the *Ratnāvalī*, it is quite mistaken to suppose that Buddhist ethics has no interest in everyday virtue and happiness, or that we can escape the obligation to take an interest in this. In fact, this picture as a whole cuts against a common picture of Buddhism as offering a life-denying ethics of *nirvāṇa*, and a distinct life-affirming ethics of *karma*.[33] If the *nibbanic/kammic* distinction is true to the Theravāda it was conjured to describe, then we may have here a way of capturing what could deserve to be called a distinctively Mahāyāna ethical outlook—distinctively Madhyamaka if, as suggested above, the mutuality of the two distinct ends rests on the distinctively Madhyamaka claims that ultimate reality is itself empty (dependent), and there is nothing to distinguish *saṃsāra* and *nirvāṇa*.

Of course, we may well wonder whether, on the above picture, well-being can maintain any distinctive identity, and what normative work happiness—elevated state—is actually doing, if any at all. If what counts as well-being is determined by what will set us on the way to the wisdom that is liberating, why not conceive of the whole as a single complicated path, organized by a single final end? And if that is in fact what we are doing, then what sort of distinctness is left to happiness so conceived? It is merely another stage on a long path, picked out quite arbitrarily.

One clear suggestion of the work that "high status" does which warrants its being picked out as a distinct end can be found in the text's way of handling concerns related to well-being. Because happiness, even transformed and informed by faith and virtue, remains rooted in *sukha*—joy, pleasure, positive affective states generally—it will be intelligibly desirable even when the good of liberation remains opaque.

> Liberality, morality, patience, truthfulness, are said to be the
> religion chiefly for the householder; the essence of this (religion)
> is compassion; it must be taken hold of with energy. (IV.99)

Such goods are intelligible as desirable, even by those who do not have an inkling of wisdom. It may even be that there is some point here in referring to this state as an "elevated" one—for elevation is a comparative notion, and this brings out the way that true happiness can be *recognized* as desirable because it compares favorably to other familiar possibilities. At any rate, the ways in which the goodness of high status manifest give it an appeal even to those unmoved by thoughts of liberation, even when the ultimate worth of that state rests on its relation to liberation.

33. As, for instance, Richard Gombrich (1975) depicts in relating the Theravāda view.

In fact, this state of limited understanding of the grounds legitimating one's commitment to high status may in some cases be preferable. For, as Nāgārjuna reminds us, a false wisdom is more damaging than no wisdom at all.

> If one does not thoroughly understand this doctrine, egotism is originated; from this, *karma*, both moral and immoral is derived, and from this a new life which will accordingly take place in good conditions of existence or in bad ones. Therefore as long as this doctrine, which annihilates egotism, is not thoroughly understood, so long apply yourself with great care to the *dharma*, which consists in liberality, moral conduct, and patience.[34] (II.24–25)

There is, then, no suggestion of the *Suhṛllekha*'s view that adhering to morality alone is a positive obstacle to liberation, like belief in a self (*Suhṛllekha* v. 51). The view is rather closer to the *Mūlamadhyamakakārikā*'s claim that

> [t]he Buddha's teaching of the *dharma* is based on two truths: A truth of worldly conventional and an ultimate truth. Those who do not understand the distinction drawn between these two truths do not understand the Buddha's profound truth.
>
> *Without a foundation in the conventional truth, the significance of the ultimate cannot be taught.* Without understanding the significance of the ultimate, liberation is not achieved. (*MMK* 24.8–10)[35]

In the *Ratnāvalī*, this is because adherence to moral practice was all along conceived of as informed, more or less explicitly, by the ultimate good of liberation. The structure of *Ratnāvalī* itself makes the point by putting an outline of ultimate reality right up front—taking up the greater part of Book I—where the fact of it, its role, and some approximate grasp of its nature inform the mundane considerations of virtue and happiness that follow in the whole text. This structure is reiterated again, on a smaller scale, in Book II (vv. 1–20), which introduces what is primarily a discussion of virtuous practice with another synopsis of the right view of ultimate truth (the concern of wisdom). This is itself the seed within the exhortation of the *Ratnāvalī*, which we see popping up again and again to set the discussion of virtue in its proper perspective.

> By having faith in the Great Vehicle and by following the precepts enjoined in it one attains to the supreme illumination and midway to all happiness. (IV.98)

34. *aham, ahamkara* are used for "egotism."
35. Translation from Garfield (1995), emphasis mine.

3

The Dismal Slough

Koji Tanaka

Ethics in the Context of Conventional Truths

Throughout this book, we are investigating the nature of ethics in the context of the Madhyamaka form of Buddhist philosophy. Our investigation into Madhyamaka ethics was initiated in *Moonshadows: Conventional Truth in Buddhist Philosophy* (2011). While that book is devoted to developing an understanding of conventional truths focusing crucially on the issues in epistemology and the philosophy of language, as the investigation progressed, we started to examine the nature of Madhyamaka ethics in the context of conventional truths. Depending on how one understands conventional truths, we can see a difficulty with ethics that can be based on conventional truths. As we saw in the previous chapter, the difficulty stems from Nāgārjuna's identification of conventional truth/reality and the ultimate truth/reality (*MMK* XXIV.18–19), while an understanding of the distinction between ultimate and conventional is also necessary for the understanding of the Buddha's teachings (*MMK* XXIV.8–10). In *Moonshadows*, we investigated a negative implication of Nāgārjuna's position in the context of Candrakīrti. We interpreted Candrakīrti as a relativist and articulated the problem that arises from such an interpretation. The interpretation of Candrakīrti offered there is certainly not the only one, as we have noted. Nevertheless, if we are to investigate the nature of Madhyamaka ethics in a positive light, the negative

The author of this chapter is grateful to Bronwyn Finnigan and Tom Tillemans for helpful personal conversations.

conclusions that we reached in *Moonshadows* need to be dispelled. Before we begin our investigation of Madhyamaka ethics, thus, we re-present the concerns that we raised in *Moonshadows*, which we need to deal with in the current book. In doing so, this chapter will connect this book with *Moonshadows* and will set the stage for what follows.

Kamalaśīla's Complaint

A good place to start in order to establish the theme of this book, while linking it to the theme of *Moonshadows*, is the complaint that the eighth-century Mādhyamika Kamalaśīla made against a particular conception of conventional truths. As we have seen in *Moonshadows*, Kamalaśīla's complaint applies not only to conventional *truths* but also to ethics understood in the context of conventional truths.

In the *Sarvadharmaniḥsvabhāvasiddhi*, he writes:

> One should analyze the production of entities logically (*rigs pa* = *yukti*) and scripturally (*lung* = *āgama*). Suppose it were thought, "Why should we analyze it, when such things as the production of sprouts being conditioned by seeds and so forth is just simply acknowledged (*grags pa* = *prasiddha, pratīta*) by everyone from cowherds on up? Judicious people (*rtog pa dang ldan pa* = *prekṣāvat*) should not analyze in order to ascertain the natures of entities (*dngos po* = *vastu, bhāva*) because it would follow that [such an analysis] would be endless and that it would not be judicious." This is not right, for they would not ascertain anything through valid means of cognition (*tshad ma* = *pramāṇa*), and moreover it is possible that what is [generally] acknowledged is wrong. Otherwise [if analysis using valid means of cognition were unnecessary], no one who applied themselves to what they had themselves acknowledged would ever end up being unreliable about anything at all. . . . As for scripture without any logic, it would leave judicious people discontent. It is scripture grounded by logic that cannot lead one astray, and so first of all we should analyze logically.[1]

In this passage, Kamalaśīla emphasizes the importance of logical analysis. He argues that we need to engage with valid means of cognition (*pramāṇa*) in

1. *Sarvadharmaniḥsvabhāvasiddhi*, p. 312a 8–312b 6, translated and quoted by Tillemans in Chapter 9 of Cowherds (2011), pp. 153–154.

order to ascertain the truth of the matter. If we were to understand the production of sprouts, for example, we would need to activate valid means of cognition (perception and inference) and provide logical analysis of how and why certain seeds lead to certain sprouts (e.g., how and why sunflower seeds produce sunflowers rather than oak trees). Logical analysis that plays an integral role in inferential reasoning is an indispensable part of the acquisition of knowledge according to Kamalaśīla.

Kamalaśīla's argument for the importance and the need of logical analysis proceeds by undermining a certain view about the means of knowledge. In the above passage, he criticizes those who hold the view that we need to leave the matter of truth to cowherds and that judicious people should not engage in logical analysis. According to his opponent, if we were to understand the nature of the production of sprouts, we should appeal only to what cowherds and people on the street would acknowledge. This is not because cowherds know more about the production of sprouts. Rather, it is because, according to the opponent, there is nothing more to "truths" than what cowherds would accept.

Putting aside examining the strength of Kamalaśīla's argument for the importance of and the need for logical analysis for knowledge acquisition, if we look at Kamalaśīla's complaint from outside Madhyamaka tradition, it looks like a plausible complaint to make. In fact, it is hard to imagine that anyone seriously holds the view he is arguing against. So who is his opponent? Why does the opponent hold the view that Kamalaśīla argues against? And what exactly is the problem that Kamalaśīla is pointing out? We answered these questions in *Moonshadows*. We rehearse them in the next three sections.

Kamalaśīla's Opponent

The view that Kamalaśīla criticizes looks so implausible that it is hard to imagine anyone actually holding such a view. We may be inclined to think that Kamalaśīla is attacking a straw man. Even a hardcore conventionalist about truths, perhaps a Carnapian, would not accept the view that one's claim to truth is just a matter of appealing to what people on the streets accept prior to conducting logical analysis. For a Carnapian, an internal structure, which can provide a mechanism to answer any (internal) question, must be set up with a careful arrangement of language, and such an arrangement cannot be made by simply appealing to what cowherds and everyone else happen to think.

Surprisingly (at least from an outsider's perspective), there seems to be someone who held the view. More surprisingly, it is a very influential figure in the tradition (from a Tibetan point of view, in any case). Tillemans in *Moonshadows* argues that Kamalaśīla's opponent is the sixth-century Prāsaṅgika-Mādhyamika philosopher Candrakīrti (or someone like him) who understands what is acknowledged by the world (*lokaprasiddha*) as the sole criterion for truth and knowledge.[2] In the *Prasannapadā Madhyamakavṛtti*, Candrakīrti approvingly cites a passage of the *Ratnakūṭa*:

> The world (*loka*) argues with me. I do not argue with the world. What is agreed upon (*saṃmata*) in the world to exist, I too agree that it exists. What is agreed upon in the world to be nonexistent, I too agree that it does not exist.[3]

Tillemans argues that, according to the view that Candrakīrti endorses, what is true and what we can know can be settled only by taking inventories of what is acknowledged by the world (*lokaprasiddha*). By approvingly citing the passage, Candrakīrti seems to accept a *lokaprasiddha* account of truth and knowledge. If this interpretation is correct, Candrakīrti is accepting an account that reduces truth and knowledge to mere opinions and beliefs.

We can ask whether or not that was indeed Candrakīrti's view. In fact, he seems to acknowledge that there is something more to truth than *lokaprasiddha*, for example in his *Catuḥśatakaṭīkā* (the first four chapters) and *Madhyamakāvatāra*, VI.25. Tillemans suggests, however, that texts provide enough evidence to read him as accepting a *lokaprasiddha* account.[4] If Tillemans is correct, it was Candrakīrti (or someone like him) whom Kamalaśīla had in mind in the passage quoted above.

But why did Candrakīrti come to accept such an account (assuming that Candrakīrti did hold such an account)?[5] The answer lies in his understanding of the notion of two truths (*satyadvaya*). The two truths—conventional and ultimate truths—played an important role in the history of Buddhist philosophy and the Madhyamaka ("Middle Way") school has put them to vital use.[6] As we have seen in *Moonshadows* and as we shall revisit in the next section, Candrakīrti understands conventional truth (*saṃvṛtisatya*) in terms of *lokaprasiddha* (at least according to one plausible reading of him). If all truths are conventional truths, all there is to truth and all we can know is *lokaprasiddha*.

2. See Chapter 9 of Cowherds (2011).

3. Translated and quoted by Tillemans in Chapter 9 of Cowherds (2011), p. 151.

4. See Chapter 9 of Cowherds (2011).

5. For the rest of the chapter, we talk as if Candrakīrti held a *lokaprasiddha* account of truth. We require a careful historical examination in order to determine the accuracy of this assumption. Our purpose, however, is to articulate the implications of the *lokaprasiddha* account, assuming that Candrakīrti held such a view, rather than determining whether or not he indeed held such a view.

6. See Cowherds (2011) for a contemporary study of the two truths that is historically responsible and philosophically rich.

The Two Truths

In the famous passage of *Mūlamadhyamakakārikā* (*MMK*), the second-to-third-century South Indian Buddhist Nāgārjuna writes:

> The various buddhas' teaching of the Dharma relies upon
> two truths: the conventional truth of the world and what
> is true from the ultimate perspective. (XXIV.8)[7]

The central thesis of *MMK* is emptiness, and Nāgārjuna explains it in terms of the two truths. The thesis can be stated as the following: anything that exists is empty of essential, independent property (*svabhāva*). This property is what allows us to establish something as true from the ultimate perspective. If everything is empty of such property, however, there is nothing that can be established as ultimately true. Thus, the thesis of emptiness can be understood to mean that anything that can be said to exist is not ultimate.

This does not mean that nothing exists according to Nāgārjuna. The appeal to two truths is his way of analyzing how things exist. He claims that nothing can be said to have ultimate existence. Yet anything that can be said to exist has conventional existence. Thus, if something can be said to exist, it has only conventional existence.

In order to understand the notion of conventional existence and truth, we need to acknowledge that Nāgārjuna presents emptiness not only as an ontological thesis but also in terms of semantics. Even though Nāgārjuna does not elaborate on semantics (or language), we must examine the semantics of emptiness in terms of two *truths*. The distinction between two truths was first developed by the Abhidharma schools. The semantics that Ābhidharmikas adopt in developing two truths is the correspondence theory of truth. That is, a statement is ultimately true if it corresponds to the ultimate way in which things exist, and a statement is conventionally true if it corresponds to a conventional way in which things exist. Thus, an ultimate truth is concerned with what ultimately exists, and a conventional truth is concerned with what conventionally exists. This means that, even though ontology and semantics may be understood separately, under the Abhidharma semantic principle, the distinction between existence and truth collapses. We can think of the Abhidharma semantics as Russellian (as opposed to Fregean). Russell (1904) rejects Frege's *sense* that mediates between a statement and the things that are referenced by the statement. For Russell, it is only reference (objects and their properties, including

7. *dve satye samupāśritya buddhānāṃ dharmadeśanā / lokasaṃvṛtisatyaṃ ca satyaṃ ca paramārthataḥ//* Translated and quoted by Newland and Tillemans in Chapter 1 of Cowherds (2011), p. 3.

the way the objects are arranged) that determines what is true. Similarly, under the Abhidharma semantics, it is the reference relation between statements and referents that sufficiently determines the truth values.[8]

Nāgārjuna does not seem to introduce a new semantic principle while arguing against Abhidharma ontology. He simply adopts the Abhidharma reference-based semantic principle. This means that what is true can be determined by investigating the way things exist. For Nāgārjuna, however, nothing has ultimate existence. So there is no ultimate truth for him. This means that, from the ultimate perspective, analysis of anything, how sophisticated and robust it might be, cannot reach an ultimate answer. Regardless of how "deep" our analysis can go, we cannot reach a stage where an ultimate answer can be given in response to a question about the nature of the existent. This can be contrasted sharply from the Abhidharma thought according to which we can provide an ultimate answer by appealing to the ultimate way in which things exist.

This means that employment of analysis cannot ultimately be put to bear fruit. If no analysis can provide the ultimate answer, then there does not seem to be much point in engaging in analysis. For example, people may have different conventional opinions about why sunflower seeds give rise to sunflowers rather than oak trees. However, there is no ground in which they can adjudicate whose conventional opinion to accept. If there is no way to settle the issue, then there is not much point in arguing with each other. So all we have are the conventions in the form of opinions that people mundanely accept and believe (*lokaprasiddha*).[9]

We can now see that the position that Kamalaśīla criticizes is derivable from Nāgārjuna's thesis of emptiness explained in terms of two truths. Whether or not Candrakīrti advocated a *lokaprasiddha* account of truth and knowledge and whether or not he derived it from Nāgārjuna's thesis of emptiness in the way that it is argued here, we can see that Kamalaśīla was not necessarily attacking a straw man. Rather, he was criticizing a view that can be made sense of from a Mādhyamika point of view. Given the prominent status that Candrakīrti enjoys within the Madhyamaka tradition (at least from a Tibetan point of view), Kamalaśīla's criticism is directed toward a respectable Mādhyamika position.[10]

8. See Tanaka (2014) for the suggestion to understand the Abhidharma semantics as Russellian. Garfield (1996) and Westerhoff (2009, ch. 9) suggest that the Abhidharma semantics was the orthodox account in Indian philosophical circles around the time of Nāgārjuna.

9. See also Dreyfus's discussion of this issue formulated in terms of skepticism in the context of Patsab Nyimadrak (*pa tshab nyi ma grabs*), the translator and promoter of Candrakīrti in Tibet, in Chapter 6 of Cowherds (2011).

10. While a no-analysis view entailed by a *lokaprasiddha* view might have been entertained by many Mādhyamikas, a *lokaprasiddha* view may not be the only Mādhyamika view on two truths. Nāgārjuna's doctrine

Dismal Slough

In the previous section, we saw a derivation of a *lokaprasiddha* account of truth from the two truths of Nāgārjuna. It involves defining truths in terms of *lokaprasiddha*. All there is to truth, according to a *lokaprasiddha* account, are the opinions and beliefs that people happen to have. Even if it may make sense from a Mādhyamika point of view, a *lokaprasiddha* account of truth—whether the account was actually held by Candrakīrti or not—is hard to accept, however. As Kamalaśīla points out in the passage quoted at the beginning, there are mainly two reasons for this.

First, there is no doubt that our opinions are unreliable. For a long time, scientists (and mathematicians) believed that the geometric nature of the existent was Euclidean. They used to recommend calculating the shortest distance based on Euclidean geometry. When mathematicians discovered geometries whose curvature was non-zero (meaning that these geometries can accommodate the non-flat nature of the Earth), the thought about the essentially Euclidean nature of what exists was put into doubt. The thought that geometry is just Euclidean was also questioned. What the "experts" used to think to be the shortest distance between two points according to Euclidean geometry may not be the shortest distance once we take into account the non-zero curvature of the Earth. Examples such as this show that even the experts' opinions, let alone the opinions of the cowherds and people on the street, may be unreliable and may need revision.

Second, a *lokaprasiddha* account entails not just the unreliability of conventional truth but also an extreme relativism. According to a *lokaprasiddha* account, all there is to truth are mere opinions (or beliefs). Since there is no analysis that can be given to establish the "real" truth of the matter, no one can have any privileged status with respect to their opinion (except, perhaps, the buddhas[11]). Any criticism or rejection is just another opinion. According to a *lokaprasiddha* account, there is no possibility of providing an analysis—whether on an empirical ground or any other ground—that can establish whether the geometry to be used for aviation should be Euclidean or non-Euclidean.

A *lokaprasiddha* account entails not only an extreme relativism but also conservatism. If all we can do in search of truth is simply "read off the

of two truths has also been interpreted in many different ways. However, a *lokaprasiddha* account of two truths is the account that became one of the focal points of investigations in *Moonshadows*, and we follow that analysis in this chapter.

11. The buddhas' alleged omniscience is a complicated issue. For discussions of omniscience, see McClintock (2000) and (2010).

surface" (Siderits 1989, p. 244), there is no room for analysis, and the "principal epistemic task [is] just to passively acquiesce and duplicate" (Tillemans in Cowherds 2011, p. 152). This means, as Tillemans points out, that "nothing the world ever endorsed could be criticized or rejected" (Cowherds 2011, p. 152). This means that no one can successfully criticize a Euclidean expert who suggests the shortest route for an aircraft based on Euclidean geometry (using a Euclidean map) except in the case of miscalculation. According to the *lokaprasiddha* account, since Euclidean geometry is used to explain why some route is the shortest by this expert and the Euclidean measurement is internal to the geometry having no applicability outside Euclidean geometry,[12] non-Euclidean measurement cannot be used to reject such a suggestion. Since an empirical observation does not have a privileged status, one cannot even appeal to our observation to adjudicate which geometric measurement should be used for aircraft navigation. Thus, a *lokaprasiddha* account removes the role of normativity that the notion of truth is said to play. It undermines the authority of epistemic practices by reducing normativity to consistency internal to the set of one's opinions or beliefs—hence the view that what people say and believe is indeed so is a dismal view. As Tillemans puts it aptly, what the *lokaprasiddha* account entails is a *dismal slough*.[13]

If truth is stripped of normative roles other than simple consistency checking in our epistemic practice, the notion of *justification* also loses its normative status. This is not to say that truth or justification loses *all* normative roles. One might think of consistency as normative. Nevertheless, no analysis can establish *why* something is the way it is, other than simply pointing at the mere fact about someone holding an opinion and claiming that it is consistent with other opinions one has. This means that dismal slough flattens out any meaningful distinction between truth and falsity that can be relied upon to acquire knowledge. The mere facts that someone believes that the shortest route for an airplane is the shortest Euclidean distance (on a Euclidean map) and that Euclidean geometry is consistent do not tell us what one is *justified* in believing. It just says that someone has that opinion and it is consistent with other beliefs one has.[14]

In the last chapter of *Moonshadows*, Finnigan and Tanaka argue that the threat of extreme relativism and conservatism applies not only to truth but also to ethical norms. In the same way that the dismal slough flattens out any

12. See Hilbert (1902).

13. The term "dismal slough" was coined by Tillemans in Chapter 9 of Cowherds (2011).

14. A similar complaint was raised against Hilbert's approach to mathematics by Frege. See their exchanges in Frege's *Philosophical and Mathematical Correspondence*.

meaningful distinction between truth and falsity, it also flattens out the possibility of meaningful distinction between good and bad conduct. Thus, Finnigan and Tanaka write, "[i]f a precept counts as morally sound just in case somebody somewhere [consistently] adopts it, then *any* practice could turn out to be virtuous. In such a case, there would be no moral distinction between different practices and types of actions" (Cowherds 2011, pp. 223–224).

It is true that some Mādhyamikas *do* make claims about good and bad conduct. As Finnigan and Tanaka acknowledge in *Moonshadows*, Śāntideva and Tsongkhapa, as well as Nāgārjuna, accept such a distinction. In his *Bodhicaryāvatāra* (*BCA*), "Śāntideva explicitly and repeatedly disavows certain actions as wrong (*BCA* II.63), cruel (I.33), and evil (II.28) and prescribes certain other behaviors as good (I.31), meritorious (IV.9), and skillful (IV.18) with respect to certain ethical codes (V.42) or precepts (III.23)" (Cowherds 2011, p. 222). Candrakīrti himself claims in the *Madhyamakāvatāra* that a bodhisattva "possesses the quality of perfect morality, and therefore has extirpated the stain of immorality even in his dreams" (II.Iab).[15] Tsongkhapa explains this verse by assuming that ethical precepts distinguish good and bad conducts.[16] Moreover, Candrakīrti argues for (or, perhaps, simply spells out Āryadeva's views about) a substantive reform in people's ethical opinions and conduct via *prasaṅga* (a form of *reductio ad absurdum*).[17]

Now, there is nothing that one needs to be *committed* to in the employment of *prasaṅga*. One can simply acknowledge what is involved in the opponent's position and argue, purely on the opponent's own ground, that the opponent's position is inconsistent. This does not bind the opponents to change their views. Thus, an employment of *prasaṅga* does not necessarily invoke any sense of normativity other than consistency. Nevertheless, while engaging in meaningful ethical discourse, we might voluntarily adjust our ethical opinions on our own accord when presented with the inconsistency of our position based on *prasaṅga*. This shows that the suspension of normativity is not necessarily incompatible with a substantive reform in people's ethical opinions and conduct.

Despite this, as Finnigan and Tanaka argue, *lokaprasiddha* offers no resources to *justify* ethical claims and conduct beyond mere facts about us having certain opinions and conducting ourselves in a certain way. There is no room for analyzing *why* one should have certain ethical opinions and behave in a certain way. All we can do is survey and observe what people believe about how

15. Translated and quoted in Cowherds (2011), p. 222.

16. See Cowherds (2011), pp. 222–223.

17. See Tillemans (2010), p. 365, and Tillemans (2011), p. 160, footnote 16.

one should act. Nothing anyone (perhaps barring the buddhas themselves) says and does has a privileged status that would trump other opinions and conduct. And it is not just that the opinions of anyone *else* cannot trump our opinions. It is also that we cannot justify our own behavior. Just like the case of truths, we cannot provide a justificatory ground for our own behavior under a *lokaprasiddha* account. So it is not just that no ethical claim or opinion is suasive; it is also that no ethical claim or opinion is normative. No ethical claim or opinion can serve as the standard in terms of which all our behaviors can be evaluated and directed. An acceptance of *lokaprasiddha* thus does not allow any possibility of reform in our ethical life.[18]

This ethical extreme relativism and conservatism is more problematic than the extreme relativism and conservatism about truths. As Finnigan (2015) argues, in the case of truths, there seems some convergence regarding what exists. We can all agree that rice exists and that sunflower seeds give rise to sunflowers (rather than oak trees, for example), though we may disagree about why that is the case. The case of ethics seems different. Many of us disagree about how we should conduct ourselves. We do know that "giving," for example, is an ethical precept for the Mādhyamika (and the Buddhist). But not everyone believes that giving is a good thing. Otherwise, classifying "giving" as an ethical precept would be an empty gesture.

These disagreements pertain not only to difficult cases like abortion and euthanasia but also to our day-to-day conduct. Should we say "hello" to a stranger? Should we shake hands or hug each other or simply bow? These questions may not be raised in ethics class, but they are, nonetheless, all questions about our ethical conduct broadly construed. And Buddhist precepts also apply to these questions. Given that there are a wide variety of opinions about how to conduct our day-to-day life, there is not any convergence regarding how we should behave and conduct our ethical life except in a limited conversation among Mādhyamikas who already share the same views. This means that we cannot even appeal to the opinion of the majority in order to come to a consensus about what to do.

A *lokaprasiddha* account of truth, thus, entails a *lokaprasiddha* account of ethical justification. Under this account, whatever we do is *ipso facto* a "justified" conduct. The "rightness" of our conventional behavior is accounted for only by what cowherds and people on the street would acknowledge. We would be trapped in extreme relativism and there would be no possibility of justifiably reforming our conduct. That is indeed a dismal slough.

18. See Chapter 14 of Cowherds (2011).

Madhyamaka Ethics?

Nāgārjuna advanced the thesis of emptiness—that things exist empty of essential, independent property. In order to make sense of this thesis, he explained it in terms of two truths—conventional and ultimate truths. The thesis can then be understood to mean that anything that can be said to exist not ultimately but only conventionally. Candrakīrti seems to interpret this to mean that there are only conventionally accepted opinions (what is acknowledged by the world [*lokaprasiddha*]) to account for truth. As we have seen, his *lokaprasiddha* account of truth reduces truth to mere consistency and strips normativity from truth. It also removes the possibility of justifying ethical claims and conduct. This means that there cannot be justified ethics from Candrakīrti's perspective (assuming, in the way we did in *Moonshadows*, that he did hold a *lokaprasiddha* account of truth).

How can we account for Madhyamaka ethics if Mādhyamikas cannot account for justified moral claim and conduct? How can we understand, for instance, Śāntideva's *Bodhicaryāvatāra*, which appears to be an ethical treatise? A serious challenge to any distinctively Mādhyamika ethics is the extreme relativism and conservatism. This is the challenge with which *Moonshadows* ended its discussion. Can a Mādhyamika meet the challenge by offering anything distinctively Mādhyamika?[19] In the rest of the book, sophisticated analytical and historical tools are used to respond to this challenge as attempts to escape from the dismal slough.

19. Finnigan and Tanaka provide a positive answer to this question. Instead of justification, Mādhyamikas can focus on the "instantiation" or the enactment of moral claims. See Chapter 14 of Cowherds (2011). See also Garfield (2010/2011) for an account of moral phenomenology that can be seen as answering the challenge in a similar way. One can also meet the challenge by providing a different account of truth. For various semantics of emptiness that were developed in response, see Tanaka (2014).

4

The Śāntideva Passage

Bodhicaryāvatāra VIII.90–103

Jay L. Garfield, Stephen Jenkins, and Graham Priest

The passages from the *Bodhicaryāvatāra* (*BCA*) on "exchanging self and other" have been a center of debate in the study of Buddhist ethics; they play a major role in this volume, and are read very differently by different Cowherds. In this chapter, we consider these passages, their role in the *BCA,* three ways in which they might reasonably be interpreted, and what hangs on their interpretation. We direct the reader, in particular, to Chapters 7 and 8 of this volume for alternative readings, and we encourage the reader to consult the translation of Prajñākāramati's commentary on these verses, included as an Appendix to his volume. First, we offer some comments on the composition of the whole text and on its author or authors. Next, we consider the central passage at issue. We then turn to a discussion of the three possible interpretations. We close with a few comments on what is at stake.

Śāntideva and *Bodhicaryāvatāra*

The importance of the *BCA* in the Buddhist world is demonstrated by its distribution and influence across the Indian subcontinent over Buddhism's last four or five centuries there, as well as in Tibet, Central Asia, and perhaps Sumatra. Its influence is reflected in an abundance of Indian commentaries that span five centuries. There are also two short summaries, the *piṇḍārthas*.

Little can be historically confirmed about the life of Śāntideva. Traditional hagiographies portray him as a monk at Nālandā University in the eighth century, which is consistent with the dating of works attributed to him. According to one tradition, Śāntideva is said to have recited the *BCA* and then to have disappeared into empty space, leaving no manuscript. On this story the text we have was memorized from its oral performance. The first part of this account is, presumably, fiction. This leaves us with the fact, and the problem, of the text. Its various Sanskrit and Tibetan editions differ significantly from one another. Three different versions of the text, varying between 700 and 1,000 verses, circulated across the subcontinent. Indian and Tibetan commentators also record different versions of the text and cross-reference them.

The oldest version yet discovered is dramatically shorter than *BCA* and is attributed to Akṣayamati, a possible epithet of Śāntideva, under the title *Bodhi-sattva-caryāvatāra* (*BsCA*). This version circulated independently of the longer text, and a commentary remains in the Tibetan canon. The name Śāntideva, as we use it now, merely personifies the voice of a later version of the text, a version that was redacted, bowdlerized, and amended by an editor with views almost certainly different from those of the author of the earlier version.

Harrison (2007) suggests that the longer version is a later revision by Śāntideva (taken to be the author of the original, short version) himself. Many of the additions, however, including the 70 verses added to the wisdom chapter, seem to be either unnecessary or out of context. They often break its flow, and fail to clarify—or even obfuscate—the arguments. One would expect Śāntideva to have done a more elegant job in revising his masterwork. Indeed, it appears that the later version of the text was more focused on debates with rival traditions than the earlier version, which was more focused on individual practice.

These considerations suggest a distinct redactor of the later edition. The original author, whoever he was, recommends that the text be used in conjunction with a compendium of scriptural passages, the *Sūtrasamuccaya* (Anthology of *Sūtras*) attributed to Nāgārjuna; the later redactor adds a further recommendation of the *Śikṣāsamuccaya* (*Training Anthology*), a text also attributed to Śāntideva. These anthologies provided students with a pedagogical guide to the massive Mahāyāna *sūtra* literature, and were central to the curricula in Indian monastic universities for the study of key scriptural themes. It would thus appear that *BCA* was written as a training manual in the practice of a *bodhisattva* and, together with the anthologies, was used as a textbook in a course of study and practice.

The *piṇḍārthas*, composed by Dharmapāla of Sumātra, show that it was important to summarize the text in an easily memorable form. The *BCA*, hence, may well have been composed to function in the same way as a *sūtra*, and so was probably written to be recited. Since the text had important ritual and performative roles, it may be important to interpret its conceptual content in relation to these roles.

For present purposes, it is most important to note that the anonymous editor's extensive additions to the *BsCA* on "exchange of self and other" diverge from that earlier text in arguing for compassion from a selfless perspective. All of the passages to which we refer in this volume on ownerless suffering appear to be later interpolations. Saitō notes that, of the more than twenty verses deleted by the reviser from the *BsCA*'s wisdom chapter, most are on a single subject, *anātman*.[1]

Any hermeneutical approach to the text must therefore be very cautious. We cannot automatically assume internal consistency in the works attributed to Śāntideva, or that they were the work of one mind, or that they constitute a single coherent project. A certain level of internal dissonance might be expected. This is certainly the case in the passage on exchange of self and other, which may not even be internally consistent. What we can attempt, as does the commentarial tradition, is to address the text we have in front of us—a text which, whatever its origins, has been treated for many centuries as a unity—and to take Śāntideva not as a historical figure whose intention we might wish to divine, but as an authorial center of gravity for a text that may have coalesced through the contributions of a transhistorical committee of scholars with divergent aims and views.

The Meditation Chapter and the Passage That Is our Concern

So much for the text as a whole. Let us now turn to the Meditation Chapter, which contains our target passage. *Bodhicaryāvatāra* is, first and foremost, a guide to the conduct and attitude necessary for following the *bodhisattva* path, the way of life committed to cultivating and acting on *bodhicitta*, the aspiration to attain awakening for the benefit of all sentient beings. It is structured largely by the rubric of the six perfections to be cultivated on this path—the perfections of generosity, mindfulness, patience, effort, meditation, and wisdom—in that order. The text begins by characterizing the nature of benighted life in *saṃsāra*, and presenting the motivation for embarking on the *bodhisattva* path. Most of the book is devoted to explaining the perfections to be cultivated on that path, the reasons for cultivating them, and the means for doing so.

1. For detailed treatments of the philological issues addressed above, see Eimer (1997); Wallace and Wallace's discussion in *Śāntideva* (1997); Saitō (1993, 1996, 2006); Harrison (2007); Liland (2009); Ishida (2010).

The passage we will examine in detail comes late in the text, a bit more than midway through the eighth chapter (of ten), the chapter on meditation. The chapter is neither a manual on meditative technique, nor a brief for the importance of meditation per se. Instead, the bulk of the chapter is devoted to a discussion of objects of meditation, images or ideas upon which one is to meditate in order to cultivate dissatisfaction with sensual pleasures, commitment to practice, and positive motivations toward others. In this context, this set of verses can be read either as one more object of meditation, or as containing arguments for the value and probity of the moral attitude to be achieved through meditation.

The Meditation chapter comprises about 58 verses in *BsCA*, but 186 verses in *BCA*. Some 60 percent of the increase in length from *BsCA* to *BCA* constitutes additions to this chapter (Crosby and Skilton 1996, p. 77). The original and emended versions of this text seem to reflect very different views about the place of self in this discourse. In the earlier version there is an emphasis on the conventional "self" as central to an ethical perspective, for instance in exchanging identity with another, or meditating on the sameness of self and other. In the later version, on the other hand, the ownerlessness of experiences is emphasized, and it is argued that the perspective of self is to be *eliminated*. The passage in question is, indeed, one of the most dramatically altered sections of the *BsCA* of Akṣayamati. The reviser, who gave us the *BCA* as we know it today, created the first half of verse 90 to introduce a section of verses, 90b to 99, which he moved from the earlier version's chapter on *Vīrya* (effort) to the *BCA*'s chapter on meditation (Ishida 2010). Except for verse 101a, verses 100 through 113 were then added by the reviser.

If we ignore the verses 100 through 113 that are added in the later version, an elegant continuity appears between verses 99 and 114, which reflects the original *BsCA* verses VI.43–44. Just as the hand protects the foot as part of one body, other beings should be protected as part of one world, and, since others are no more different from us than our own future selves are different from our present selves, we should address their suffering just as we would our own. The *bodhisattva* is encouraged to identify with the body of another, rather than take a selfless perspective. The reviser appears to argue instead that self-identity is itself the ethical problem and should be rejected.

While the original text emphasized the wholeness of the body or the world, the later reviser emphasized that, because the wholeness of persons is unreal, the proper perspective for compassion is one of ownerless sufferings. Perhaps the second layer of thought was added as a corrective. It is not at all obvious that these positions can be reconciled: nonetheless, they are treated as a unity in the Indian and Tibetan commentaries, and some Cowherds regard them as complementary rather than inconsistent.

Here is the passage in full. Words in italics are unique to the *BCA*.[2]

VIII.90 *First, one should earnestly meditate*
On the similarity of self and others:
Everyone, subject to similar happiness and suffering,
Should be protected by me like myself

VIII.91 Just as the body, having many parts, divided into
hands etc.
Should be protected as one.
The world, though divided, is undivided
With respect to the nature of suffering and happiness.

VIII.92 Even if my own suffering
Does not hurt others' bodies,
That suffering is still mine and is hard to bear
Because of self-love.

VIII.93 Just so, even though I do not experience
The suffering of another myself,
It is still his;
His suffering is hard to bear because of self-love.

VIII.94 The suffering of others should be eliminated by me,
Because it is suffering like my own suffering.
I should help others
Because they are sentient beings, as I am a sentient being.

VIII.95 When the happiness of myself and others
Are pleasing in the same way,
Then what is so special about me
That I merely strive for my own happiness?

VIII.96 When the fear and suffering of myself and others
Are not pleasing in the same way
Then what is so special about me
That I defend myself, but not others?

VIII.97 If they are not defended
Because their suffering does not hurt me,
So why defend against the suffering of a future body
That does not hurt me?

2. Translations are from the Sanskrit with reference to the sDe dge edition of the Tibetan.

VIII.98 It is vain fantasy
To think "that is me then."
Only another died
From which only another is born.

VIII.99 If it is thought that only the suffering which is his
Should be protected,
When a pain in the foot does not belong to the hand,
Why should it protect that?

VIII.100 *"Even though it is wrong,*
This happens because of self-construction [ahaṃkāra]."
But that which is wrong, whether one's own or others',
Should be avoided as far as possible.

VIII.101 A continuum and collection,
Just like such things as a series or an army, are unreal.
The one for whom there is suffering does not exist.
Therefore to whom will that suffering belong?

VIII.102 *Since all ownerless sufferings are*
Without distinction,
They should be alleviated just because of being suffering,
What restriction can be made in that case?

VIII.103 *"Why should suffering be alleviated?"*
Because it is undisputed by everyone that
If it is to be alleviated, all of it is to be alleviated.
After all, I am just like everyone else.

The Three Readings

The *Bodhicāryāvatāra* passage in question, as it was read by canonical commentators, appears to advocate adopting an impartial attitude toward the suffering of oneself and others, and treating the suffering of others as a motivation for action to relieve it—just as one might treat one's own suffering as a motivation for relieving it. The question is how, exactly, it is to be understood as doing this. Reasonable scholars disagree. Three distinct interpretations are encountered in this volume. One, which we call "the meditation reading," treats this passage not so much as containing an argument or arguments for the adoption of a particular position regarding suffering and happiness, but instead as an instruction for meditation—meditation intended to cultivate this attitude.

A second interpretation, which we call the "*Abhidharma* reading," takes the passage indeed to contain arguments, the crucial one appealing to what appears to be an *Abhidharma* metaphysics. A third interpretation takes it to contain an argument for adopting the attitude in question on the grounds that it is the only rational attitude to take: self-interest is arbitrary. We call this the "rationality reading."

In exploring these readings we will consider two canonical commentaries on *BCA*, Prajñākaramati's (eleventh century) *Bodhicaryāvatāra-Pañjikā* (*Commentary to Bodhicaryāvatāra*), and the influential Tibetan commentary by the fifteenth-century scholar rGyal tshab Darma Rinchen, *Byang chub sems pa'i spyod pa la 'jug pa'i rnam bshad rgyal sras 'jug ngogs* (*Gateway to the Glorious Explanation of Bodhicaryāvatāra*) (1999).

The Meditation Reading

First, we consider the Meditation reading. The eighth chapter is structured around a set of objects of meditation, including the transience of relationships (5–10), the repulsiveness of the body (40–85), and so forth. It therefore makes sense to understand this passage as one more object of meditation. We may see these verses not primarily as containing *arguments* for the conclusion that I ought to regard others as morally and motivationally identical to myself, and to take their weal and woe as motives for action, just as I do my own, but rather as a set of images which, if contemplated carefully in meditation, would *cause* me to adopt such attitudes. On this reading, Śāntideva does not *argue* for the value of these attitudes, but *assumes* them, and provides a practical way to cultivate them in meditation.

There are several reasons to like this reading. First, the passage begins and closes with admonitions to meditate in this way. The passage is at least part of a set of meditation instructions, whatever else they are. Ishida (2010, p. 3) observes that in the *BA*, this passage, which was transplanted to the meditation chapter, is introduced and characterized by meditational terms that are absent in the *BsCA*.

This supports the thought that this section should be read as meditation guidance and should be evaluated as such, not as a philosophical argument, which would be written in the style of a debate manual, as is the ninth chapter on wisdom. Buddhist meditation manuals, it should be noted, often urge the use of imagination to generate motivation, and this may simply be a case in which *bodhisattvas* are asked to imagine taking on the identity of another person and to observe themselves through another's eyes. On this reading, then, the entire section should not be taken as containing philosophical arguments, but as an imaginative motivational technique (see Harris, 2011).

We might note, also, that rGyal tshab (a disciple of Tsongkhapa, whose commentaries on Indian texts are central to the dGe lugs monastic curriculum)—who, we shall argue, himself supports the rationality reading—begins his commentary on verse 90 as follows:

> "How should one meditate on this?," one might ask. One should first meditate on the fact that self and others are alike. "How?," one might then ask. Just as one attempts to increase one's own happiness and reduce one's own suffering, one should attempt to increase others' happiness and reduce others' suffering. Thus, since to achieve others' happiness and to dispel their suffering is similar, one should see that all sentient beings are like oneself, and so one should protect them.
>
> The second part of this discussion divides into four: The explanation of the meaning of meditating on the similarity of self and others; how to meditate on the similarity of self and other; the benefits of meditating in this way; having meditated on the similarity of self and others, how to see things this way.[3] (1999, p. 329)

We need go no further into rGyal tshab's commentary at this point. The important issue is this: he characterizes the structure of the discussion as a set of meditation instructions in the classic mold of explaining the meaning, method, benefits, and consequences of the meditational practice.

Though there is good reason to take this passage simply as a description of a meditational practice, and although the reviser's intentions in moving the material to a chapter on meditation and his use of meditational language are clear, we should also remember that the passages that were relocated were not originally framed, composed, or intended in this way. Moreover, note that taking them as concerned with meditation is not inconsistent with taking them also to present arguments, for many Buddhist meditational practices are analytical in character, and the mind can be transformed as much by familiarization with argument as by visualization.

Indeed, the fact that this passage figures in a chapter on meditation and in the context of the introduction of a set of meditation practices does not entail that it itself is merely of practical use. After all, the *BCA* generally defends the

3. *thabs gang gi sgon nas bsgom zhe nab dag dang gzhan du mnyam pa ni dang po nyid du 'bad de bsgom par bya'o/ji ltar zhe na bdag gi bde ba ched du bsgrub cing sdug bsngal ched du 'gig pa bzhin du bzhan gyi bde sdug la yang 'dor len de ltar byed pas gzhan gyi bde ba bsgrub pa dang sdug bsngal sel bar mnyam pas na sems can thams cad bdag bzhin gces par gzung nas bsung bar bya'o//nyis pa la bzhi/bdag bzhan mnyam par sgom pa'i don bshad pa dang/bdag gzhan mnyam par sgom tshul dang/de ltar sgom pa'i phan yon dang/bdag gzhan mnyam par goms na de lrat bskyed nus pa'o//* All translations of rGyal tshab are our own from the Sarnath edition.

positions it sets out through argument. We can expect it as well to *argue for,* not merely *describe,* the meditational practices it recommends and the goals at which it takes them to be aimed. The ideas here seem too deeply interlaced with basic Buddhist teachings on selflessness to be taken simply as practical imaginations. Furthermore, Prajñākaramati's commentary clearly analyzes the verses as if they contain the technical components of a logical argument. We now turn to two readings of this passage as argument.

The *Abhidharma* Reading

The first argumentative reading we consider is one that appeals to an *Abhidharma* understanding of what it is to be a person. This is the way it is interpreted by Williams (1999). On this interpretation, the passage is to be understood roughly as follows. VIII.90 states the major conclusion of the passage—that we should be equally concerned with everyone—at (d); (c) also gives a reason for this, though an apparently fallacious one. The reason is that everyone experiences happiness and suffering in the same way. It follows that everybody is motivated to act in the same way. This could be achieved in two distinct ways, though: (i) if everybody is motivated to alleviate only his or her own suffering; (ii) if everyone is motivated to alleviate everyone's suffering. Śāntideva clearly wants the stronger conclusion (ii), but this does not follow if (i) is a possibility.

VIII.91 then gives an independent argument for (ii). This is by analogy. Just as each part of the body looks after the well-being of each other part, so each person should look after the well-being of all others. This analogy is a poor one, though. Each part of the body looks after the well-being of the others because they all constitute an integrated functioning whole. This is not (or not obviously) the case with a group of people. To take it to be obvious would be to beg the question: for each of us, unlike the parts of our bodies, appears to have our own interests.

One can hear VIII.92 as an objection to these arguments, since it states that every person does indeed have something that makes her relationship to her own suffering different from her relationship to the suffering of others. I feel my suffering, in a way that I do not feel others' suffering. VIII.93 then replies that everyone is in the same boat. And VIII.94 then concludes that since this is the case, I should alleviate everyone's suffering. This, however, just repeats the argument of VIII.91, and is problematic for the same reason.

VIII.95 and 96 ask why I should treat others differently from myself. This is effective rhetoric, but a rhetorical question is not an argument. As long as the objection of VIII.92 has not been answered, the interlocutor can simply respond, "because it is mine." VIII.97 and 98 do, however, give an argument that would undermine the objection raised against the argument in VIII.90. I am in the same situation with respect to others as I am with respect to my future self. I am literally identical with neither. Nonetheless, it clearly makes sense to take steps to alleviate future suffering. After all, I cannot alleviate the suffering of my present self: that is *already now* happening. So if I act to alleviate my own suffering, it must be the suffering of my future selves. But since I am no more identical with those selves than with the selves of others, I should act to alleviate their suffering as well. Prajñākāramati glosses VIII.97 as follows:

> "No harm—i.e., injury—comes to me by means of the suffering of that other person"—if consequently for this reason I do not protect someone else, then there would be the following difficulty. "There is no harm whatsoever to this [presently] appropriated body [of mine from suffering] of a future body marked by suffering of birth in hell, etc., in a future life," since this is what is said in the world, or what follows from that. This being so, for what purpose does one protect it from that? Because, with respect to what is called the body, evil is to be avoided and the good promoted.[4]

This is an interesting argument, but it is problematic. For all that I am not identical with my future selves, my present self has a causal relationship with those that it does not have with others: it lies in the same causal continuum. It is my present self who suffers with a hangover today because of what my past self did last night. In the same way, if I drink to excess now, it is my future self that will pay the price. This causal continuity is what grounds my prudence. At least *prima facie*, I am not in the same situation with respect to others. There is still, then, a difference between myself and others. So there is no compelling argument yet for treating others as I do myself.

VIII.99 repeats the argument by analogy of VIII.92. VIII.100 imagines someone saying that something or other happens only because of a false sense of self. Prajñākāramati glosses the point as follows:

> The sense of "I" with respect to this body is due to conceiving of an "I" even though there is no self. Protective attention toward the foot etc. results, i.e., is produced. This [conceiving of an "I"] is not correct. Since what is mistaken does not meet with success, it is to be abandoned, i.e., removed, with respect both to oneself and to others, to the best of one's ability, i.e., to

4. See the Appendix to this volume for context.

> the extent that one is capable. Only because of insufficiency of power is it acceptable to overlook it. This is the meaning.

He then imagines an objection:

> Perhaps it will be said: "While there is no self or the like, still there is a single series, and likewise the collection of many things such as hands and feet is a single body. In this case such things as warding off harm and the like as one's own will be restricted to the pair that is suitably linked in this world and the next. Hence your 'for there is no difference' [between the case of another person and the case of the hand and the foot] has an unproven reason, and the previous reason ['because it is suffering'] is inconclusive."

This takes us into the core argument of VIII.101 and 102, which he interprets as a reply, and where the appeal to self-interest is finally laid to rest.

Since it asks us to take instances of suffering seriously, while pointing out that the owners of suffering do not ultimately exist, many have taken VIII.101 to contain an implicit appeal to *abhidharma* metaphysics. Prajñākāramati explains:

> The series does not exist as a single ultimately real entity. But this is just a stream-like succession of resultant moments in the relation of effect and cause, for nothing distinct from that is apprehended. Thus in order to express with a single word these moments, the buddhas create a "series" as a conventional designation, for practical purposes. This is only nominally existent. So attachment to this is not right. That is not appropriated by anything other than a self. The collection is likewise not someone ultimately real thing over and above the things that are collected, for it is not apprehended apart from them. But the mistaken concept with respect to this is understood by means of the analysis of the partite, which is not laid out here. And so this is also just conventionally real, like the former [the series]. He then says there are numerous examples of both—the queue, the army, etc. The series is like a queue, the collection is like the army and the like. Due to the term "and the like," such similes as that of the necklace and so on are grasped. Just as, apart from the form of ants arranged one after another, there is no queue resembling a single continuous thread, and as apart from assembled elephants, horses, foot-soldiers and so on there is no other single thing whatsoever to be an army, the collection is so as well. And [since] this is analyzed extensively elsewhere, it is

> not analyzed here. Thus since it lacks an ultimately real object, the thought is mistaken. Alternatively this means that it does not hold up under analysis. Hence, since there is nothing whatsoever like a self that could be an owner, there is nothing to which suffering is connected. Hence "whose will this suffering be that is thought to be one's own?" The meaning is that there is no one at all.

He then infers correctly at VIII.102 that, given this fact, the argument of VIII.92 does not work. Prajñākāramati glosses this verse as follows:

> The analysis [of "ownerless"] is that owners do not exist for those [sufferings] under discussion; the meaning is that those [sufferings] that are not "mine" are utterly lacking in a counter-positive. Why? Not for any? No, all are indeed ownerless, for there is no difference. There is no such thing as being an owner of anything on the part of anyone, for there is no difference. Having obtained the non-distinction between self and other, they are to be prevented, i.e., to be warded off, just because they are suffering. There is here no other ground, mineness and the like. How can this limitation be imposed—in virtue of what difference is it imposed—by which sufferings of one's own are to be prevented and not sufferings of others? Thus it is determined that the reason "because it is suffering" is not inconclusive.

The claim that each person has a special relation to his or her own pain fails, because there are literally no people. If any pain should be alleviated, then all pain should. VIII.103 states this conclusion.

On this interpretation, the central argument is that of VIII.101 and 102. Let us spell out the metaphysical picture apparently appealed to more carefully. On an *Abhidharma* metaphysics, composite entities, such as armies, forests, and persons, are merely conventionally or nominally (*saṃvṛti/prajñapti*) real (*sat*). Their identity conditions depend upon decisions about what entities to aggregate. Nonetheless, composite entities reduce to momentary property instantiations, *dharmas*. These are substantially (*dravya*), or ultimately (*paramārtha*) real (*sat*). Of course many palm leaves were used to work out the details of this picture, but those details are beside the point of the present discussion.

All endurants—indeed, all macroscopic entities—are composites, since all reduce to sequences or aggregations of *dharmas*. Therefore, all endurants and macroscopic entities are merely conventionally real. Ultimate reality is constituted by an interdependent array of momentary instantiations of properties. *Dharmas* are ultimately real; all else is ultimately unreal. Moreover, since *dharmas* are *dravyasat,* or substantially real, they each are characterized by a *svalakṣaṇa,* or essential individual characteristic that makes them the *dharma* that they are.

Momentary experiences of suffering and happiness are *dharmas.* They are hence ultimately real. Suffering has the *svalakṣaṇa* of being unbearable, happiness the *svalakṣaṇa* of being desirable. Persons are composites; they are hence ultimately unreal, albeit conventionally real. They have no *svalakṣaṇa* at all. For this reason, we should be concerned with suffering and happiness—they are ultimately real—but not with any distinctions between their bearers: they, and the distinctions between them, are only conventionally real.[5]

There are certainly reasons to take this reading seriously. The passage so read develops an intelligible and continuous line of thought. Moreover, *abhidharma* metaphysics was important in the history of Buddhist philosophy and would have been foundational to the training of Śāntideva (that is, whoever is the first author of the text) and his reviser. It is not implausible that they would have appealed to it when necessary. So this framework does provide a natural parsing of the verses in the passage in question. Finally, this is the reading that appears to be endorsed by Prajñākaramati in his commentary, a commentary that carries a great deal of weight in the Indian and Tibetan traditions.

But there are also reasons to worry about this reading. First, usual *abhidharma* discourses about ethics, and notably compassion, insist that compassion is conventional and that its *ālambana,* or objects, are sentient beings.[6] This would therefore be an unusual use of abhidharma ideas, and fits better with Mahāyāna constructions of *dharmālambana* of *karuṇā.*

Second, and more important, the central argument is at least *prima facie* fallacious from a Madhyamaka standpoint, as Williams and others note. The argument, on this understanding, appeals to the fact that the *dharmas* of suffering are ultimately real; but selves are only conventionally real. This is not something that a Mādhyamika can endorse. For a Mādhyamika, all things have the same ontological status: empty, but conventionally real. And Śāntideva, like his reviser, is not an *abhidharmika* but a Mādhyamika. Once again, Cowherds are not unanimous regarding the force of this argument. In particular, see Chapter 7 for a contrary view.

5. VIII.101 says that persons are unreal. It does not say explicitly that *dharmas* are not. Indeed, neither the root text nor commentaries speak in terms of *dharmas* or their relative reality. But if they were unreal, too, the contrast in the passage would appear to lose all force. Moreover, in that case, if the people do not exist, neither does the pain!

6. *Sphutārthā: Abhidharmakośavyākhyā by Yaśomitra.* ed. Unrai Wogihara (Tokyo: Publishing Association of *Abhidharmakośavyākhyā,* 1932–1936 [reprinted 1971]), Part 2, VII:12a–b, p. 687:12.

For a Mādhyamika, from the fact that persons are not *ultimately* real, it does not follow that they are not real *in any sense*. And since action is conventional, and is undertaken by conventional agents, there is no reason to think that merely conventional distinctions are irrelevant to action and its goals. Indeed, if it were the case that we could disregard things that exist merely conventionally, then we could disregard suffering, since this has no ultimate existence either!

If one is persuaded by these considerations (and, as we note, not all Cowherds are), the Principle of Hermeneutical Charity militates against this reading. The composite nature of the text could, however, be seen as mitigating this point. This is the most heavily revised section of *Bodhicāryāvatāra*, and it is plausible that the reviser found the original arguments either unacceptable or inadequate and tried to repair or supplement them with arguments related to ownerless suffering.

Third, this interpretation, while endorsed by Prajñākaramati, is arguably at odds with that of rGyal tshab Darma Rinchen. When two such influential commentaries disagree, arguments from canonicity are fraught, and the fact that a Tibetan commentator felt free to diverge in this way (although, to be sure, without acknowledging that divergence) suggests that the *Abhidharma* reading may already have been suspect. In any case, while this reading is plausible and well-attested, it is not the only one on the table, either philosophically or historically.

The Rationality Reading

Let us now turn to the other argumentative reading: the "rationality reading." This takes these verses to be advancing a different kind of argument, one that works by shifting the burden of proof from the bodhisattva to those who appeal to self-interest, and arguing that egocentrism itself is unmotivated rationally. It hence shares insights both with Humean ideal observer theory and with Schopenhauer's argument in *On the Basis of Morality*. This reading is articulated by rGyal tshab.

rGyal tshab labels the section of the text comprising these verses "the explanation of the meaning of meditating on the similarity of self and others." He begins his commentary on this section with the following challenge:

> Suppose one asked, "How does it make sense to consider
> increasing the happiness and reducing the suffering of others
> as just like increasing my own happiness and reducing my own

> suffering? After all, since there are infinitely many sentient beings, it makes no sense to visualize them all as *me*."[7] (329)

The interlocutor here is the naïve egoist, who takes it for granted that self-regarding action is intrinsically justified, and that other-regarding action requires justification. It simply makes no sense on this view to regard others' harms or benefits as motivations for *me*. In his commentary to VIII.91, rGyal tshab articulates what he takes to be Śāntideva's reply:

> Just as my body has many parts, such as hands and feet, since it constitutes only one person, it is to be protected as a whole. In the same way, although beings such as deities and humans are indeed distinct living things, it makes no sense to say that their *suffering* is different. Once one has seen that there is no difference, since they [deities and humans] are all similar to oneself, once one takes them as oneself, one should work to bring about their happiness. Since they are suffering, one should work to eliminate that, and one should think this way of all of [deities and humans]. This is the meaning of this meditation.[8] (329)

rGyal tshab suggests that Śāntideva asks us here to focus not on the identity of the being as the ground of motivation, but on the identity of the state of suffering. If suffering is taken to be a bad thing, then it is a bad thing wherever it occurs, and if something is bad, that itself is a reason to eliminate it. Note the affinity here to Nagel's (1989, p. 159f) account of the grounds of altruism. rGyal tshab then has his interlocutor continue, in an introduction to VIII.92, by pointing out that even if suffering is all bad, the harm it causes is to particular people:

> Suppose one argued as follows: Since others' suffering does not harm oneself, and similarly, one's own suffering doesn't harm others, it makes no sense to say that dispelling one's own suffering and that of others is similar.[9] (330)

7. *Sems can mtha' yas pa du ma yin pas de la nga'o snyam pa'i blo bskyed du mi rung pa'i phyir/ de dag gi bde sdug gi 'dor len la rang dang mtshungs par ji ltar rung zhe na//*

8. *rang gi lus la rkang pa dang lag pa sogs pa'i dbye ba rnam pa mang yang nga'i snyam du gang zag gcig gis yongs su bsrung bya'i lus su gcig pa ltar/de bzhin du lha dang mi la sogs pa'i 'gro ba tha dad kyang de dag gi bde sdug dag la tha dad med pa ste/khyad par med par dmigs nas thams cad bdag dang 'dra bar bdag tu gzung nas bde ba 'di bdag gis bsgrub par bya/sdug bsngal 'di bdag gis bsal bar bya'o snyam du 'di kun de dang 'dra bar sgom pa'i don to//*

9. *gshan gyi sdug sngal gyis bdag la mi gnod pa rang gi sdug bsngal gyis gzhan la mi gnod pa dang 'dra bas/de ched du sel ba rang gi sdug sngal sel ba dang mtshungs pa mi 'thad do zhe na//*

But, rGyal tshab continues, in VIII.92 and 93, presenting the following reply:

> . . . Consider the claim that others' suffering does not harm oneself. Even though one's own suffering does not harm others' *bodies*, it is nonetheless *their* suffering: Since they are different from oneself, they do not need to bear one's own suffering. Nonetheless, if other sentient beings meditate on taking others as oneself, their own suffering and those of others such as oneself will not appear different. And for this reason, they will strive to eliminate the suffering of sentient beings because it is suffering. Since sentient beings are taken to be as oneself, when suffering arises, one should protect them from enduring it.[10] (330–331)

The point is straightforward. If everyone responds to the suffering of all others, then even though nobody will be physically harmed by anyone else's suffering, all will suffer sympathetically. The only question then, is whether it makes sense for everyone to do this meditation. Of course, if it makes sense for any random individual, it makes sense for all, and it is to establishing that claim that rGyal tshab takes Śāntideva now to turn. He calls VIII.94–96 "explaining the argument that meditating on this makes sense," further subdividing the argument in ways that need not concern us here.

Commenting on VIII.94, rGyal tshab writes:

> Consider the suffering of others. It makes sense for one to eliminate it, because it is suffering. Take one's own suffering, for instance: it is the same. And it makes sense for one to bring about the happiness of others: since other sentient beings are indeed sentient beings. Take one's own body, for instance: bringing about its happiness is the same.[11] (331)

We can clarify this terse debate–courtyard style commentary by Prajñākaramati's commentary on the same verse, a commentary rGyal tshab is condensing:

> If my suffering does not cause hurt in other distinct bodies, still it is indeed my suffering. Why? Through love of self it is difficult to bear,

10. *gzhan gyi sdug sngal gyis rang la mi gnod pa ltar/gal te bdag gi sdug sngal gyis gzhan gyi lus la mi gnod pa de ltar na'ang de bdag gi sdug sngal yin te/rang la bdag tu zhen pas rang gi sdug sngal la mi bzod pa 'byung ba nyid yin pa de bzhin du sems can gzhan yang bdag tu gzung ba goms pas gzhan gyi sdug sngal dag bdag la 'bab par mi 'gyur yang/ de ltar na'ang sems can gyi sdug sngal de bdag gis bsal bar bya ba'i sdug bsngal yin te/ sems can la rang gis bdag tu zhen pas de la sdug sngal byung na bzod par dka' bag 'gyur ro//*

11. *sems can gzhan gyi sdug sngal cos can/bdag gis bsal bar rigs te sdug sngal yin pa'i phyir/dper nab dag gi sdug bsngal bzhin no//bdag gis gzhan la phan pa dang bde ba bsgrub bar bya rigs te/sems can pa rol po sems can yin pa'i phyir/dper na bdag gi lus la bde ba bsgrub pa bzhin no//*

> i.e., intolerable. This states the reason. The meaning is that activity with respect to some does not set aside the nature of suffering . . .
>
> Hence having rejected the distinction between self and other, the intrinsic nature of suffering is by itself a reason for averting it.
>
> Whatever suffering occurs is to be prevented by me, just as one's own suffering. That the suffering of others is suffering—this is the consequence of a reason based on intrinsic nature (*svabhāvahetu*). It is to be prevented solely in virtue of possessing the intrinsic nature of suffering. And the reason is not unestablished (*asiddha*), for it is proven that suffering has this intrinsic nature undifferentiatedly. Nor is [the reason] inconclusive (*anaikāntika*), since the proposition that one's own suffering is not to be prevented due to non-difference [from that of others] is rejected as erroneous. For this reason there also can be no fault of contrary reason (*viruddhatā*) [i.e., a reason for the opposite conclusion].
>
> There is this further consequence: . . .
>
> Whatever beings there are, all are to be shown benevolence by me, just as one is oneself a being. That all beings are also living things is a reason based on intrinsic nature as well. In the mere state of having the nature of a being is found the intrinsic nature of being deserving of benevolence. And this [reason] is not unproven, for it is established in the locus of having the nature of a being. [The reason] also could not be inconclusive, since that would lead to the absurd result that one should not help oneself. And as before, there could be no contrary reason.[12]

The commentarial point is this: the text is arguing that suffering is bad, per se, and this gives a *prima facie* reason for its elimination. To privilege one's own suffering over others would require one to take oneself to be different from others in a morally relevant respect. But the only morally relevant fact is that one is a sentient being, and we are all the same in that respect. There is hence no reason to privilege one's own suffering as a motive. This reasoning is available to anyone, and so it is rational for everyone to think this way. If so, the suffering of anyone in fact is a source of suffering for everyone. rGyal tshab continues, commenting on VIII.95:

> Having seen the suffering of oneself and others, it follows that it makes just as much sense to alleviate each and to bring about

12. See Appendix for full translation.

> the happiness of each. When one maintains that both self and others are similar in desiring happiness, it would make no sense to distinguish between oneself and other persons. Therefore, for this reason, if it makes sense to pursue one's own happiness, it makes no sense not to pursue that of others.[13] (332)

He concludes with these remarks on VIII.96:

> Since self and others are similar in not desiring suffering, one cannot distinguish between them in this respect. For this reason, without protecting the happiness of others, one cannot imagine increasing one's own happiness, and so one should protect it. We have established rationally that they are similar.[14] (332)

It is clear that rGyal tshab take these initial verses to be offering an argument; that the argument is one that shifts the burden of proof to one who invokes self-interest, challenging him to present a reason to take his own suffering and happiness as special sources of motivation; and urging that no such reasons can be forthcoming.

rGyal tshab takes VIII.97 ff to contain refutations of anticipated objections to this argument. The commentary on VIII.97 gives the flavor of this interpretation:

> Suppose one replied that since when the suffering of other sentient beings occurs it does not hurt oneself, one should not guard against it. This makes no sense. A young man may doubt that when he is old he may suffer from such things as poverty. In the same way, it makes no sense to doubt that one should ignore suffering that will occur tomorrow or later because it is now today. Since later suffering is still suffering, it makes no sense for a person, at an earlier time, if he does not want to be harmed, not to avert it.[15] (332–333)

The analogy is clear. Just as it is arbitrary and irrational to refrain from averting suffering because it is not present in time, it is arbitrary and irrational to

13. *gang gi tshe bdag dang gzhan gnyis ka bde ba 'dod du mtshungs pa la bdag dang gang zag gzhan khyad par ci yod na ci yang med pa'i phyir/rgyu mtshan gang gi phyir na bdag gcig pub de bar brtson par byed cing gzhan gyi bde ba la mi brtson pa mi rigs so//*

14. *gang gi tshe bdag dang gzhan gnyis ka sdug sngal mi 'did par mtshungs pa la bdag dang gzhan khyad par ci yod na ste ci yang med pa'i phyir ro//rgyu mtshan gang gi phyir gzhn gyi bde ba bsrung ba min par bdag gi bde ba ched du bsgrub cing mi nams par srung bar byed//*

15. *gal te sems can de la sdug bsngal byung bas bdag la mi gnod pa'i phyir mi bsrung ngo zhe na//de ni chas mi rigs te rgos pa'i tshe sdug bsngal byung dogs nas gzhon pa'i tshe nor gsog pa dang/de bzhin do sang dang phyi dro sdug sngal byung deogs nas de ring dang snga dro'i dus nas sdugs sngal sel ba'i thabs la 'bad pa mi rigs par thal// phyi ma'i dus kyi sdug bsngal ma 'ongs pa'i sdugs sngal yang snga ma'i dus kyi gang zag de la gnod par mi byed ba de byung dogs nas cis bsrung mi rigs par thal lo//*

refrain from averting suffering because it is not present in space. In either case, an argument for the special value of the here and now would be necessary; in neither case is it forthcoming.

VIII.101 may also be interpreted as anticipating an objection, and rGyal tshab's commentary is ambiguous here. On one reading, the interlocutor is represented as worrying that, since on a Madhyamaka analysis the person is ultimately unreal, there is a problem about explaining the origin of suffering, which should be the result of past actions, and should be the suffering of *someone*. On this understanding, VIII.102 replies that this issue is beside the point. Suffering clearly occurs; it is bad per se, as noted above, and so its very existence, regardless of its relation to any particular continuum, is always a reason to alleviate it. On the other hand, if we read rGyal tshab as following Prajñākāramati, he would be read as taking VIII.101 and 102 together as a response to an anticipated objection, arguing that the ownership of suffering can never, on its own, figure as a reason for its alleviation. Either reading is plausible, and the text is ambiguous. rGyal tshab writes:

> For this reason, suffering is without an independent self that endures it. Thus there is no distinction between one's own suffering and that of another. But since conventionally, the self and others exist in mutual dependence, their suffering exists; therefore, there is reason to eliminate one's own suffering.[16] (336)

Locating suffering in a particular continuum cannot add anything to its badness or provide any additional reason for its alleviation. rGyal tshab concludes the exegesis with the following remark on VIII.102cd and 103:

> Thus, since others' suffering is indeed suffering, it makes sense to eliminate it. And why would you distinguish between the suffering of oneself and others? . . . If there is no reason to eliminate the suffering of others, then one's own suffering is not to be eliminated either, since it is just like the suffering of other sentient beings.[17] (336)

The summary is nice. There is either reason to care about the suffering of others or not. If there is, fine. If not, then suffering itself is not what is bad. And if that is the case, there is no reason to worry about one's own.

16. *rgyu mstan des na sdug bsngal la longs spyod pa'i rang dbang ba'i dbag po med par ni bdag dang gzhan gyi sdug bsngal thams cad bye brag med pa nyid yin la tha snyad du phan tshun ltos pa'i dbag gzhan de dag gi sdug sngal yang yod pas/ rang gi sdug sngal sel ba la 'bad par rigs so//*

17. *des na gzhan gyi sdugs bsngal de yang sdug bsngal yin pa'i phyir de rang gis bsal bar bya ba rigs kyi rang gzhan ris su gcod pa'i nges pas der ni ci zhig bya//. . . gzhan gyi sdug bsngal sel ba de min na bdag gi sdug bsngal kyang sems can gzhan gyi sdugs bsngal bzhin du/*

So, on the "rationality reading" articulated by rGyal tshab, the argument can be reconstructed like this:

(1) Suffering is bad per se (by definition).
(2) Suffering is hence a motive for action. (1)
(3) To take one's own suffering as a *special* motive requires that there be something *morally special* about one's oneself.
(4) All sentient beings are fundamentally alike in *desiring happiness and not desiring suffering.*
(5) There is hence nothing *morally special* about oneself. (4)
(6) There is hence no reason to take one's own suffering as a special motive. (3) and (5)
(7) So, one should take all suffering as a motive for action.

This reading shares with the "*Abhidharma* reading" the view that this passage presents arguments for abandoning self-interest and embracing *karuṇā*. It differs regarding what those arguments are.

This interpretation also has in its favor the fact that it is endorsed by an influential canonical interpreter, and, most important, the fact that it does not have Śāntideva appealing to an *Abhidharma* metaphysics that is unacceptable to any Mādhyamika. These considerations, however, are not conclusive.

First, even canonical commentators misinterpret texts, especially when the text and the commentators are separated by countries and centuries (as is the Tibetan commentary in this case). One need think only of the interpretation of Plato given by Neo-Platonists such as Plotinus. They might have thought they were being faithful to Plato. Modern scholarship has disagreed. Disputes abound between Buddhist commentators, such as that between Candrakīrti and Bhāviveka regarding how to read Nāgārjuna. We also need to remember that the traditional commentaries were operating on the assumption of a single author working from an enlightened perspective, rather than a work subjected to massive revision.

Second, this interpretation faces *prima facie* cogency problems of its own. Recall the very first step of the argument, (1) above: suffering is bad per se. Suffering is always *someone's* suffering—for a Mādhyamika anyway. It makes no sense for suffering to float free in midair, as it were. So *whose* suffering is it that is bad per se? The answer is simply that anyone's suffering is bad, no matter whose. Once this has been granted, the rest of the argument is, in fact, otiose. Of course all bad things should be eliminated if possible. But as now becomes clear, when properly spelled out, (1) just smuggles into the argument the very conclusion to be established, and so begs the question.

What Is at Stake?

Of course, there is much more to be said about all three of the interpretations we have spelled out. And we do not rule out the possibility that there are other possible interpretations as well. Indeed, in the last analysis, the two halves of the text may simply be at odds with each other. But the aim of this introductory discussion is not to settle the question of which, if any, of these interpretations is the correct one (or to develop detailed exegesis of the text). That matter gets taken up in a number of the chapters that follow. We close by commenting on what is at stake in choosing between these readings.

The meditational reading gives ethics a kind of subjective flavor. That is, on this view, the role of these verses is to transform the way one sees others, and the nature of one's moral experience, not by giving reasons for seeing others in a new way, but by inducing a moral gestalt shift, presuming that that shift is salutary.

The two more analytical readings give ethics a more objective flavor, arguing (in different ways) that reason itself determines that one should adopt this proper ethical standpoint. One should remember that most Buddhist thought is framed by soteriological intentions and functions. This suggests another distinction between two views of ethical cultivation. On the meditational reading, ethics is a matter of spiritual practice, to be cultivated through meditation. On the two analytical readings, ethical sensibility is to be developed through argument and analysis.

Now, these are not, of course, mutually exclusive. The standard account of personal cultivation in the Buddhist tradition is the three-stage process of study, analysis, and meditation, with analysis as the necessary mechanism for ascertaining and clarifying the views one encounters in study, and meditation as the mechanism for internalizing those views and rendering them operative in engagement with the world.

In choosing between the two analytic readings, two issues seem central. First, there is the question of the degree of continuity or discontinuity between early Buddhist *Abhidharma* thought and Śāntideva's or his editor's own thought. If one takes Śāntideva's Madhyamaka to be a continuous development of the ideas articulated in the *Abhidharma,* the first reading is more plausible. If one takes his view to be part of a radical critique of that tradition, the second is more plausible. And indeed, it is therefore not surprising that commentators likely to thematize the divide between the Mahāyāna and earlier schools, and to valorize the later, tend to adopt the second reading. It may be useful to keep that agenda in mind.

Second, one way to think of what is at issue between the two argumentative interpretations is a question of *onus probandum*. On the *Abhidharma* reading, the reasons to be prudent are obvious; the burden of proof is on the ethicist to show why one should be moral. On the rationality reading, moral considerations are, by default, universal and motivating; self-interest requires justification. This debate is familiar in Western ethics as well. How one thinks it should come out might well incline one to one reading over the other.

5

Buddhist Ethics in the Context of Conventional Truth

Path and Transformation

Jay L. Garfield

Introduction: The Problem to Be Dissolved

Why are we worried about ethics, per se, in the context of conventional truth and the Madhyamaka understanding of the two truths? What is the *special* problem about ethics, once we understand that to take the two truths seriously is to take the conventional truth seriously as a *truth?* (Cowherds 2011). In this chapter, we argue that there is nothing to worry about; there is no special problem. Instead of *solving* a problem about ethics in the context of conventional truth, the project in this chapter is to *dissolve* an *apparent* problem. But this is Madhyamaka analysis, and so, following Tsongkhapa's practice (Cowherds 2011, esp. chapter 5) we must begin by identifying the object of negation, that is, to be clear about what we are arguing does *not* exist—in this case, the apparent problem. As we will see in subsequent chapters, however, demonstrating that the problem about ethics is not *special* does not by itself show that there are no difficulties in seeing how ethics is meant to go in the context of conventional truth.

The problem before us concerns the degree to which ethical truths or injunctions can be binding on us if they are "only" conventionally true. That is, does the conventional status of ethical truth take us straight to ethical relativism, or at least to ethical "optionalism?" We want to know that it is *really true* that torturing children is wrong, that generosity is to be cultivated, and that suffering is bad. Adding "conventionally" to any of these claims appears to weaken their force and to render ethics insufficiently important. And of course for any non-Mādhyamika, for whom there is a substantial *difference* between conventional and ultimate truth, this *would* be a weakener. On the other hand, as we will see, for a Mādhyamika, for whom these truths are in an important sense *identical*, it is not.

This initial observation should lead us to be suspicious of the worry with which we began right off the bat. Despite its apparent origin in a laudable moral seriousness, it is a bit precious to insist that while it might be only *conventionally* true that the earth is round, that we all die, and that the speed of light is constant across inertial frames, moral truth demands more than this. If the qualifier "conventional" really is a *weakener*, then, as epistemic agents, we should be as worried about it as we are as moral agents. Of course the burden of Cowherds (2011) is that it is *not* a weakener, and that conventional truth is indeed truth in the full sense of the word. We cannot, as we emphasize in Chapters 3 and 11 of this volume, fall into the dismal slough against which Kamalaśīla warns us. That should, perhaps, end the story in the case of ethics, and I think it does close one chapter in the proceedings. But there is a lingering worry. Let me put that worry into relief before finally setting it aside.

The conventional status of ethical truth seems to pose a special problem for two reasons. First, in part because of its normative character—because of the fact that, as we note in Chapter 2, there is implicit reference to an *ideal* of ethical behavior, to a state of perfection, perhaps of buddhahood—it appears to take us beyond the "merely" conventional. That reference to an ideal might suggest that ethical truth answers to a higher standard than does empirical truth. (We might also compare Kant's insistence on the regulative role of the idea of a holy will, or a kingdom of ends, in constituting a doctrine of moral obligation.) In virtue of its responsibility to a kind of perfection to which we are called, and in virtue of the absolute nature of perfection, ethics may demand more than conventional reality can deliver. This, I think, is the interesting motivation for a special worry about ethics in the context of the two truths. We can and will dissolve this worry, and doing so will allow us to bring the structure of Madhyamaka ethics into clearer focus, allowing us to answer more specific questions as we proceed.

A second reason for this worry is the specter of relativism. No (informed, sane) person suggests that the earth is flat, or that the speed of light varies with inertial frame, or even that these are reasonable *options*—conventions that (informed, sane) people might rationally adopt. But there are apparently informed, sane people who disagree deeply with one another about ethical matters: about the permissibility of abortion or infanticide; about the permissibility of certain kinds of non-consensual genital mutilation; about the obligations of the rich to the poor; about whether patriotism or fundamentalism are virtues or vices; about whether rights are trumped by utility, and so on. And while some argue that—dispute about such matters notwithstanding—there are correct answers to these questions, others argue that this plurality of views and intractability of dispute should lead us to adopt relativism, anti-realism, moral skepticism, or worse. It might then appear that when ethics is relegated to conventional truth, we have no basis for any kind of moral realism.

Now we are not here concerned directly with the metaethical questions of moral realism or relativism. But we must be concerned with the question of the logical connection between a Madhyamaka understanding of ethics and these positions. In particular, we should wonder whether, as the Cowherds (2011) argued, although Madhyamaka does not lead to relativism or to anti-realism in the metaphysical and epistemological domain, it does so in the moral domain. Part of the burden of this chapter is to suggest that there is parity between these domains in this respect. While Madhyamaka locates ethics firmly in the conventional, this does not entail that ethical truth is any *less* robust than empirical truth.

In this chapter, we will be concerned with the ethical thought of each of the four important Madhyamaka philosophers toward whose views this volume is addressed—Nāgārjuna, Āryadeva, Candrakīrti, and Śāntideva. While Nāgārjuna, as we saw in Chapter 2, initiates Madhyamaka ethical reflection in *Ratnavalī* (*Garland of Jewels*), and, as we will note below, also in *Mūlamadhyamakakārikā* (*Fundamental Verses on the Middle Way*), Āryadeva in *Catuḥśatika* (*Four Hundred Verses*) is the first Madhyamaka philosopher to think ethics through systematically, and particularly to address the relationship between ethics and the two truths. Candrakīrti, of all Indian Mādhyamika philosophers, inquires most deeply into the status of conventional truth and into the relationship between the two truths. In his *Madhyamakāvatāra-bhāṣya* (*Commentary on Introduction to the Middle Way*) and his *Catuḥśatika-tika* (*Commentary on the Four Hundred Verses*), he addresses ethical concerns in the context of his Madhyamaka ontology and epistemology. Śāntideva in *Bodhicaryāvatāra* (*How To Lead an Awakened Life*) follows Candrakīrti closely metaphysically, and indeed is always classified with him as a dBu ma thal "gyur pa, or Prāsaṅgika Mādhyamika (reductio-wielder) in Tibetan doxography. But he, more than any other Indian Mādhyamika, develops the ethical side of Madhyamaka in detail. The reading of these texts presented in this chapter is certainly inflected by Tibetan commentarial literature, and especially the commentaries of Tsongkhapa and rGyal tshab.

Path versus Fruition as the Domain of Ethics

It is important when thinking about Buddhist ethics to focus on the distinction between path and result, or fruition. It is tempting, given the normative character of ethics, and the role of ideals in the specification of norms, to think that the consideration of the motivation, psychology, or action of a Buddha is what drives Buddhist ethics. After all, one might think, since a Buddha is perfect, hence ethically perfect, and since Buddhahood is the ideal toward which a Buddhist strives, the way to figure out the content of Buddhist ethics is to figure out what a Buddha does, why she or he does it, and what she or he is like. Once again, a comparison to Kant, and his insistence on measuring our motivations against those of a will, or a legislator for a kingdom of ends is apposite, as is the Aristotelian perfectionism to which we compare Buddhist ethics in Chapter 2.

But this would be wrong, and would be to ignore the structure of Buddhist moral theory. Buddhist ethics is about *path*. After all, Buddhism, as we note in the Introduction to this volume, from the very beginning, is about solving a problem—that of the universality and pervasiveness of *dukkha,* and the route to solving the problem is the eightfold noble path. That path articulates the domain of ethics; hence ethics is a *means* to the achievement of liberation, not something to be fully achieved *upon* liberation. For that reason, we focus not on perfection when addressing Buddhist ethics, but upon the means of self-cultivation.[1]

Now, of course path and goal are intimately bound up. Paths are paths to goals, and the Buddhist path is a path to liberation (and, in the case of more specific paths, paths to specific intermediate goals necessary to that final goal). It is therefore necessary to conceptualize and to reflect on the nature of the goal in order to motivate the structure of the path. Buddhahood is therefore not *irrelevant* to Madhyamaka ethics. Nonetheless, we will argue, its relevance is only indirect: the point of Madhyamaka ethics is not to characterize buddhahood, but rather the path thereto; the content of Madhayamaka ethics does not

1. One might reply that the prominence of the *paramitās*, or *perfections*, in Mahāyāna ethics undermines this claim. But in that context, the *paramitās* are aspirational: goals toward which we strive, not conditions of ethical life.

directly reflect the motivation of a *Buddha*, but rather that of the *bodhisattva*. It is therefore much more intimately connected to path than to goal.

This is an important difference between Buddhist ethics and most (though not all) Greco-European ethical theory. While most Western ethical theory concerns itself with ordinary conduct, it generally takes its point of departure from the ideal, rather than from the standpoint of the aspirant. Aristotle, for instance, as we saw in Chapter 2, focuses on the highest good as the guiding principle of the *Nicomachean Ethics*.[2] The corresponding focus in Buddhist ethics would be the state of awakening. But that state does not figure in ethics from a Buddhist standpoint—it is rather para-ethical, to coin a useful term. Kant in the *Foundations of the Metaphysics of Morals* asks us to take a transcendental standpoint, thinking of ourselves as pure rational beings. Buddhist moral theorists instead ask us to take the standpoint of those who could do better—of practitioners who recognize their own moral imperfection and see a route to progressive improvement. Utilitarian moral theory adopts an absolute standard of moral excellence, requiring a calculus performed by an ideal hedonic accountant. Buddhist theory asks us to attend to more local matters (but note the connections we find between Buddhist ethics and consequentialism in Chapter 8 of this volume). It may well be that the closest we can come to Buddhist approaches to ethics in the Western tradition would be Humean moral theory, possibly in its more particularist incarnations. But our concern here is not with comparison or indeed with Western ethics at all. These remarks are intended only to forestall false starts that are all too common as those of us raised on a diet of European ethics approach Buddhist moral theory.

Moreover, the Buddhist idea of path (*mārga/lam*) is complex on at least three dimensions. First, we encounter at least two principal versions of the path to awakening—one in the *Dhammacakkapavatanna-sutta* (*Discourse Setting in Motion the Wheel of Doctrine*) in the context of the articulation of the four noble truths[3] and one in the context of the Bodhisattva path that structures much Mahāyāna thought. Second, path is not simply conceptualized as an *external* route along which one *travels*, but also as an *internal* state of being that one *cultivates*. So one often reads of a path "arising" in a practitioner, as well as of a practitioner attaining or traversing a path. Attending to this internal dimension

2. Stoic and Epicurean thought are important counterexamples to this trend. And indeed there are intriguing affinities between Hellenistic and Roman ethical thought and Buddhist ethical thought that are outside the scope of this chapter.

3. Of course it is not the truths themselves that are noble; rather they are truths to be taken seriously by those who would be noble. They are ennobling truths. The same goes, *mutatis mutandis*, for the eightfold noble path.

of the idea of path helps us to focus on the role of Buddhist ethics in personal cultivation.

Third, the three principal divisions of the eightfold path—*śīla/tshul khrim, samādhi/ting nge 'dzin and prajñā/ye shes*—are often translated as *ethics, meditation*, and *wisdom*, while the three principal aspects of the Mahāyāna path as articulated in the Tibetan *sa lam* (*grounds and path*) literature—*blos gtong/saṃtyāga, byang chub sems/bodhicitta*, and *stong pa nyid/śūnyatā*—are often translated as *renunciation, altruistic aspiration*, and *emptiness*. While these are not entirely erroneous, in this context they tend to give the impression that in the case of the *Śrāvakayāna* (Disciples' Vehicle) tradition only the first aspect is specifically ethical, and that in the Mahāyāna tradition only the first two are. Nothing could be further from the truth. Let us take these three points in turn.

First, consider the two paths: the first is the eightfold noble path. It comprises right view, intention, speech, action, effort, livelihood, attention, and meditation. By characterizing this as a path, and in virtue of glossing *samyak* (*right*, or *correct*) in terms of being conducive to awakening, and in virtue of a rather laconic approach to filling that content out in each case, the eightfold path encourages thinking about ethics in terms of concern and attention to a range of domains, the domains of view, intention, speech, and so on—each a domain in which what we do matters ethically. This eightfold path metaphor thus encourages us to see ethics as comprising all of life—how we think, our aspirations and goals, what we say and do, how we organize our lives professionally and socially, and the thoughtfulness we bring to life. In each of these domains, self-improvement is possible.[4] In each of these domains, there are right and wrong ways to conduct ourselves, and to take responsibility for our cognitive, verbal, and physical conduct in each of these domains is the principal demand of moral agency.

The bodhisattva path, as articulated in the *Avataṃsaka sūtra* and its many commentaries, and which structures all of Mahāyāna Buddhist moral thought, is divided into five, two of which are preparatory to the first bodhisattva stage or ground (*bhūmi/sa*) and the final three of which comprise the ten bodhisattva stages. Unlike the eightfold path, which one practices all at once, the bodhisattva path is set out as a sequence of practices, achievements, and goals. The first two are the paths of accumulation and preparation. On these paths one first accumulates the merit and understanding necessary to undertake the arduous further paths to perfection and then undertakes the

4. See Dreyfus (1995) for more specific discussion of why meditation per se is a matter of *moral* concern and Garfield (2012) for parallel discussion of mindfulness and morality.

practices necessary to toughen one's resolve. The third path is the path of insight, associated with the first bodhisattva stage of joy at which the practice of generosity dominates moral life. The fourth is the path of meditation. This path comprises a number of stages: the stainless, luminous, radiant, challenging, transcendent, and far-gone, at which proper conduct (*śīla/tshul khrim*), patience, energy, meditative concentration, wisdom, and liberative skill (*upāya/thab mkhas*) dominate life, respectively. The final path is that of no more learning, comprising the two stages of discriminative wisdom and of the domain of reality (*dharmadhātu/chos dbying*), where transcendent power and primordial wisdom predominate.

The bodhisattva path so articulated differs in structure and content from the eightfold path. It is sequential, rather than simultaneous,[5] and the moral domains on which it focuses are primarily internal, concerned directly with self-cultivation.[6] Nonetheless, it is important to note first that the eightfold path is not *replaced*, but rather is *supplemented* by the bodhisattva path, and so its domains of concern remain in place when we turn to bodhisattva practice. They constitute the spheres within which the cognitive and affective states cultivated on the bodhisattva path operate. Second, while the paths and stages of the bodhisattva path are indeed sequential, the moral characteristics that dominate each stage are not strictly sequential. They are mutually implicative, and their salience at various stages is a matter of emphasis, not of exclusive manifestation.

Nonetheless, juxtaposing the bodhisattva path and the eightfold path allows us to see clearly the double aspect of the notion of path itself. On the one hand, it is to be traversed, a way from an initial state to a goal state—whether that is from *saṃsāra* to *nirvāṇa* or from confusion (*avidya/ma rig pa* or *moha/gti mug*) to awakening (*bodhi/byang chub*). The stages on the bodhisattva path are markers of progress on a spiritual journey. In this sense, the path is a temporally extended object to be traversed, and the moral agent is the one who traverses it. On the other hand, the path is also an inner phenomenon, an aspect of the

5. But not *strictly* sequential. While the sub-paths identified as comprised by the Bodhisattva path are traversed in sequence, the perfections that are to be cultivated and the attitudes that are dominant on each path are not *unique* to that path; nor are they completed at the ends of the paths to which they each pertain. So, while generosity, for instance, predominates on the path of insight, it is necessarily practiced before that path is undertaken, and it attains greater perfection on subsequent paths. While merit is accumulated on the first path, it continues to accumulate on subsequent paths. So, while the paths are sequential, the practices, perfections, and results are all interdependent, and the achievement of each facilitates the development of the others.

6. Of course there are such inner dimensions to the eightfold path as well, but they occur in the context of explicitly verbal and physical domains as well—the point is that the bodhisattva path is more explicitly inner-directed.

agent herself. That is, the path is itself a quality of mind, a focus on particular traits of character and ways of taking up with the world. Ethical life consists in cultivating these states of mind and modes of engagement.[7]

We noted earlier the broad sweep of ethics in a Buddhist framework. It is easy to overlook this if, for instance, one translates *śīla* as *ethics* in the narrow sense in which that term is generally used in English, and then dismisses, in the context of the eightfold path, the aspects of the path comprised under *samādhi* and *prajñā* from the ethical domain. But that is simply an error of translation. *Śīla* is better translated as *proper conduct*, indicating action appropriate to one's status, standing, and circumstances. *Ethics*, coming from the root *ethos*, denotes *habit*, or *way of life*. Derivatively, of course, it indicates those habits or aspects of life that conduce to making one a better person, a better citizen, and so those aspects of one's life that are evaluable simply in virtue of one's humanity. And indeed all aspects of the path, whether the eightfold or the bodhisattva path, satisfy this description. Buddhist paths are paths to a kind of human perfection, and inasmuch as one's ability to attend, or one's grasp of the nature of reality, is in part constitutive of one's perfection or lack thereof, these are *all* ethical matters.

Buddhist Ethics as Phenomenology

The Mahāyāna understanding of moral life that underpins all Madhyamaka ethical thought is distinctive, and as we have seen, it is different in important respects from many of the accounts of the moral or the exemplary life most familiar in the European tradition. It does not focus in the first instance on obligation; nor does it focus on action; nor again does it focus on states of character manifested in habits; and finally, it does not take as its focus an ideal state, but rather the state of the practitioner in a non-ideal moment. I have argued earlier that it is primarily a *phenomenological* account of moral life (Garfield 2010/2011, 2012, 2015). While the context for moral discourse is the theory of path, as we

7. It is worth asking at this point whether this sense of "ethical life" makes sense only for a Buddhist, or indeed for a Mahāyāna practitioner, in view of the explicit tie to the Bodhisattva path and the goal of awakening for the benefit of all sentient beings. I think that the answer is a definite "yes and no." Yes: a Mahāyāna practitioner must be internally committed to the view that the Bodhisattva path is the highest ethical commitment, and so must recognize other ethical commitments as inferior, despite their value and even appropriateness to those who practice them. (And it is important to note that part of path theory is the view that different paths are appropriate to different people, in virtue of different levels of moral and intellectual capacity.) No: the specific traits of character, insights, and commitments identified on the path are largely independent of Buddhist soteriology. And if the ethical perspective articulated in the Mahāyāna is correct, they are valuable to *anyone*, Buddhist or non-Buddhist, Śrāvakayāna or Mahāyāna.

have seen, the central moral *phenomenon* in the Madhyamaka tradition is *bodhicitta*, a term we will leave untranslated. This term is usually translated either as *the awakened mind* or as *the mind of awakening*. But that is not very helpful, in part because of the different connotations of *citta/sems* and *mind* in Sanskrit/Tibetan and in English philosophical usage, respectively, and in part because of the unclarity of the bare genitive construction in English. A gloss will do better than a translation.

Bodhicitta is a complex psychological phenomenon. It is a standing motivational state with conative and affective dimensions. It centrally involves an altruistic aspiration, grounded in *karuṇā* or *care*—a term we will discuss in more detail below—to cultivate oneself as a moral agent for the benefit of all beings.[8] That cultivation demands the development of the set of skills in moral perception, moral responsiveness, traits of character, and insight into the nature of reality that we have noted in our discussion of the path. This is a transformation so deep that it reconstructs our way of seeing ourselves and others, and issues in a radically new form of what might be called practical wisdom—*upāya/thab mkhas*, perhaps best translated, following Thurman (1976), as *liberative skill*. In short, *bodhicitta* constitutively involves a commitment to attain and to manifest full awakening for the benefit of others. It is the engine of progress on the path, as well as its goal. A bodhisattva is simply one who has cultivated *bodhicitta*.

Āryadeva is the first Mādhyamika to develop a systematic account of ethics in this sense, and of the cognitive discipline that enables that cultivation. His account is extended and deepened by Śāntideva, and receives careful—if eccentric—exegesis by Candrakīrti, and a systematic treatment much later by rGyal tshab. It is the image of moral life that emerges from the texts composed by this group of philosophers that will concern us, and we will see that this vision of morality is one that takes conventional truth seriously and can itself be taken seriously in the context of conventional truth.

Buddhist ethics, as we have seen, is best conceived as an attempt to solve a deep existential problem—the problem of the ubiquity of suffering—and as an attempt to solve that problem by developing an understanding of our place in the complex web of interdependence (*pratītyasamutpāda*) that is our world. This is the world of conventional truth itself in the context of which the path to liberation makes sense in the first place. The triune root of suffering is represented in the familiar Buddhist representation of the Wheel of Life with the

8. We must tread with care here, however. Jenkins argues (1998) that "altruism" may be a bit strong, since, as we shall see below, *bodhicitta* and the motivations and skills connected to it are beneficial to the bodhisattva as well as to others. It is, as Śāntideva will emphasize, always in the end in one's own interest to cultivate *bodhicitta*.

pig, snake, and rooster at the hub, the six realms of transmigration representing aspects of the phenomenology of suffering—brutality; pain and despair; insatiable need; arrogance and the need for recognition; insensitivity to the pain of others in our own happiness; and the vulnerability and imperfection that comes with being human—revolving around them, structured by the twelve links of dependent origination (a detailed psychology of perception and action), all of which is depicted as resting in the jaws of death, the great fear of which propels so much of our maladaptive psychology and moral failure. This iconic representation is ubiquitous in Indo-Tibetan Buddhist culture, and serves as a representation of the Buddhist phenomenology of *saṃsāra*. It represents the starting point of the path to liberation, and represents that path as a path of inner transformation.

Mahāyāna moral theory, per se, is innovative in its reconstruction of the path as an internal sequence of psychological transformations and in the installation of *karuṇā* as the central moral value and the model of the bodhisattva's engagement with the world. *Karuṇā* is not a passive emotional response, and not a mere desire. Instead it is a genuine commitment manifested in thought, speech, and physical action to act for the welfare of all sentient beings, founded upon the insight that suffering is bad, per se, regardless of whose it is.[9] We will return to Āryadeva's exposition of the relationship between these ethical commitments and metaphysics below. But first let us consider Śāntideva's account of the rationality of adopting this attitude. We now turn to the important passage in Chapter VIII of *Bodhicaryāvatāra* that we considered in Chapter 4 of this volume, adopting for the purposes of the present chapter what we called there "the rationality reading."

9. This gloss on *karuṇā* is, we must admit, controversial. In much meditational practice devoted to cultivating *karuṇā*, emphasis is placed on the cultivation of *affect*, as opposed to *commitment* or *action*. And so one might conclude that the attitude simply consists in a sympathetic wish that sentient beings be free from suffering and have happiness, to paraphrase a common formula in such meditative traditions. I do, however, think that this is too narrow a reading.

First of all, there is no reason to take the affect or the mere wish as the *goal* of the meditation that cultivates *karuṇā*, as opposed to an *instrument* for its cultivation. After all, someone who—however sincerely—mumbles the formula, and who weeps at the woe of sentient beings, but who takes no action at all to alleviate their suffering, even when the opportunity presents itself, has not completed the cultivation of *karuṇā* by anyone's standards.

Second, the etymology of the term itself suggests an internal connection to action, as opposed to mere cognition. While the term is most often translated as *compassion*, this is a serious error. *Karuṇā* derives from the root *kṛ, to act*, and connotes a commitment to act for the benefit of others; *compassion*, on the other hand, derives from *passio, to feel*. To translate a term so clearly associated with action by one so clearly associated with passivity is seriously misleading.

Finally, we can use a cheap (and admittedly, for a number of reasons, non-demonstrative) argument from authority and note that HH the Dalai Lama frequently glosses the term this way in public teachings in order to distinguish the state from what he often calls in English "mere sympathy."

On this reading, to fail to take another's suffering seriously as a motivation for action is, Śāntideva argues, itself a form of suffering—a kind of mental illness that manifests in irrationality. This irrationality goes beyond the mere "enlightened self interest" we discuss in Chapter 7, and that may also lie behind the argument from interdependence we develop in Chapter 11. The point is not that I myself would be happier, or have more pleasure, if other sentient beings were happy, and that this responsive pleasure or happiness should be the motive for action. The irrationality at issue, that is, is not the irrationality of acting against my own hedonic self-interest. Instead, Śāntideva thinks, it is the irrationality of failing to be able to give a reason for any distinction between the treatment of similar cases. Once I grasp the fact that suffering is bad, that is by itself a reason for its alleviation. Whose suffering it is is therefore simply irrelevant.

The central argument in chapter VIII of *Bodhicaryāvatāra* is presented, as we saw in Chapter 4, in verses 90–103. Here is a recap of what we there called the "rationality reading" of the argument:

VIII.90 "Self and others are the same,"
One should earnestly meditate:
"Since they experience the same happiness and suffering,
I should protect everyone as I do myself."

Here Śāntideva introduces the conclusion: there is no moral or motivational difference between moral subjects. He then offers several arguments or analogies to make this point: First, the ontology that takes individual organisms as the relevant unit of analysis for the purpose of moral assessment of motivation is arbitrary:

VIII.91 Divided into many parts, such as the hands,
The body is nonetheless to be protected as a single whole.
Just so, different beings, with all their happiness and suffering,
Are like a single person with a desire for happiness.

Second, it is not the *locus* but the *fact* of suffering that makes it bad. So worrying about whether it is mine or someone else's is simply beside the point:

VIII.92 Even if my own suffering
Does no harm to anyone else's body,
It is still my own suffering.
Since I am so attached to myself it is unbearable.

VIII.93 Just so, even though I do not experience
The sufferings of others,
It is still their own suffering.
Since they are so attached to themselves, it is hard for
them to bear.

VIII.94 I must eliminate the suffering of others
Just because it is suffering, like my own.
I should work to benefit others
Just because they are sentient beings, as am I.

Third, to single myself out as uniquely deserving of moral concern, or as a unique source of motivation for action, is arbitrary:

VIII.95 Since I am just like others
In desiring happiness,
What is so special about me
That I strive for my happiness alone?

VIII.96 Since I am just like others
In not desiring suffering,
What is so special about me
That I protect myself, but not others?

VIII.97 If, because their suffering does not harm me,
I do not protect them,
When future suffering does not harm me,
Why do I protect against it?

Fourth, the facts of personal identity militate against egoism. There is no strict identity relation between successive stages of the continuum I regard as denoted by "I." So, the fact that I take my future self seriously in practical reasoning already suggests that I take the welfare or suffering of those not numerically identical to myself seriously in these ways. It is therefore irrational to distinguish motivationally between temporally distinct states of my own personal continuum and states of others' continua.

VIII.98 The idea that this very self
Will experience that suffering is false:
Just as when one has died, another
Who is then born is really another.

VIII.99 If another should protect himself
Against his own suffering,
When a pain in the foot is not in the hand,
Why should one protect the other?

VIII.100 One might say that even though it makes no sense,
One acts this way because of self-grasping.
That which makes no sense with regard to self or to others
Is precisely the object you should strive to abandon!

Finally, and perhaps most germane to the present topic, neither the self nor others, nor the relations of identity or differences among persons, exist ultimately. All are conventional. But that conventional status is not a reason *not* to take suffering seriously. It is, on the other hand, a reason to take *all* suffering seriously. Conventional reality is not *unreality*. It is the only way that things can be real. But once we see that, we see that all suffering has precisely this kind of reality, and hence precisely the same claim on us. *Karuṇā,* or *care,* is therefore the only appropriate reaction to the actual mode of existence both of sentient beings and their mode of being in the world. It is the only rational mode of *mitsein* and hence of *dasein.*

VIII.101 The so-called continuum and collection,
Just like such things as a forest, or an army, are unreal.
Since the sufferer does not exist,
By whose power does it come about?

VIII.102 As the suffering self does not exist,
There are no distinctions among anyone.
Just because there is suffering, it is to be eliminated.
What is the point of discriminating here?

VIII.103 "Why should everyone's suffering be alleviated?"
There is no dispute!
If it is to be alleviated, all of it is to be alleviated!
Otherwise, I also am a sentient being!

Karuṇā, grounded in the awareness of our individually ephemeral joint participation in global life, Śāntideva argues, is hence the wellspring of the motivation for the development of all perfections, and the most reliable motivation for morally decent actions. *Karuṇā* is also, on the Mahāyāna view, the direct result of a genuine appreciation of the essencelessness and interdependence of all sentient beings. And this is so simply because *egoism*—its contrary—is rational if, and only if, there is something very special, very independent about the self, something that could justify the distinction between my suffering or well-being and that of others as a motive for action.

Karuṇā on Śāntideva's account emerges not as a positive phenomenon, but as the *absence* of the irrational egoism born of taking the self to exist ultimately, and to be an object of special concern, just as emptiness is not a positive phenomenon, but the absence of intrinsic nature.[10] This is why Candrakīrti opens *Madhyamakāvatāra* by praising *karunā* as the seed, the rain as well as the harvest, of a bodhisattva's practice.

This transformation of vision (and consequent transformation of mode of being), even though it both conduces to and issues from a direct understanding of ultimate reality, and an understanding of the relation between this ultimate reality and conventional reality, amounts not to seeing a distinct truly existent reality *behind* a world of illusion, but rather to coming to see a world about which we are naturally deceived just as it is, not being taken in by the cognitive habits that issue in that deception. In particular, in the ethical domain this transformation amounts to coming to see ourselves as individual sentient beings among multitudes, and our own concerns as minor affairs in the grand scheme of things; it amounts to seeing all beings as equally objects of our rational care.

For this reason, just as the historical Buddha, in the presentation of the eightfold path at Sarnath, emphasized that one's view of the nature of reality is a moral matter, Śāntideva, in his analysis of an awakened life, urges that our metaphysics and epistemology are central to our moral lives. It is the metaphysical and ethical insights at which Madhyamaka is directed that enable us to cultivate the moral vision necessary for *karuṇā*. And it is partly for this reason that ethics is so deeply implicated in conventional reality. There is no other reality in which it can be grounded, and all that good metaphysics can ever deliver in the end is a precise understanding of the nature of conventional reality.

Ethics and Conventional Truth: Āryadeva and Candrakīrti

Śāntideva inherits this account of ethics as concerning conventional reality, per se, from Āryadeva's *Catuḥśataka*, together with Candrakīrti's commentary. We will approach those texts through rGyal tshab's commentaries. Candrakīrti in a verse explaining the method of Āryadeva's treatise, writes:

> By explaining the precise mode of existence of the everyday world,
> The ultimate is gradually presented. (rGyal tshab 50)

10. The parallel of this account to that of Schopenhauer in *On the Basis of Morality*—perhaps the most unjustly neglected moral treatise in the Western tradition—is intriguing.

rGyal tshab, after a summary of the topics of the first eight chapters, returns to this idea, saying "Therefore, the first eight chapters present the path for maturing the continuum, while the last eight present the path for overcoming negativities and obstructions to wisdom through the presentation of the ultimate truth" (51). Here and in the exegesis that precedes this remark, rGyal tshab emphasizes that the first half of the book, that which deals principally with ethics, as opposed to the metaphysics that underlies it, is not concerned at all with the ultimate truth, but rather with the conventional. rGyal tshab concludes his introduction with a remark on the structure of the text that reinforces this point: "The second part of this treatise, the explanation of the meaning of each of the chapters individually, has two parts: the explanation of the stages of the path according to the conventional truth, and the explanation of the stages of the path according to the ultimate truth" (52). It is clear that the first of these refers to the first eight chapters, those concerned with ethics. The discussion of the ultimate truth in turn provides the deeper analysis that grounds, but does not displace, the ethical discussion.

This reading of Āryadeva's intention makes good sense. The first chapter of the text is concerned with the importance of cultivating mindfulness of death, and hence of the impermanence of life and the urgency of practice. Āryadeva links moral failure in this chapter to the illusion of immortality, and moral progress to the realization of our finitude. There is no pretense here of attention to emptiness, or that ethics has some transcendent ground; rather, the foundation of ethical consciousness is, according to Āryadeva, squarely in an understanding of the fundamental fact about *saṃsāra*: all of us are mortal.

The opening of the second chapter reinforces this location of ethical concern in the conventional realm:

1. Although one might regard the body as an enemy,
   One should care for it.
   By maintaining ethical discipline for a long time
   Great merit is achieved.

rGyal tshab comments (78) that too much attention to impermanence, and to the role of physical attachment in the genesis of suffering, might lead one to deprecate the body, but that one must remember that it is only through the proper use of the body that an agent can perform morally beneficial actions. Of course, this is not, according to Āryadeva or his commentators, a rejection of the body or the pursuit of sensory pleasure as sources of suffering, as the remainder of the chapter makes clear. This is Buddhist ethics, after all. Nonetheless, it is an affirmation of the importance of the mundane in ethics, and of the mundane as the domain of ethical thought.

The third and fourth chapters are devoted to the dangers of sensory attachment and of pride, and the need to abandon them. Once again, the arguments all concern their deleterious effects on our own psychology—the tendency of attachment to sense pleasure to issue in addiction, narcissism, and frustration, and of pride to undermine our concern for others and our ability to lead a contented life.

In the fifth chapter, we encounter the importance of intention (*cetanā/sems*) to ethical life.

4. Without intention, such actions as going
Would therefore not be found to have such characteristics
as merit.
Therefore, in all action
The mind should be understood to be the most important factor.

5. In the case of bodhisattvas, in virtue of their intentions
All actions, whether they accord with virtue or vice,
Are in fact perfectly virtuous.
This is because they have achieved control over their minds.

This emphasis on intention is important in this context because of the fact that buddhas lack *cetanā*, in virtue of its conceptual character. *Cetanā* is central to karmic formation, because our intentions have the greatest effect on who we become. It is therefore important to develop positive intentions, intentions that are morally beneficial. But *cetanā* is also *cognitive, conceptual.*[11] Morally positive action, however free from duality we might hope it can become, is hence *intentional*, hence *conceptualized*, hence implicated with subject-object duality, objectification, always conditioned by ignorance, and therefore, in the end, with *saṃsāra.*[12] Moral action, its basis, and its point, that is to say, are bound to the conventional domain.

Even appropriate conception is *conceptual*; even positive karma is *karma*, and a Buddha does not generate karma, does not objectify, does not engage conceptually. A Buddha, therefore, acts without *cetanā, non-intentionally.* Now a great deal of debate about how to understand the subjectivity and agency of a Buddha without the category of intentionality has been generated by this conundrum[13] (see Griffiths 1994; Siderits 2011; Garfield 2010/2011; Myers 2010). We need not worry

11. For an exceptionally clear treatment of the role of *cetanā* in Buddhist theory of action see Myers (2010).

12. This is why the relevant distinction, as is so often the case in Buddhist epistemology, is that between *perception* and *reflection* or *conceptual thought*. When we perceive, we engage directly with particulars, and hence with *reality*. When we reflect, we *conceive*, and apprehend unreal universals. For unawakened human beings, the morally salutary finger pointing to the moon of perfection remains, for all that, a finger.

13. Buddhaghosa attempts to resolve the conundrum of a Buddha's motivation being at the same time intentional but not karmic by introducing a new "neutral kind of intention and karma that characterizes the Buddha's and arhat's actions: *kirīyakarma* or *kirīyacetanā*, which are neither the fruits of other karma nor generative of future fruits. This karma is also called "path karma" (*maggakarma* or *maggacetanā*). This device is used by

about this, as this is not an essay in Buddhology. The point is just this: given the centrality of intention to Madhyamaka ethics, given the conceptual character of intention, and given the fact that conceptuality is bound to the conventional truth, ethics is purely a matter of conventional truth[14] (see Garfield 2012.)

The sixth and seventh chapters of *Catuḥśataka* are concerned once again with the abandonment of attachment to the apparent pleasures of samsāra. The eighth, the final chapter in the set concerned with ethics, makes the transition from ethics to metaphysics, and lays the foundation for the account of the metaphysical basis of ethical life. Note the following two central verses:

> 8. Whatever concerns the everyday world
> Is said to involve engagement.
> Whatever concerns the ultimate
> Is said to involve relinquishment.
>
> 9. When you say "since everything is nonexistent, what's the use?"
> You have become afraid.
> But if actions existed [ultimately],
> This dharma could not engender abandonment.

Engagement is not, Āryadeva emphasizes, a bad thing! The entire purpose of ethical training is to facilitate productive engagement with the everyday world, the world we inhabit. Discussion of the ultimate is important as well. But that discussion concerns fruition, the transcendence of the mundane in Buddhahood. That is beyond the level of ethical engagement.[15] Ethical engagement is, I have been arguing, a matter of pursuit of path, and a Buddha has no need for a path. Action exists

Vasubandhu in *Abhidharmakośa* as well. This move to something that is supposed to be just like an intention, directing action to its object, only without objectification or conceptualization, does appear rather desperately ad hoc, only emphasizing the difficulty and the importance of the problem.

14. There are two additional points worth making in this context. First, the fact that ethics pertains to the conventional does not mean that in ethics "anything goes." After all, as the Cowherds (2011) are at pains to point out (see esp. chapters 2, 3, 4, 12), the fact that conventional truth is a kind of *truth* means that there are standards of correctness and incorrectness within the conventional. This is the heart of Candrakīrti's epistemology and metaphysics of the two truths. Just so in the case of ethics: the fact that ethics is bound to conventional truth means that there are, within the bounds of convention, standards of rightness (*samyak*).

Second, the fact that ethics is "purely a matter of conventional truth" does not mean that the ultimate truth is *irrelevant*. Once again, as the Cowherds were at pains to argue in (2011), the ultimate truth is that the conventional truth is merely conventional. It is not a separate domain. To understand the ultimate truth is to understand the mode of existence of the conventional. It is for this reason that an understanding of emptiness is essential for an understanding of conventional truth. But ultimate truth is unconceptualizable, since all conception is falsifying. And *cetanā* is conceptual, and fundamental to ethical conduct. Ethical thought is hence bound to conventional truth. But clear ethical thought and motivation in turn therefore require a thorough understanding of conventional truth and hence an understanding of the ultimate.

15. Once again, this indicates the para-ethical nature of Buddhahood. After all, one might wonder: Isn't a Buddha *perfect*, and so possessed of all of the perfections? And isn't *śīla* one of the perfections? And isn't that *ethics*? So, how could a Buddha not be supremely *ethical*? There are two problems with this line of reasoning. First,

only conventionally, and ethics concerns action—physical, verbal, and mental. Dharma is about action, and engenders abandonment—awakening—precisely because it concerns the conventional. So, to say that because the conventional is not ultimately existent, there is no use in taking it seriously is to give up not only on the conventional, but upon the ultimate as well.

Taking Ethics Seriously

Of course Nāgārjuna saw this. He makes the same point in a metaphysical register in *Mūlamadhyamakakārikā* XXIV:

8. The Buddha's teaching of the Dharma
Is based on two truths:
A truth of mundane convention
And an ultimate truth.

9. Those who do not understand
The distinction between these two truths
Do not understand
The Buddha's profound teaching.

10. Without depending on the conventional truth
The meaning of the ultimate cannot be taught
Without understanding the meaning of the ultimate,
Nirvana is not achieved.

Nāgārjuna here warns against the disparagement of the conventional in favor of the ultimate in the metaphysical domain, and reminds us that the understanding of ultimate truth does not replace, but rather depends upon our grasp of conventional truth. He is, of course, on the way to an account, a few verses later, of the non-duality of the two truths. But at this point, he is emphasizing not their *unity*, but their *difference*. The conventional is the domain of conceptual thought, of objectification, of language, and of intention. The ultimate transcends all of that. But one cannot achieve transcendence (especially that transcendence which amounts to a return to immanence) without a firm grasp of the immanent world to be transcended (and reaffirmed).

as we noted earlier, there is the translational problem. If we translate *śīla* not as *ethics*, but as *proper conduct*, there is no problem in saying that a Buddha is perfect in *śīla*. His or her conduct is perfectly proper. But second, inasmuch as ethics is concerned with the *path* to perfection, we can say that a Buddha has accomplished all that ethics is intended to enable. She or he therefore does not continue to practice ethics, but transcends it. The para-ethical is the goal, not the continuation of the ethical.

Āryadeva (and Candrakīrti) are after the same point in the ethical register. We might be tempted to disparage ordinary ethical life, or the ordinary motivations for ethical life—a better life for ourselves and those around us, less suffering, a clearer understanding of reality, the possibility of advancement of our most fundamental projects and values—because all of that is ultimately empty, and because the only *real* values are unconditional ultimate values.

But that impulse to disparagement must be resisted. And this for two reasons. First, we are on our way to a non-dual understanding of the relation between the ultimate and the mundane, and so to disparage the latter is to disparage the former. But more important, the state of transcendence that one might think can validate all values can only be achieved through conventional engagement in conventional actions, directed by conceptually involved, hence conventional, intention. This is the domain of the path, and this is the domain of ethics. If we disparage this, we have no ethical world left. In the end, a conventional account of ethics, and a conventional ground of ethical motivation must be accepted, simply because that is the only ethical domain that makes any sense.

But this does not amount to an abandonment of a commitment to serious ethical principles, of a distinction between right and wrong, or a descent into trivial relativism. Just as conventional truth requires and enables a distinction between truth and falsity, it enables a distinction between paths that lead to liberation and those that do not, and a distinction between actions, attitudes, and states of character that are consistent with a correct understanding of the world and those that are not. The eightfold noble path is ennobling because of the kinds of beings we are and because of the way the world is, not optionally, not ultimately, but conventionally. The bodhisattva path is the means to cultivate a liberative way of being in the world because of the kinds of beings we are, and because of the nature of reality. Ethical engagement then requires us to take our ultimate nature and the ultimate nature of reality seriously. But to take our emptiness and the emptiness of all around us seriously is to take our conventional reality and the conventional reality of the world seriously. To take the conventional world seriously is to take seriously the distinction between conventional truth and conventional falsehood and to do so in all domains, including the ethical. To take the conventional world seriously is therefore to take ethical considerations to be conventional, and hence to be as serious as any concerns could ever be. In the following chapters, we take these considerations seriously, first considering the object of *karuṇā*.

6

Waking into Compassion

The Three *Ālambana* of *Karuṇā*

Stephen Jenkins

Anyone who becomes familiar with Buddhist thought eventually has to deal with the question of how compassion can be meaningful, if both its agent and its object are ultimately unreal. The ultimate truth of Buddhism, whether that truth is no-self or emptiness, seems to deny both the object of compassion and the compassionate subject. The Buddhist ethic, which takes the suffering of sentient beings seriously, seems to be at odds with its ultimate truth, which denies the very existence of those beings. This chapter begins by taking up how this presents itself to us as a philosophical and interpretive problem, and then investigates Indian Buddhist sources that recognized and directly addressed these problems in systematic thought. The motif of the three objects, or *ālambana*, of *karuṇā* served as a frame for discussing how compassion made sense to Mādhyamika thinkers such as Candrakīrti, Śāntideva, and Prajñākaramati.

The apparent problem with the concept of no-self is obvious: Who is the object and who is the agent of this compassion? In Abhidharma thought, this is moderated by the affirmation of an incessantly self-renewing causal continuity of temporally ephemeral and physically microscopic elements, the negation of macro-realities and affirmation of micro-realities. It is this continuity that is the referent for the word "self," and it is a substantial basis. The whole effort to understand and control that causal continuity, saṃtāna, is based on the fact that it is taken seriously as a relentless and perpetual process, an almost inescapable *karmic* continuum. The strength of this continuity is the principal challenge in the quest for *nirvāṇa*.

From the Madhyamaka's standpoint of emptiness, finding a meaningful object for compassion is apparently more difficult, since here even the evanescent microscopic elements of the psycho-physical continuum dissolve under analysis. Abhidharma thinkers maintained confidence in the ability of objective linguistic concepts to ultimately describe reality, even if only at an atomic level. They engaged in projects to catalogue and systematically analyze the minute components or *dharmas*, whose combinations make up the gross perceptual objects we mistake for objects in themselves. If accused of nihilism when teaching selflessness, an Ābhidharmika can simply point to the *dharmas* that are the objectively real basis of our lives. The Śūnyavādins, however, rejected the idea that "reifying thought" could ultimately describe reality. For them, objectifying thought itself is the principal challenge in the quest for *nirvāṇa*. However useful the human mode of linguistic thinking in terms of objects may be, objects are merely an aspect of our thought that we naturally and habitually project on the world. The world as such ("suchness") is empty of the objectivity that is a basic aspect of human thought. Every "thing" dissolves under analysis and proves to be empty of objectivity, even the *dharmas* that insulate the Ābhidharmika from nihility. So, in Abhidharma contexts, the problem of compassion and no-self rarely comes up, but it constantly appears in the literature of emptiness.

Emptiness and selflessness have been broadly interpreted as providing an ontological rationale for compassion. This is a very attractive and compelling idea. In Euro-American vernaculars, we naturally and intuitively connect the capacity for compassion with self-conception. We use terms such as selfless, unselfish, self-sacrifice, and self-forgetting, and their opposites: egotistical, egocentric, self-centered, selfish, self-seeking. This can lead to ironic misinterpretation, when the Buddhist ontological negation of the self is conflated with the ethical negation of self-interest in Western ethics, which is in fact based on a very strong ontological conception of the self. In Buddhist thought, selfless is not something one can become, it is ontologically the way things are in the first place.

Surprisingly, when we look at what Buddhists themselves say, the view that the realization of emptiness and compassion are actually incompatible has good grounds for argument. Perhaps the most common formulation of *bodhicitta*, the compassionate resolve to become enlightened for the sake of others, is that the *bodhisattva* should vow to save all sentient beings, even though no sentient beings exist. Their compassion can appear to be in spite of emptiness, not because of it. The Perfection of Wisdom in Eight Thousand Lines says:

> This is difficult, indeed supremely difficult, for *bodhisattva-mahāsattvas*. They put on the armor [of *bodhicitta*], thinking "Immeasurable, countless, infinite sentient beings I must cause to [enter] *parinirvāṇa*." Yet those sentient beings ultimately do not exist; ... If even when this is being taught a *bodhisattva* is not despondent ... that *bodhisattva* courses in the Perfection of Wisdom.[1]

If there is a positive relationship between emptiness and compassion, it is "supremely difficult," not a natural or intuitively obvious idea. In fact, Buddhist texts recognize the apparent incompatibility between the two, and often revel in it, perhaps playfully, as a kind of conundrum. So we can certainly comfort ourselves, as we work on these issues in this text, that the classical thinkers themselves saw the relationship between emptiness and compassion as extremely difficult to understand and practice.

On the other hand, there are textual resources to point to that suggest a very positive relationship of emptiness and compassion, even to the point of suggesting that *karuṇā* has a kind of ultimacy. For example, when the *Vimalakīrtinirdeśa Sūtra*, using a stock scriptural allegory, says that *bodhisattvas* should regard all beings as a master illusionist sees a person created by illusion, even Mañjuśrī, the celestial *bodhisattva* of wisdom, is puzzled. He asks the natural question:

> If *bodhisattvas* should consider sentient beings in this way, how then are they going to generate great loving kindness, *maitrī*, for them? (Vimalakīrti answers:) Mañjuśrī, a *bodhisattva* generates a *maitrī* that accords with reality, ... a Tathāgata's *maitrī* that understands thusness, ... a self-arisen *maitrī* because it is self-enlightened, a *maitrī* with enlightenment because it has a uniform flavor, ... a *maitrī* with *mahākaruṇā* because it is the full illumination of the Mahāyāna, that is without weariness because it considers emptiness and no-self, ... This, Mañjuśrī, is the *maitrī* of a *bodhisattva*.[2]

1. Rajendralal Mitra, ed., *Aṣṭasāhasrikā* (Calcutta: Asiatic Society of Bengal, 1888), p. 444. Cf. Edward Conze, trans., *The Perfection of Wisdom in Eight Thousand Lines* (Bolinas, CA: Four Seasons, 1973), p. 259.

2. Lal Mani Joshi and Bhikṣu Prāsādika, ed. and trans., *Vimalakīrtinirdeśasūtra: Tibetan Version, Sanskrit Restoration, and Hindi Translation*, Bibliotheca Indo-Tibetica, v. 5 (Sarnath: Central Institute of Higher Tibetan Studies, 1981), pp. 128–129; cf. Étienne Lamotte, trans., *The Teaching of Vimalakīrti*, English tr. Sara Boin (London: Pali Text Society, 1976), pp. 153–155; cf. Robert Thurman, trans., *The Holy Teaching of Vimalakīrti* (University Park: Pennsylvania State University, 1976), p. 56.

Although it is presented as confusing even to the great Mañjuśrī, this description makes it clear that this goodwill for dream-like sentient beings is possible. It even seems to give ultimacy to *maitrī*. But another important aspect of this common allegory, an illusionist seeing an illusion, is that it describes how *bodhisattvas* see nonexistent sentient beings, not that they do not see them. This is a crucial point. Even in the context of the compassion with no object, discussed below, this will hold true. A distinction highlighted by David Schulman between awakening into, rather than awakening from, an illusion may be useful:

> Unlike the Advaita System, for example, which seeks to awaken us from the illusion that we take for normal reality, the *Yoga-vāsiṣṭha* . . . seeks to wake us into the illusion that the mind creates. In much the same vein, the famous Buddhist philosopher Nāgārjuna and his successor Vasubandhu seem to want us to internalize a reality that is continuously reimagined and thus neither empty nor full (to use their language) but rather a beginningless series of what we might call true illusions.[3]

This suggests the analogy of a lucid dreamer who, rather than waking from a dream, recognizes the dream, and, rather than being bound by it, takes it as an opportunity for playful creativity.

Prajñākaramati and Candrakīrti on the Three Ā*lambana* of *Karuṇā*

Sources that give detailed concrete explanation of the relationship of emptiness and compassion are rare, but by looking at them we get a different sense than if we look at compassion and emptiness independently and then make inferences about their correlation. Prajñākaramati's tenth-century commentary on the *Bodhicaryāvatāra* is such a source. It raises many of the questions that we would want to ask. If everything is empty, then for whom is there compassion? If illusory sentient beings are the object of compassion, does that root the ethic in ignorance, creating a gulf between the highest truth and the highest values? Since Prajñākaramati answers from the Madhyamaka perspective, we can see how these questions are dealt with from the most uncompromising interpretation of emptiness.

3. David Shulman, *More Than Real: A History of the Imagination in South India* (Cambridge, MA: Harvard University Press, 2012), p. 113. He cites a forthcoming article by Gary Tubb, "The *Laghu Yogavāsiṣṭha* and Its Relation to the *Yogavāsiṣṭha*."

The scheme of the three *ālambana* provides the basic structure of Prajñākaramati's presentation of the relationship between various ontological perspectives and compassion. Here compassion is classified as threefold according to its referent. The first referent, object, or basis of compassion in this scheme is simply conceived sentient beings. The second basis, incorporating the Buddhist view that all beings are compounded, is *dharmas* as the constituent elements of the personal continuum. The third and highest compassion is *anālambana-karuṇā*, compassion with no referent. By incorporating the third level, this scheme seems to suggest that compassion can operate even from the ultimate standpoint of emptiness. This threefold scheme is found in Mahāyāna *sūtras*, in the treatises of the Madhyamaka and Yogācāra, and in the Tathāgatagarbha literature.[4] It is also well known in Chinese and Tibetan sources. Although it appears in the *Bodhisattvapiṭaka Sūtra*, which may be earlier, the best-known source of the "three *ālambana*" is the *Akṣayamatinirdeśa Sūtra*, on which it is cited in the *Śikṣāsamuccaya* and the *Mahāprajñāpāramitopadeśa Śāstra*.[5] According to the *Akṣayamatinirdeśa*:

> There are three *maitrī*.[6] . . . *Maitrī* having beings for its basis, having *dharmas* for its basis, and having no basis. *Bodhisattvas* who have generated the first *bodhicitta* have *maitrī* with beings for its basis. *Bodhisattvas* who have practiced the way have *maitrī* with *dharmas* for its basis. *Bodhisattvas* who have attained acceptance of the nonarising of *dharmas* have *maitrī* with no basis.[7]

The *Akṣayamatinirdeśa* assumes that there are different ontological perspectives for different levels of the path, not between schools, but for all *bodhisattvas*. The highest perspective, objectless compassion, is limited to the rare

4. For an extended study with extensive cross-referencing, see Stephen Jenkins, "The Circle of Compassion: An Interpretive Study of Karuṇā in Indian Buddhist Literature" (PhD diss., Harvard University, 1998), pp. 196–236.

5. Ulrich Pagel, *The Bodhisattvapiṭaka*, Buddhica Britannica V (Tring, UK: Institute of Buddhist Studies, 1995), p. 141, fn. 84, gives *sTog Palace bKaḥ-ḫgyur*, dKon-brtsegs, Ga, (Leh, 1979), v. 37, folio 269; see <IBT>Étienne Lamotte, *Le Traité de la grande vertu de sagesse de Nāgārjuna (Mahāprajñāpāramitāśāstra)*. Tome III (Louvain: Université de Louvain, 1970),</IBT> p. 1245, notes 1 and 2; *ibid.*, p. 1250, note 1, gives a rich bibliography on the three *maitrī*. Sometimes cited as *Akṣayamati Sūtra*, as in the *Śikṣāsamuccaya*, the *Akṣayamati-nirdeśa* is occasionally mistaken for the *Akṣayamati-paripṛcchā*, as here by Lamotte.

6. *Maitrī*, commonly translated "loving kindness," is the first of the "four immeasurables," including compassion, sympathetic joy, and equanimity. Texts often state the others are implied. For the purposes of this chapter, the treatment of *maitrī* and *karuṇā* are in common.

7. Cecil Bendall, ed., *Śikṣāsamuccaya: A Compendium of Buddhist Teaching Compiled by Śāntideva Chiefly from Earlier Mahāyāna Sūtras* (Indo-Iranian Reprints, 1957), p. 212:12; cf. Cecil Bendall and W. H. D. Rouse, trans., *Śikṣāsamuccaya* (Delhi: Motilal Banarsidass, 1971), p. 204. Here the pioneering, but badly dated, translation obscures the motif; cf. Jens Braarvig, trans. *Akṣayamatinirdeśa Sūtra: The Tradition of Imperishability in Buddhist Thought*, Vol. II. (Oslo: Solum Forlag, 1993), pp. 351–352.

few that reach the realization of emptiness, or "tolerance of the nonarising of *dharmas*," on the eighth of ten stages of progress toward Buddhahood. For most Mahāyāna Buddhists, then, ethical thinking would be in relation either to the simple perspective of persons, or an *abhidharma* deconstruction into *dharmas*. Buddhist thought assumes the possibility of multiple, even competing ontologies, and allows for monks of various perspectives to live within the same *vinaya* code. Laity and monks would not have the same ontology, nor would monks of different schools, or monks at various levels of understanding or realization. This internal diversity makes suspect any effort to put forth a general theory of Buddhist ethics based on a particular ontology. The kinds of ethical thought agreed upon by Buddhists of all varieties, and most ignored by modern studies, are based on the first type of compassion with beings for its object.

Sattvālambana-karuṇā: Compassion with Beings for Its Object

In the Wisdom Chapter of the Bodhicaryāvatāra, we find the question of how there can be compassion if there are no sentient beings.[8] Prajñākaramati expresses the objection of a Mahāyāna Buddhist as follows:

> If [when] examined in every way a being, self, or person were not found, were not existent, then towards whom would the compassion and pity of *bodhisattvas* be? Having what basis other than sentient beings could it function? Compassion is the practice, *sādhana*, for accomplishing complete enlightenment . . . all the qualities of a Buddha evolve preceded by compassion.
>
> As it is said in the *Ārya Dharmasaṃgīti Sūtra*: ". . . Oh Bhagavan, . . . If a *bodhisattva* holds a single *dharma*, and understands it well, then all the *dharmas* of a buddha will be there in the palm of their hand. . . . just so when great compassion is present all the other *dharmas* that produce enlightenment will develop."

8. This section of the *BsCA*, like the Meditation chapter's treatment of "exchange of self and other," was radically altered by a later reviser. Here, of about twenty-one original verses, only five and a half are retained. The first half of *BsCA* VIII.53, questioning how there can be compassion if there are no beings, was retained as *BCA* verse IX.76ab [v. 75 in English translations], but the earlier answer was deleted. *BsCA* VIII.55 was then placed before the verse it used to follow, and became *BCA*.IX.75 [v. 74 in the Eng. tr.]. See Akira Saitō, "Śāntideva's Critique of 'I' or Self in the Early and Later Recensions of the *Bodhi(sattva)caryāvatāra*," *Studies in Indian Philosophy and Buddhism* 13. no. 3 (2006): 35–43. The reviser clearly shows an aggressive interest in correcting the BsCA on this issue. I focus here on Prajñākaramati's response to the *BCA* as he knew it.

And in the *Ārya Gayāśīrṣa Sūtra* it says:

> . . . The origin of the practice of *bodhisattvas* is great compassion, Oh Devaputra, and sentient beings are its basis." . . .
>
> So certainly one ought to accept that from the first compassion refers to sentient beings. Its origination is based on suffering sentient beings. [IX.76.][9]

As we will see, Prajñākaramati basically agrees with this objection, which he has embellished with authoritative scriptural citations, and will respond in three different ways. The apparently simple statement that at first compassion refers to sentient beings actually has a technical significance. Prajñākaramati is applying the scheme of the three bases of compassion, which provides a structure for his whole presentation. He begins by presenting beginners' compassion for sentient beings; next he will discuss compassion for persons seen as a collection of aggregates; and finally he deals with the objection that even these aggregates are empty. From the outset of the path, compassion is for sentient beings as they are conventionally perceived. Compassion is the means of accomplishing the realization of ultimate truth, and precedes the realization of emptiness that negates sentient beings. Compassion is not a response to emptiness, it is a prerequisite for realizing it.

It is this simplest and too often unappreciated form of compassion that is also given the deepest reverence by the great Mādhyamika Candrakīrti. In the opening salutary verses of his *Madhyamakāvatārabhāṣya*, which are usually reserved for praise, gratitude, and invocation of *buddhas* and patriarchs, Candrakīrti explains that he chooses instead to praise compassion. Using the frame of the three *ālambana*, he especially praises the first compassion of a *bodhisattva*, which is not based on dependent origination or emptiness, but simply perceives sentient beings. It is this compassion, he says, that leads to *bodhicitta*, which in turn leads to the pursuit of wisdom.[10] Compassion is the seed, water, and harvest of the *bodhisattva* path.

Following the root text, Prajñākaramati gives a second reason for accepting compassion even though ultimately there are no beings, that is, because it is

9. S. Tripathi, ed., *Bodhicaryāvatāra of Śāntideva with the Commentary Pañjikā of Prajñākaramati*, Buddhist Sanskrit Texts # 12, 2nd edition (Darbhanga: Mithila, 1988), p. 234.

10. Louis de la Vallée-Poussin, ed., *Madhyamakāvatāra par Candrakīrti*, Bibliotheca Buddhica 9 (St. Petersburg: Academy of Sciences, 1907–1912); (reprint Osnabruck: Biblio Verlag, 1970), pp. 10–11; cf. C. W. Huntington Jr. and Geshe Namgyal Wangchen, *The Emptiness of Emptiness* (Honolulu: University Hawaii, 1989), pp. 149 and 219 note 3; cf. Guy Newland, trans., in *Compassion: A Tibetan Analysis* (London: Wisdom, 1984), p. 120.

practical. Compassion for simply conceived sentient beings leads to the pursuit of higher wisdom.

> The purpose here is the supreme goal of humanity, Buddhahood liberated from all obscurations and free from the net of all false imaginings. However, that is not accomplished without the non-grasping of all *dharmas*. [Buddhahood] is attained from undertaking excellence in wisdom; and that arises from long uninterrupted devoted study. But taking on that [study] arises from the power of compassion. And [compassion], which is directed at first toward suffering sentient beings, initiates the process. . . . So, for the sake of a purpose, the illusion having the form of conventional truth is accepted. Therefore at first there is the compassion focused on sentient beings, then after that focused on *dharmas* and [finally] without any referent.[11]

His first point is that compassion has a clear temporal priority on the path. Compassion does not derive from emptiness or self-deconstruction, but from the perception of suffering sentient beings. As with Candrakīrti, compassion precedes the understanding of emptiness and leads to its study. Conventional truth is affirmed, and so sentient beings, because it serves the purpose of attaining Buddhahood. (We will return to this crucial point later in the discussion of compassion without an object.)

Prajñākaramati's commentary on *BCA*.IX.4–5 contains an important related discussion.[12] There it is asked how a *bodhisattva* can practice the perfections, such as giving, and so on, if there are no beings. The answer is interrelated with the question of how yogins see conventional reality differently than ordinary people. Here again, the acceptance of sentient beings is justified because it is practical, that is, leads toward Buddhahood. But the acceptance of sentient beings suggests participation in ignorance. So Prajñākaramati adds the following natural objection: "If the illusory things that yogins perceive are the very same ones perceived by ordinary folk, then what's the difference?"[13] The root text answers that the difference is that ordinary people take things as real, while *yogins,* though they see the very same things, perceive them as illusory. Prajñākaramati elaborates using the familiar example of an illusionist who sees the elephant that he produces for his audience, but, unlike them,

11. *BCAP*, ed. Tripathi, p. 234.

12. See P. R. Oldmeadow, "A Study of the Wisdom Chapter (*Prajñāpāramitā pariccheda*) of the *Bodhicaryāv atārapañjikā* of Prajñākaramati" (PhD diss., Australian National University, 1994), pp. 33–38; *BCA*, ed. Tripathi, p. 185.18. Prajñākaramati uses the motif *trimaṇḍalapariśuddhi*, giving without giver, gift, or recipient.

13. Oldmeadow, "A Study of the Wisdom Chapter," 38; *BCA*, ed. Tripathi, p. 186.6.

also sees its essential nature.[14] Again, there is a sense here of waking into an illusion, rather than from an illusion. Persons do not disappear from Buddhist ethics.

Dharmālambana-karuṇā: Compassion with *Dharmas* for Its Object

Following the scheme of the three *ālambana*, Prajñākaramati next defends compassion for illusory sentient beings as in Abhidharma thought. Continuing, he says:

> Beings are not nonexistent in every way. The aggregates are conventionally designated with the word *ātman*. . . . So even if sentient beings when defined ultimately by wisdom have no *ālambana*, even so, they are not denied conventionally. . . . Therefore, those [aggregates such as] form, *et cetera*, are conventionally designated with the word "being," and, so, compassion is not without its sphere [of activity].[15]

Here, as in Abhidharma literature, Prajñākaramati simply resorts to the aggregated components as a basis of the conventional person. We saw above that the *Akṣayamatinirdeśa Sūtra*, with which Śāntideva had a special affinity, tells us that *dharma-ālambana-karuṇā* is the type of compassion characteristic of *bodhisattvas* who have made progress on the path up until the eighth stage, where emptiness is directly realized.[16] It would be natural then for this Abhidharma perspective, which at first seems inconsistent for the Mahāyāna, to play a major role in its ethical thought, since exceedingly few *bodhisattvas* reach the eighth stage. This bears on the passages from the *Bodhicaryāvatāra*'s Meditation Chapter, discussed in Chapter 3 of this volume, that have been the subject of so much debate. Why, in those earlier verses, is deconstructive analysis only taken as far as *dharmas*? For a Mādhyamika to be consistent, those "ownerless sufferings" must also dissolve under analysis. But perhaps, in a text composed for

14. *Ibid.*

15. *BCAP*, ed. Tripathi, p. 234.

16. Akira Saitō, *A Study of Akṣayamati (= Śāntideva)'s Bodhisattvacaryāvatāra as Found in the Tibetan Mansuscripts from Tun-huang* (Grant-in-Aid for Scientific Research (C), Mie, 1993), pp. 21–22; Akira Saitō, "Śāntideva in the History of Mādhyamika Philosophy," in *Buddhism in India and Abroad: An Integrating Influence in Vedic and Post-Vedic Perspective*, ed. Kalpakam Sankarnarayan, et al. (Mumbai: Somaiya Publications Pvt. Ltd., 1996), p. 258; Paul Harrison, "The Case of the Vanishing Poet: New Light on Śāntideva and the *Śikṣāsamuccaya*," in *Indica et Tibetica: Festschrift für Michael Hahn, Zum 65*, edited by Konrad Klaus and Jens-Uwe Hartmann (Vienna: Arbeitskreis für tibetische und buddhistische Studien Universität Wien, 2007), pp. 224–229.

training purposes, Śāntideva is addressing those of us below the eighth *bhūmi*. Paul Griffith concluded that the ideal reader for the companion volume that the *Bodhicaryāvatāra* recommends for study, the *Śikṣāsamuccaya*, was a monk at an early stage of training, pointing out that the text itself tells us that it is of special benefit to beginners, *śikṣārambhakas*.[17]

Prajñākaramati used the Abhidharma perspective to offer a positive ground for references to persons, which is the stock approach of Abhidharma traditions. However, many scholars believe the *Bodhicaryāvatāra* used the Abhidharma perspective in a different, perhaps even opposite, way in the Meditation Chapter, particularly in passages attributed to its reviser.[18] It has been taken to say that, from a selfless ontological perspective, "ownerless" sufferings should be the object of compassion. Since persons do not exist, compassion should be directed to the sufferings themselves, which have no personal owners. We might then expect Prajñākaramati to use this same argument here or in the discussion of giving noted earlier in BCA.IX.4–5. It would seem to be a ready argument, already employed earlier in the text, and an important place to redeploy it, but no such approach appears here. Instead, in the more philosophical context of the Wisdom Chapter, he says the *dharmas* referred to in *dharmālambana-karuṇā* provide a meaningful basis for referring to conventional persons. Unlike ordinary people, who view persons with naïve objectivity, *bodhisattvas* who have progressed on the path see the conventional persons who are the concern of compassion, while also realizing that they are a dynamic continuity of aggregates. This is not meant to imply the absence of conventional persons; rather, it validates them. As always, we must assume that conventional and ultimate are paired.

The idea of compassion for ownerless *dharmas*, without reference to a conventional person, appears to be inconsistent with Abhidharma thought. In discussion of the *ālambana* of compassion, the *Abhidharmakośa* and other classic sources specifically rule out this approach. In these contexts, compassion takes a conventional object, *ālambana*, and the elemental atomic components leave no meaningful referent for such an attitude. The *Abhidharmakośa*, a core text for late Abhidharma discourse and a foundational text for Mahāyāna education, offers a two *ālambana* scheme, with which scholars such as Prajñākaramati and Candrakīrti would have certainly been familiar.[19] It contrasts the conventional perspective of compassion, which has sentient beings for its object

17. Paul Griffiths, *Religious Reading: The Place of Reading in the Practice of Religion* (New York: Oxford University Press, 1999), p. 137. He cites P. L. Vaidya, ed., *Śikṣāsamuccaya of Śāntideva*. Buddhist Sanskrit Texts 11 (Darbhanga: Mithila Institute, 1961), p. 3.

18. See Chapter 4 of this volume "The Śāntideva Passage," on the BsCA's reviser.

19. Prajñākaramati often cites or paraphrases the *Kośa*. See Oldmeadow, *A Study of the Wisdom Chapter*, xiv.

(*sattvālambana*), with ultimate truth, which has the universal characteristic of *dharmas* for its object (*dharma-sāmānya-lakṣaṇa-ālambana*).[20]

> The defilements, *kleśas,* are destroyed by focusing on reality. The [immeasurables, compassion etc.,] do not destroy them because their *ālambana* is sentient beings. The established fact is that the *kleśas* are destroyed by focusing on the universal characteristic of *dharmas.*[21]

The same point is made by several other important Abhidharma sources.[22] The intellectual training of Mahāyāna intellectuals was grounded on the Abhidharma, and masters such as Śāntideva, and the later redactors of his work, would have been well aware of this. In Abhidharma thinking, compassion is definitively regarded as a conventional perspective, and its objects are persons. Ownerless *dharmas,* the perspective of ultimate truth, cannot function as the objects of emotional attitudes.[23] For example, Buddhaghosa uses deconstruction into elements as a technique to overcome the anger that may arise when attempting to generate compassion for an enemy. The great teacher seems to have fun with the idea:

> One who is not able to extinguish anger [by the other techniques] ought to perform the dissolution into elements (*dhātu-vinibhogo*). Look here, renunciant, when you are angry with this [person], what is it you are angry with? Are you are angry with head hair, or perhaps body hair, or fingernails? . . . or are you mad at urine? Then again, maybe you are angry with the earth element within the head hair, or the water, fire, or air element. Among the five aggregates, the twelve sense-fields (*āyatana*) or the eighteen elements (*dhātu*), in regard to which this venerable person is

20. For a general discussion see Jenkins, "The Circle of Compassion," 177–185.

21. Unrai Wogihara, ed., *Sphutārthā: Abhidharmakośavyākhyā by Yaśomitra* (Tokyo: Publishing Association of *Abhidharmakośavyākhyā*, 1932–1936) [reprinted 1971], Part 2, VII:12a–b, 687:12; P. Pradhan, ed., *Abhidharmakośa of Vasubandhu,* revised second edition, ed. Aruna Haldar, (Patna: K. P. Jayaswal Research Institute, 1975), p. 454.

22. See Louis de la Vallée-Poussin, trans., *Abhidharmakośabhāṣyam,* trans. Leo Pruden, (Berkeley: Asian Humanities Press, 1990), p. 1302, note 174, which cites *Mahāvibhāṣā,* TD 27, 819b10. Here also the immeasurables cannot destroy the defilements because they concentrate on helping (*anugrahamanasikāra*), not on reality (*tattvamanasikāra*), and do not have the uncompounded (*asaṃskṛta*) for their object; cf. Padmanabh S. Jaini, ed., *Abhidharmadīpa with Vibhāshāprabhāvṛitti* [*sic*], Tibetan Sanskrit Works Series Volume IV (Patna: Jayaswal Research Institute, 1959), pp. 427–429, verses 588–592.

23. According to Lambert Schmithausen: "When the spirituality of '*not*-Self' became dogmatized into a *doctrine* of '*no*-Self' in which holistic persons and living beings were dissolved into mere bundles of factors, this resulted in a certain tension or even incompatibility between this level of ultimate denial of Selves or holistic living beings on the one hand and compassion as essentially referring to just living beings on the other, with the tendency to relegate compassion to the conventional level." "Buddhism and the Ethics of Nature—Some Remarks," *The Eastern Buddhist,* New Series, XXXII, no. 2 (2000): 26–78.

> called by name, which are you angry with? . . . For one who does the dissolution into elements, there is no basis for anger, like a painting on space, or a mustard seed on the tip of an arrowhead.[24]

The idea that ownerless body parts, or the elements they are composed of, could be objects of anger is found humorous.[25] So, either we are misunderstanding the argument in the *Bodhicaryāvatāra*'s Meditation Chapter, or perhaps there is the deliberate deployment of a way of thinking that Ābhidharmikas explicitly rejected. For Prajñākaramati, as in normative Abhidharma thought, the appearance of beings is based on the aggregates. As noted above, according to one of the *Bodhicaryāvatāra*'s key scriptural sources, the *Akṣayamatinirdeśa*, and multiple other treatments of the three *ālambana*, it is quite normal and appropriate for most Mahāyāna practitioners, that is, all those who have not reached the eighth *bhūmi*, to apply Abhidharma perspectives in their ethical thinking. This, and the importance of compassion for simply conceived beings, raises doubts about the general tendency to treat emptiness as if it were the key to understanding Mahāyāna ethics.

Anālambana-karuṇā: Objectless Compassion

Still we are left with the problem that, according the Mahāyāna's highest truth, the *dharmas* that serve as the referent for persons must also dissolve under analysis. Fortunately, Prajñākaramati raises the objection for us. He last defended the idea of compassion for selfless beings by saying that the elemental *dharmas* serve as a basis for what we refer to as persons. But his next hypothetical objection moves to the perspective of emptiness, by raising the natural objection that the aggregates used in Abhidharma thought as a referent for the word "self" are denied by a Śūnyavādin. Such a perspective seems to deny the owner of the action and the fruit of the action. This implies moral nihilism, since the basis of Buddhist ethics is the cause and effect of *karma*.

> Objection: "If there are no sentient beings" . . . and since the arising of [the aggregates such as] form, *et cetera*, is abolished, whose is the goal? The sense is, it would be nobody's.

24. Henry Clarke Warren, ed., *Visuddhimagga of Buddhaghosācariya*, Harvard Oriental Series, vol. 41, revised Dharmananda Kosambi (Cambridge, MA: Harvard University Press, 1950), pp. 253–254, ix.38; cf. Bhikkhu Nyanamoli, trans., *The Path of Purification: Visuddhimagga* (Berkeley, CA: Shambala, 1976), pp. 331–332.

25. This resonates with the view held by Candrakīrti and many later Mādhyamikas that the conventional satisfies only as long as it is not analyzed.

> Exactly! That is precisely our intention! Indeed, ultimately the goal is nobody's, because all *dharmas* are ownerless, *asvāmika*. . . . the effort, is activity from delusion. . . . [but] even if beings do not [ultimately] exist, conventionally they have the nature of illusion (*māyā*), . . . exertion for the sake of a goal is only conventional.[26]

Prajñākaramati simply agrees to the objection; ultimately compassion has no referent at all. But, his point is that the ownerless nature of *dharmas* does not eclipse the conventional appearance of beings.

Candrakīrti similarly cornered himself by raising the same problem. At several points in his writing, when the balance of the middle path threatens to shift toward over-negation, he pauses to address the problem of the apparent ethical nihilism implied by the denial of the existence of the self. He rephrases a hypothetical objection originally put forward by Nāgārjuna as follows:

> If all this is empty, when everything does not even exist, then, because of falling within "everything," right and wrong [actions] would not be conjoined with the desired and undesired fruits that they cause.[27]

His response is that the basis of this kind of objection is a misunderstanding of the meaning of emptiness.

> You wrongly attribute [to us], only by your own false discrimination, the view that the meaning of emptiness is nonexistence (*nāstitva*). . . . But this . . . is not the meaning of emptiness detailed by us in the treatise, . . . Dependent arising is that which we regard as emptiness. It is a procedure based on verbal convention; it is the very middle. . . . That which is born of conditions is unborn. . . . Thus the meaning of the term "dependent-arising" is the same as the meaning of the term "emptiness." But the meaning of the term "nonbeing" is not the meaning of the term "emptiness." Having superimposed the meaning of the word "nonbeing" on the meaning of the word "emptiness," you find fault with us.[28]
>
> . . . The *yogi*, having realized that conventional truth arises merely from ignorance and is without own-being [and] practicing emptiness which is the defining characteristic of the ultimate truth of that [conventional reality], does not fall into

26. *BCA IX.76*, ed. Tripathi, p. 235.
27. *MMK*, ed. la Vallée Poussin, 490:1–2.
28. *MMK*, ed. la Vallée Poussin, 490; cf. Sprung, *Lucid Exposition*, p. 228.

> the two extremes [of over-reification and over-negation]. Because [*yogis*] do not reject the conventions of the world, which have the mode of a reflection, they also do not reject *karma* and its fruit, right and wrong, *et cetera*. Nor do they attribute [them] with ultimately having the nature of an existent, because they see the fruit of *karma* and the rest as without self-existence and the object of words; and do not see them as self-existent.[29]

He goes on to describe emptiness as being like a snake, which must be carefully handled in order to avoid misinterpretation and the consequent disaster of moral nihilism.

Candrakīrti's defense, that what he means by emptiness is dependent origination, is sometimes taken as a comforting version of emptiness. In the struggle to maintain middleness, Candrakīrti is generally pulling on the negative end of the rope, and here he shows that this should not be taken too far. But we should remember that, throughout the Mahāyāna *sūtras, śūnyatā* is spoken of as terrifying, a dangerous idea that is difficult to accept or tolerate. Candrakīrti's version of dependent origination is also non-dependent non-origination; as he put it above, because all things arise dependently, no things arise. This is part of a thoroughgoing rejection of objectifying thought that is profoundly challenging to our basic cognitive relationship to the world. However, he rejects the interpretation that this is nihilistic and insists that rejection of conventional reality is a grave ethical error. In the *Prasannapadā*, Candrakīrti even agrees with his critic that those who so negate the self, thinking that the world is not real and that ill actions bear no fruit, constantly perform evil actions "and are headed for a mighty plunging into the hells."[30] Candrakīrti, like Nāgārjuna before him, clearly recognized the ethical challenges raised by emptiness. His response was to charge his critics with exaggerating or misinterpreting his anti-realism.[31] We will return to this issue below.

Returning to Prajñākaramati for now, what will he do next, having so bluntly accepted a premise that seems to imply moral nihilism through the destruction of the *karmic* scheme? Like Candrakīrti, he resorts to the so-called "provisional acceptance of sentient beings." Compassion can function because we conventionally accept beings that according to our highest truth do not

29. *MMK*, ed. la Vallée Poussin, 495–497; cf. Sprung, *Lucid Exposition*, pp. 232–233.

30. Mervyn Sprung, trans., *Lucid Exposition of the Middle Way* (Boulder, CO: Prajñā, 1979), p. 175; see also pp. 232–233; Louis de la Vallée Poussin, ed., *Mūlamadhyamakakārikās de Nāgārjuna avec la Prasannapadā de Candrakīrti* (St. Petersburg: Academy of Sciences, 1903–13), p. 356.

31. In Chapter 9, we discuss another aspect of Candrakīrti's defense, which is that, without emptiness, karmic causality is incoherent, and we return to the issue of anti-realism.

exist. But then a strictly conventional compassion seems to have been relegated to the realm of illusion; and so the highest truth of Buddhism and its ethic seem to be in conflict. Prajñākaramati anticipates this and takes the analysis a step further, offering his most interesting hypothetical objection of all.

> Objection: Since it has the nature of ignorance, that which is called delusion (*moha*) should not be accepted in any way. So how is it that you accept it? Śāntideva says:
>
> "For the sake of relieving suffering,
> The delusion of a goal is not rejected."
>
> There are two kinds of delusion, [one is] the cause of the process of *saṃsāra* and [the other is] the cause of the quieting of *saṃsāra*. [Delusion] that is a causal link of *saṃsāra* is to be eliminated. However, [delusion] for the sake of relieving suffering, . . . ending the birth *et cetera* of sentient beings, and realizing the goal . . . of ultimate truth is neither rejected nor denied. Indeed, it is accepted because it is conducive (*upayogitvāt*) toward ultimate truth . . . for the sake of quieting absolutely every suffering of all sentient beings, the realization of ultimate truth is undertaken and . . . there is no attainment of the ultimate truth, except through conventional truth.[32]

So the compassionate perspective is not a matter of falling back on ignorance per se, since not all conventional perspectives are the same. Some delusions cause suffering, while others relieve it. All conventional discourse may be illusory relative to ultimate truth, but conventional "truth" quiets *saṃsāra* and leads to the ultimate human goal. Conventional discourse is acceptable to the degree that it is liberating. This gives epistemology a strong relationship to compassion. Ronald Davidson has described this quality of leading toward *nirvāṇa* as the "final touchstone" for what constitutes *dharma* and even the word of the Buddha.[33] As we point out in the preceding chapter, this is also a basic discriminating factor for what qualifies as auspicious, *kuśala*, or inauspicious moral action in Mahāyāna Buddhism. Auspicious action mitigates against *saṃsāra*, while inauspicious action augments it.[34]

32. *Bodhicaryāvatāra*, ed. Tripathi, 235:28. Paraphrased for the sake of brevity.

33. Ronald Davidson, "An Introduction to the Standards of Scriptural Authenticity in Indian Buddhism," in *Chinese Buddhist Apocrypha*, ed. Robert Buswell (Honolulu, University Hawaii, 1990), p. 295.

34. This means that even inflicting suffering rather than removing it, to the extent of torture and taking life, may be auspicious if they are in the compassionate service of liberation. Pain and suffering are not bad per se, since they may be in the use of a surgeon, parent, or righteous king. Stephen Jenkins, "On the Auspiciousness of Compassionate Violence," *Journal of the International Association of Buddhist Studies*, 33, no. 1–2 (2010 [2011]): 299–331.

Prajñākaramati used the term *upayogitvāt* to describe the positive relationship between conventional truth and ultimate truth. This can mean "suitable, applicable, conducive, useful, or necessary." The ultimate cannot be taught and buddhahood cannot be attained without resort to the conventional. Conventional truth is conducive toward ultimate truth, and the conventional truth that constitutes the Buddhist *dharma* has its source in the Buddha's realization of ultimate truth. Conventional truth both comes from and leads toward ultimate truth. Prajñākaramati might accept the description found in the Abhidharma that conventional truth "flows out of," *niṣyanda*, ultimate realization, and that therefore ultimate truth participates in, *bhajanam*, conventional truth. Yaśomitra put it like this:

> When an ascetic departs from the contemplation in which the knowledges of the absolute truth are realized, through the force of these knowledges, later knowledges are produced which are of the conventional truth: . . . The two knowledges, the knowledge of destruction and the knowledge of nonarising therefore participate in the conventional level of truth, not in and of themselves or through definition, but through their outflowing [*niṣyandena*].[35]

It may seem that relegating compassion to the conventional cuts it off from the ultimate perspective, but although conventional truth is of a different order, it is also in a circular relationship with ultimate truth. Compassion finds its highest sphere in conventional reality viewed from an enlightened perspective: as Vimalakīrti put it, compassion for beings seen as a master illusionist sees an illusory person. Rather than seeing nothing, the magician sees through his own illusions as a set of causes and conditions that produce a certain appearance of objective reality, waking into an illusion rather than waking from it. Even though both cowherds and *buddhas* perceive sentient beings, the conventional perspective of one who has realized the ultimate perspective is not the same as the conventional perspective of someone who has not. The magician may see the same visual effect as his audience, but he also sees through it.

Candrakīrti's praise of the three types of compassion also gives this kind of perspective. Having given the highest praise to beginners' compassion with sentient beings for its basis, he speaks of the other two in a way that shows that

35. *Abhidharmakośabhāṣyam*, trans. la Vallée Poussin, p. 1108, 7:12a–b; *Abhidharmakośa of Vasubandhu*, ed. Pradhan, p. 399; *Sphutārthā: Abhidharmakośavyākhyā by Yaśomitra*, ed. Wogihara, p. 625.6. By Wogihara's edition, Poussin writes the subcommentary into the autocommentary. This is Yaśomitra, not Vasubandhu; see also Poussin, p. 1128 and preceding: "When one cultivates conventional knowledge at the end of the comprehension of a certain truth, the conventional truth takes on the aspects of this truth and has this truth for its object."

even compassion without a personal object is still a way of looking at sentient beings. As is typical for the opening verses of a text, he makes a play on his own name, which might be rendered "Moonshine."

> To explain the aforementioned compassion with *dharmas* for its object and with no object:
>
> Homage to compassion produced for creatures,
> like the moon in rippling water,
> Seen as empty of self-existence and rippling. (4a)
>
> When a reflection of the moon [appears] on the surface of pristine water covered with waves from a gentle breeze, . . . the true see [that it] abides according to two revealed essential characteristics, i.e. moment-to-moment impermanence and emptiness of self-existence.[36]

Consistent with his statement in the *Prasannapadā*, that *yogins* do not reject "the conventions of the world, which have the mode of a reflection," each mode of compassion "sees" sentient beings in a different way. Reflections do not disappear when they are recognized as such. The three types of compassion all refer to sentient beings, not to *dharmas* or emptiness per se.

A reflection, provisionally accepted as real for pragmatic purposes, hardly sounds like a compelling basis for ethical thought. However, any "charitable" interpretation also has to consider that Candrakīrti was someone who obviously cared about social justice and individual suffering, who insisted that he affirms karmic causality, who expressed a keen awareness of the moral danger of not taking the world and persons seriously enough, and who strongly challenged social norms. His vitriolic rant against the violence of kings in the *Catuḥśatakaṭīkā* is sufficient example. Clearly he is not someone who simply "read off the surface" and left moral conventions unchallenged.

So how do we account for this from someone who sees the world as a rippling reflection? His own response to the criticism that he fails to take the world seriously enough was that his anti-realism is being exaggerated. Candrakīrti's negations have a clear and specific target, the objectivity characteristic of human linguistic thought. It is the objectivity of beings that is taken as like a reflection, a conventional mode of linguistic thought. It is this illusory objectivity that must be provisionally accepted and which cannot stand

36. *MMK.4a*, ed. la Vallée-Poussin, pp. 10–11; thanks to John Dunne for consulting on the translation; cf. Huntington Jr. and Wangchen, *The Emptiness of Emptiness*, p. 149, and p. 219 note 3; cf. Newland, *Compassion: A Tibetan Analysis*, p. 120.

analysis.[37] If the objectivity characteristic of human thought is the only way we can conceive things to be, then this is indeed nihilism. But for Candrakīrti, the lack of objectivity in the world does not imply its absolute nonexistence, *nāstitva*. Although Mādhyamikas are generally railing against realism, they regard this kind of anti-realism as just as significant a mistake. Emptiness describes the nature of the mundane world. An important scripture for Mādhyamikas, the *Kāśyapaparivarta Sūtra*, addresses this in a humorous way by mocking those who are terrified by the idea of emptiness, when they have been in emptiness all along. "If a *brāhmaṇa* is terrified of emptiness, I say that he is acutely mentally deranged. If you ask why, Kāśyapa, it is because they are terrified by that very emptiness while they course in it." [38]

Candrakīrti's resort to dependent origination as a basis for accepting the conventional is consistent with one of three qualities of conventional reality that later became generally accepted by Mādhyamikas after the eighth century, that is, that it satisfies only when unanalyzed, arises dependently, and leads to effective action.[39] Looking to the two more positive aspects of the conventional, that it arises dependently and leads to effective action, we can see persons also as dependently arisen and related by effective action. The second two aspects are positive and balance the first, which seems to undermine the ability to engage in penetrating analysis, or even to take the conventional seriously. In considering the "dismal slough" raised in Chapter 3, we should take care not to conflate the general lack of modern-style ethical analysis in Buddhist thought for a special lack among Mādhyamikas, and also avoid mistaking their particularistic narrative based mode of ethical thought for lack of depth and subtlety. As opposed to the Western tradition of using abstract analysis to clarify the ambiguities of narrative contexts, Candrakīrti used narrative to illuminate abstract principles. For example, in explaining the idea of killing with compassion, he offers narrative cases of a loving father who kills a sick son by hugging him too hard, of stopping a mass murderer, of a father faced with shooting one son so that both do not die, and of defense against wild animals, and so on.[40]

37. See Chapter 3 of this volume.

38. *The Kāśyapaparivarta a Mahāyānasūtra of the Ratnakūṭa Class*, ed. Baron A. von Stael-Holstein (Shanghai: Shanghai Commercial Press, 1926), pp. 99–101; cf. "The Sūtra of Assembled Treasures," in *A Treasury of Mahāyāna Sūtras*, edited by Garma Chang (London: Penn State, 1983), p. 396.

39. David Eckel, "The Satisfaction of No Analysis," in *The Svātantrika Prāsaṅgika Distinction: What Difference Does a Difference Make*, ed. George Dreyfus and Sarah McClintock (Boston: Wisdom, 2003), pp. 189–190 and 200, fn. 36. David Eckel, *Jñānagarbha's Commentary on the Distinction Between the Two Truths* (Albany: State University of New York, 1987). See pp. 89–96 on *avicāramanohara* and p. 137, note 104, for extensive cross-referencing. Thanks to Tom Tillemans for clarifying these issues.

40. Jenkins (2010).

In response to incisive objections, Candrakīrti and Prajñākaramati never resort to the idea that emptiness provides a rationale for compassion: perhaps that ontological boundaries are broken down, or that all are interconnected in a cosmic soup of *dharmas*, or dissolve into a radiant realm of emptiness. Instead, consistent with the emphasis in Chapter 5, they make a case for taking conventional truth seriously. Both thinkers also point to the importance of compassion based on ordinary undeconstructed persons. Since the vast majority of Buddhists have no idea about emptiness or no-self, the normal unanalyzed construction of persons must be the basis of most Buddhist ethics. Furthermore, for *yogins*, the path toward the realization of emptiness is initiated from compassion, and must start before such higher truths are realized.[41] This casts suspicion on the overwhelming attention to these higher truths in trying to understand Buddhist ethics. The three *ālambana* scheme assumes that there are multiple levels of practitioners with different ontological perspectives. None of these perspectives eclipses the conventional, but each constitutes a different way of seeing persons. Compassion, in fact, precedes the realization of emptiness and is the motivation for achieving it. So compassion has to begin by making sense from an ordinary standpoint, and then must evolve until it incorporates first the perspective of the compounded nature of beings, and finally the emptiness of even their components.

Compassion and emptiness are understood in Mahāyāna texts to be related in both complementary and problematic ways. Compassion functions from conventional perspectives, and so, in a sense, is excluded from the perspective of emptiness, but the conventional wisdom or truth that most fully informs and empowers compassion both leads to and flows from the ultimate truth of emptiness. Furthermore, the realization of emptiness is the single most powerful tool for the compassionate relief of suffering through understanding and relieving its most subtle causes. Therefore the compassionate strive for it.

Many modern scientists might agree that human beings are a dynamic collection of psychophysical processes and that therefore linguistic designations, like self, oversimplify their referents by reducing them to the simple objectivity that only obtains in language itself. We think in linguistic constructs and therefore project the objective qualities of language on the world. The Mādhyamikas insist that the objective structures of language do not ultimately obtain at any level of reality. Objects are only the way human beings simplify into thinkable form a world that does not ultimately conform to objectivity. But this does not

41. Compare the discussion in Chapter 2 on the gradually phased development of interrelated ethical perspectives and that in Chapter 5 on the path.

mean that linguistic structures are useless or meaningless. The phenomenal world's ultimate lack of referents for the configurations of our mental processes, its emptiness of them, only implies nihilism if we are convinced that the only way the world can be is in the manner that we think it, an anthropocentric conceit the size of Mount Meru and, for Mādhyamikas, the keystone of *saṃsāra*. One thinks of the cognitive dissonance of a sentient computer upon discovering that the world is empty of ones and zeroes.

A physicist knows that a table consists mostly of space, that it is a temporary conglomeration of ephemeral atomic and subatomic particles that endlessly dissolve under ever more minute levels of analysis, that its designation as a table is a subjective human label, and that there is no inherent tableness to be found among its countless billions of components, which themselves dissolve into ever more elusive and insubstantial constructions such as "space-time foam." The physicist might also agree with Candrakīrti that simple objective thinking satisfies as long as one does not analyze the table down to space-time-foam. But, their analytic dissolution of the phenomenal world hardly implies nihilism. The usefulness of the human convention "table" is acknowledged, as is the whole level of discourse related to such objects. The "truth" of such a convention has nothing to do with whether its referent is ultimately objectively real, but everything to do with its conventional practical use, or the lack of it. Even in her deconstructive analysis, a physicist might recognize that all she finds are ever more refined conceptual constructions that are only true relative to other theories and concepts to the degree that they are more or less useful. Pragmatism provides a solid anchor for conventional truth claims. Mādhyamikas also saw value in the sophisticated atomic analysis of the Abhidharma, as long as those components are also recognized as being just as liable to dissolution under analysis as the table.

In a sense, the projection of linguistic thought structures on the environment creates a realm of illusion, but that does not mean that language cannot be formulated in ways that are pragmatically expedient. As Prajñākaramati put it, some illusions lead to the cessation of suffering, and some are the cause of suffering. There is no more contradiction between a *bodhisattva*'s assertion that ultimately there are no objective beings and their compassion for conventionally accepted beings, than there is between the physicist's assertion that there is no objective table and her sitting down to eat at the same table. The physicist also has incredible power and freedom in her work with the material world that would be impossible without seeing beyond the frame of conventional objective thought. She might create a table that is biodegradable or resistant to bacteria. The *bodhisattva* seeks a similar kind of power and freedom from the limitations of our psychological programming. The recognition of our imaginative powers to create delusional identities and intersubjective worlds characterized as *saṃsāra* also suggests, for those who awaken into the illusion but are no longer bound by it, a powerful creative freedom to manifest awakened identities compassionately at play with those same powers of imagination.

7

Does "Buddhist Ethics" Exist?

Mark Siderits

A central question of this work is what a specifically Madhyamaka Buddhist ethics might look like, given that Madhyamaka denies there is much if anything that can be said to be ultimately true. Ethical theorists commonly resort to metaphysical claims to support their views about ethics: think, for example, of the role of the Forms in Plato, of God in divine command theories, of *li* in neo-Confucianism. The Madhyamaka claim that there are no ultimately real entities (*dharmas*), with its implication that the metaphysical enterprise simply makes no sense, suggests to many that Madhyamaka must lead to moral nihilism. (Chapter 3 of this volume raises that question in an especially dramatic form.) The present chapter responds to that charge. But it does so in a roundabout way. It begins with the question of whether there is such a thing as ethical theory in the Buddhist tradition as a whole. The answer turns out to be a qualified yes, but insofar as what it identifies as a distinctively Buddhist contribution to ethical theory relies on the metaphysics of non-self, one wonders whether a Mādhyamika can endorse it. The rest of this chapter addresses that question.

The Problem of "Ethical Theory"

What can Buddhist ethics contribute to current discussions in ethical theory? Some, like Tom Tillemans and Michael Barnhart, are not convinced that there is much by way of ethical theory—at least not what is nowadays considered ethical theory—in the Buddhist tradition.[1] There are, of course, many pronouncements in the various Buddhist canons concerning normative matters: rules that prohibit various activities for lay followers; edifying tales, used in moral education, of former lives of the Buddha and of other bodhisattvas; precepts that monastics are expected to follow; lists of virtues that advanced practitioners are to cultivate, and much practical advice concerning how to cultivate them; accounts of the anti-nomian conduct of highly advanced practitioners; and much else besides. But there is not much that would be generally recognized as ethical theory. Now there may be an important lesson for ethical theorists that can be extracted from the Buddhist material. But the extraction will involve a good bit of rational reconstruction—which is a polite way of saying that we will have to do much of the work ourselves. Before coming to what that important lesson is, though, more needs to be said about why it might be that the work has not already been done.

What do we want an ethical theory to do? There is a tendency today to think that the job of ethical theories is to give an answer to the question of moral motivation (Why should I be moral?) and to provide decision criteria that help us solve moral dilemmas. This makes of ethics something whose chief focus is *moral* reasons—reasons that concern other-affecting actions—and not *prudential* reasons. It was not always so in the Western tradition.[2] For Plato and Aristotle ethical theorizing begins with the question, How should I live my

1. Tom Tillemans discusses some of the sources of his skepticism concerning a substantive "Buddhist ethics" in "Madhyamaka Buddhist Ethics," *Journal of the International Association of Buddhist Studies* 33, nos. 1–2 (2011): 353–372. As for Michael Barnhart, in "Theory and Comparison in the Discussion of Buddhist Ethics" *Philosophy East and West* 62, no. 1 (2012): 16–43, he claims that because Buddhism does not unequivocally subscribe to any ethical principles, either we must say that its concerns are orthogonal to those of ethics, or else it is a form of ethical particularism. The first possibility, which bears some resemblance to my own view, he describes as follows:

> The emphasis is on achieving a state of enlightenment that has nothing to do with moral or ethical conduct in itself. Buddhism is not primarily interested in achieving a moral objective, making people behave better or even doing good or some such. It is about enlightenment, even the relief of existential suffering, but not because it is the right thing to do. Rather, these are desirable states or goals that exhibit a kind of impersonal gravitational attraction on our psychology—they are good therapeutic ends. (Barnhart 2012, p. 30)

Of course if we substituted "human flourishing" for "enlightenment," we could say much the same of Aristotle, yet few are skeptical about the existence of "Aristotelian ethics." So while I largely agree with the characterization of Buddhism in the above passage, my own reasons for skepticism run deeper.

Barnhart rejects this view in favor of the characterization of Buddhism as ethical particularist, largely because of the prominent role of *upāya* in accounts of the conduct of fully enlightened beings. I shall have more to say about this when I discuss his reasons for rejecting the characterization of Buddhist ethics as consequentialist.

2. For the claim that in ancient ethics no sharp distinction is drawn between moral and non-moral reasons, see Julia Annas, "Ancient Ethics and Modern Morality," *Philosophical Perspectives* 6 (1992): 119–136.

life? Or to be more accurate, it begins when we realize that the obvious answer to this question—that we want to live the life that leads to happiness—leaves almost completely undetermined just what we ought to do.

Now while it seems clear that the broader Indian philosophical tradition likewise does not have very much to say about ethics as currently understood, it could be added that the focus on happiness or *eudaimonia* that one finds in classical Greek philosophy likewise characterizes the beginnings of what theorizing about ethics one does find in Indian philosophy. The first steps in Indian ethical theorizing are to be seen in the original list of three human ends (*puruṣārthas*):

> *kāma*, or sensual pleasure;
> *artha*, or material wealth and power;
> *dharma*, or virtue and good repute.

It is significant that this list was not intended to represent a hierarchy of ends; it simply records a presumed fact about human variation in basic orientation. One then finds a literary corpus growing up around each, with the *Kāma Sūtra* and its commentaries, for instance, representing a body of theorizing concerning how best to achieve one such distinctive form of human flourishing.

But this pluralism about ends comes to a halt at the point when a fourth human end was added to the list:

> *mokṣa*, or liberation from the cycle of rebirth.

Those who promulgate this end—which includes most of the schools of classical Indian philosophy—claim that this is the supreme aim for humans (and for that matter all other sentient beings as well). The wheel of rebirth is understood to represent a form of suffering, and while the pursuit of any of the other three human aims may yield satisfaction in the short run, it also contributes to bondage on this wheel and is for that reason poisoned. Only liberation from *saṃsāra* can guarantee perpetual absence of suffering.

There has been much speculation as to what triggered this new focus on liberation, but we need not go into any of that here. The one point that is important for our purposes is that this focus came with the introduction of the ideas of karma and rebirth into Indian thought. Without this conception of human existence, it becomes difficult to maintain that liberation is intrinsically superior to the other three human aims.[3] There are, after all, instances of single lives that

3. This claim does not hold for the Buddhist conception of liberation (*nirvāna*), which can plausibly be held to constitute the highest human end without presupposing rebirth. The reason has to do with the point that Buddhist ethics is not *eudaimonistic*, about which I have more to say below.

are successes when measured by the standards offered by one or more of those three aims. Only when it is added that each life is followed by another, the conditions of which are determined by the actions of the prior, does it become at all plausible to suppose that a life filled, for instance, with sensual pleasure must necessarily be followed by something far less pleasant. And only with the notion of a beginningless and potentially endless succession of lives does the threat of cosmic ennui (or worse) begin to infect the pursuit of mundane ends.

Yet it is still possible to fit most Indian liberatory projects into the mold of *eudaimonistic* ethics. For the most part, the state of liberation is depicted in positive terms, as one of unalloyed happiness or even pure bliss. And its achievement is said to depend on coming to understand one's true nature or identity—as not the empirically given psycho-physical complex, the states of which are involved in the attainments of *kāma, artha,* and *dharma.* So, just as with Plato and Aristotle, the good life for humans is understood as something one arrives at through coming to understand the nature of the soul and its relation to the rest of the cosmos, and then learning to act accordingly. We even find in the Indian tradition the same disagreement we see between Plato and Aristotle over whether this state is to be achieved through knowledge alone, or instead through the cultivation of a new set of habits.[4]

What does mark a difference, though, is what happens to the question of moral motivation once the ideas of karma and rebirth are on the table. For then there is a very simple answer to the question of why one should be moral: because otherwise one is certain to get something bad in return. Here it is important to be clear about the (virtually) pan-Indian conception of karma. In discussions of the Buddhist conception of karma, one often encounters the claim that actions of a certain sort can be habit-forming: cruel actions tend to foster more of the same on the part of the agent, and likewise for acts of generosity. This claim can be included under the rubric of karma theory insofar as it involves an alleged causal connection between an action (*karman*) and a fruit (*phala*), an effect in the agent caused by that action. But this is not the core conception of karma. The heart of the theory of karma lies in the claim that every (intentional) action is the cause of a later fruit for the agent that takes the specific form of a feeling of pleasure, pain, or indifference, this hedonic character of the fruit being determined by the moral character of the action. Whether my act of unmitigated cruelty becomes habitual or not, performance of this evil act will cause me to experience great pain, either in this or a subsequent life.

4. This is not to suggest that classical Indian ethics is in all respects like classical Greek ethics. The point is just that what we see in the non-Buddhist Indian systems is consistent with Annas's claim that *eudaimonistic* ethics is the starting point for ethical theorizing.

Rebirth is a necessary part of this view, since we know that many agents escape this life without receiving the due reward or punishment for their actions.[5] The standard view of rebirth is that at death those actions one performed in the present life whose fruit has yet to appear serve as the cause of one's rebirth in a particular form (male or female, human, non-human animal, god, inhabitant of one of the hells, etc.) in particular material circumstances (e.g., healthy and to a family of wealth and privilege, etc.). And the connection between actions and situation of rebirth is strictly causal; a cosmic bookkeeper and judge is no more required here than in the case of the laws of motion.

Given the widespread acceptance of this view, one can perhaps see why the question of moral motivation did not loom especially large in Indian ethics. Once one knows what the karmic causal laws are, it will be just as obvious why I should refrain from undetectable theft as why I should not drink automobile antifreeze (which apparently tastes good going down). Of course, it is hard to come by knowledge of the karmic causal laws; one must learn to recall many past lives and then look for the patterns. This helps explain the prevalence of immoral conduct. Many people simply do not know of rebirth, or of the karmic causal laws that govern the process. Had Gyges known, he would not have become a tyrant. But it is not philosophy that gives us such knowledge. Its acquisition belongs to the technical expertise of the *yogi*.

The fact that classical Indian philosophy is principally concerned with the project of liberation provides another reason that the questions of morality will not loom especially large. For notice that the question of moral motivation is now answered in terms of benefits in the form of pleasure and avoidance of pain: I should refrain from harming others because I thereby avoid a painful rebirth. On the standard Indian analysis of liberation from rebirth, it is identification with the psycho-physical complex—the part of the person that is thought to benefit from pleasure and to be harmed by pain—that prevents one from attaining the ideal emancipated state.

When morality is understood in karmic terms, it becomes aligned with the mundane world. It is of course also true that Indian theories of liberation generally claim that immoral actions tend to reinforce those beliefs and habits that perpetuate bondage, and that other-regarding actions may help undermine such beliefs and habits. To this extent, the cultivation of such moral virtues as forbearance and generosity may play an important role in the prescribed path

5. To call karmic fruit reward or punishment may seem unjustified given the impersonal nature of karmic causation. Still, this is how the process seems to have been taken. Otherwise the karma-rebirth ideology would not have performed its function of rationalizing inequality of birth; this requires that karma be seen as a force of cosmic justice.

to liberation. Still, there may be individual cases where the demands of morality (as specified by what produces a pleasant fruit) conflict with those of path to liberation. An act of noble self-sacrifice might win one rebirth as a god, but the gods are usually depicted as not particularly interested in attaining liberation. If the point of philosophical rationality is to deliver us from bondage to *saṃsāra*, then concern with ethical theorizing may seem like something of a distraction.

Ethics and Liberation in the Buddhist Tradition

The emancipatory projects of much of classical Indian philosophy can thus be fit into the mold of *eudaimonistic* ethics. This is not, however, true of Indian Buddhism. The reason is to be found in its conception of the suffering that is attendant on bondage to *saṃsāra*. The ubiquity of suffering is, of course, a central theme in the Buddha's analysis of human existence. And the subsequent tradition includes a wide variety of negative hedonic states under this category. But as the legend of the four sights makes clear, the core conception of *duḥkha* is existential suffering. The young prince Siddhārtha is said to have been inspired to abandon the householder's life by seeing first an old person, then a sick person, then a corpse, and finally a wandering ascetic. The first three indicate that it is the threat of meaninglessness in light of one's mortality that is at issue. (Note that rebirth merely compounds the problem.) Now the same could be said of the understanding of suffering at work in the Brahmanical systems, yet these were said to be compatible with a *eudaimonistic* approach to ethics. What makes the case of Buddhism different?

What all the Indian emancipatory projects share is the idea that suffering arises because we identify with something we are not—a psycho-physical complex that is inherently prone to unsatisfactory states. The standard solution (common to the Brahmanical systems and to Jainism) is to claim that we are something else. This is compatible with a *eudaimonistic* approach in ethics because it can then be claimed that the discovery of what we essentially are is the key to determining the ideal state for humans.[6] Liberation is the state of true human flourishing because only in it does our nature find full expression. This is thought to represent a solution to the problem of existential suffering because then the threatened loss of meaning can be stanched: when I express my essence, I can see myself as doing what I am *for*. This was the thought

6. Interestingly, some Indian systems insist that only through the exercise of philosophical rationality can one attain this ideal state. Others, though, deny that the path of knowledge (*jñāna yoga*) is the only way to attain liberation.

behind Aristotle's defense of his version of virtue ethics. It is possible to see something akin to it in the standard solution that the Indian schools offer to the problem of suffering. Consider, for instance, Kṛṣṇa's efforts to get Arjuna out of his existential funk in the *Bhagavad Gītā*. Not only is Arjuna told to follow the path of *karma yoga* because that is best suited to his nature, this pursuit will (temporarily) instill new meaning in his life precisely because it leads to the state of eternal bliss that comes with realization that his true self is just the non-dual being/consciousness that is Brahman (*Bhagavad Gītā* 5.24).

What sets the Buddhist tradition apart is that while it agrees that we suffer because we identify with something we are not, the mistake lies not in what we identify with, but that we identify with anything at all—that there is "appropriation" (*upādāna*). The Buddhist doctrine of non-self is the view that the sense of "I" and "mine" is fundamentally mistaken. Liberation from *saṃsāra* comes about through coming to see the continued existence of a person as no more than the occurrence of a complex causal series of impermanent, impersonal psycho-physical elements.

Existential suffering is thereby extirpated because one comes to see that questions of meaning simply do not arise for the sort of thing one turns out to be (namely, a sort of fiction). There being nothing that the events in my life could have meaning for (it not being *my* life at all), the threat to meaningfulness that my transitoriness represents loses all sting. While Buddhist liberation (*nirvāṇa*) is sometimes depicted in positive terms, it is most fundamentally the state of living without existential suffering.

Interestingly, Buddhists do offer an explanation for the ignorance they claim perpetuates suffering. They claim that the personhood concept behind our sense of "I" and "mine" is a useful fiction, but that we suffer because we take it too seriously. It is useful, they claim, for the elements in a causal series of impersonal impermanent psycho-physical elements to think of themselves as a single enduring thing because this fosters identification with past and future stages in the series. And such identification leads to the sort of behavior we call responsible and prudent—behavior that typically results in less overall pain.

Two examples from *The Questions of King Milinda* (*MP* 40) illustrate this. We agree that the future life of the child will be better if he or she becomes educated. But the child typically feels no concern for the young adult who will either get a good job or else be consigned to casual labor and unemployment. Fostering a sense of identification with the future stretches of this causal series is a way of preventing pain and suffering that might otherwise occur. We also agree that preventing recidivism in criminals is an effective strategy for preventing future pain caused by future criminal behavior. And this requires that the apprehended criminal acknowledge responsibility for his or her past misdeeds. What we may fail to notice is that this in turn requires an act of identification on the part of the present elements in the series with past elements of that series. We fail to notice this because we take it as obvious that the present convicted criminal and the earlier miscreant are the same person; failure to identify and accept responsibility can, we think, only represent bad faith on the criminal's part. In the absence of an enduring self, however, there is no fact that makes this the same person. Adoption of the conceit that they are is part of a strategy for lowering the overall amount of pain and suffering that occurs.

The personhood concept and the sense of "I" and "mine" that it fosters are a kind of cognitive shortcut that is effective at preventing pain and suffering. We could of course learn to do the math ourselves. We could try to teach everyone to do the computations that show the overall pain and suffering produced by Gyges's tyranny vastly outweigh the pleasure. But given our cognitive capacities, the likelihood of this succeeding on a large scale seems dim. So instead we bring it about that everyone takes it as obvious that the causal series represents the continued existence of a single thing, me. This does at least make prudent behavior more likely. It also gives us conceptual tools that prove useful in moral training.

But it has two problematic results. First, it fosters existential suffering. To think of oneself as a person is to see the events in the causal series as unified by a narrative. My present hardships as I pursue my education, for instance, are justified by the ultimate goal they are meant to serve, my brilliant career. Socialization of the child is principally a matter of transforming a pleasure-seeking animal into a happiness-seeking person. And happiness comes from seeing past and present events in one's life as having meaning for the future, as having their place in the story arc. This strategy does, once again, have its benefits. But it also sets the stage for the crisis of meaninglessness triggered by the realization of transitoriness (or endless repetition). The quest for happiness turns out to be a hedonic Ponzi scheme.[7]

The second difficulty that comes from taking the personhood fiction too seriously is that it drives a wedge between prudential and moral reasons. Self-regard we take to be innate, other-regard as merely a welcome add-on. This is the predictable result of the shortcut we adopted. Since present events in the causal series are more reliably linked to good or bad results in future stretches of the same casual series than to events in other series, it makes good practical sense to start with minimization of pain in the single series—to start by fostering prudential reasoning and the search for happiness. What this obscures is

7. This may rule out the possibility that Buddhist ethics might be thought of as *eudaimonistic*. But for a somewhat more sympathetic look at the possibility, see Chapter 2 of this volume.

that the point all along was to minimize overall pain and suffering—not that of this or that person, but pain and suffering themselves, regardless of where and when they occur. We take it as given that each of us has a reason to minimize our own pain and suffering, whether now or in the future.

The question of moral motivation is the question of why we should take ourselves to have any reason whatsoever to minimize the suffering of others. But this bit of common sense rests on the mistake of taking too seriously what is merely a useful fiction. This is the point of Śāntideva's argument in Chapter VIII of his *Bodhicaryāvatāra* (*BCA*), to which we will turn in a moment. But first we need to consider a question concerning what has been said so far.

We began with the claim that the Buddhist tradition does not have very much to contribute to current discussions in ethical theory. We then presented a case against the view that Buddhism espouses a kind of *eudaimonistic* ethics. It will be clear, though, that that case represents Buddhism as instead espousing a variety of negative consequentialism, and hence attributes to Buddhism a commitment to a substantive ethical theory.[8] Is there a tension here? Two things can be said in response. The first replies to the objection that any evidence that Buddhist ethics is consequentialist is indirect at best. The reply is that in a tradition marked by the absence of major controversies over the nature of morality, it is hardly surprising that Buddhists should fail to say very much about their own approach to ethics, especially when that approach does not differ markedly from those of their philosophical rivals. When all Indian philosophers save the Materialists agree that the ideal state for humans is the state of liberation from *saṃsāra*, and also agree that conduct that accords with the rules of conventional morality is generally instrumental in bringing about that state, an argument from silence carries little probative value. Theorizing is usually sparked by open and protracted disagreement.

The second part of the reply is in response to Barnhart's argument against characterizing Buddhism as consequentialist, which is one part of his larger argument for the claim that Buddhists do not subscribe to any ethical theory. Barnhart argues that utilitarians (and presumably consequentialists more generally) claim as a major strength of their view that moral calculation is rendered "transparent and dependent on a mere ability to reason" (2012, p. 23), whereas in much Buddhist literature we are told that only a fully enlightened being can be counted on to know what should be done in a particular case. Barnhart is here referring to the so-called skillful means (*upāya kauśala*) of the

8. For more on the classification of Buddhist ethics as consequentialist, see Chapter 8. For a cautionary note concerning attempts to categorize Buddhist ethics using terms taken from Western ethical theory, see Chapter 5.

bodhisattva, the ability of such individuals to discern, in any given situation, the course of action that best leads to liberation and that thus should be done. This, Barnhart claims, is specialist knowledge that cannot be captured in an algorithm, and so is not transparent. It is for this reason that Barnhart thinks Buddhism represents a form of ethical particularism, the no-theory ethical theory.[9]

The reply is that if this is a reason to deny that Buddhist ethics is consequentialist, then it is equally a reason to deny that anyone is a consequentialist. For there simply cannot be a usable algorithm that will always give the right results. Should I lie to my friend about his partner's infidelity? Not only does this involve such imponderables as the effect of my friend's continued ignorance on his partner's behavior. (If the friend found out sooner rather than later, would that make a reconciliation more likely by making the infidelity seem more like a casual fling? And would reconciliation make the partner less likely to stray in the future?) Then there are the effects on my own character should I engage in what I judge to be a justified case of deception. (Will this make me more likely to tell self-serving lies in the future, some of which will no doubt be detected, causing me harm?) Publicity effects compound the difficulties exponentially. How will those who know of my deception be affected, not only in their behavior toward me, but in their standing policies with respect to lying? Now suppose we add into this mix the karmic effects of the action. For all we know, lacking as we do any specialist knowledge of the karmic causal laws, it might be that all of my past conduct makes this one lie something that will cause me to be reborn in circumstances from which liberation is quite unlikely. Once we begin to think about all the possible ramifications of the action, the classical three-body problem in Newtonian mechanics looks like a no-brainer by comparison.

And yet we do have our ways of making seat-of-the-pants judgments in these matters. A sane consequentialism tells us this is what we must do—but that in doing so we must be open to the possibility that there might be better ways of arriving at knowledge of the ideal outcome. This may be the real point behind what Barnhart takes as evidence that Buddhism espouses ethical

9. Barnhart characterizes ethical particularism as follows: "Ethical deliberation follows neither specific rules nor principles, exactly. Rather, it takes a more case-based approach to ethical reasoning—that the relationship of theory to practice is the reverse of what ethical theories say it is. Principles proceed out of cases and provide limited guidance in terms of how we adjust to new cases." (2012, p. 30) But it is possible that particularism is not incompatible with the commitment to ethical theory that stands behind this construal of Śāntideva's ownerless suffering argument. In "The Metaphysics of Ethical Love," *Sophia* 48 (2009): 221–235, Vrinda Dalmiya argues that a feminist care ethics whose notion of care is modeled on maternal love (and which thus lays great stress on caring as involving relation to a particular other) may require supplementation by an answer to the problem of moral motivation.

particularism—the claim that only a fully enlightened being can know what is best in each particular case. The point is not that we must defer to these experts for counsel on what to do. Since such perfected beings appear to be quite rare in our world, this would be pointless advice. The figure of the fully enlightened one may be just a sort of regulative ideal, serving to remind us of the existence of an objectively best choice in every case. The fully enlightened being has presumably lived countless lives honing the skills required to help others overcome suffering, and is thus never taken by surprise by a novel case. The fact that such a being is logically possible vividly illustrates the fact that for the consequentialist there is a right answer in each case, but that working out just what it is takes great effort and not a little luck. It makes us both diligent and humble in our practical deliberation.

Śāntideva's Argument

It was claimed earlier that despite the relative paucity of explicit theorizing about ethics in the Buddhist tradition, there is nonetheless an important lesson we can draw from it. That lesson is to be found in Śāntideva's argument for impartial benevolence. (For the argument, see the Appendix, which contains a translation of the relevant verses of *BCA* as well as the commentary by the tenth-century C.E. philosopher Prajñākaramati. For other ways of interpreting the argument, see Chapter 4.) Perhaps *argument* should be put in quotation marks here. Much of the *Bodhicaryāvatāra* has the flavor of the road-show PowerPoint of a motivational speaker.

His "argument" for hard determinism is a case in point.[10] That Śāntideva was himself aware that what he says in *BCA* VI.22–31 does not constitute a good argument is shown by the fact that in the immediately following verse 32 he grants that hard determinism is incompatible with his own Buddhist practice. Likewise, if we take *BCA* VIII.58 as an argument, we attribute to him the fallacious reasoning that since one does not want to touch soil that is defiled with feces, it is irrational to wish to touch another person's body, since that is the source of feces. What this suggests is that he is not always in the business of giving arguments; sometimes he is merely supplying useful advice for meditators.[11] When lustful thoughts arise spontaneously in someone trying to

10. The passage in question, *BCA* VI.22–31, is construed as an argument in Charles Goodman, "Resentment and Reality: Buddhism on Moral Responsibility," *American Philosophical Quarterly* 39, no. 4 (2002): 359–372.

11. And sometimes an argument might also prove useful for meditators.

achieve distance from their passions, the thought about feces might be better than a cold shower.[12]

Yet while it is possible that Śāntideva did not mean what he says at *BCA* VIII.90–103 to serve as an argument, we can nonetheless, in rational reconstruction mode, use it as the basis of an argument for impartial benevolence.[13] (Indeed, Prajñākaramati's commentary interprets it in just this way.[14]) This argument proceeds from the assumption that non-self is true, that "I" has no real referent: there is no substantial self or soul-pellet, and the person, as a composite entity, is a mere conceptual fiction, a many masquerading as a one. It then attempts to demonstrate that it is irrational not to seek to prevent suffering in others.

Of course the common assumption is that while it is irrational not to seek to prevent one's own suffering, whether present or future, indifference toward suffering in others may be rational. The strategy is to show that this asymmetry in the common assumption—temporal neutrality with respect to one's own states, but locational partiality with respect to global distribution of states—has no rational basis. It is commonly assumed that one is justified in seeking to prevent one's own future pain by virtue of one's ownership of that pain. Ultimately, though, there is nothing that justifies that assumption: the series consisting of impermanent psycho-physical elements in complex causal relation is, as a composite entity, itself a mere conceptual construction, something we superimpose on reality for ease of calculation.

The opponent will respond that at least one is justified in a bias toward one's present states, but this too turns out to be based on taking a mere useful fiction too seriously. As Śāntideva points out, a present pain in the foot does not give the presently existing hand a reason to intervene if such reasons depend on ownership; it is only the present person who can be thought to own this pain, and it is likewise a conceptual construction. Thus we must choose: either all suffering is to be prevented, or else none is.

12. This is not meant to downplay the importance of what Śāntideva has accomplished in *BCA*. In the project of attaining cessation of suffering, good philosophical arguments may be less important than useful advice about how to meditate. But we shall return to the question of how to assess Śāntideva's work later.

13. Here we refer to this as an argument for impartial benevolence, but the passage is often described as giving an argument for *compassion*, e.g. in Chapters 4, 6, and 12. The term *karuṇā* is usually translated as "compassion," and *karuṇā* plays an important role in Mahāyāna ethics. But it is far from clear that Śāntideva sees himself as giving an argument in support of *karuṇā* (a perfection of the bodhisattva) as opposed to the *maitrī* (benevolence) that is part of the path to *arhat*-hood (the goal of practice for the Abhidharma schools). Neither Śāntideva nor his commentator Prajñākaramati uses the term *karuṇā* in this passage. Śāntideva's term for the disposition that is to be cultivated is *anugraha*, which is synonymous with *maitrī*. For more on the translation of *karuṇā*, see Chapters 1, 4, and 6.

14. In Chapters 4 and 6 we consider the question of whether these verses in this arrangement are authentically Śāntideva's and not those of some later redactor. We shall ignore that issue here and instead address the argument as Prajñākaramati finds and interprets it. Those who share the suspicion that this is not authentic Śāntideva might want to put scare-quotes around the use of the name in this context.

Here it is taken as a given that at least some pain is bad and thus is to be prevented. From this it is then said to follow that all pain is to be prevented; the question for the agent is just how they can most effectively deploy their limited resources. But what if one were to deny that pain is intrinsically bad? One might, for instance, take Hume to have given grounds for such a denial when he says (in his defense of the permissibility of suicide) that it is no more obviously wrong to divert a few ounces of blood from their natural channel than to divert the waters of the Nile or Danube from their natural channel.[15] But this is not precisely to the point, since the question is whether pain is intrinsically to be prevented, not whether the diversion of liquid is intrinsically to be prevented. It might still be thought that the pain of slitting one's wrists is not to be prevented if one's future is sufficiently grim. But this is merely a matter of balancing, which presupposes that pain is intrinsically bad.[16] So if there are grounds for questioning this premise of the argument, they must be sought elsewhere.

The place to seek them is Madhyamaka, which, ironically, is the author Śāntideva's school.[17] It will be clear that the argument depends on the claim that composite things such as persons are not strictly speaking real, are mere *façons de parler.* The Abhidharma schools of Buddhist philosophy developed a two-tiered ontology in support of this claim. Composite entities such as chariots, forests, and persons are said to be conventionally real (mere "conceptual fictions"), while the simples of which they are composed (called *dharmas*) are said to be ultimately real.[18] And the mark of something's being ultimately

15. "Of Suicide," *Two Essays: Of Suicide and Of the Immortality of the Soul* (London, 1777) par.12. www.david-hume.org/texts/suis.html.

16. Likewise for Nietzsche's "Anything that does not kill me makes me stronger" (cited in Chapter 12), which is also a matter of balancing. As for Nietzsche's claim that making others suffer may be good (also discussed by Priest), this does not conflict with the claim that pain is intrinsically bad, as long as one presupposes a real difference among subjects.

17. While many (including some fellow Cowherds) have pointed out the apparent incongruity of Śāntideva's argument given his Madhyamaka sympathies, to our knowledge the first to do so was Paul Williams, in *Altruism and Reality: Studies in the Philosophy of the Bodhicaryāvatāra* (Richmond, Surrey: Curzon Press, 1998). His 1998 critique does not, however, depend on the point that for Śāntideva suffering cannot have an intrinsic nature; Williams believes the Madhyamaka denial of *svabhāva* is incoherent. Instead, he claims that the thoroughly impersonal nature of the ultimate truth supposedly revealed by Śāntideva's argument is incompatible with the personal care and concern exhibited by bodhisattvas. See Chapter 12 for discussion of a later Williams criticism, and see Chapter 11 for an extended discussion of Williams's 1998 critique.

18. "Abhidharma" in this context means the mature philosophical theories developed by such figures as Vasubandhua, Saṃghabadra, and Buddhaghosa. (Arguably Dignāga and Dharmakīrti can also be included.) Of course, as Tse-fu Kuan makes clear in his "Abhidhamma Interpretations of "Persons" (*puggala*): with particular reference to the *Aṅguttara Nikāya*," *Journal of Indian Philosophy* 43 (2015): 31–60, the earliest strata of Abhidharma in the Theravāda school do not assert the asymmetry between the ontological status of the person and that of the psycho-physical elements that is central to mature Abhidharma theories. Early Abhidharma may have been a more purely hermeneutical enterprise. What is common to the Abhidharma theories of the mature schools, however, is the theses that (1) only things that bear their nature intrinsically can be ultimately real; (2) persons do not bear intrinsic nature; and (3) there are *dharmas*, things that do bear intrinsic nature. Madyamaka accepts (1) and (2). Its core claim that all things are empty is the rejection of (3).

real is said to be that it bears its nature intrinsically—that it has *svabhāva* or intrinsic nature. The central claim of Madhyamaka is that nothing has intrinsic nature—everything is empty or devoid of *svabhāva*. Supposing that at least some of the arguments given in support of this claim are sound, it might then be said that the argument for impartial benevolence falsely assumes that pain is ultimately real, with badness as its intrinsic nature.

We can see how this criticism would go by reconstructing the argument, which has the following *prima facie* structure:

(1) At least some pain is bad and to be prevented.
(2) It is not the case that some pain is mine and other pain is someone else's.
(3) Nothing else could justify a bias in favor of preventing my own pain.
(4) Therefore all pain is to be prevented.

To make the argument work, we must recast it by bringing in the distinction between conventional and ultimate truth:

(1') It is ultimately true that at least some pain is bad and to be prevented.
(2') It is not ultimately true that some pain is mine and other pain is someone else's.
(3') Nothing else could justify a bias in favor of preventing my own pain.
(4') Therefore it is ultimately true that all pain is to be prevented.

(2) must be understood as (2'), that is, as couched in terms of ultimate truth, since it would be false if understood through the lens of conventional truth; the conventional truth about pain is that it always has an owner. This means (1) must likewise be understood as involving the ultimate-truth operator. And this requires that to-be-prevented-ness be taken as the intrinsic nature of an ultimately real entity, pain.[19] Now this might seem like an innocent

19. Contrast this with the argument that could be reconstructed out of *BCA* VIII.90, the argument of the sameness of oneself and others (*parātmasamatā*): "All are equally subject to suffering and happiness, and should be protected just like myself." On one natural interpretation of this verse, the premise—that happiness is characterized by to-be-promoted-ness and suffering is characterized by to-be-prevented-ness—is acceptable to all (i.e., is conventionally true) precisely because the badness here attributed to suffering is actually badness for its owner. This is something everyone, even the psychopath and the sadist, acknowledges. But for precisely this reason, the argument fails. While everyone agrees that each person has a reason to promote her own happiness and prevent her own suffering, the moral skeptic questions whether this can be universalized. Of course if the passage is construed as advice for the meditator on the bodhisattva path (as Śāntideva may have intended it), then it works. But this is because such an adept will already be motivated to develop concern for the welfare of others. What the appeal to the sameness of self and others cannot do by itself is provide a reason for developing such concern.

Moreover, if we follow Prajñākaramati's interpretation, the argument of VIII.90 is precisely the argument that is more fully elaborated in VIII.97–103. As he understands "the sameness of others and oneself," the point is just to establish that all suffering is characterized by to-be-prevented-ness and all happiness by to-be-promoted-ness, not to assert anything like equality of moral status for all sentient beings.

assumption. For surely anyone who claims that pain is not in and of itself bad, something it would be better to be rid of, simply does not know what pain is. But a Mādhyamika will nonetheless insist that absurd consequences follow from the seemingly innocent assumption that there are irreducibly simple entities with natures they bear independently of all facts about other things. So while the argument might be acceptable to an Ābhidarmika, it seems like something that a Mādhyamika cannot endorse. And a premise of this book is that the sort of Buddhist ethics we are here exploring is something that would be acceptable to a Mādhyamika.

Now since the argument is novel and interesting, it seems worthwhile to explore the possibility that it might after all prove acceptable to a Mādhyamika. But the route to supporting the claim that it is will be somewhat circuitous, first exploring what other ethical consequences the doctrine of emptiness might be thought to have. The strategy will be to defend an interpretation of emptiness that is sufficiently conservative as to leave a place for the argument for impartial benevolence, by showing that the more radical interpretations are problematic.

Making the Argument Safe for Madhyamaka

It is quite natural to suspect there to be a connection between the Madhyamaka doctrine of emptiness and ethics. Madhyamaka is historically the first of the two major Indian Mahāyāna philosophical schools, and Mahāyāna claims superiority over the Abhidharma schools due to its teaching of emptiness and its advocacy of the career of the bodhisattva, the ideal expression of impartial benevolence. Madhyamaka understands the teaching of emptiness as the denial that reductive analysis ever bottoms out. Why should this be thought to support the claim that the supremely rational aim is the career of the compassionate bodhisattva? To address this question, we must survey the available interpretations of emptiness, of which there are now several.

One popular view is that the emptiness of all things means that the ultimate nature of reality is inexpressible, something that can only be captured in non-conceptual intuition. This seems like a reasonable extrapolation from the one thing Nāgārjuna does tell us about the soteriological point of emptiness (at *Mūlamadhyamakakārikā* [hereafter *MMK*] XVIII.5cd): that grasping emptiness brings about the end of *prapañca*, a term often translated as "verbal proliferation" or prolixity. Now in this context *prapañca* might just be hypostatization or reification, the tendency to take as real what is just a way of talking. But some have taken it to instead mean all conceptualization. In that case, to grasp the emptiness of all things would be to understand the nature of things to be beyond all language and concepts.

If this is right, then any connection between emptiness and benevolence will likewise be unconceptualizable and so inexpressible, something we can "get" only by becoming fully enlightened and thereby acquiring the requisite intuitive insight. This would bring us no closer to understanding the connection between emptiness and benevolence, but at least we would know of a connection. But there is reason to doubt that this is what Mādhyamikas mean by emptiness. To say that the ultimate nature of reality is inexpressible is to express something about the ultimate nature of reality. Mādhyamika philosophers were well aware of this "paradox of ineffability," and used it against those of their opponents (namely, certain Yogācārins) who do explicitly affirm that the nature of reality is ultimately inexpressible. That they should do so is evidence that they do not share this view of the ultimate nature of reality.

Indeed, Mādhyamikas are fairly explicit about rejecting all views about the ultimate nature of reality (which would include the view that it is inexpressible). Thus Nāgārjuna declares "incurable" those for whom emptiness, supposedly the ultimate truth about things, is itself a metaphysical view (*MMK* XIII.8). This suggests that perhaps the lesson to be learned from the emptiness of all things is that the very notion of ultimate truth is incoherent. If there are no things with intrinsic nature, then there can be no ultimate truth-makers, so the expression "ultimate truth" must itself be vacuous. This might in turn be taken to mean that there is only conventional truth: that "how things are" necessarily reflects human interests and cognitive limitations, and that the very idea of "how things are *anyway*" is at best merely a useful regulative ideal.

This seems to be on the right track, but what connection could there be with ethics, let alone with the great compassion of the bodhisattva? One suggestion might be that if there is only conventional truth, then the person as object of benevolence is reinstated in our ontology. The thought here is that Abhidharma's valorizing of what they call ultimate truth results in a bloodless impersonal world of subjectless *dharmas*, while the exercise of compassion requires that one take sufficiently seriously the concrete particularity of the owner of those states.[20] The Madhyamaka critique of the Abhidharma notion of ultimate truth could then be seen as paving the way for benevolence by giving us back our common-sense world of chariots, rivers, mountains, and persons. Unfortunately, this strategy would also, by reinstating the common-sense conception of the person, give us back existential suffering, as well as the classical

20. For more on this way of understanding Madhyamaka ethics, see Chapter 5.

self-interest theory of rationality, with its asymmetry of temporal neutrality and locational partiality.

It might be thought that insight into emptiness will not result in the reinstating of an unrevised common sense. For, it could be claimed, common sense includes its own share of *prapañca* in the form of belief in things that have intrinsic natures and so resist reductive analysis. The point of the doctrine of emptiness, it might be claimed, is that nothing is like that—having a nature that is independent of the natures of other things. Instead, each thing is in relations of thoroughgoing interdependence with all other things. This might in turn supply the sought-after connection between emptiness and benevolence by fostering the sense that my own welfare is inextricably intertwined with that of others. Indeed, some hold that this "Indra's net" interpretation of emptiness serves as the basis for a Buddhist environmental ethic.[21] But more needs to be said about how this is to work. Is it that since what befalls others must affect me, I should be concerned about the welfare of others? But this is just enlightened self-interest, and its shortcomings as a basis for benevolence are well known. One such deficiency is that with some others, any adverse impact on me is likely to be negligible, and can safely be ignored when assessing actions that benefit me while harming others. For the "Indra's net" strategy to work, it must somehow undermine the distinction between my welfare and that of others. One way it might be thought to do this is by erasing all distinctions between "this" and "other," by way of the point that any such distinction requires that the entities in question have their own determinate identities. Determinate identity requires intrinsic nature, so if there is no intrinsic nature there can be no numerical distinctness. This would dissolve the distinction between my own welfare and that of others, but at too high a price. For then there could likewise be no distinction between benefit and harm, and agents could have no reason to prefer one course of action over any other. A second difficulty with this strategy is that it seems to indulge in what sounds suspiciously like the sort of metaphysical theorizing that Mādhyamikas reject. While the "Indra's net" picture may look like the rejection of metaphysics when seen against the background of Abhidharma views, when we step back from the Buddhist context it is no longer clear just how it differs from the non-dualism of Advaita Vedānta.

The alternative, conservative interpretation of emptiness starts with the idea that if nothing has intrinsic nature, then the very idea of ultimate truth—of

21. For a survey and critique, see Christopher Ives, "In Search of a Green Dharma: Philosophical Issues in Buddhist Environmental Ethics," in *Destroying Māra Forever*, ed. John Powers and Charles S. Prebish (Ithaca, NY: Snow Lion, 2009), pp. 165–185. Some of these criticisms of the "Indra's net" strategy echo those of Ives.

"how things are *anyway*"—is incoherent. Now Mādhyamikas are quite insistent that realization of emptiness is essential for liberation from *saṃsāra*. If this is not in order to clear the way for some other metaphysical vision, and is also not to take us straight back to the common-sense view of our existence, why might this be? The suggestion is that *prapañca* be understood as the subtle form of self-affirmation that results from the metaphysical realist conception of truth,[22] but that adherence to this conception is itself the outcome of a certain degree of progress on the Buddhist path to liberation from *saṃsāra*. The upshot will be that the assertion that nothing has intrinsic nature will be warranted only when addressing individuals who are stuck at the *arhat* stage due to *prapañca*. It will not be warranted in contexts generated by questions concerning what one should do. In such contexts, there is no difficulty in asserting either that pain is real and intrinsically bad, or that persons are mere conceptual constructions. Such assertions are warranted in contexts where the interlocutor is someone just approaching the *arhat* stage. So the emptiness of all *dharmas*, which *prima facie* conflicts with the intrinsic badness of pain, does not after all represent a bar to Śāntideva's argument going through.

Let us start with the claim that adherence to the metaphysical realist conception of truth is a predictable result of following the Buddhist path to liberation. The portion of the path I have in mind is the one described in early Buddhism and the Abhidharma schools. Now it is important to note that not only do Mādhyamikas never reject this path, Nāgārjuna himself explicitly endorses it (e.g., in *MMK* XVIII 1–5ab and in *MMK* XXVI). His complaint is not that this path is misguided, but that it does not conduct one all the way to liberation, for which insight into emptiness is required. Suppose that Ronald Davidson is right and the ordinary conception of truth is perfectly transparent, something that calls for no theoretical articulation. The two-truths scheme implicit in early Buddhism and explicit in Abhidharma clearly deviates from this minimalist stance toward truth, leading instead to metaphysical realism. It is understandable why this should be so. The "I"-sense is among the most powerful intuition generators in our conceptual repertoire. Its extirpation, something all Buddhists agree is necessary for liberation from *saṃsāra*, seems to require the philosopher's commitment to follow the argument wherever it may lead. This explains not only the centrality of philosophy to Buddhist practice, but also how the two-truths doctrine would prove necessary to such practice.

22. Putnam defined metaphysical realism as the view that there is one true theory about the nature of the world, with truth understood as correspondence to mind-independent reality. By "mind-independent reality" he meant what others mean by the phrase "how things are *anyway*." In what follows it will be important that the conception of truth at work in the Abhidharma distinction between conventional and ultimate truth is this metaphysical realist conception.

Given that belief in the existence of persons is virtually universal, one must either explain how such a widespread error might have arisen, or else make it an article of faith that the vast majority has been deluded by Māra. Since the second route risks reinscribing the powerful affirmation of self that typically comes with faith commitments, the first is preferable. And it seems to work, at least up to a point. The two truths theory explains how the concept of an enduring subject and agent might come to be utilized by a system consisting of a causal series of impermanent, impersonal psycho-physical elements. But in doing so, it renders truth less than fully transparent. If the truth of "the cat is on the mat" does not consist in the cat's being on the mat (since cats and mats are conceptual constructions), but in something immensely more complicated, then we have begun a journey down the well-worn path to truth-makers, correspondence, and verification-transcendent truth-conditions—to real truth as conformity to how things are *anyway*.

Once again, as Mādhyamikas see things, this is all perfectly appropriate and useful. The difficulty is just that metaphysical realists are inclined to pound the table—to insist that there is such a thing as ultimate truth, that the truth is "out there." And in this insistence the Mādhyamika sees a subtle form of self-assertion—indeed so subtle as to perhaps defy detection and extirpation. For after all, the ultimate truth being insisted on is that there is nothing to which "I" refers. The discordance between propositional content and what is conveyed performatively (in the table-pounding gesture) can easily go unnoticed: when I insist on a thoroughly impersonal truth, I may miss the fact that I am thereby engaged in an act of appropriation (*upādāna*). Emptiness is the purgative that purges one of all tendencies to perform unbridled assertions. It is the cure for a metaphysical realism that may be a necessary component of the path but must still be overcome.

But emptiness, in purging one of all metaphysical views, is said to expel itself as well (see *MMK* XIII.8). This is the famous doctrine of the emptiness of emptiness. That all things are empty is not, we are told, itself ultimately true. This means that the claim that all things are empty can be asserted only in contexts where saying this will prove useful, namely in helping one make the final step from realization of non-self to full enlightenment. Its assertion is not warranted in other contexts.[23]

Among the contexts in which it is not warranted might be the context of practical reasoning in which one wonders what reason there is to prevent suffering in others. A wise Mādhyamika might not object to the claim that pain is intrinsically bad when this claim is made in the context of trying to determine

23. See Candrakīrti's comments on *MMK* XXII.11, at LVP 444–445.

what should be done.[24] Earlier, Śāntideva was compared to a road-warrior motivational speaker. The implied contrast was with the philosopher, understood as someone who aims at giving ultimately sound arguments. If the sort of contextual semantics currently under discussion represents the Madhyamaka stance, then it is open to Śāntideva to question the contrast. For the wise Mādhyamika who gives philosophical arguments against there being intrinsic nature does so only as a sort of therapeutic intervention. The efficacy of the intervention may depend on the soundness of the arguments. But the point of giving the arguments is to help this specific audience—already possessing the skills involved in exercising philosophical rationality—attain their goal, the cessation of suffering.

Some Final Remarks

This is how one might make the argument for impartial benevolence safe for Madhyamaka.[25] And since Madhyamaka holds that there is no ultimate truth, it follows that at least this much of Buddhist ethics may be based wholly in the conventional. The question, Why should I be moral? can be answered without appeal to ultimate facts; the argument's seeming resort to the ultimate can be safely domesticated. This is not to say that the answer will be equally obvious to all. Indeed, it is not clear that those for whom the answer is obvious (i.e., who understand the argument and accept it as sound) will be motivated to exercise impartial benevolence through their grasp of the argument alone. Sadly, it is all too common for us to recognize that we have good reasons to act in a certain way and yet to be unable to bring ourselves to behave accordingly. I might acknowledge the harmfulness of smoking and yet persist nonetheless. But then, while many Buddhists would agree that the exercise of philosophical rationality is necessary for liberation, very few claim that it is sufficient. Even those who take philosophy to be an important component of the path to cessation usually

24. To say this is in effect to allow that in certain contexts, certain entities are usefully thought of as having intrinsic natures. For more on the sort of contextualism at work here, and why it might be advisable for a Mādhyamika to adopt it, see Siderits, "Is Everything Connected to Everything Else? What the Gopis Know," in Cowherds, *Moonshadows: Conventional Truth in Buddhist Philosophy* (New York: Oxford University Press, 2010), pp.167–180.

25. To respond specifically to the question raised in Chapter 3, a Candrakīrti-style Mādhyamika could use the present strategy to escape the dismal slough, provided they were willing to accept the form of contextualist semantics that allows terms to denote things that are understood as having intrinsic natures in certain contexts. It is often claimed that so-called Prāsaṅgikas must refuse to countenance intrinsic natures even at the level of the merely conventional. But it is not at all clear why this could not be done wittingly—in a way that need not lead to hypostatization.

hold that the practice of meditation is also necessary. Meditational practices are designed to undermine those cognitive and affective habits that perpetuate the "I"-sense and thus suffering. Since it is precisely these habits that also stand in the way of practicing genuinely impartial benevolence, it is hardly surprising that one's motivational structure might retain a strong egoistic bias, even after grasping the argument for impartial benevolence and granting its force.

How does one come to be wholly motivated by impartial benevolence? Different schools of Buddhism give different accounts, and there is much that can be learned about moral psychology from their literature concerning the path to *nirvāṇa*. But our concern has been with a different question: Is there anything that ethical theory as currently construed can learn from the Buddhist tradition? Now a key difference between current ethical theory and the sort of ethical theorizing one finds in both the classical West and in classical India is the modern insistence on a distinction between moral and prudential reasons, with a consequent demand that ethics give some account of the normativity of moral reasons.

That this demand has proven difficult to meet is a potent source of moral skepticism. One might reject the distinction and the demand by embracing the classical conception of ethics as *eudaimonistic*. But once the distinction has been drawn, it becomes difficult not to see that move as leading to just another enlightened self-interest theory, this time based on questionable empirical premises. What Śāntideva's argument gives us is a way of directly challenging the distinction by showing it to rest on a questionable metaphysics of the self. And once the argument has been made safe for Madhyamaka through judicious application of contextualist semantics, it yields a response to moral skepticism that does not rely on appeals to queer facts of any sort.[26] Not so bad for a school that doesn't do ethical theory.

26. But see Chapter 8 for a somewhat different (though not wholly incompatible) way of making the argument safe for Madhyamaka.

8

From Madhyamaka to Consequentialism

A Road Map

Charles Goodman

Is emptiness compatible with ethics? This fundamental question has been a major concern of Buddhist scholars in the Madhyamaka tradition throughout that tradition's history in India, Tibet, and elsewhere in Asia. And the same question faces us today. The profound teaching of emptiness subtly undermines all our dogmatic convictions and beliefs, and points toward a compelling realization of the core Buddhist ideal of "freedom from view." But if we are to realize such an ideal, what will happen to our ethical commitments? Is there a danger that following the path that leads to seeing the ultimate truth will have the side effect of turning the practitioner into a monster?

These issues face anyone with any moral commitments who is attracted to the Madhyamaka view. But they seem particularly pressing for those scholars who interpret Buddhist ethical views as forms of consequentialism. Even if it is possible to reconcile compassionate action and nonviolent lives with emptiness, we may still have difficulty building consequentialist ethical theories on the empty space that is the only foundation Madhyamaka allows.

One way to put the problem starts with noticing that, in Buddhism, there are only two kinds of truth: ultimate and conventional. And it is clear that, according to Madhyamaka, ethical statements cannot possibly be ultimately true. So they must be merely conventional. What, then, does it mean to say that ethics is merely conventional? It sounds like we would be saying that ethics is a social construct within each particular society, with no basis at all outside the contingent practices and customs of that society. Such a claim leaves us with a variety of extremely unattractive metaethical options, including moral relativism, ethnocentric conservatism, and error theory. And none of these options fits well at all with any universal ethical theory that aspires to provide normative guidance, however general and abstract, across places and times.

Another concern would be that consequentialism is a grand theory that seeks to ground many diverse normative judgments and intuitions on a single underlying theoretical structure. On some ways of understanding Madhyamaka, this kind of high theory is precisely what we need to abandon. Such views could lead us to expect that the field of ethics may simply be too complex and messy to be brought into any unifying framework.

Yet another reason for concern is that recent work advocating a consequentialist interpretation of Buddhist ethics has rightly focused on Śāntideva's strategy of drawing on the doctrine of no self, in its Abhidharma form, to lend support to the universalism that is characteristic of consequentialist thinking, and to undermine intuitions about the significance of the distinction between persons. But the doctrine of no self in the Abhidharma relies on a postulated ontological asymmetry between ultimately real simple entities and conventionally posited, unreal people. If the existence of everything is in part constituted by conceptual construction, as the Madhyamaka argues, then no such asymmetry can be sustained, and we have to ask whether Śāntideva's strategy still has any viability. If not, it will be much harder to sustain any connection between Buddhist forms of life and consequentialist ethical theory.

This chapter will proceed on the basis of a particular philosophical reconstruction, in contemporary terms, of the Madhyamaka of the great Tibetan philosopher Tsong kha pa. In the most crucial chapter of the Insight section of his *Lam Rim Chen Mo*, "The Actual Object to be Negated," Tsong kha pa writes:

> Ignorance does not apprehend phenomena in this way; it apprehends each phenomenon as having a manner of being such that it can be understood in and of itself, without being posited through the force of a conventional consciousness. . . . Therefore, what exists objectively in terms of its own essence without being posited through the power of a subjective mind is called "self" or "intrinsic nature." (2002, p. 213)

In these terms, we would formulate the Madhyamaka view as the claim that there is no such thing as self or intrinsic nature anywhere.

Now this passage could be interpreted as an expression of idealism. Tsong kha pa might be saying that a chair, for example, exists only while it is being perceived by some sentient being. That reading would collapse the distinction between Madhyamaka and Yogācāra, the tradition of Buddhist idealism. We might also adopt a more pragmatist understanding of Tsong kha pa's meaning. If we approach our experience with a conceptual scheme that includes the concept of "chairs," then from the point of view of that scheme, there are right and wrong answers to questions about how many chairs are present in a given situation. Moreover, we can set up our concepts in a way that makes other concepts, not contained in our initial state of awareness, useful to us, whether we know this or not. Once we start thinking in terms of "water," we will have a use for the concept of "hydrogen," even if we do not yet have that concept. But on the other hand, there are no chairs, and there is no water, totally independently of the way we conceive of the world. It is only in relation to perceivers and thinkers with particular kinds of interests, values, and concerns that we can properly speak of chairs, water, or examples of any other concept you might name. They exist, at least in part, by being posited through the power of a conceptual scheme, not objectively, in terms of their own essences.

How is a view like this, which makes the existence even of hydrogen dependent on our conceptual frameworks, not a form of idealism? It helps to consider Hilary Putnam's famous slogan: "the mind and the world jointly make up the mind and the world" (1981, p. xi). Objects of awareness depend for their existence on other objects, and on mental processes; mental processes depend for their existence on other mental processes, and on objects. In this interdependence, there is no asymmetry. To use a Buddhist term, objects and mental processes are *born together* (Skt. *sahaja*, Tib. *lhan cig skyes pa*). Idealism makes world dependent on mind; neopragmatism and Madhyamaka make mind and world dependent on each other.

Could someone who holds a view like the one sketched here defend a consequentialist ethical theory, or indeed, an ethical theory of any kind? Perhaps it would be more natural for a form of particularism, like the views of Jonathan Dancy, to emerge from a Madhyamaka outlook. Or maybe Mādhyamikas should endorse the anti-theoretical, constructivist naturalism defended by such writers as Margaret Urban Walker.

Some could legitimately raise concerns about how well motivated this question is in relation to historical Buddhist philosophers. As Mark Siderits explains in Chapter 7 of this volume, the majority of Buddhist writers do not seem to be engaged in any activity much like the construction and defense of systematic ethical theories. This is not to say that they explicitly endorse particularism, or some other anti-theory view; rather, they are entirely silent about what we consider to be metaethical and high-level normative ethical matters. And if these Buddhist philosophers would have no interest in having any view about such questions, then it seems pointless to ask whether their other views would constrain their options in this regard. Now these concerns may be well grounded in relation to quite a few Buddhist thinkers. But there is at least one important exception in the philosopher who will be the primary focus of examination here: Śāntideva.

There is a passage in the *Śikṣā-samuccaya* of Śāntideva that is striking in the closeness of its resemblance to Western formulations of classical utilitarianism. Śāntideva writes:

> If a bodhisattva does not make a sincere, unwavering effort in thought, word, and deed to stop all the present and future pain and suffering of all sentient beings, and to bring about all present and future pleasure and happiness, or does not seek the collection of conditions for that, or does not strive to prevent what is opposed to that, or does not bring about small pain and suffering as a way of preventing great pain and suffering, or does not abandon a small benefit in order to accomplish a greater benefit, if he neglects to do these things even for a moment, he undergoes a downfall. (*ŚS* 15)

It may be superfluous to lay out again just how utilitarian this passage sounds. Nevertheless, we might wonder what Śāntideva thought he was doing in offering this formulation. Did his intellectual objectives have anything in common with those of Western ethical theorists, or did his assertions—which sound like ethical theory to us—serve some entirely different set of purposes and concerns? We can answer this question rather decisively by looking at the lines that immediately precede the above quotation:

> On this topic, for those who have taken the vow, a universal characteristic of downfalls will be stated, so that whenever they perceive anything that has that characteristic, they should abandon it, and so that they will not become confused by merely apparent downfalls, or things that merely appear not to be downfalls. (*ŚS* 15)

We could hardly ask for a clearer explanation. A downfall (Skt. *āpatti*) is a violation of the bodhisattva vow, which is no mere arbitrary collection of rules, but is the moral commitment of a Mahāyāna practitioner to awaken for the benefit of all beings. Śāntideva is trying to provide theoretical guidance to bodhisattvas who want to avoid violating this commitment, and who want to be able to distinguish between genuine and apparent breaches of their vows. This aspiration, to provide a general formulation that will be relevant to practical judgment, is exactly what particularists see as misguided and impossible. It is a form of the distinctive aspiration of an ethical theorist.

So Śāntideva is trying to do ethical theory, and consequentialist theory at that. But does he have any right to? After all, there is no question that he is a Mādhyamika; the arguments in Chapter IX of the *Bodhicaryāvatāra* are sufficient to show that. On his view, whatever exists is a product of conceptual construction. But contemporary discussions about metaethics have lent strong support to the claim that a consequentialist view about normative ethics goes most naturally with a realist view about metaethics. Given that Madhyamaka is resolute in its opposition to realism in all its forms, we might think, it would be expected to rule out the kind of metaethics that is most compatible with consequentialism. Instead, we would do better to look to an account on which morality is through and through a social product, emerging in various particular social contexts through the construction of practices of responsibility. On such a view, defended ably by Margaret Urban Walker (2007), it is worse than useless to attempt to arrive at timeless, universally valid moral principles. Doing so involves ignoring or occluding the actual social realities from which real morality emerges, and privileging the perspectives of the socially advantaged people who carry out the theorizing. We should replace grand ethical theorizing with careful empirical attention to the social contexts in which moral norms are constructed, and with a process of "transparency testing" that assesses moral assertions to see whether they are based on deceptive ideologies and false descriptive claims.

When we juxtapose this view with universalist consequentialism, there turns out to be an important area of agreement that should not be overlooked. For consequentialists, the overwhelming majority of features of our moral practices are, in fact, socially constructed. The foundational truth about morality does not include rights, property relations, desert of punishment, special obligations, or indeed, most of the duties and responsibilities that frame most people's experience of the moral life. All of these have been created by societies. Now, as a matter of descriptive historical fact, they may have been created for all kinds of proximate reasons, such as beliefs about the will of God or the whims of human rulers. But for purposes of justification, these practices, to the extent that they are justifiable at all, are so because they serve certain purposes. To utilitarians, for example, these practices are justified when they serve, promote, and protect human well-being in particular, or sometimes the well-being of sentient beings in general.

One way to explain the issue between these two views, then, is to ask whether we should try to give a theory of the human goals that the constructed norms and institutions are supposed to promote. If there is such a theory, then it seems very likely that the resulting account can helpfully be expressed in the framework of consequentialism. But if there is nothing illuminating to say about what these goals are, then consequentialism will be the wrong approach. If we are to regard the purposes of morality as eternally up for grabs—if the theory is no more insistent on specifying what the construction is for than on specifying the exact results of the construction in advance—then we will be left with a view much more like Walker's than like Sidgwick's.

Here is another way to develop, and perhaps clarify, what is at stake. The output of the theory, in the form of the rules to be followed in society and the rights that people can claim, will have been shaped in important ways by social construction. Moreover, we are ruling out the possibility that there are any inputs to the process from a human essence, conceived in a metaphysically robust way. We deny that there is any such thing as a deeply grounded, ultimately real human essence.

But could there be such a thing as the human condition—a condition shaped, in part, even by the genetic inheritance of normal humans?[1] Are there values, reasons, and normative concerns that proceed, not from a variable and unconstrained process of social construction taking place within each society, but from the existential situation of human beings as frail, impermanent, conscious creatures, confronting certain kinds of dangers, experiences, and opportunities? Could it be, for example, that there are some moral reasons that proceed, directly or indirectly, from our human susceptibility to pain and suffering?

This is not to say that the human condition is non-empty. When we subject any given element of the human condition to rational analysis—including even our crude biological susceptibility to pain—we will find that a realist perspective is unsustainable, and that what we are looking at exists in a way that involves conceptual construction. But society and the process of social construction are also empty. It can be true conventionally that the social construction of rules and rights takes inputs both from social choices

1. Rejecting a human essence is therefore not the same as rejecting human nature in the sense defended by Pinker in his *The Blank Slate*. Madhyamaka can't be committed to the idea that none of what humans are like is innate. We shouldn't understand emptiness in such a way that it requires us to deny that having two arms and two legs is genetic. On the other hand, for example, there might be no fact of the matter about whether a being with human ancestors who had been subjected to extensive genetic manipulation was still human or not. And Pinker regards "intuitive essentialism" as an innate heuristic that often leads us into error, and that conflicts with Darwinism: see Pinker (2002), pp. 230–231.

and from general features of what is conventionally true about humans everywhere. Nothing about the Madhyamaka view itself either requires us to say this, or forbids us to do so.

Given this understanding of Madhyamaka, we would be well advised to consider the possibility that its ethics should involve some form of contextualism.[2] There is much promise in this suggestion, but we should develop it in a way that does not require us to abandon one of the most fundamental commitments of Buddhism since its beginnings: the commitment to the universality of morality and to the moral equality of all humans, independent of their social status. This commitment is indirectly but clearly articulated at various places in the Pāli Canon: for example, MN 84. Everyone wants to be happy and free from suffering, and everyone is subject to the same law of karma. Simply believing that you are permitted, for example, to kill your king's enemies to aggrandize his domain, doesn't make you exempt from suffering the karmic consequences of such an action, and it won't stop Buddhists from describing your actions using evaluative terms such as *akuśala* and *pāpa*—even, as it happens, if those Buddhists are Mādhyamikas. Candrakīrti makes this clear in his commentary on Āryadeva's *Catuḥśataka* (*Four Hundred Stanzas*), where he levels some serious criticisms at the moral beliefs of his own society (for example, at CŚT 353, 389, and 414 in Lang 2003, pp. 187, 193, 199). This text alone is enough to show that even the strictest Mādhyamika should not be committed to a posture of unthinking deference to prevailing moral norms. So we have a paradox: the broader metaphysical views we are assuming require ethics to operate only within a certain context, but the overall normative picture we find in the texts requires ethics to be universal and to involve the possibility of criticizing the practices of our own and other societies.

What, then, is the context in which Mahāyāna ethics applies? Ethics applies whenever we are looking at the world in terms of folk psychology. Wherever there are beliefs and desires, thoughts and emotions, happiness and suffering—so far the scope of ethical evaluation extends, and no further.

The appropriate context, then, is not a particular culture or set of commitments, but instead a set of concepts. This approach stems from the more general, pragmatist-influenced reading of Madhyamaka that was briefly sketched above. There is no special set of concepts that captures the ultimate nature of reality. But once you adopt a certain set of concepts, there are right and wrong answers to questions you might ask in terms of those concepts. Moreover, once you adopt a certain set of concepts, there are characteristic problems,

2. As proposed in Finnigan and Tanaka (2011).

challenges, and opportunities that arise, and that may call for the development and articulation of further concepts.

That is folk psychology is an optional way of looking at the world, but one that carries with it certain commitments. We can imagine alien beings who are eliminative materialists, in the style of the Churchlands, or who are pure atomistic reductionists, and see the world merely as swarms of elementary particles. Moreover, Buddhists maintain that it is possible for humans to drop the conceptual scheme of folk psychology. In the advanced state of meditation known as the base of nothingness (Pāli *ākiñcañña-āyatana*) the conceptual processes that normally construct a physical world of objects have ceased to operate. In Kant's terms, the process of synthesizing a manifold has temporarily stopped. From the point of view of this meditative state, no sentient beings or mental states appear, and so ethics is utterly irrelevant. This is an example of a state that is outside the context in which Buddhist ethical views operate. But once the meditator rises up from her cushion and engages with the world, sentient beings appear—beings with their own world of thought, feeling, and experience. They may appear as illusory, in some more or less subtle sense; nevertheless, they appear and must be dealt with somehow. As soon as other sentient beings are encountered, ethics will come into play.

What about the fact that folk psychology is a badly imperfect theory—so that, for example, when we try to use it to understand the behavior of those who are gravely mentally ill or suffering from severe dementia, its categories seem to break down? This is just what Mādhyamikas should expect. Our frameworks for understanding the world pay their way by being useful, by leading to successful practice. Certainly folk psychology is immensely valuable to us in negotiating social interactions; no substitute seems to be at hand that could do anything like the same work. But when we push its concepts to their limits, they disintegrate. Why? Because, like everything else, these concepts and the entities they describe are empty; and the theory in which they feature is merely conventionally true.

One way to put these claims in more traditional-sounding Buddhist language would be in terms of the view that there could be a whole series of discourse practices, some of which are conventional or ultimate with respect to others, but none of which is ultimate in an absolute sense. Some would associate this view with the Svātantrika form of Madhyamaka (Tib. *dbu ma rang rgyud pa*). So we could say that concepts such as rights, freedoms, ownership, and claims are conventional with respect to well-being, and that in that context, well-being functions as if it were ultimate. But from a deeper perspective, well-being itself is merely conventional; neither the welfare of sentient beings nor anything else is ultimate in an unqualified sense.

Can Mādhyamikas, who reject the idea of ultimate, metaphysically robust objectivity, really accept that discourse about well-being is somehow more objective than, and stands as relative ground to, discourse about rights, responsibilities, and claims? Contrast how Mādhyamikas think about language, which is socially constructed and arbitrary, with how they think about the causal structure of the world. At the heart of the dGe lugs lineage's interpretation of emptiness is that the complete absence of any essence is entirely compatible with the universal, cross-cultural validity and accuracy of a very specific conception of how causality works: the twelve-linked chain of dependent arising. For Tsong kha pa, if you do not yet comprehend how emptiness is compatible with the Buddha's detailed analysis of dependent arising, "then you must understand that you have not yet found the Madhyamaka view" (2002, p. 138). And emptiness is compatible with dependent arising in the sense that dependent arising is correct; other understandings of causality that deny aspects of dependent arising would therefore be incorrect. These claims may be true only conventionally, but that doesn't stop them from being true; it also doesn't stop them from holding cross-culturally, even if some people deny them. They would fail to hold only from perspectives that don't even involve the concept of causality, such as the deepest meditative absorptions.

So even though Mādhyamikas reject scientific realist conceptions of the objective truth of physics, they can still hold that statements like "electrons have negative charge" have a different status, and a somewhat greater degree of objectivity, than statements like "a green traffic light means go." It would follow, then, that they could, consistently with their broader metaphysical and epistemological commitments, assign a different status, and a somewhat greater degree of objectivity, to statements about well-being than to statements about rights or responsibilities. Indeed, their view of well-being might turn out to look strikingly like a realist one, even if they would go on to reject a fully realist understanding of the metaphysical status of that account.

What is it like, then, to be a realist about well-being? One of the most influential realist conceptions of well-being is due to Richard Boyd. In "How to Be a Moral Realist," Boyd appeals to the concept of a homeostatic property-cluster. When there are several properties that not only tend to be observed together, but actually tend to preserve and enhance each other, and that, when found together in relevant contexts, have characteristic kinds of further effects, we can regard them as jointly making up a homeostatic cluster (1988, p. 217). This can be true even if some of these properties do sometimes occur without others; the presence of most of the properties is sufficient for the instantiation of the cluster, and the presence of a moderate number or degree of the properties would create a case falling in the vague penumbra of the concept defined by the cluster. One of Boyd's strongest examples of such a homeostatic cluster is the terms "healthy" and "healthier than" (1988, p. 218). There are many aspects of bodily condition that we can reasonably see as helping to constitute health. Some reasonably healthy people are lacking in some few of these aspects, and although we can specify necessary conditions (if your heart isn't beating, you can't be very healthy), there is no small set of aspects that are jointly sufficient for health. When various aspects of health are present, they reinforce each other.

For Boyd, well-being has this kind of structure too. There are a variety of human needs: "Some of these needs are physical or medical. Others are psychological or social" (p. 122). When some of these needs are satisfied, that often tends to make it easier to satisfy others. No one of the human goods by itself constitutes well-being, and no small set is jointly sufficient. Boyd sees this perspective on well-being as suitable to ground a form of "homeostatic consequentialism." And this understanding of the relation between goods, Boyd maintains, is helpful in a particular way, in both theoretical and practical contexts: "a concern for moral goodness can be a guide to action for the morally concerned because the homeostatic unity of moral goodness tends to mitigate possible conflicts between various individual goods" (p. 122).

Now a notable feature of Buddhist discussions of the qualities that make for admirable human lives, of which there are many, is that they pay almost no theoretical attention to the issue of conflicts between different goods. This fact, which creates quite a few interpretive difficulties for ethically interested readers of Buddhist texts, could be explained if Buddhist thinkers such as Śāntideva held something like a homeostatic property-cluster view of well-being. If the different aspects of well-being don't typically compete with each other, but if progress on one tends to contribute to progress on the others, there would be little need in practice for any theoretical guidance about balancing them against each other.

Do we have any evidence that well-being, as explained by Śāntideva, has a structure like a homeostatic property-cluster? The *Śikṣā-samuccaya* quotes a passage from the *Dharma-saṃgīti-sūtra*:

> A mind absorbed in meditation sees things just as they are. In a bodhisattva who sees things as they are, great compassion unfolds for sentient beings. Such a person thinks, "I should bring it about that all sentient beings see everything just as it is as a result of meditative absorption." Moved by that great compassion, this person quickly completes the training in higher moral discipline, higher thought, and higher wisdom, and awakens fully to highest

> genuine full awakening. "Therefore, I should be well established in moral discipline, not moving, never slacking off." In this way, one should reflect on the greatness of resting meditation for oneself and others, and in order to go beyond endless suffering in the lower realms and elsewhere, and for the sake of obtaining for oneself to the fullest extent endless, excellent worldly and transcendent happiness and success, with longing, one should practice diligently, like someone in a burning house longing for cool water. In this way, sharp attention arises in training. One also applies mindfulness, and applying mindfulness, gives up what is fruitless. And when someone gives up what is fruitless, what is harmful cannot arise for that person. Therefore, those who want to protect the body should seek out the root of mindfulness, and then should always apply mindfulness. (*ŚS* 119–120)

According to this complex passage, resting meditation (*śamatha*) leads to insight, which in turn produces compassion. Compassion, in turn, promotes progress in moral discipline and wisdom, by arousing intense motivation for practice. This motivation also leads to the application of mindfulness. Mindfulness then leads to giving up fruitless activities. This whole process of development gives rise to "worldly and transcendent happiness."

In particular, Śāntideva discusses in detail the relationship between moral discipline (*śīla*) and stable attention (*samādhi.*) He writes that "[m]oral discipline helps create the conditions for stable attention"; moreover, "[i]n the same way, someone who is aiming for moral discipline should also make an effort at stable attention." He supports this claim with a *sūtra* quotation saying that, when a practitioner attains stable attention,

> Such a person does not act badly,
> But is well established in good conduct.
> The spiritual practitioner stays in the right sphere of activity,
> Gives up inappropriate activities,
> And lives free from burning desire,
> Disciplined, with the senses protected. (*ŚS* 121)

Śāntideva concludes that "[m]oral discipline and stable attention reinforce each other."

Passages of this type could be multiplied at tedious length. We quote them in order to give partial support to the following picture. For Buddhists such as Śāntideva, there exist certain states of mind and character, such as the Six Perfections and other Buddhist virtues, that tend to produce, sustain, and reinforce each other, and therefore constitute a homeostatic cluster. These states tend, both individually and jointly, to produce happiness, understood as attitudinal pleasure—an attitude of acceptance toward what is arising in experience. The causal processes by which they produce happiness operate both internally and externally. These states constitute well-being. Individually they can produce low levels of well-being, as can happiness, however it is caused; the highest levels of well-being are characterized by most or all of these states, jointly instantiated and accompanied by deep and extensive happiness.

It is a feature of this view that well-being *has no essence*, at least in some senses of that term. For example, we will not be able to give strict necessary and sufficient conditions for the presence of well-being, though we will be able to say what features count for or against describing a sentient being's life as going well. To the extent that the English word "essence" captures at least part of the meaning of the Sanskrit word *svabhāva*, the homeostatic cluster view would leave us in a position to say that well-being is *niḥsvabhāva*. This claim may give Mādhyamikas some reason to prefer a homeostatic cluster view of well-being to the closely related but subtly different view articulated in Goodman (2009).

Moreover, the homeostatic cluster view can help address the problems some Mādhyamikas would raise about regarding particular events or states as intrinsically good. These problems may not be very serious, because the word "intrinsic" can be used in various ways, some of which are not the intended targets of the Madhyamaka critique (Goodman 2009, pp. 128–129) Nevertheless, suppose that there is a strong Madhyamaka objection against intrinsic value as such. And suppose that the virtues that help to make up well-being reinforce each other in various complicated ways. Then we could say that each of them is good, not just because of the way it is, but also because of its relations to all of the others, and to happiness. This would give the value of these virtues what could be a helpfully relational character.

Happiness itself would be more difficult to treat in this way. But suppose that, as many popular writers on Buddhism today claim, happiness tends to make our thoughts and actions better and more virtuous—for example, by making us less prone to anger (Chodron 2001, p. 60). If this claim is correct, then happiness may be a full member of the homeostatic cluster, and not just a result of its presence. That would mean that, for Buddhists, the value of happiness itself would be only partly intrinsic, and partly relational.

A homeostatic cluster view of well-being suggests that well-being is like health. It is interesting to note that the analogy with health has deep roots in Buddhism. We can find it, for instance, in the *Discourse to Māgandiya* (MN 75.)

Indeed, it would not be inaccurate to describe the goal of Buddhism generally as a kind of mental health, when that term is properly understood. And it is quite plausible, and textually motivated, to think that rules of Buddhist moral discipline, and the organization and etiquette of Buddhist organizations and institutions, are justified, when they can be justified, by their tendency to make it possible, or easier, for people to find this kind of mental health within themselves and to live in a way that nourishes and develops it.

We have argued that Mādhyamikas can legitimately regard particular moral norms as resting on a view about well-being, even though neither well-being nor any other concept can be a ground in the ultimate sense. Now we are in a position to ask whether emptiness, as understood in the Madhyamaka, can in any way help us to defend the kind of impartial concern about well-being that is characteristic of universalist consequentialism, and, of course, of many forms of Buddhist ethics as well. There are reasons to believe that emptiness cannot contribute to this goal; nevertheless, emptiness can support impartialism, if we are careful about just how.

The ownerless suffering argument is the project of using the early Buddhist and Ābhidhārmika doctrine of no-self to support impartial, universal concern to relieve suffering and bring about happiness, without regard to the distribution of these states. Clearly, if sentient beings themselves are nonexistent, or if they have only a secondary form of existence within a pragmatic and imprecise way of speaking, whereas happiness and suffering are ultimately real, then we have some reason to hold that a view of ethics that understands these facts would focus on the overall quantity of happiness and suffering, without concerning itself with illusory and insignificant claims about who experiences these states.

The result of this reasoning is a rational justification of what Mahāyāna writers called *dharma-ālambanā-karuṇā*, "compassion that takes simple entities as its object." This form of compassion does not occur in Abhidharma texts belonging to the Way of the Disciples (*Śrāvaka-yāna*); its possibility may be in conflict with some of the assumptions of those texts. Since we are dealing with an understanding of compassion that is distinctive to the Mahāyāna, we should not expect that it would be explained in a way that would be entirely consistent with Abhidharma frameworks. Instead, any interpretation of *dharma-ālambanā-karuṇā* will have to see it as a creative reappropriation and transformation of concepts originating in the Abhidharma, in order to make these concepts serve Mahāyāna intellectual and spiritual goals. In particular, Śāntideva wants to use the doctrine of no-self, in more or less its Ābhidhārmika form, to defend the rationality of working to relieve all suffering everywhere, no matter who has it, as in consequentialism.

Unfortunately, it seems that Śāntideva's own final view, the Madhyamaka view of emptiness, cannot be used to support the ownerless suffering argument. Śāntideva's strategy seems to depend on an asymmetry between the metaphysical status of persons, as merely conventional, and the metaphysical status of mental states, as ultimately real. But the Madhyamaka rejects any such asymmetry, and so cannot argue in this way. Anything that exists, exists conventionally. These claims place us in a strange and embarrassing position. Recall that Śāntideva himself is universally regarded as a Mādhyamika. Nearly all of the contemporary Tibetan Buddhists who would endorse his arguments also hold that Madhyamaka is the highest form of Buddhist philosophy. If the ownerless suffering argument cannot be used by Mādhyamikas, why did he advance it in the first place?

Some scholars have recently proposed a way out of the dilemma: denying that he ever did advance such an argument. The rationalist reading of *BCA* VIII.90–103, as explained in Chapter 4 of this volume, "The Śāntideva Passage," maintains that Śāntideva intended to argue only that, since I am not special in any morally important way, my suffering does not count any more than the suffering of others. Therefore, I should treat the future suffering of others as being just as important as my own future suffering.

The Abhidharma interpretation of the passage accepts that Śāntideva did intend to make the argument just described. On this reading, there are two arguments in the passage, rather than one. There's the reasoning that, since I am not special, my suffering is no more important than anyone else's; and the reasoning that, since in some sense there is no owner of suffering, all suffering should be treated as equally significant.

Two major commentators on this passage, Prajñākaramati and rGyal tshab, read it in a way that, though superficially different, is in fact entirely consistent with the account I want to give. They see 97–101 as responding to objections based on the distinction between self and other: that the suffering of others does not harm me; that I need to protect myself against future suffering; that certain suffering is mine and therefore has special significance to me; that self and other are distinct individuals, unlike the same series; and so on. For example, consider part of Prajñākaramati's commentary on v. 98: "due to the absence of any one thing that is the object of the concept of 'I,' this is a mistaken construction, it is attachment: 'It will also be just me then as well.'" The whole point of the Abhidharma interpretation of this passage is that the absence of any true unity in the person is a crucial step in showing that concern for all sentient beings is uniquely rationally justified. Given how the reasoning in verses 97–101 is supposed to function, it is an entirely verbal and inconsequential issue whether we think of this reasoning as a response to objections raised in defense of selfishness, or as a second argument intended to refute the rational justifiability of selfishness.

It would also be possible to concede that the *Bodhicaryāvatāra* as we have it contains an ownerless suffering argument, but to deny that such an argument was part of Śāntideva's original authorial intention. We know that the first version of the text, the *BsCA*, was altered, and a number of verses were added by a reviser. These include the core verses that advance the ownerless suffering argument. If the reviser was not Śāntideva, then perhaps we should see the argument in question as a spurious addition to an otherwise great classic text.

We may never know for sure, but it is relevant to note that the ownerless suffering argument is not confined to the *Bodhicaryāvatāra*: it occurs in the *Śikṣā-samuccaya* as well. Indeed, the argument is so structurally important there that it acts as a frame for the entire text. The very first verse of the root text of *ŚS* duplicates *BCA* VIII.96. And the long verse passage that concludes the *ŚS* contains duplicates of *BCA* VIII.97–98 (at *ŚS* 358.) Shortly thereafter, at *ŚS* 360, comes a verse that, though it raises significant linguistic issues, we may translate thus:

> Therefore, in this way, living beings should be understood as
> Like collections of sense-spheres (*āyatana*).
> Since that suffering is not owned,
> It should be prevented for oneself and others.[3]

This verse is not in the *BCA*. The verse that follows immediately after it is closely similar, though not identical, to *BCA* VIII.100.

The existence of an ownerless suffering argument in the *ŚS* does not settle the question of the identity of the reviser. What it shows is that the reviser, whoever he was, had control, not only over an ancestor of our manuscripts of the *BCA*, but also over an ancestor of our manuscripts of the *ŚS*. At least, whoever composed the version of the argument that appears near the conclusion of the *ŚS* did not limit himself to quoting the *BCA*, but was willing also to produce a version of the argument in his own words.

Assuming, then, that Śāntideva did intend to advance an ownerless suffering argument, how could a Mādhyamika have any right to argue in this way?

3. In Sanskrit, *tasmād-evaṃ jagat jñeyaṃ yathā-āyatana-saṃcayaḥ/aprāptam-eva tad-duḥkhaṃ pratikāryaṃ para-ātmanoḥ*. In Tibetan, *de phyir skye mched tshogs bzhin du/'gro ba gcig du shes par bya/ma byung nyid nas sdug bsngal de/gzhan gyi bdag las phyir bzlog bya*. The key term here is Skt. *aprāptam*, translated above as "not owned." It is odd that the term is represented in the Tibetan by *ma byung*. However, the Nitartha Tibetan Dictionary lists "gained, obtained, got" as possible meanings of *byung*.

One could try to use the idea, explored above, that discourse about persons is conventional *relative to* discourse about mental states. To develop this argument, we would have to pay careful attention to issues about the proper level of discourse at which to make ethical claims, and the exact nature of the appropriate relationships between different discourses. Such a task may be too difficult to undertake here.

Instead, we can make progress by exploring what we might take to be the polar opposite of the ownerless suffering argument: the attempt by modern non-consequentialist ethicists to attack utilitarianism for ignoring the separateness of persons. Two of the most prominent political philosophers of the twentieth century, Rawls and Nozick, are often framed as bitter intellectual opponents. But they are both critics of utilitarianism, and they criticize utilitarianism in strikingly similar ways. Rawls writes:

> [The utilitarian] view of social cooperation is the consequence of extending to society the principle of choice for one man, and then, to make this extension work, conflating all persons into one through the imaginative acts of the impartial sympathetic spectator. Utilitarianism does not take seriously the distinction between persons. (1971, p. 27)

Nozick argues as follows:

> But there is no social entity with a good that undergoes some sacrifice for its own good. There are only individual people, different individual people, with their own individual lives. Using one of these people for the benefit of others, uses him and benefits the others. . . . To use a person in this way does not sufficiently respect and take account of the fact that he is a separate person, that this is the only life he has. (1974, p. 33)

Because we are fundamentally separate beings, with our own lives, this argument goes, it is inappropriate to treat the boundaries between lives as unimportant, by aggregating benefits and burdens across persons, or by burdening some to cause greater benefits to others.

What these writers object to in consequentialism is not that it rejects the distinction between persons, but that it fails to take that distinction with what they regard as sufficient seriousness. What is necessary to generate Rawlsian complaints against consequentialism is not merely that there should be a distinction between persons, nor even that the distinction should have some sort of normative significance. Rather, it is necessary to assume that the distinction between a benefit to person A and benefit to person B is *of greater significance* than the distinction between a benefit to person A at t_1 and a benefit to person

A at t_2.[4] This is because these writers accept that it is entirely rational and appropriate to give up small benefits or accept small burdens at one time, in order to bring about greater benefits or avoid greater burdens at some other time in the same life. Yet they reject the view that we can similarly balance benefits and burdens between different lives. So their position rests on the assumption that there is a kind of metaphysical asymmetry in which the separateness of different lives is more fundamental than the differences between the parts of the same life.

Mādhyamikas are well placed to deny this claim. Though they may have rejected some aspects of the formulations of no-self in other Buddhist schools, they certainly would accept that the distinction between separate persons is no more fundamental, metaphysically, than the distinction between "the same" person at different times. If the logical structure of the debate is indeed as I have characterized it, then Mādhyamikas need have no more sympathy than other Buddhists for Rawls's "separateness of persons" critique of consequentialism.

We can frame these considerations in a different, more psychological way. Like other Buddhists, Mādhyamikas such as Tsong kha pa hold that sentient beings have two innate, very strongly held wrong views, known as self-grasping and self-cherishing. By self-grasping, I mean the view that *I am one, real, unitary, permanent, independent thing*. By self-cherishing, I mean the view that *that thing is the most important thing in the world*. Self-grasping and self-cherishing are inconsistent with the early Buddhist teaching of no-self, and they are also inconsistent with the Madhyamaka teaching of emptiness. A crucial goal of the Buddhist path is to eradicate these innate mistakes. Buddhists hold that this goal is possible, but very difficult to achieve.

In light of these views, Mādhyamikas, like other Buddhists, could claim that the source of some anti-consequentialist intuitions is self-grasping and self-cherishing. It would not be plausible for them to make this claim about all anti-consequentialist intuitions. But where this claim would be plausible, they would have a non-justifying, undermining explanation for the existence of these intuitions. And that would help to defend consequentialism.

It will be helpful to focus on one particularly important example. Simple, well-known, and powerful arguments suggest that we should all be devoting a large share of our resources to helping the world's poorest people (Singer 1972). These arguments, while not wholly dependent on consequentialist ethical theories, are broadly consequentialist in spirit. Most people, when they encounter these arguments, regard them, at least initially, as much too demanding.

4. For example, the arguments cited by Jeremy Waldron in a number of his writings fit this pattern. See, e.g., Waldron (2010), pp. 134–135, especially fn. 49 and 53.

Morality, they think, could not ask so much of us. Many ethical theorists have built on these emotional reactions to construct theories that carve out a personal moral space for us to pursue our own projects, relegating the demands of morality to the margins of our lives.

Notoriously, though, Buddhist teachings uphold lofty and sometimes even terrifying ideals of generosity. For Buddhists, morally ideal people would in fact practice extreme generosity; and if we are not like these people, that is actually a misfortune for us. So, it seems to me, Buddhists should have little sympathy with most of the philosophical opponents of very demanding moral views. And they could argue that the intuition that arguments for generosity are inappropriately demanding is largely based on self-cherishing. If each of us has the irrational, emotionally based belief in our own superior importance, that would help explain our emotional resistance to the demand to do more for the very poor. And this explanation would undermine the credibility of that resistance, to the extent that it would take an anti-consequentialist form. Left intact, of course, would be rule-consequentialist considerations about how much it would be best to ask people to give on a social level, taking into consideration what people's motives are going to be. So we would still have resources, perhaps, to moderate the demands on most people to some degree—but only in a way that would be consistent with an indirect consequentialist perspective.

Our conclusion, then, could be this. Someone who accepted an unqualified version of the early Buddhist doctrine of no-self could use the ownerless suffering argument to provide a powerful positive argument for universalist consequentialism. Mādhyamikas cannot use the argument in this way, but that does not mean that their doctrine of emptiness is irrelevant to ethics. A Madhyamaka understanding of the emptiness of the person can be used to block one of the most popular objections against universalist consequentialism, and to give a non-justifying psychological explanation of some of the emotional resistance to such views. And a proper Madhyamaka view of the relationship between well-being and social norms can be quite hospitable to consequentialism. Consequentialism is certainly not the only possible moral view that a Madhyamaka could have; and some would argue that Mādhyamikas should have no view about ethics at all. But if they do have an ethical view, universalist, welfarist consequentialism is an entirely viable option for them to choose, and it may well be the option that fits best with their overall Buddhist worldview.

9

The Prāsaṅgika's Ethics of Momentary Disintegration (*Vināśa Bhāva*)

Causally Effective Karmic Moments

Sonam Thakchöe

In *Moonshadows: Conventional Truth in Buddhist Philosophy* (Cowherds 2011), we argued that the linchpin of the Prāsaṅgika's epistemology is its thoroughgoing commitment to ontological non-foundationa lism.[1,2] We showed that according to the Prāsaṅgika system, only cognitive processes that are both ultimately and conventionally empty of intrinsic reality can perform epistemic functions: we can make sense of epistemic praxis only within the context of the rejection of the intrinsic reality of subject and object—both conventionally and ultimately. In this chapter we argue that the Prāsaṅgika's moral philosophy is also strictly non-foundational, as the causal efficacy of karma requires its momentary arising and disintegrating, which in turn depends on its lack of any intrinsic nature.

In Buddhist ethical literature we find two ethical standpoints: (1) moral foundationalism, and (2) moral

1. All translations are mine, except where indicated otherwise.

2. Also cf. Thakchoe, "Through the Looking-Glass of the Buddha-mind: Strategies of Cognition in Indo-Tibetan Buddhism" *Octa Orientalia Vilnensia* 11, no. 1 (2012): 93–115; Thakchoe, "Prāsaṅgika Epistemology: A Reply to Stag tsang's Charge Against Tsongkhapa's Uses of Pramāṇa in Candrakīrti's Philosophy" *Journal of Indian Philosophy* (2013) 41: 535–561.

non-foundationalism. Moral foundationalism is the view according to which ethics and the momentariness of karma are incompatible. On this view, there is a need to posit a real ontological basis in order to explain karmic causation. This is, for instance, the Sautrāntika position. Moral non-foundationalism is the view according to which ethics and the momentariness of karma are complementary: ethics works naturally within the framework of momentary karmic process, and there is no need to posit anything extra in order to explain how an earlier action can serve as a cause of an immediate or much later effect. Prāsaṅgika, we will argue, is committed to a form of moral non-foundationalism.

Momentary Disintegration and the Problem of Moral Causality

In the *Abhidharmakośa-bhāṣya (Commentary to the Treasury of Abdhidharma)* (AKB IV.2b–3b), Vasubandhu presents the Sautrāntika's position on momentariness as follows:

> All conditioned things are momentary (*kṣaṇika/skad cig pa)* . . . To exist for a moment (*kṣaṇa/skad cig*) is for a thing to perish immediately after having acquired its being; to be momentary is to be dharma that has moments, as a staff-wielder (*daṇḍika/dbyug can*) is one who has a staff (*daṇḍa/dbyug pa*). (Vasubandhu, AKB IV.2b. Skt. ed. Swāmī Dvarīkā Śāstri)[3]

According to the Sautrāntika, karma is momentary, for it is a conditioned process. And whatever is a conditioned process must disintegrate (1) *spontaneously* and (2) *causelessly*. First, karma disintegrates spontaneously because a conditioned thing does not exist beyond the attainment of its existence: it perishes on the spot where it arises; it cannot go from this spot to another

3. *Na gatiryasmātsaṁskṛtaṁ kṣaṇikaṁ ko'yaṁ kṣaṇe nāma? Ātamalābho'nantaravināśī, so'syāstitī kṣaṇikaḥ|daṇdikavat|* (cf. *mNgon pa* Ku 166b). Similarly, according to Śāntirakṣita's *Tattvasaṁgraha* VIII.388: "Moment is so-called for it is that form of the thing which does not persist after its production; and that which has this form is held to be *momentary* (*kṣaṇika*)." *Utpādānantarāsthāyi svarūpaṁ yacca vastunaḥ/ taducyate kṣaṇaḥ so'sti yasya tat kṣaṇikaṁ matam*||*Tattvasaṁgraha* VIII.388 (Skt. ed. Svāmi Dvarīkā Śāstri) (cf. *Tshad ma* Ze, 16b). Elaborating on this point further, Kamalaśīla's *Commentary* (*Tattvasaṁgraha-Pañjikā*) says: "what is called moment is the character of the thing which is destroyed immediately after it has been produced, and that which has this characteristic is called momentary. Therefore the physical action is not a mov ement."||*Utpādānnataravināśasvabhāvo vastunaḥ kṣaṇaḥ ucyate, sa yasyāsti sa kṣaṇika iti/tathā coktam—"ātmalā bhānantarvināśī kṣaṇaḥ sa yasyāsti sa kṣaṇikaḥ" iti*||Kamalaśīla, *Tattvasaṁgraha-Pañjikā* VIII.388 (Skt. ed. Svāmi Dvarīkā Śāstri) (cf. *Tshad ma* Ze, 232a).

(AKB IV.2b. Skt. ed. Svāmi Dvarīkā Śāstri).[4] Consequently, karma is devoid of any spatiotemporal movement.[5]

Second, karma disintegrates *causelessly* because its disintegration does not depend on anything external; it does not depend on a cause (AKB IV.2b. Skt. ed. Svāmi Dvarīkā Śāstri).[6] That which depends on a cause, argues Vasubandhu, is an effect, something "done" or "created." Disintegration of karma is, however, a *negation*, and a negation cannot "be done," or be "created." Thus karmic disintegration does not depend on a cause (AKB IV.2b. Skt. ed. Svāmi Dvarīkā Śāstri).[7]

The Sautrāntika defense of this position goes as follows:

> we have said that disintegration, being a negative state, cannot be caused. We would further say that if disintegration were the effect of a cause, nothing would not perish without a cause. *If, like arising, disintegration proceeds from a cause, it would never take place without a cause.* Now we hold that intelligence, a flame or sounds, which are momentary, perish without their disintegration depending on a cause. Hence, disintegration of the kindling, etc., is spontaneous. (AKB IV.3a. Skt. ed. Svāmi Dvarīkā Śāstri)[8]

If we accept the Sautrāntika argument, however, momentary disintegration would appear to bring karma to a complete standstill, since no causal movement is possible from one time to another. Disintegrating karma does not achieve any new ontological presence. Disintegrating karma is a negation: since it is not a cause, it does not produce any subsequent effect.

Karmic disintegration, the Sautrāntika argues, has no actual existence. Each instant of karmic activity intrinsically perishes where it arises. Hence the preceding moment cannot causally influence the subsequent moment. With no time to move and no space for any causal influence to occur, whatsoever, any change in the spatiotemporal dimensions and the location of the momentary instants of

4. *Sarvaṁ hi saṁskṛtamātmalābhadūdharvaṁ na bhavatīti yatraiva jātaṁ tatraiva dhvasyate|tasyāyuktā deśāntarasaṁkrāntiḥ/tasmānna gatiḥ kāryaṁ|* (cf. *mNgon pa* Ku 166b).

5. Objecting to the Vatsīputrīya's position which takes a bodily action (*vijñāpti/lus kyi rnam par rig byed*) to be a movement (*gyo ba*), Vasubandhu asserts that a bodily action is not movement at all on the ground that it is momentary, and that whatever is momentary spontaneously self-destroys, causelessly.

6. *Syādetadeva, yadi sarvasya kṣaṇikatvaṁ sidhayet? Siddhamevaitad viddhi|kutaḥ? saṁskṛtasyāvaśyaṁ vyyāt/ākasmiko hi bhāvānāṁ vinaśaḥ|* (cf. *mNgon pa* Ku 166b).

7. *Kiṁ kāraṇaṁ? kāryasya hi kāraṇaṁ bhavati, vināśacābhāvaḥ|yaścābhāvastasya kiṁ kartavyam| so'sābākasmiko vināśo yadi bhāvasyotpannamātrasya na syāt, paścādapi na syād; bhāvasya tulyatvāt|* (cf. *mNgon pa* Ku 166b).

8. *Punaḥ na kasyacidahetoḥ syāt yadi vināśo hetusāmānyānna kasyacidahetukaḥ syādutpādavat|kṣaṇikānāṁ ca buddhiśabdāciŕsa drasṭa ākasmiko vināśa iti nāyaṁ hetumupeśate|* (cf. *mNgon pa* Ku 167a).

karmic action is impossible. Consequently, for the Sautrāntika's philosophy, as Vasubandhu rightly concludes, any real karmic *causation*, real *motion*, real *continuity*, real *identity*, and so on, are impossible.[9] There is no real relation between momentary karma as a cause and its momentary karmic effect; thus there is no direct causal correlation between arising karma and disintegrating karma. Thus an unbridgeable causal gap between karma and its effect seems inevitable.

For this reason, Sautrāntika does not attempt to offer an explanation of moral causation on the basis of natural causal relationship between karma and its effect. Rather, it explains moral causation by means of positing a karmic foundation (*karmaphālālaya/las 'bras kyi brten*). Depending on the details, either the mental continuum or basic consciousness (*ālayavijñāna*) bridges the causal gap between momentary karma and its effect.[10] In the latter case, karma leaves its impressions upon this basic consciousness. The ripening of those impressions at a later stage gives rise to karmic effect. Thus karmic effect is no other than the maturation of karmic impressions deposited by karmic activity upon *ālayavijñāna*. Thus, according to the Sautrāntika, karmic consequences are possible even though karma ceases long before the arising of its effect, because the *ālayavijñāna*, as a moral foundation, brings momentary karma and its effect into a relationship.

Karmic Disintegration Is Causally Effective

Let us now consider the second view. Candrakīrti's philosophy inspires moral non-foundationalism, defended later in Tibet by Tsongkhapa. On this view, disintegrating (*vināśa/zhig pa*) karma is naturally causally effective (*bhāva/dngos po*) precisely because a disintegrating karma *is an actual presence* (*bhāva/dngos po*), and not, as per the Sautrāntika position, an absence (*abhāva/dngos med*). On the Prāsaṅgika view, karmic disintegration is causally effective without the need of any extraneous metaphysical foundation. Both karma and karmic effect, according to this view, are equally insubstantial and mutually dependent and thus there exists a natural causal relationship between disintegrating karma and arising karmic effect.

Arising effect and disintegrating karma, on this view, are two interdependent aspects of the same momentary karmic event: the process of arising of

9. Vasubandhu, AKB IV.2b (Skt. ed. Svāmi Dvarīkā Śāstri): *sarvaṁ hi saṁskṛtamātmalābhādudharvaṁ na bhavatitī yatraiva jātaṃ tatraiva dhvasyate|tasyāyuktā deśāntarasaṁkṛāntiḥ|tasmānna gātiḥ kāryaṁ* (cf. *Mngon pa khu* 166b).

10. The Sautrāntika-Yogācāra posits *ālayavijñāna*, the Vaibhāṣika posits indestructible (*chud mi za ba*), and obtainment (*thob pa*), some Sautrāntika, Kaśmīrī Vaibhāṣikas posit the continuum of mental consciousness.

effect is "heading toward" the arising (*janmonmukhaṃ/skye bzhin pa de skye la phyogs pa*), which does not yet exist (*na sa*); the process of disintegrating karma is "heading toward" the disintegration (*nāśonmukhaṃ/'gag bzhin pa ni yod kyang 'jig la phyogs*), although it still does exist. The two processes are explained to be analogous to that of simultaneously interdependent activities of the ascending and descending ends of a scale.

Just as there is no ascending activity of a scale without its descending activity, there is no karmic moment, which is exclusively of arising karma. Just as there is no descending activity without the ascending counterpart, there is no karmic moment—viz., arising and distintegrating—that is exclusively a moment of disintegrating karma. Thus, the two activities of each karmic moment cannot be separated from each other.

According to Candrakīrti, disintegrated karma (in the previous karmic moment) and the subsequent karma that arises from it presently exist and have not yet disintegrated (*bhāva/ma zhig pa*), and are not distinct: both are causally produced as effects and both are efficient causes. Both the previous karmic moment and the later karmic moment are causally conditioned and interdependent. Thus, all karmic moments are empty of intrinsic nature (*svabhāva/rang bzhin*). If karma were intrinsically real—whether it is disintegrated karma (the previous karmic moment) or disintegrating karma (the present karmic moment), or arising karma (the future karmic moment)—it could be neither a *cause* nor an *effect*. The former karmic moments would lack the ability to causally condition and influence the subsequent ones. And consequently the later karmic moments would not arise dependently from the previous karmic moments.

Now we shall have a closer look at Candrakīrti's defense of this claim—the causal efficacy of disintegrating karma. We shall first explore Candrakīrti's five principles of karmic relation and then turn to the *Prasannapadā Lucid Exposition (PP)* and the *Yuktiśāṣṭīkāvṛtti (Commentary on the Sixty Stanzas of Reasoning)* (*YŚV*) where Candrakīrti supplies his substantive arguments for the defense of his account.

The Relationship Between Disintegrating Karma and Its Effect

The *Śālistambakakārikā* (*Rice Seedling Discourse*) XV *and Śālistambakavistarākhyāṭīkā Detailed Commentary on the (Rice Seedling Discourse)* (canonically attributed to Nāgārjuna) employ the five principles to explain moral causation, the relationship between conditioned disintegrating and conditioned arising.

(1) Non-persistence;
(2) Non-annihilation;

(3) The cause is not transferred to the effect;
(4) A larger effect can develop from a smaller cause; and
(5) The effect must be similar to the cause. (*Śālistambakakārikā* XX Skt. ed. Sonam Rabten)[11]

We will consider each of the five principles briefly in reverse order and will take a closer look at the implications of the first two in particular upon the karma-effect relationship. The first two, Candrakīrti says, provide us with a more sophisticated explanation of the karma-effect relationship.

According to the fifth principle, there is an established homogeneity between karma and its effect. The character of the karmic effect must be similar in kind to the ethical content of karma. Whatever kind of karma is performed, the same kind of result is experienced, just as whatever type of seed is sown causes that type of fruit to develop. Negative karma produces destructive effects (suffering, agony, poverty, and so on), while positive karma produces wholesome effects (joy, wellness, prosperity, and so on) (*Śālistambakavistarākhyāṭīkā* XX Skt. ed. Sonam Rabten).[12]

The fourth principle says that a large karmic effect develops from a small quantity of karma: just as few seeds sown produce many fruits under the right circumstance, the development of a large karmic effect occurs from a small quantity of karma as cause (*Śālistambakavistarākhyāṭīkā* XX Skt. ed. Sonam Rabten).[13]

The third principle of non-transmigration (*na saṁkrāntitaḥ/'pho bar ma yin*) indicates the nature of the relationship between karma and its effect. Karma does not become the effect, and karmic effect does not come and take karma's place. Moral causation is therefore without any transmigration from here (cause) to there (effect).

The possibility of transmigration requires that karma (like a seed) and karmic effect (like a sprout) are not dissimilar in nature. In fact, they would have to be identical—the effect would be no different whatsoever from karma (just as a sprout would not be different from its seed). Thus the *Śālistambakavistarākhyāṭīkā* argues that there is nothing whatever that transmigrates from this world to another world. There is (only) the appearance of the effect of karma, because of the non-deficiency of causes and conditions,

11. *Śāśvatato na coccedān na saṃkranteḥ parīttataḥ/hertormahāphalāvāptiḥ sadṛśānuprabodhataḥ*|| (cf. *dMo 'grel* Nge 18b). Nāgārjuna paraphrases the *Śālistambasūtra's* words almost identically, with a minor exception in the last principle.

12. *Sadṛśānuprabodhād iti tu yādṛśaṁ bījamupyate tādṛśameva phalābhinirvṛtiriti* | *atastatsadṛśānuprabandhaḥ* | *sadṛśāphalābhinirvṛttiḥ* | (cf. *mDo 'grel* Nge 37a).

13. *Parīttataḥ hetoriti—parīttabījavapanān mahāphalāvāptiriti tatparītta—hetorbahuphalābhinirvṛttiḥ, parīttānmahāphalābhi- nirvṛttitvāt, tasmāt parīttahetormahāphalābhinirvṛtiḥ* | (cf. *mDo 'grel* Nge 37a).

just as in the case of a reflection, there is no transmigration of the face into the mirror; instead, there is an appearance of the face because the causes and conditions required for this phenomenon of reflected image are satisfied (*Śālistambakavistarākhyāṭīkā* XX Skt. ed. Sonam Rabten).[14]

The second principle—*non-annihilation* (*nocchedato/ched par ma yin*)—asserts that the arising of karmic effect does not manifest from the previous cessation of karma, nor without its cessation. But still, karma ceases, and at just that time simultaneously, the effect composed of arising manifests (similar to the ascending and descending of the two ends of a scale). Therefore, causal annihilation does not occur (*Śālistambakavistarākhyāṭīkā* XX Skt. ed. Sonam Rabten).[15]

The scale analogy neither suggests the arising of effect by virtue of unique (*svalakṣaṇa*) and intrinsic (*svabhāva*) reality. Nor does it show the simultaneous arising of intrinsic effect from intrinsically real karma. *Śālistambakakārikā* XXI makes use of the scale analogy only to show the simultaneity of the disintegrating non-intrinsic karma and the arising non-intrinsic karmic effect. Hence the analogy illustrates, in Candrakīrti's words, "simultaneity of dependent origination (*cig car du brten nas 'byung ba*) of non-intrinsic effect and the cessation of non-intrinsic karma" (*Madhyamaka-bhāṣya* VI.19d; *dBu ma* 'a 251b).

We will have more to say on this point a little later. Here we just emphasize that the ascending and the descending ends of a scale are two mutually dependent actions that occur simultaneously. These two actions are meant to illustrate that arising karmic effect and disintegrating karma occurs simultaneously and interdependently. So the *simultaneity* at issue is between two mutually dependent *activities*—disintegrating karma and arising karmic effect—rather than between two *entities*—karma as one entity and karmic effect as another entity. Interpreted *simultaneity* as between two discrete entities would lead to an absurd conclusion that cause and effect exist concurrently, which the Prāsaṅgika vehemently and consistently rejects.[16]

14. *Na saṁkrāntitaḥ iti tu bījāṅkurau tu asadṛśau eva | tasmāt ' na saṁkrāntitaḥ* | (cf. *mDo 'grel* Nge 37a).

15. *Na cocchedāditi na ca pūrvaniruddhādbījādaṅkuro niṣpadyate nācāpyaniruddhād | api tu bījād niruddhāt tasminneva samaye'ṅkuro utpadyate | ato nocchedataḥ* | (cf. *mDo 'grel* Nge 37a). Karmic causation is comparable to any other natural causation in which conditioned arising of a sprout can be easily seen as non-annihilated. The sprout does not arise from the prior cessation of the existence of the seed, nor indeed without any prior cessation of its existence. But still the seed ceases, and at just that time the sprout arises, just as in the case of the ascending and the descending of two ends of the scale.

16. Another way to put the argument is this. Although the dying aggregates ceases to exist during the rebirth, it is not case that the aggregates that are reborn also cease to exist as a result. This is because, as a general principle, when the process on which something depends ceases, that which is dependent on them also ceases (see Tsongkhapa 2004, p. 208). Argued in this way, the principle of non-annihilation shows the incoherence of the Sautrāntika's claim, for according to its reading, disintegrating karma meets its dead end, a absolute absence, and it has no causal power to produce its effect naturally.

Finally, according to the first principle of non-persistence (*na śaśvatato/ rtag pa ma yin*), karma is one activity, and the karmic effect that arises from it is quite another, even as the seed is one thing and the sprout from which it arises quite another. Where karma *disintegrates*, there and then simultaneously arises karmic effect. Therefore *eternity* is not the case (*Śālistambakakārikā* XX Skt. ed. Sonam Rabten).[17]

The Buddha illustrates the possibility of causation without intrinsic reality with a dream example.[18] It is said that a person dreams of having sexual intercourse with a beautiful woman. When he wakes up from his slumber, he still remembers the woman and develops even more intense infatuation toward her. The woman, of course, is only his fabrication in the dream, and she is not even conventionally real. He thus cannot really enter into sexual intercourse with a woman who does not exist.

Nevertheless, what are conventionally real are the cognitive events—the memory of the woman and the psychological processes, including the rise of passionate fixation toward the woman—that followed, even after the dream had ended. Even though there appears to be a considerable lapse of time between the dream of having sex with the woman and the recalling of her while awake (the dream having long been ceased), it still causally triggers passion in the mind of the person. This is possible because there is no temporal or ontological chasm between each moment; as each moment is constituted by mutually dependent dual activities—disintegrating karma (desires, clinging) and arising karmic effect (emotional fixation)—they mutually regenerate each other, causing a series of uninterrupted and invariable phenomenological processes.

17. ' *śāśvatato na ' iti yasmādanyadbījam, anyo'ṅkuraḥ, na ca ya evāṅkurāstadeva bījam, bījamevāpi nā'ṅkuraḥ | aniruddhād bījādapi aṅkuro notpadyate | na ca niruddhād, tathāpi bījanirodhe aṅkura utpadyate | tasmān na śāśvatato* (cf. *mDo 'grel* Ngi 36b–37a). This third principle challenges the plausibility of the Naiyāyika's claim according to which eternal substances are the locus of causal relation. The Naiyāyikas have unanimously rejected the Buddhist theory of universal momentariness. The *Nyāya-Sūtra*, for instance, rejects the universal momentariness on the ground that the eternal substances cannot be denied and that there is no evidence of cognition of the universal momentariness (*Nyāyasūtra* IV.i.28 cited Kher 1992, p. 15) The *Nyāya-Bhāṣya* of Vātsyāyana says that "[t]hings such as the elemental substances in their subtle forms, *Ākāśa*, Time, Space, Soul, and Mind—and some qualities of these, such as Generality (*Sāmānya*), Particularity (*Viśesa*) and Intimate Union (*Samavāya*) are not cognised by any means of right knowledge to ***be subject to origin and destruction. Therefore, they are eternal***" (Kher 1992, p. 15). Vācaspati Miśra's *Nyāyavārttikatātparyāṭīkā* also claims that enduring character of things by chiefly criticizing the impossibility of action and production on the theory of momentariness (Kher 1992, p. 107). Things' enduring character is Uddyotakara's chief argument against momentary production and destruction (Kher 1992, p. 49). For these reasons, it is important that the Naiyāyika's claim that destruction and production are causal should not be confounded with Candrakīrti's thesis that momentary disintegration is causal. The Naiyāyika's claim that disintegration has a cause must not be interpreted as a causation within the context of momentary disintegration of Candrakīrti's kind.

18. Candrakīrti's *Madhyamakāvatāra-bhāṣya* draws this from *Discourse on the Saṁsāric Migration* (*Bhavasaṃkrānti-sūtra/'phags pa srid pa 'pho ba'i mdo*). In this *Discourse* Bimbisāra, king of Magadha, approaches the Buddha and put forward this question. "How does karma that was performed and accrued with a considerable lapse of time endure and be mentally appropriated during the time of death? Why is karma not constrained given all conditioned phenomena are empty?" (*mDo sDe*, Tsa 284b).

In this way, disintegrated events or processes that seem to go out of existence are causally productive in the same way that the disintegrated dream girl who had long ceased still causally produces passion to arise in the mind of the passionate (*mDo sDe*, Tsa 284b).[19] Candrakīrti concisely puts the argument in this way:

> Just as a naïve person may remember the objects apprehended during his dream and become attached to them even though he is awake, even so, an effect may arise out of karmic action *that has already ceased and that had no intrinsic nature.* (Candrakīrti, *Madhyamakāvatāra (Introduction to the Middle Way)* VI.40 Skt. ed. Xuezhu, Li)[20]

But these karmas are constitutionally series of disintegrating and arising causal events, which on ceasing leave impregnated impressions. When all the conditions are appropriate, in spite of the considerable lapse of time, disintegrated karma in the form of impregnated karmic dispositions ripens and produces its effect, in the same manner in which attachment to a dream woman is causally produced in the mind of a person even while awake. Candrakīrti puts the point this way:

> It must be understood that *because no action ceases intrinsically*, even without any foundation and despite the lapse of considerable period of time following the cessation, karmic effect arises somewhere. (*Madhyamakāvatāra* VI.39 Skt. ed. Xuezhu, Li)[21]

Glossing this passage in *Madhyamakāvatāra-bhāṣya* VI.39, he explains that

> *[b]ecause karmic action (las) does not arise inherently (rang gi bdag nyid)*, it does not cease [inherently either]. Because it is not impossible to arise effect from what is not [inherently] disintegrated (*ma zhig pa*), karma that has not been [inherently] disintegrated indeed very plausibly maintains its causal connection with its effect. (*Madhyamakāvatāra-bhāṣya (Autocommentary to the Introduction to the Middle way)* VI.39 *dBu ma* 'a: 260a)[22]

In more concise terms, the thrust of Candrakīrti's argument is this. Karma produces its effects because it *does not cease intrinsically: both ultimately and*

19. Cited in Candrakīrti, *Madhyamakāvatāra-bhāśya* VI.40 *dBu ma* 'a.

20. *Svapnopalabdhān viṣayān avetya bodhe 'pi mūḍhasya yathaiva saṅgaḥ | saṃjāyate tadvad asatsvabhāvāt | phalaṃ niruddhād api karmaṇo 'sti |||*

21. *Yasmāt svarūpeṇa na tan niruddhaṃ ciraṃ niruddhād api karmaṇo 'taḥ / kvacid vinaivālayam asya śakteḥ phalaṃ samutpadyata ity avaihi ||*

22. *Gang gi ltar na las rang gi bdug nyid kyis ma skyes pa de'i ltar na ni de 'gag pa yod pa mu yin zhing, ma zhig pa las 'bras bu 'byung ba mi srid pa yang ma yin pas, las rnams mi 'jig pas las dang 'bras bu'i 'brel pa ches shin tu 'chad par 'gyur ro//*

conventionally. For this reason, there is no need to posit any real moral foundation, such as *ālayavijñāna (foundation consciousness)* or the *ātman*.

> *Since there is no intrinsic reality in terms of both the truths*, not only are the views of reification [of the Naiyāyika] and nihilism [of the Sautrāntika] discarded afar, despite the lapse of a considerable period of time following the cessation of actions, it is also reasonable not to conceive the continuum of basic consciousness (*kun gzh rnam she skyi rgyun*), the indestructible (*chud mi za ba*), the *attainment* (*thob pa*) and so forth as the anchor or relata (*'brel ba*) of the effects of the actions. (Candrakīrti, *Madhyamakāvatāra-bhāṣya* VI.39 *dBu ma* 'a: 260a)[23]

So, as we can observe from these passages, the key to Candrakīrti's argument for the karma-effect relationship is its *non-intrinsic* character: karma does not disintegrate intrinsically; even so, effect does not produce intrinsically. Being mutually dependent, dependent arising of effect from karma is reasonable, without positing *ālayavijñāna*, *ātman*, and so on, as the basis for moral efficacy.

Advancing the same argument, Nāgārjuna's *Mūlamadhyamakakārikā* (*MMK*) states:

> Why is karma without *arising*? This is because it does
> not exist intrinsically. Since it does not arise it does
> not cease. (*MMK* XVII.21. Skt. ed. P.L. Vaidya)[24]

Furthermore,

> If karma had intrinsic nature, it would, without doubt, be eternal.
> Karma would be unproduced, because there can be no production
> of what is eternal. (*MMK* XVII.22, Skt. ed. P. L. Vaidya)[25]

The reason that there can be a relationship between karma and karmic effect is that they both lack intrinsic nature, and thus exist codependently.[26]

23. *De phyir de ltar bden pa gnyis kar yang rang bzhin med pas rtag pa dang chad par lta ba rgyang ring du spangs pa 'ga' zhig tu ma zad kyi, las rnams 'gags nas yun ring du lon yang las rnams kyi 'bras bu dang 'brel pa ni kun gzhi'i rnam par shes pa'i rgyun dang chud mi za ba dang thob pa la sogs par yang yongs su rtog pa med par yang 'thad pa yin no //*

24. *Karma notpadyate kasmāt niḥsvabhāvaṁ yatastataḥ | yasmācca tadanutpannaṁ na tasmādvipraṇaśyati ||* (cf. *dBu ma* Tsa, 10b).

25. *Karma svabhāvataścetsyācchāśvataṁ syādasaṁśayam | akṛtaṁ ca bhavetkarma kriyate na hi śāśvatam ||* (cf. *dBu ma* Tsa, 10b).

26. Empty entities such as reflections do not appear without depending on collocations. In the same way, from an empty reflection, cognition of that form (i.e., color and shape) can be seen to arise. In the same way, since all phenomena are empty, everything arises from emptiness | *śūnyāḥ padārthāḥ pratibimbakādyāḥ sāmagryapekṣā na hi na prasiddhāḥ | yathā ca śūnyāt pratibimbakādeś cetas tadākāram upaiti janma || evaṃ hi śūnā api sarvabhāvāḥ śūnyebhya eva prabhavaṃ prayānti* (Candrakīrti, *Madhyamakāvatāra* VI.37–38ab. Skt. ed. Li Xuezhu; cf. *dBu ma* 'a 206a).

The Arguments for the Status of Disintegration as a Cause

There are two central arguments to support Candrakīrti's thesis that disintegrating karma is causally effective *(bhāva/dgnos po)*:

(1) The argument that shows non-intrinsic disintegrating karma has a cause (*hetu/rgyu*), therefore it is a causally conditioned process;
(2) The argument that shows that disintegrating karma has an effect and so causally conditions other subsequent karmic processes.

Candrakīrti advances the first argument in the *Prasannapadā* in his examination of the causes of disintegrating previous moments of karma. The second argument he advances in the *Yuktiśāṣṭīkāvṛtti* in his examination of the causes of the subsequent moments of karma, or causes of the continuum of disintegrated karma. Both the arguments are developed on the understanding that disintegrated karma (often described as "karmic destruction," or "karmic cessation") and karma that is yet to be disintegrated (or not ceased or undestroyed) have the same ontological status: both are causally produced and both are causally productive. Thus it will be argued that both disintegrating karma and arising karmic effect are causally produced and are causally effective. Both are equally capable of being a cause as well as having an effect. In the remaining part of this chapter we shall more closely examine these two arguments in turn.

The Argument Showing That Disintegrating Karma Has a Cause

In *Śālistambakavistarākhyāṭīkā*, disintegrating seed is shown to proceed from the coming together of six elements (*dhātu*)—the earth, water, heat, wind, space, and seasonal factors (*ṛtu*). The earth element supports the seed, the water element moistens the seed, the heat matures the seed, the wind brings out the seed, the space performs the function of not obstructing the seed (by providing the space in which it grows), and the season performs the function of transforming the seed. Without these conditions, the seed *does not disintegrate*. But with these conditions satisfied, the seed disintegrates, allowing the development of the organism, until the disintegration of a *flower*, when the six conditions are appropriately together, and there is the development of a fruit.[27]

27. The sprout disintegrates when all six conditional factors appropriately come together, along with the development a leaf. *The leaf disintegrates* when all six conditions come together and there is the development of a

Disintegrating karma is no different from a disintegrating seed in that both are causally conditioned. Disintegrating ignorance, when all the necessary conditions are satisfied (*avidyā/ma rig pa*), conditions (*pratyayāḥ/rkyen*) karmic formations (*saṁskārāḥ/'du byed gis las*). Similarly, disintegrating volitional formations condition consciousness (*vijñānam/rnam shes*). Disintegrating consciousness conditions name-form (*nāmarūpam/ming gzugs*)—material and mental aggregates. Disintegrating name-form conditions the six senses (*ṣaḍāyatanam/skye mched drug*). Disintegrating six senses condition contact (*sparśaḥ/reg pa*). Disintegrating contact conditions sensations/feelings (*vedanā/tshor ba*). Disintegrating feeling conditions desire (*tṛṣṇā/srid pa*). Disintegrating desire conditions grasping/clinging (*upādānam/len pa*). Disintegrating grasping conditions existential becoming (*bhavaḥ/srid pa*). Disintegrating existential becoming conditions birth (*jātiḥ/skye ba*). Disintegrating birth conditions decay (*jarā/rga*), and disintegrating decay conditions death (*maraṇam/shi ba*), grief (*śoka/mya ngan*), lamentation (*parideva/smre snags 'don pa*), mental discomfort—associated with old and death, as well as separation from what is pleasant, union with the unpleasant, poverty, and so on (*Āryaśālistambasūtratīkā* XXII. Skt. ed. Sonam Rabten).[28]

If ignorance did not disintegrate (i.e., was not subjected to momentary flux), karmic formation would not arise, and if karmic formation did not disintegrate, consciousness would not arise, and so on, until when there is no disintegrating aging and death, birth and sorrow, and so forth, would not arise. However, with ignorance disintegrating, karmic formations come to be, and with karmic formations disintegrating, consciousness comes to be, and so on, until with aging and death disintegrating, birth and sorrow, and so on, come to be.

In the *Prasannapadā* VII.32, Candrakīrti advances his argument partly as a refutation of his Sautrāntika opponent.

> There are those who having accepted disintegration is
> uncaused, still assert momentariness of what is produced.

shoot. The *shoot disintegrates* when all the conditions are appropriate and the development of a stalk occurs. The *stalk disintegrates* when the six appropriate conditions and the development of a bud come together. The *bud disintegrates* when all the six conditions come together and there is the development a flower. The *flower disintegrates* when the six conditions are appropriately together and there is the development of a fruit.

28. *Avidyāpratyayāḥ saṁskārāḥ | saṁskārapratyayaṁ vijñānam | vijñānapratyayaṁ nāmarūpam | nāmarūpapratyayaṁ ṣaḍāyatanam | ṣaḍāyatanapratyayaḥ sparśaḥ | sparśapratyayā vedanā | vedanāpratyayā tṛṣṇā | tṛṣṇāpratyayamupādānam | upādānapratyayo bhavaḥ | bhavapratyayā jātiḥ | jātipratyayaṁ jarāmaraṇam | jarāmaraṇapratyayāḥ śoka—parideva-duḥkha—daurmanasyopāyāsāḥ sambhavanti* | (cf. *Toh.* Derge 3986. *mDo 'grel nge* 37b).

> On this view, there would be no cause, analogous to the sky-flower; therefore there would be no disintegration. It would follow that things would not be momentary and would not disintegrate. How could entities that are not momentary and do not disintegrate, be produced? Therefore all of this would be inconsistent. (*Prasannapadā* VII.32, Skt. ed. P. L. Vaidya)[29]

Candrakīrti's refutation points out inconsistencies in the Sautrāntika's position. It is contradictory, he argues, for the Sautrāntika to claim that disintegrating karma is uncaused and still assert the momentariness of what is produced. If disintegrating karma were uncaused, karma would not be produced, like a sky-flower. Moreover, he charges, the Sautrāntika claims that disintegrating karma is causeless; if this were the case, he asks, how could karma be momentary? If karma were not momentary, it would not disintegrate. However, karma does disintegrate.

Now, Candrakīrti charges, if disintegrating karma were uncaused, arising karma would also have to be uncaused; if arising karma were caused, disintegrating karma must also be caused. This is because, he argues, arising karma and disintegrating karma are two mutually entailing activities of the same karmic moment; if one is caused, so is the other.

The same argument, Candrakīrti charges, also exposes a contradiction in the Sautrāntika's claim that disintegrating karma is nonexistent, whereas arising karma is existent and therefore a produced phenomenon. If disintegrating karma were nonexistent, by the same argument, the Sautrāntika must also accept arising karma to be nonexistent.

To claim that karma is a produced phenomenon in virtue of being momentary is to claim that karma is constitutive of a series of fleeting moments without any enduring properties. Of those moments that collectively define karma, the latter moments are as integral a part of karma as are the previous moments. As argued earlier, each karmic moment is characterized by two mutually entailing interdependent activities—arising karma and disintegrating karma—analogous to the ascending and the descending ends of a scale. Wherever is present an arising karma, there also is present a disintegrating karma; wherever is present a disintegrating karma, there also is present an arising karma—thus two activities of each karmic moment inseparably entail each other.

29. *Yastu vināśasya ahetukatvamabhyupetya kṣaṇikatāṁ saṁskārāṇāmāha, tasya nirhetukatvāt | khapuṣpavadvināśābhāvāt kutaḥ kṣaṇikatvaṁ bhāvānāṁ setsyati, kuto vināśarahitānāṁ saṁskṛtatvamapīti sarvameva asamañjasaṁ tasya jāyate* | (cf. *dBu ma* 'a 59a).

According to Candrakīrti, the Buddha also clearly said that disintegrating karma has a *cause* when he announced that

> [t]hrough birth as the condition, aging and death come about, and the characteristics of a produced phenomena are included among the composite aggregate. (*Prasannapadā* VII.32, Skt. ed. P. L. Vaidya)[30]

Just as the arising and the momentary endurance of produced phenomena are included within the composite aggregate, so, too, are aging and death, which are disintegrating produced phenomena. If aging and death were uncaused, because they are disintegrating moment by moment, aging would not cause death, and birth would not cause aging. Similarly, the *Daśābhūmi-sūtra* says,

> Death also involves two activities: it destroys the compounds and it provides the cause for an unbroken continuum of ignorance. (Cited in the *Prasannapadā* VII.32, Skt. ed. P. L. Vaidya)[31]

These texts also argue that disintegrating karma, since it can perform a function, must have a cause (cited in the *Prasannapadā* VII.32, Skt. ed. P.L. Vaidya).[32] Accordingly, Tsongkhapa's *Illumination of Thought* (*dGongs pa rab gsal*) explains that these texts show two aspects of karmic disintegration: (1) that disintegration *has a cause* that gave rise to it, and (2) that disintegration *has an effect*, therefore acting as a cause for the continuum of karma (Tsongkhapa 2004, pp. 281–282).[33] We will take up this latter point as part of the discussion of the next argument.

Both birth and death are causally dependent processes—brought into existence by virtue of their causal conditions. Disintegrating aging and death are conditioned by birth. Therefore, by reason of the assertion that aging and death are conditioned by birth, disintegration at the latter moments depends on it having arisen at the earlier moment.

30. *Jātipratyayaṁ jarāmaraṇaṁ saṁskṛtalakṣaṇānāṁ ca saṁskāraskandhāntarbhāva varṇayatā bhagavatā nanu sahetukatvaṁ spaṣṭamādarśitaṁ vināśasya* | (cf. *dBu ma* 'a 59a).

31. *Api ca* | *maraṇamapi dvividhakāryapratyupasthāpanaṁ saṁskāravidhvaṁsanaṁ ca karoti* | *aparijñānānupacchedaṁ (?)* (cf. *Phal chen* Kha 221b). Death's two activities are, however, not ontologically distinct. Death destroys the unity of corporeal compounds; at the same time, it causes birth with the unbroken continuum of ignorance.

32. *Cetyāgamāt kathaṁ na sahetuko vināśaḥ? api ca* || (cf. *dBu ma* 'a 59b).

33. *Zhig pa la skyed pa'i rgyu yod pa dang, zhig pas 'bras bu skyed nus pa yin te, 'di ni rgyun gyi zhig pa yin yang skad cig ma dang po dus gnyis par zhig pa la yang 'dra la, skad cig ma dang po dus gnyis par zhig pa'i rgyur yang bstan no//des na sems can skyes pa dang shi ba gnyis dang skad cig ma gnyis par mi sdod pa dang, skad cig ma gnyis par ma bsdad pa rnams la dngos por 'jog mi 'jog dang, rgyus skyed mi skyed kun nas mtsungs so//*

> Because it is easy to prove that momentary entities that do not remain for a second moment cease, so all of this fits together nicely in this system. (*Prāsannapadā* VII.32, Skt. ed. P. L. Vaidya) [34]

Since karma is characterized by four activities—arising, enduring, aging, and ceasing—it is a produced phenomenon. Karma arises where it has been previously absent, endures while it exists, ceases without remaining for the second moment after the moment when it comes into existence, and ages, becoming different from what it was earlier. Since it has been shown that non-disintegrating karma (while it exists) and disintegrating karma (at the second moment) are *similar* with respect to the fact that both exist, and are causally effective, it follows that karma's disintegration is its impermanence.

As we observed above, Candrakīrti's argument turns on the similarity between a disintegrating and non-disintegrating karma. It is therefore incoherent, according to the Prāsaṅgika position, for the Sautrāntika to assume that disintegrating karma is an absence (*abhāva*), and to ask: "What could causes do for disintegrating karma (*kim hetunā kartavyamiti*)?" (*Prāsannapadā* VII.32, Skt. ed. P. L. Vaidya).[35] But now, suppose the Sautrāntika objects to this point as follows:

> if that were the case, then, because disintegrating is an activity would it not constitute an existent (*bhāvaḥ/dngos por*)?
>
> Our reply is "yes." Disintegrating is an existent (*bhāvaḥ/dngos po yod*) in virtue of its nature, although it is a nonexistent (*na-bhāvaḥ/dngos po med pa*) with respect to the things such as material form which is excluded from its nature. (*Prāsannapadā* VII.32, Skt. ed. P. L. Vaidya)[36]

Notice that Candrakīrti characterizes disintegrating (*vināśa/'jig pa*) as "nonexistent" (*na-bhāvaḥ/dngos por med pa*) only insofar as it is an *epistemic exclusion* of the affirmative properties such as material form, and so on. Contrary to the Naiyāyika's theory of nonexistence[37] (a pure *ontological exclusion* of any form

34. *Jātimātrāpekṣatvāccāsya kṣaṇabhaṅgo'pi sukhasādhya iti sarvaṁ susthaṁ jāyate* || (cf. *dBu ma* 'a 59a).

35. *Yaccocyate—yaścābhāvaḥ tasya kiṁ hetunā kartavyamiti, tadayuktam* || (cf. *dBu ma* 'a 59b).

36. *Nanvevaṁ sati kriyamāṇatvādvināśo'pi bhāvaḥ prāpnotīti cet, iṣyata evaitat | vināśo hi svarūpāpekṣayā bhāvaḥ, rūpādidharmanivṛttisvabhāvatvāttu na bhāvaḥ* || (cf. *dBu ma* 'a 59b).

37. The Naiyāyika's account of disintegrating, Vācaspati Miśra says is an *absence* or *nonexistence*, "*Disintegration is a* form *of non-existence. When non-existence arises, the thing or existence is disintegrated.* As for the question as to how the rise of one thing can lead to the disintegration of another, the reply is simple—it is the 'nature' (*svabhāva*). Entities which constitute mutual negation (*paraparaparihāra*) arise from their own causes. Thus fire produces 'ashes' but not the 'seed' though both are equally different from fire. In the same way *non-existence is produced from its own respective causes*, just as existence is produced. Similarly *the rise of non-existence means the same as the absence of existence*" (Kher 1992, p. 169 n. 12). Vācaspati Miśra's assertion that disintegrating,

of positive existence and therefore an exclusion of any form of causal activity), Candrakīrti characterizes the ontological status of disintegration in positive terms. Thus, while for both the Sautrāntika and the Naiyāyika, disintegrating karma is entirely different from the activity of karma—the difference between nonexistence and existence—for Candrakīrti, karmic disintegrating is itself its activity; the two are not different. Thus disintegrating karma is an ontological presence, and has a cause. Whatever has an ontological presence can perform functions, and thus it is causally effective.

Thus, the argument that disintegrating karma has a cause can be briefly stated as follows:

- Whatever is not disintegrated intrinsically (both conventionally and ultimately) is only disintegrated dependently through causes and conditions (analogous to a disintegrating barley seed). Karma is not disintegrated intrinsically; therefore it is disintegrated dependently through causes and conditions.
- Whatever is disintegrated dependently through causes and conditions is a conditioned phenomenon. Karma is also disintegrated dependently through causes and conditions; therefore its disintegrating is conditioned.

The argument thus far establishes that disintegrating karma has a cause. Now we turn to the second argument.

The Argument Showing That Disintegrating Karma Has an Effect

The argument showing that disintegrating karma has an effect is no different from the argument by means of which we can prove that a momentary disintegrating seed naturally has its effect. In the *Yuktiśāṣṭīkāvṛtti* XX, Candrakīrti employs the same kind of argument to show that disintegrating karma is able to sustain its subsequent continuum. There it is argued that exhaustion (*kṣīṇam/zad pa*) is a cause of disintegrating karma, which Candrakīrti says is

on the Nyāya's account, is entirely deprived of any positive (*satta*) feature is a crucial point to be noticed, notwithstanding its claim that nonexistence (*abhāva*) is a reality, an objective counterpart of the notion of nonexistence that exists in the external world: "Non-existence is neither *intimately* united with its causes (*kāraṇassamāvāyaḥ*) nor does it have the relation of intimate union with being (*sattāsamāvāya*) which are the characteristic feature of 'existence' or a positive thing. *It assumes its own form of non-existence (svarūpapratilaṁbhaḥ) and that is the only feature common to existence and non-existence.* But there are other points of difference so that the two categories are available. 'Knowability,' 'namability,' and having a cause are common to the existents and non-existents, but the former have 'satta' a positive Being in which the latter are deficient" (Kher 1992, p. 169 n. 14).

analogous to the exhaustion of the butter and the wick acting as a *cause* of the extinguishing (*shi ba*) of the butter lamp. Nāgārjuna's *Yuktiśāṣṭīkā (Sixty Stanzas of Reasoning)* XX states the argument as follows:

> It is perceived that from the exhaustion of causes comes
> the exhaustion of tranquility. How come it is called
> "exhaustion" if it is not exhausted (*yatkṣīṇam/ma zad*)
> intrinsically (*svabhāvena*)? (*Yuktiśāṣṭīkā* XX)[38]

In exploring the implications of Nāgārjuna's argument in detail in the *Yuktiśāṣṭīkāvṛtti (Commentary to Sixty Stanzas of Reasoning)* XX, Candrakīrti makes the following points. If a produced karma can arise from its conditions, its continuum sustained by disintegrating also must solely depend on its conditions. When the sustaining conditions of karma are exhausted, karma is disintegrated. In the same way, when the sustaining conditions of disintegrating karma (which sustains the continuum of karma) are exhausted, the disintegration proceeds. Accordingly, it is argued that the world recognizes tranquility (*śāntam/zhi ba*) and liberation (*nirvāṇa*) in terms of "the exhaustion of causes" (*rgyu zad*) that bear the fruit of afflictions. Any karma that is exhausted (*zad pa*) in the absence of sustaining afflictive conditions is surely dependent on the exhaustion of sustaining conditions. Hence the exhaustion of karma, as Nāgārjuna puts it, is not intrinsic (*svabhāvena*) (Candrakīrti, *Yuktiśāṣṭīkāvṛtti* XX *dBu ma* Ya 15b).[39]

> If exhaustion [of karma] were intrinsic, it could not depend on its
> conditions, and could not come from the complete exhaustion
> of the causes [of *saṁsāra*]. Consequently one could attain *nirvāṇa*
> even without the elimination of karmic and afflictive dispositions,
> since the attainment of liberation would proceed without any
> effort. (Candrakīrti, *Yuktiśāṣṭīkāvṛtti* XX, *dBu ma* Ya 15b)[40]

Furthermore, it would be possible for a well-protected butter lamp to die out without fully consuming its oil and wick! But this does not happen because

38. *Śāntam hetukṣayādeva kṣīṇam nāmāvabudhyate | svabhāvena hi yatkṣīṇam tat kṣīṇamucyate katham ||* (cf. *dBu ma* Ya 15b).

39. *Skyes pa'i dngos po skye ba yod na 'jig la dngos po'i gnas pa yang rkyen gyi kho na las te gnas pa'i rkyen med na 'jig par 'gyur bas de ltar na 'jig rten na rgyu zad nas zhi ba dang mya ngan las 'das pa gang yin pa de nyid zhi ba zhes bya bar dmigs te, gang yang gnas pa'i rkyen med na zad par 'gyur ba de gnas pa'i rkyen med pa la rag las pas rang gi ngo bor grub pa med par khong du chud nas, rang bzhin gyis ni gang ma zad // de la zad ces ji skad brjod // ces bya ba smos so //*

40. *Gal te rang bzhin gyis zad pa zhig yod na ni de rkyen la ltos par mi 'gyur ro // de rgyu yongs su zad pa las ma yin par 'gyur ro // de'I phyir las dang nyon mongs pa'i dngos po med par ma gyur kyang mya ngan las 'das par 'gyur te, de bas na 'bad mi dgos par thar bar 'gyur ro //*

there is no intrinsic disintegrating or ceasing (Candrakīrti, *Yuktiśāṣṭīkāvṛtti* XX, *dBu ma* Ya 15b).[41]

The Sautrāntika may object by stating that the disintegrating butter and the wick are *not the causes* of the extinguishing of the butter lamp; instead, the cause of the disintegrating butter and the wick is the *incompleteness* of the set of cooperative conditions for the final moment of the butter lamp that give rise to a similar subsequent moment. Accordingly, a future karma—action yet to come—is also not arisen just because the set of *conditions* for it to arise is *incomplete*; when the set of conditions for karma is *not incomplete* that karma must *certainly arise*. Therefore, on this view, the incompleteness of the set of conditions is the *cause of the non-arising of the karma that is yet to come* (i.e., the future). The cause of the future karma that is to arise—not arisen at present, and yet to come—is also regarded as the incompleteness of its conditions due to conditions that existed earlier (*Yuktiśāṣṭīkāvṛtti* XX, *dBu ma* Ya 15a).[42]

As we can observe, the Sautrāntika's objection presupposes that disintegration is *nonexistent*, and *uncaused*, and therefore incompleteness is regarded as its cause in the above argument. As argued earlier, for Candrakīrti, disintegrating karma is a causally effective existence. He applies the same argument in the case of non-arising of the future karma, that which is yet come. Just as disintegrating karma is caused by its conditions, non-arising karma is a *cause* that produces effects. Thus Candrakīrti responds to the Sautrāntika's objection by advancing his counterargument.

> If the incompleteness of conditions for the future [karma] serves as a cause of non-arising, then if there were no incompleteness of causes, [karma] will have to arise undoubtedly. Therefore *non-arising* is also a *cause*. Advocating this [position] is tantamount to accepting [Nāgārjuna's statement (*Yuktiśāṣṭīkā* XX) which says:] "Tranquility (*śāntam*) which is called 'exhaustion' [is attained] through exhausting *(kṣīṇam/zad)* the cause." (*Yuktiśāṣṭīkāvṛtti* XX, *dBu ma* Ya 15b–16a).[43]

41. *Mar dang ras yongs su ma zad par mar me 'chi bar 'gyur ba'i rigs na de yang de lta ma yin pas rang gi ngo bor grub pa'i 'gag pa med do //*

42. *Ci ste mar dang ras yongs su zad pa ni mar me'i 'chi ba'i rgyu ma yin te, ji lta zhe na, mar dang ras lhan cig tu 'gags la mar me'i skad cig ma tha ma de'i rigs kyi mar me skad cig ma ma 'ongs pa'i lhan cig byed pa'i rgyu med pas skye ba'I yan lag gi dngos por ma gyur pa ma 'gags so // ma 'ongs pa yang skye ba'i rkyen med pas ma skyes te, de lta bas na ma 'ongs pa'i rkyen med pas 'di la skye ba med ces bya'o // snyam du sems na //* Some sections of the translation are Garfield's from Tsongkhapa's *Ocean of Reasoning* (2006, p. 282).

43. *De ltar ma 'ongs pa'i rkyen med pa mi skye ba'i rgyur 'gyur na ni gal te rkyen med par ma gyur[16a] na gdon mi za bar skye bar 'gyur ro // de ltar na mi skye ba yang rgyu nyid du khas blangs pa yin no de ltar khas len na rgyu zad nas zhi ba gang yin pa de zad pa zhes bya bar khas blangs pa yin no //*

The non-arising of karma and the exhausting karma are *causes* and thus are causally effective. *Nirvaṇic* peace is a state of exhaustion, but it is attained only through the non-arising of karma or the exhausting of the afflictive karma. If the non-arising of karma and the exhausting of afflictive karma are not causes, and not causally effective, the attainment of *nirvaṇa* through the non-arising of the afflictive defilements would be incoherent. Since both the parties to this debate accept that peace is attainable through the exhausting of afflictive defilements, it must follow that the disintegrating afflictive defilements are causally effective.

> Moreover for those who maintain that thing's cessation is an uncaused (*rgyu med pa*), because it is uncaused like the sky-flower, cessation must not depend on the things. This could not be the case, for they are known to have causes in the world. Otherwise there would be a problem [like their notion of the uncaused] cessation; they themselves would not depend on things. (*Yuktiśāṣṭīkāvṛtti* XX, *dBu ma* Ya 16a)[44]

Moreover, for the Sautrāntika who insists that a thing's disintegration is uncaused, it would follow that the disintegrating afflictive defilements are not dependent on the existence of defilements, or that the attainment of *nirvāṇa* is not dependent on the disintegrating afflictive defilements. If this consequence were to be accepted, then for the Sautrāntika, *nirvāṇa* would be no different from the sky-flower—a state of utter nonexistence. Just as the sky-flower is an uncaused, *nirvāṇa* would have no cause.

An opponent may mount another challenge as follows: "How could you apply the term "cause" (*rgyu*) to an absence (*med pa*)?" This opponent could conceivably be either the Sautrāntika or Naiyāyika.[45]

> [Candrakīrti:] "How could you also apply the term 'cause' to an existence (*yod pa*)?" At such time as when a seed has existence, it cannot be recognised as a material cause of sprout; it has served as a cause when it has become absent. (*Yuktiśāṣṭīkāvṛtti* XX, *dBu ma* Ya 16a)[46]

44. *Gang dag dngos po rnams kyi 'gag pa rgyu med pa yin par 'dzin pa de dag gi 'gag pa de dngos po la brten par mi 'gyur te, nam mkha'i me tog la sogs pa bzhin du rgyu med pa'i phyir ro // 'jig rten na rgyu dang bcas pa grags pas de dag ltar ma yin no // yang na de dag kyang 'gag pa bzhin du dngos po la brten pa med pa'i skyon du 'gyur ro //*

45. They both assert disintegrating to be negative, an utter absence and therefore causally ineffective. In their view, the term "cause" can be applied to something that positively exists, but not to disintegration.

46. *Gal te med pa la rgyu zhes ji skad du bya zhe na, yod pa las yang rgyu zhes ji skad du bya; sa bon yod pa'i dus nyid na / myu gu'i rgyu'i dngos por ni shes par mi rung ste, med par 'gyur ba'i tshe rgyur 'gyur ro //*

However, for Candrakīrti, disintegrated karma is a causally efficient phenomenon, just in the same way as a past mental faculty (*mano-indriya*), the moment of mental consciousness immediately preceding the present visual faculty, which is identified with the antecedent condition of the present moment of visual consciousness, although it has been disintegrated in the present.

> It is like asserting that the very [moment of] consciousness which has come to pass is the antecedent condition (*samanatara-pratyaya/ de ma thag rkyen*) of another [moment of] consciousness. As long as consciousness persists, it cannot be defined as being a cause of another consciousness, since two [moments of] consciousness cannot occur simultaneously, [for one constitutes the present and the other the future]; it is impossible for another consciousness conceiving the domains of both existent and nonexistent. (*Yuktiśāṣṭīkāvṛtti* XX, *dBu ma* Ya 16a)[47]

Since momentary disintegration is an ontological presence (not an utter nonexistence), the meanings associated with alternative terms such as "exhaustion" (*zad pa*) or "cessation" (*'gag pa*) or "absence" (*med pa*) also have this positive sense of existence. Since even the cessation (*'gag pa*) or "absence" (*med pa*) of karma may be a cause, it is incoherent," argues Candrakīrti, "to deny that the cessation (*'gag pa*) of [karma] is causally efficient" (*Yuktiśāṣṭīkāvṛtti* XX, *dBu ma* Ya 16a).[48] Each of them has a cause and has the ability to cause other subsequent processes. When a bud is disintegrating and all other conditions come aright, only then, a flower develops as the effect. When the flower is disintegrating and the other conditions are appropriate, only then there is the development of a fruit as the effect. If the disintegrating bud and the flower are absences, as both the Sautrāntika and the Naiyāyika claim that they are, the disintegrating bud could not cause the development of a flower. Likewise, the disintegrating flower could not be a cause for the development of a fruit.[49]

47. *Dper na med par 'gyur ba'i rnam par shes pa nyid rnam par shes pa gzhan gyi de ma thag pa'i rkyen du khas blangs pa lta bu ste, rnam par shes pa de yod pa'i dus na rnam par shes pa gzhan gyi rgyu yin no zhes ni brjod par mi nus so // rnam par shes pa gnyis cig car du mi 'byung ba'i phyir ro // yod pa dang med pa gnyis kyi gnas brtogs pa'i rnam par shes pa gzhan ni mi srid do //*

48. *La la rgyu 'gags ma thag pa ni 'bras bu skye ba'i rkyen yin no zhes bya bar mi rigs so zer ba yang yod, de bas na med pa yang rgyur srid pas med pa rgyur mi rung ngo zhes bya bar mi rigs so //*

49. Unlike the Sautrāntika (for whom absence is both uncaused and deprived of any causal efficacy), for the Naiyāyika absence is real and has a cause. However, Vācaspati Miśra says that the Nyāya's absence (or nonexistence) "is not intimately united with its causes (*kāraṇassamāvāyaḥ*) nor has it the relation of intimate union with Being (*sattāsamāvāya*) which are the characteristic feature of 'existence' or a positive thing . . . that nonexistence assumes its *own form of non-existence (svarūpapratilaṁbhaḥ) and that is the only feature common to existence and non-existence*" (Kher 1992, p. 169 n. 14). Adding further: "'Knowability,' 'namability,' and having a cause are common to the existents and non-existents, but the former have 'satta' a positive being in which the latter are

This argument appeals to the way things are presented in the ordinary convention (*laukika-vyavahāra/'jig rten pa'i tha snyad*) in which Candrakīrti argues that absence is recongized *as a cause* (*Yuktiśāṣṭīkāvṛtti* XX, *dBu ma* Ya 16a).[50] Consider these examples. Ordinarily we say: "Since there was no water my crops failed." Alternatively we may say: "Without food, my son died."

Here what we are saying is that because of the absence of water the crops failed; because of the absence of food, the son died. Inasmuch as a non-exhaustion of water and a non-exhaustion of food, respectively, are regarded as the causes of good crops and the life of the son, in just the same manner their exhaustion (therefore their absence) is also recognized as the cause of the respective losses (*Yuktiśāṣṭīkāvṛtti* XX, *dBu ma* Ya 16ab).[51] Likewise Nāgārjuna states:

> It is perceived that from the exhaustion of causes comes the exhaustion of tranquility. (Nāgārjuna, *Yuktiśāṣṭīkā* XX, *dBu ma* Ya 16b)[52]
>
> That which is not intrinsically (*svabhāvena*) exhausted, how could it be called "exhaustion"? (Nāgārjuna *Yuktiśāṣṭīkā* XX, *dBu ma* Ya 15b)[53]

Glossing these concise passages of Nāgārjuna, Candrakīrti writes:

> exhaustion is specifically presented as the exclusive exhaustion of a cause. Such exhaustion is impossible in a state prior to their exhaustion of causes; and since it only exists through their exhaustion, it has no intrinsic nature. (*Yuktiśāṣṭīkāvṛtti* XX, *dBu ma* Ya 16b)[54]
>
> What is not exhausted intrinsically is not exhausted independently of its causes by virtue of its own account. So how could it then be exhausted extrinsically by virtue of

deficient" (Kher 1992, p. 169 n. 14). Such absence, according to Candrakīrti, could not be causally productive because it assumes its own intrinsic form (*svarūpa*), therefore not amenable to conditionality. Only when absence in virtue of disintegrating is entirely non-intrinsic that it can be a causal.

50. *Gal te rigs pas rnam par dpyad na rgyur mi srid do zhe na yang de ni de lta ma yin te, 'jig rten gyi dngos po rnams ni rnam par brtag cing khas blang par mi bya ste, 'jig rten ji lta ba bzhin du'o //* "That is not the case. We do not accept the things of the world on account of critical investigation, [they are accepted] rather according to the ways in which they are represented conventionally."

51. *'jig rten na yang med pa la rgyu zhes bya bar yod de, 'di ltar chu med pas 'bru ma rung bar 'gyur ro//zan med pas nga'i bu shi'o // zhes de skad du chu dang zan med pas 'bru dang bu ma rung bar byas so zhes zer ro // 'jig [16b] rten pa'i tha snyad thams cad la 'thad pa med pas, 'jig rten na grags pa'i don rnams kyang 'jig rten na grags pas rnam par gzhag par bya ste, 'thad pas ni ma yin no //*

52. *Chu la sogs pa med pa ni 'jig pa'i rgyu zhes bya ba yod de, de bas na, rgyu zad pa yis zhi ba ni, zed ces bya bar mngon ba ste / zhes bya ba grub po //*

53. *Rang bzhin du ni gang ma zad // de la zad ces ji skad brjod //*

54. *Rgyu zad pa nyid nye bar bzung nas zad pa zhes bya bar rnam par gzhag ste, zad pa de ni rgyu zad pa'i snga rol gyi gnas na mi srid la zad nas yod pas rang gis grub pa'i ngo bo nyid med do //*

others' account? The nature of things that are not exhausted are not the same as the nature of things that are exhausted, therefore [the latter] are not presented as having the nature of exhaustion. (*Yuktiśāṣṭīkāvṛtti* XX, *dBu ma* Ya 16b)[55]

Therefore arising and disintegrating are possible neither intrinsically (*rang gi dngos pos*) nor extrinsically (*gzhan gyi dgos pos*). From the perspective of a contemplative (*yogin/ī*) who sees dependent origination as it really is, nothing arises and nothing ceases when examined logically. (*Yuktiśāṣṭīkāvṛtti* XX, *dBu ma* Ya 16b)[56]

The defense of the thesis that disintegrating karma has an effect (or it is causally effective) can be stated as follows: Whatever produces its effect through causes and conditions is disintegrated dependently. Whatever is disintegrated dependently is not intrinsically disintegrated. Whatever is not intrinsically disintegrated is not annihilated intrinsically. Whatever is not intrinsically annihilated does not become intrinsically nonexistent or absent either.

Whatever is not intrinsically nonexistent is causally productive of its subsequent effects, like a disintegrating seed that, when other conditions are satisfied, produces a sprout. Disintegrating karma is not intrinsically nonexistent because it is not intrinsically annihilated. It is not intrinsically annihilated because it is not intrinsically disintegrated. It is not intrinsically disintegrated because its disintegration is dependently brought about by virtue of its causes and conditions. Since it is causally dependent, disintegrating karma is, therefore, causally effective in producing its subsequent effects.

Whatever produces its effects non-intrinsically, produces its effects naturally (without intrinsic nature, substances, essence, etc., as its foundation) by virtue of causes and conditions. Whatever produces its effect naturally (as in the case of a disintegrating barley seed) does not require any extraneous metaphysical foundation (like the Sautrāntika's *ālayavijñāna*, the Naiyāyika's *ātman*). Through its connection with other appropriate conditions, it naturally produces a sprout as its effect without any extraneous intervention. Disintegrating karma produces its effects non-intrinsically, naturally, and dependently upon necessary causes and conditions. Thus there is no need to posit any moral foundation, such as the *ālayavijñāna* or the *ātman*.

55. *Gang rang bzhin gyis ma zad de rgyu la mi ltos par ngo bo nyid kyis zad pa yang ma yin pa de dag gzhan gyi ngo bo gang gis zad ces bya bar rnam par gzhag, zad pa ma yin pa'i ngo bo'i chos ni zad pa'i ngo bo nyid mi mthun pas zad pa'i ngo bor rnam par gzhag par mi nus so //*

56. *Gang gi phyir de ltar skye ba dang 'gag pa 'di rang gi dngos pos kyang srid pa ma yin la, gzhan gyi dngos pos kyang ma yin pa de'i phyir rnal 'byor pas rten cing 'brel par 'byung ba ji lta ba bzhin du mthong ste 'thad pas rnam par dpyad na, de ltar gang yang skye ba med // gang yang 'gag par mi 'gyur ro //*

Conclusion

Since no one disputes that the *arising* of karma constitutes a cause and that it is productive of effects, in this chapter we did not concern ourselves with settling this issue with the Prāsaṅgika's arguments. The same, however, cannot be said about the causal efficacy of disintegrating karma. As we have briefly noted, both the Sautrāntika and the Naiyāyika deny the causal efficacy of disintegrating and disintegrated karmas. Although the Naiyāyika accepts disintegrated karma as having a cause, it agrees with the Sautrāntika that a disintegrated karma is entirely negative, devoid of any causal efficacy.

In this chapter we have provided the Prāsaṅgika's case for the causal efficacy of the disintegrated and the disintegrating karma. We have attempted to show, on the Prāsaṅgika's account, how and why karmic moments (the ones disintegrated in the past and the ones disintegrating in the present) can be causally effective. We have argued that, because the Prāsaṅgika characterizes both the arising and disintegrating karma as non-intrinsic and mutually dependent, and because it accords these two activities the same ontological and causal significance, just as arising karma is causally effective, so, too, is disintegrating karma.

We have thus considered two substantive arguments. The first argument shows that disintegrating karma has a cause because disintegrating karma is a causally conditioned process (just as arising karma is a causally conditioned process). Both arising karma and disintegrating karma are relations between certain preceding or contemporary causes and conditions. A disintegrating barley seed has a cause because only when the appropriate conditions come together (one of which, among others, is arising of the sprout) does the disintegration of a barley seed proceed.

The second argument shows that disintegrating karma has an effect because disintegrating karma has an ability to cause or to condition its subsequent moments (just like arising karma has an ability to produce disintegrating karma, which is its subsequent moment), for the reason that both arising and disintegrating karma are non-intrinsic and causally dependent. Both have causal efficiency to produce their succeeding moments.

Central to both the arguments is the Prāsaṅgika's thoroughgoing non-foundationalism in which disintegrated karma, disintegrating karma, and arising karma are all conceived as part of one causally relational process, dependent upon each other.

10

How Does Merely Conventional Karma Work?

Guy Newland

In this chapter we consider the problem of making sense of karma within a Madhyamaka conception of conventional truth, focusing on the tradition running from Nāgārjuna through Candrakīrti to Tsongkhapa. We begin with some remarks on why understanding emptiness is essential to understanding the possibility of ethics, and how the Madhyamaka doctrine of the two truths illuminates the consistency of a conventional ethical framework with ultimate emptiness. We then turn to Tsongkhapa's analysis of how to understand karma within this framework, an analysis that relies on Candrakīrti's understanding of Nāgārjuna's account of causality. After considering Gorampa's (Go ram pa bsod nams seng ge's) critique of Tsongkhapa's analysis and arguing that this critique misses the mark, we will conclude by reflecting on what we learn through philosophical engagement with the distinctive complex of Buddhist notions about karma.

Without Emptiness There Is No Virtue

In Madhyamaka philosophy, the relationship between emptiness and conventional reality is articulated through a pair of theses that might appear in tension with one another, but which in fact are complementary:

(1) Conventional categories—such as persons, virtue, karma—are convenient pedagogical devices, or rungs on a ladder, that lead us to liberating knowledge of the ultimate emptiness. (Some Mādhyamikas in India and Tibet press this so far as to say that conventional entities do not appear at all to awakened minds—or that they appear only in a second-order way, as the nonexistent intentional objects of unawakened minds.)

(2) Conventional things exist precisely as *that which is empty*, the very bases of emptiness (*stong gzhi*); ultimate emptiness is not self-existent, but simply the empty quality (*stong chos*) that characterizes these conventional things. Without real conventional things, there could be no emptiness. Awakened wisdom here entails recognition of the conventional *as* conventional; knowledge of emptiness matters because it strips away false superimpositions about how these conventional things exist.

For any Mādhyamika, nothing withstands Madhyamaka analysis of how things ultimately exist; analysis comes at last only to emptiness, which is itself also empty of any ultimately findable nature. From the standpoint of emptiness, there are no persons, no virtue, no nonvirtue, no karma. There is no good or evil, no death or rebirth. So did the Buddha speak of such things only as compassionate fictions? This is the point of thesis #1.

On the other hand, according to thesis #2, these things actually exist and function despite, or perhaps even because of, their emptiness. This means that we need to take conventional things very seriously. But if empty things are the only things that can exist and function, to what extent can we investigate them and learn *how* they work without, through such analysis, arriving again at only their emptiness and a blank silence? To answer this question is to explain the consistency of these two theses and is the central project of Tsongkhapa's ethical theory.

The Indian Madhyamaka Context

Cyclic rebirth—driven by the power of virtuous and non-virtuous karma (action)—is a salient instance of dependent arising, the Buddhist account of how the world works. The *Rice Seedling Sutra* (*Śālistambasūtra*) glosses "dependent arising" through the formula "in dependence upon this, that arises." Nāgārjuna's Madhyamaka arose in part as a response to Abhidharmika Buddhist understandings of this dependent arising in terms of intrinsically real causal connections between intrinsically real fundamental constituents of reality called *dharmas*.

On this view, while the person is a mere nominal imputation on the basis of a collection of ever-changing constituents, these constituents themselves are simple, irreducible momentary entities. Dependent arising then, is a relation between these actual elemental *dharmas*, by means of which one collection of *dharmas* gives rise to another. Insight, arising through the use of introspection and meditative analysis, ascertains how these processes work in fine detail. This insight, in turn, liberates one from the delusion of an autonomous person and thus from the grip of cyclic rebirth.

Nāgārjuna instead argues that there is nothing at all that can be found under analysis of the mode of existence of things. Not only are composites such as persons empty; any constituents into which a composite such as a person can be analyzed, no matter how far that analysis proceeds, are also empty in exactly the same sense. Nāgārjuna (*MMK* XXIV.18) argues that this universal emptiness, rather than eviscerating dependent arising as one might expect, is in fact the most profound, and the only coherent, articulation of that doctrine: things are not self-existent, but are contingently designated. The three jewels and the four noble truths, including the workings of karma, are not undermined by emptiness; they are shown to be possible only because of emptiness. Emptiness is what makes conventional reality possible. It is the being that allows beings to be. Nāgārjuna (*MMK* XXIV.10) says:

> Everything makes sense for someone to whom emptiness makes sense; nothing makes sense for someone to whom emptiness does not make sense.

This because emptiness is only the absence of intrinsic reality, or independent existence, that—were it present—would freeze entities in autonomous isolation. Nāgārjuna is quite explicit that he is not refuting *existence*, but rather the idea that entities can exist *independently*, in virtue of their own intrinsic nature. He argues that such self-existence contradicts the observed functioning of the world. He (*MMK* XXIV.16–17) says:

> If you regard things as existing *in virtue of their own nature*, then you will regard things as being without causes and conditions. Effects and causes, agents, instruments and actions, and arising and ceasing . . . will be impossible.

Nāgārjuna's *Fundamental Wisdom of the Middle Way (Mūlamadhyamakakārikā)* is a series of demonstrations of the impossibility of intrinsically existent entities. Without any existence or boundaries of their own, distinct entities and events exist only in dependence on parts, and upon conditions, and upon being organized into units and named. They exist only conventionally. But it is precisely because they are empty, free of any ultimate reality, that they can be real at all.

Nāgārjuna therefore defines Madhyamaka, the middle way, as the equivalence of dependent arising and emptiness. For all Buddhists, the most preeminent instances of dependent arising are the processes through which we are bound to cyclic rebirth and liberated from it. These notions constitute important elements of what the tradition accepts as the "conventions of the world." Crucial among these conventional, interdependent processes is the working of karma. Thus, Nāgārjuna argues that only emptiness makes action, virtue, and non-virtue possible. He (*MMK* XXIV.33a–c) asks rhetorically:

> If all this were nonempty, then no one could perform any virtuous
> or nonvirtuous actions. What could anyone do?

Nāgārjuna concludes that it is wrong to advocate a position that undermines conventional existence, and it is precisely those who deny emptiness that end up in that position. And (*MMK* XXIV.40) conversely,

> [w]hoever understands dependent origination understands suffering,
> its cause, its release and the path.

Nāgārjuna's commentator Candrakīrti follows him closely in this doctrine. His *Introduction to the Middle Way* (*MAV* VI.38ab) says, "Even though all things are empty, from those empty things effects are definitely produced." And his *Clear Words* (*PP* 501) explains that it is only within the context of emptiness that one can make sense of "all worldly conventions," including "proper and improper conduct and its consequences."

All of this reflects thesis #2. But we must not lose sight of thesis #1, according to which teachings about conventional existence—including virtuous and non-virtuous actions and their effects, but also other conventional relationships—are compassionate concessions to an ignorant and terrified world, a world unable as yet to penetrate the profound, transcendent, and inexpressible mode of existence of reality. Candrakīrti (*PP* 263.5–264.4), having identified emptiness as the final nature of things, then asks whether one can say that fire has emptiness as its nature. One might expect him to say in this context, "Yes, emptiness alone is the final nature of fire, water, persons, chairs, and so forth." But Candrakīrti is careful and nuanced:

> Does fire have such a final nature? It neither essentially has it nor
> essentially lacks it. Nevertheless, to avoid frightening listeners,
> I reify it and say, "It exists conventionally."

Candrakīrti's approach reflects the sensibility of an important remark of Nāgārjuna (*MMK* XIII.8):

> We do not assert "empty." We do not assert "non-empty." We assert neither "both" nor "neither." These are used only nominally.

He follows Nāgārjuna in arguing that to assert even emptiness as a real quality is already to engage in a distorted superimposition.[1] The awakened person indulges in such conventional discourse only as a compassionate concession and skillful aid to those who would otherwise be utterly terrified by the utter impossibility of finding anything under analysis.

A Mysterious Bird

Tsongkhapa is the Tibetan philosopher who most forcefully articulates and defends the thesis that the conventional reality of karma and other instances of dependent arising are not sheer fables to comfort frightened children, but actualities within the empty world. But he came to this view gradually. In his early works, he suggests that the fact that things cannot withstand Madhyamaka analysis entails that they have no determinate mode of existence. He also suggests in his early works that all things are illusory and unfindable, yet "for the sake of others" the bodhisattva assumes the reliability of dependent origination.[2] Like Candrakīrti's reference to the danger of frightening others, this seems to imply that the wise speak of the reliable operation of virtue, non-virtue, karma, and other worldly conventions only as compassionate fictions, and not because such discourse makes any sense at all from their own perspective.

In his mature works, on the other hand, Tsongkhapa emphatically refutes this view, hammering home the point that a proper understanding of emptiness entails that it is the very meaning of dependent arising, rather than something that supersedes it.

Tsongkhapa argues that prior Tibetan interpretations of Madhyamaka involve a nihilistic understanding of emptiness that fails to take the conventional seriously. In *Three Principal Aspects of the Path* (1999, p. 136) he argues that as long as conventional dependent arising and ultimate emptiness *alternate*

1. In his *Clear Words*, Candrakīrti's gloss on this verse makes it clear that the point is that emptiness cannot be taken to be one more intrinsic nature among others, but rather the absolute absence of any intrinsic nature, *including emptiness itself.*

2. These views are attributed to the early Tsongkhapa in the Dalai Lama's *From Here to Enlightenment* (Snow Lion, 2012), p. 156.

within the mind, like the shuffling feet of a weaver, one has not reached a fully awakened understanding. Full understanding of either the conventional or the ultimate demands an understanding of their identity.

Tsongkhapa (1985, pp. 582–584) argues at considerable length that the very heart of Madhyamaka is the "non-contradictory admissibility within emptiness" of all teachings about how cyclic existence works. The perfect virtue and perfect wisdom of buddhahood are possible only because practical knowledge of how specific helpful and harmful effects arise from their particular and respective causes is fully compatible with profound knowledge of how all things are empty of any essential nature.

It is one thing to assert this and another to explain it. Emptiness is said not only to be compatible with, but in some way equivalent to, conventional dependent arising. But how does this actually work in the case of karmic cause and effect? Given the utter emptiness of all things and persons, there is no permanent substrate connecting the karmic agent to the result-experiencer. How do empty actions in one lifetime give rise to empty rebirths, or other consequences in a distant future? Or even in the near future? In short, how can there be any connection between actions and their results? Or to put it another way, what is the basis of morality in an empty universe?

Tsongkhapa's first mature work, the *Great Treatise on the Stages of the Path* (1985, pp. 730–741), addresses this question in the context of the argument that there is no intrinsically existent self of persons because such a self is neither one with the mental and physical aggregates nor essentially different from them. Tsongkhapa points out that the personal self cannot be identical to the mental and physical aggregates because there is a constant flux of mental and physical events. If the self were identical to the aggregates, it would likewise be subject to constant change, arising and disintegrating instant by instant. Suppose, on the other hand, Tsongkhapa argues, there were an essentially real self that is one with the mind and body. Since at each instant the mind and body are in a new situation, there would have to be at each instance a new intrinsically real self that is identical to that new mind-body state.

Each of these successive selves would have to be intrinsically real and identical to the mind and body of that instant; therefore, the new self of each moment would be essentially different from the self of the moment before. It would follow that when one person acts, an intrinsically different person—identical to a different mind-body state—would at a later time experience the effect of that action. In each moment, every person would experience the karmic effects of actions committed by some other person. This, Tsongkhapa points out, would be just as absurd as waking up in the morning with some other person's memories. In such a circumstance we could not make sense of even the minimal conventional identity needed to make sense of action theory or of morality. Hence, Tsongkhapa concludes, there can be no intrinsically real self.

At this point, Tsongkhapa (1985, p. 735) imagines a possible objection to this analysis: In our Madhyamaka system, where all is empty of essential or intrinsic existence, do we not have this same problem? The person who does an action and the person who experiences the result cannot be identical, of one essential nature. And so we also have no way to explain how a person undergoes at a later time the effects of that same person's earlier actions.

Tsongkhapa replies that this problem does not arise in the Madhyamaka system because the karmic agent and result-experiencer are parts of a single personal continuum. Moreover, he argues that this answer is not available to the advocate of intrinsic existence, for if the self were intrinsically real, it could not plausibly be placed in a single continuum with other selves from which it is intrinsically different. If two selves are intrinsically different, then they are really two separate persons, in the same sense in which President Obama and Mitt Romney are different persons. On the other hand, in an emptiness-based system where intrinsic existence is refuted, it is perfectly viable to have the karmic agent and result-experiencer conventionally coexist within the same personal continuum. They are neither intrinsically identical nor intrinsically different; they are instead moments of a single, conventionally designated continuum. One is put in mind here of Hume's church.

But how are we to imagine karma working within this conventionally existent personal continuum? Tsongkhapa (1985, p. 736) produces an analogy that seems at first glance astonishing and deeply perplexing:

> If a dove has been on the thatched roof of a house within which there is a container of yogurt, one can see its footprints there in the yogurt even though its feet did not enter the container of yogurt. Similarly, the person of this life has not gone back to a former life, yet it is not contradictory that such a person should remember experiences there.

A conventionally existent person can recall the experiences of an earlier conventionally existent person, without going back in time, simply by virtue of being a successor in the same continuum. Likewise, earlier experiences can produce karmic effects as well as mnemonic ones. Tsongkhapa here draws directly from Candrakīrti's *Commentary on the Four Hundred Stanzas* (1986, pp. 96–97):

> We dispense with any notion that causes and effects are the same or different. It is just that there is an impermanent stream of

> conditioned factors, each brought about by its particular causes. This being the case, it is reasonable to say that the imputedly existent self . . . remembers its [past] lives. Things do not exist by way of intrinsic character; it stands to reason that they encounter various conditions and are changed. Therefore, you should carefully examine the astonishing fact that things have causes that do not exist by way of intrinsic character. Inside a house, you can see in a container of yogurt—as though it were in wet clay—the footprints of a dove that has been on the heavily thatched roof. Yet the dove's feet have not at all entered the container.

Candrakīrti and Tsongkhapa simply assume that members of their respective audiences have common knowledge that this sort of thing sometimes happens. (Indeed, anecdotal evidence indicates that most contemporary Tibetans living in traditional communities take this for granted as well, and some seem astonished that their Western interlocutors, for all of their scientific sophistication, are ignorant of this commonly known fact.) For author and traditional audience, it is an incomprehensible but nonetheless *given* fact that the world includes cases of unmediated causation between distant phenomena. Candrakīrti deploys this as a model for imagining mnemonic and karmic efficacy within the personal continuum even when, like the dove and the yogurt, cause and effect make no contact.

Today, Candrakīrti's and Tsongkhapa's audience is global and includes many who do not participate in this tacit knowledge that certain doves can, in some ordinary but mysterious manner, sometimes transmit their footprints through thatched roofs into yogurt pots. So in our context, Candrakīrti's analogy may not illustrate, but rather rhetorically undermine his thesis by suggesting to readers the *implausibility* of karma-driven rebirth.

But we should not be so hasty in our dismissal, and we should focus not on the details of the example, but on its structure. Our contemporary scientific worldview (Rosenblum and Kuttner, 2006) also includes instances of apparently inexplicable causal "entanglement" (as dubbed by Edwin Schrodinger) between certain objects apparently cut off from one another in space/time. The work of John Stewart Bell eliminated the last qualms about this phenomenon, which Albert Einstein had called "spooky action at a distance."

It is not clear why or how certain particles that were once part of a pair can remain entangled even when widely separated. We can construct astonishing and inevitably counterintuitive explanations, as some theorists have done. Or else we can accept that this is, mysteriously, inexplicably, but very predictably and reliably, simply how the world works. The question becomes, what are the outer limits of our ability to imagine, conceptualize, analyze, and explain the world? In the case of traditional Buddhist philosophy, the problem of non-local karmic efficacy raises a similar challenge. Just as in the case of quantum entanglement, there are those who say, "this is just how karma works," and there are those who are dissatisfied with that and think that analysis can, and therefore at some point must, push further and conceptualize its exact mechanism. But then again, there may just be brute facts about causation that will remain inexplicable.

For Candrakīrti and his followers, the key to understanding action at a distance is emptiness, entailing that there is never any objectively real sameness or objectively real difference between a cause and its effect. Cause and effect, upon analysis, can never make contact in time without becoming, at the contact point, simultaneous and identical. Neither are they truly different in nature; for, if they were, then striking a match might just as well produce darkness as light. The workings of karma are an instance of dependent arising: in dependence upon this, that arises. *This*, the cause, is neither essentially one nor essentially different from *that*, the effect. We cannot find a place in time where *this* and *that* are together; conventionally, we say they are different moments within one continuum. Nonetheless, they are somehow related to one another. Greed leads to poverty, violence to hell, sexual misconduct to having an unruly spouse—just as the dove walking on the roof generates, in the impressionable surface of the yogurt directly below, the distinctive marks of a dove's feet. There is a congruency in that the tracks do not appear in some other house, nor are they the tracks of some other creature.

On one view, that is all we can say. Tsongkhapa's *Great Treatise* gives elaborate explanations of what constitutes good and bad karma and of the specific sort of effects they generate. However, this merely transmits general Buddhist traditions from common Mahāyāna sources; it is the received conventional knowledge of the tradition. It does not speak to the question of how karma works within the context of the Madhyamaka emptiness. Tsongkhapa's *Great Treatise* was his first major, mature work, and as far as this particular tome is concerned, the dove/yogurt analogy is the whole story of how karma works in an empty world. Standing alone, it leaves readers with a sense that the functioning of karma is a simply an amazing but true fact that we cannot get behind. And this amazing fact is *not* that just anything produces anything anywhere. Rather, it is that *without any possible contact between cause and effect*, specific actions astonishingly give rise to specific and congruent effects along an identifiable continuum.

Explaining the Inexplicable

Perhaps in the wake of the *Great Treatise*, Tsongkhapa and his followers had a sense that something more was needed. To see why, we have to recall that a central theme in Tsongkhapa's mature work is the vital importance to the path of detailed *conventional* analysis. We need analysis to sort out just what is helpful and harmful at the conventional level. Ultimate analysis does not discriminate virtue from non-virtue (since all is empty), but to practice virtue just such discrimination is needed. It cannot be the case that there are only analytical perspectives—which correctly penetrate to the ultimate nature of things—and useless non-analytical minds that are deluded by appearances. There must be something else, something that analyzes not things' basic ontological condition, but their relative helpfulness in producing light, or oak trees, or awakening. Good and evil, hot and cold, north and south, awakened and unawakened: all of these are completely and equally empty of any intrinsic reality. If we cannot analytically determine which is which, then we can make no progress on the path or make any sense of morality.

This is the very reason that Tsongkhapa is never content with a dichotomy between (1) analysis showing that all is empty and (2) non-analytical, conventional perspectives that just go along with whatever the world assumes to be the case. He (1985, p. 628) says, "If you want to know what a conventional perspective is, you cannot just ask worldly elders who have no philosophy." Hence he stresses the need for *conventional analysis*. Such discernment operates within the context of how things appear to ordinary minds, but uses the information available there to sort out the practical and ethical utility of various explanations or courses of action. Even arguments for the thesis that all things are ultimately empty have to be grounded in our ordinary, conventional experience. After all, no other basis is available.

To return to the analogy, we really have no idea *how* bird footprints get into the yogurt. It is just how dependent arising works—full stop. But is this really the outer limit of our ability to explain? Tsongkhapa taught his followers to seek deep conviction about the efficacy of karma, and then to maintain and deepen that understanding within their exploration of emptiness. And given his emphasis on analysis, even at the conventional level, there was a need for further clarification as to how, in conventional terms, one might conceptualize the mechanism of karmic causation.

In his *Great Treatise* (1985, p. 584), Tsongkhapa states that when essentialists and Mādhyamikas debate, their differences all come down to one point: Is emptiness contradictory to, or rather instead requisite for, the karmic processes of cyclic existence and the liberating practice of the path? Following through on this idea, Tsongkhapa (2010, pp. 185–206) later lectured on a list of points he identified as critically differentiating Candrakīrti's Prāsaṅgika Madhyamaka from other Buddhist systems. The idea was to show how, when deeply understood, all of these differences derive from—and thus implicitly demonstrate—the non-Prāsaṅgika's failure to understand emptiness.

In this context, the very first point Tsongkhapa (2010, pp. 185–187) adumbrates is the Prāsaṅgika denial of a foundational consciousness (*kun gzhi, ālaya-vijñāna*) as the medium within which karmic potency lies dormant between the time of the action and the time of its karmic fruition. This leads Tsongkhapa right into the question of how karma actually *does* work within Prāsaṅgika emptiness. Now the magic bird is gone—but we might still be astonished. First Tsongkhapa (2010, p. 185) imagines an interlocutor posing a perennial problem:

> If a virtuous or non-virtuous action remained up until the time it came to fruition, then it would have to be permanent and so one would fall to the extreme of permanence. On the other hand, if an action has disintegrated in the very instant after its completion, then, inasmuch as what has disintegrated cannot be a functioning thing, it would be impossible for action (karma) to produce a result. Actions (karma) go to waste.

In order to get from the time of commission to the time of fruition, karma would seem to have to be durable, immune to moment-by-moment disintegration. Yet a Buddhist who took such a view would be falling from the middle way to the extreme of reification. On the other hand, if one says that the potency of an action expires immediately, then there would be no means for karmic fruition, and hence one would fall to the extreme of nihilism. Any Buddhist system needs some answer to this dilemma. It is essential to reconcile conviction in karma with insight into emptiness and momentary impermanence.

In response, Tsongkhapa (2010, pp. 185–186) reviews the standard Buddhist answers:

> Some claim there is a foundational consciousness that, even after actions have disintegrated, carries forward the force of those actions moment by moment. Others say that this function is carried out by the continuum of the mental consciousness. Then there are some who say that the action has disintegrated, but the condition of having acquired (*thob pa*) the action still exists. And some

> answer the objection by saying that there is another factor, called "non-wastage," which is like a promissory note recording a debt.

He rejects all of these and offers his own (2010, p. 186):

> Our answer is that we assert neither a foundational consciousness nor those other three positions, yet actions that have been committed do not go to waste. This is because it is not contradictory for a disintegrated action (*las zhig pa*) to generate an effect.

Tsongkhapa then links the efficacy of disintegrated action to the Prāsaṅgika position that all things are utterly empty, even conventionally, of any intrinsic nature (*rang bzhin, svabhāva*). Disintegration (*zhig pa*) here means the nonexistence now of something that existed a moment ago. Non-Prāsaṅgikas, holding that things exist intrinsically, he claims, must accept that nothing that is disintegrated can be effective. This is because if one is committed to intrinsic existence, and to the inherence of causal powers in their basis, anything that is disintegrated, while it once had an actual nature of its own, is no longer real and so is causally impotent.

On Tsongkhapa's reading of Candrakīrti, on the other hand, when emptiness is understood as the utter lack of any intrinsic nature in anything, anywhere at any time, even conventionally, then "actions that are disintegrated and those that are not disintegrated are equivalent in regard to whether they may be considered functioning things" (2010, p. 186). That is, if causal power is detached from intrinsic identity, there is no reason to see the causal potency of something present as any greater than that of something that is absent. Each is equally nonexistent intrinsically; each may be connected through spatiotemporally extended chains of dependent origination to other phenomena.

As Tsongkhapa sees it, proponents of intrinsic nature do not consider disintegration a functioning, effective thing because for them a functioning thing must be able to function *in its own right*, without being contingent upon anything else. When we speak of a disintegrated *action*, we recognize that there at one point *was* an action and that this immediately led to an initial moment in which the action has already happened and had disintegrated. In other words, in thinking of a disintegrated action, the mind must take hold of the action and negate it. So the disintegrated action appears to mind only in dependence upon apprehension of the original action; it cannot appear in its own right, by way of its own nature.

In contrast, Tsongkhapa argues that in Candrakīrti's Prāsaṅgika Madhyamaka, where nothing has any intrinsic nature, disintegrated action and undisintegrated action have *equivalent functionality*. Disintegrated action and undisintegrated action are equivalent insofar as all action (disintegrated or otherwise) lacks autonomous efficiency, and all action (disintegrated or otherwise) has merely conventional efficiency.

Tsongkhapa (2010, p. 186) imagines a rebuttal from an interlocutor who argues that disintegration is simply the stopping, the coming to an end, of some effective thing. It is therefore the sheer termination of an entity's effectiveness and is itself utterly incapable of any causal activity.

But Tsongkhapa (2010, p. 186) sticks to his line that the effectiveness of actions does not depend on their being undisintegrated. Their effectiveness is simply a matter of conventional designation. We speak of "effects" as things that arise dependently after the time of their causes. But if the causes are gone, how can the causes have any effective power at the time the effect arises? So then, how could *any* action produce *any* effect? In other words, the same analysis that shows that actions that have already happened can produce no effect would render *all* action ineffective.

Any analysis, therefore, showing that actions that have already happened have no effects is already an *ultimate analysis*, pointing at the ultimate emptiness of all things. On the other hand, in conventional terms, actions do produce effects. Empty actions, whether disintegrated or not, whether happening or already happened, give rise to empty effects. Actions have no inherently existent arising or passing away; their very emptiness is what allows the interrelated flow of the world. In Tsongkhapa's conclusion (2010, pp. 186–187), he claims not just Candrakīrti, but also Nāgārjuna as a predecessor in this view:

> Therefore, even though we do not assert a foundational consciousness or the like, a disintegrated action produces a karmic effect and so actions are not wasted. It was with this in mind that the Master Nāgārjuna said, "Since actions are not produced, they have no nature. Since actions are unproduced, they are not wasted."

This may all seem like a sleight of hand. How can the claim that nonexistent phenomena have causal power save dependent origination? This is not as crazy as it might seem. We can ask ourselves, "Does Martin Luther King exist or not?" If we say that since he is dead he does not exist, then this might seem to put King in the same camp with the imaginary venomous turtles that live on Mars. Clearly, we want to say that he *did* exist—and that *this* is what actually matters. Moreover, even though he *no longer exists*, that his life *happened* is causally relevant to what is happening now. So, even though he has *disintegrated*, as have his actions, he and they are efficacious. To deny this is to forgo obviously useful explanations of our present social situation.

Indeed, since things *constantly* arise and vanish, vanishing as they arise, it is hard to say what exists and what does not; to be arising is already to be disintegrating, a point Tsongkhapa makes forcefully in his *Ocean of Reasoning* (1987, p. 157) as he comments, closely following Candrakīrti's *Clear Words*, on the seventh chapter of Nāgārjuna's *Fundamental Treatise*.[3] What has already happened is always shaping what is happening next. To be *disintegrated* is not to be *obliterated*; it is rather to enter the vital class of *what has actually happened* and thus to give birth to the next moment.

Implicit in Tsongkhapa's explanation, and spelled out by his successors such as 'Jam byang bzhad pa, is a crucial twist (Cozort 1998, 181–219). The very condition of *having just happened* is not a stable one; like everything else that arises, in its very arising is its disintegration. Immediately then, that condition of having just disintegrated itself disintegrates. Then the disintegration of the prior disintegration definitely disintegrates. This, Tsongkhapa seems to be saying, is how karma works. Everything, including disintegrations and that which has disintegrated, has disintegrated by the time it is efficacious. Everything that happens depends upon that which has disintegrated.

Gorampa's Critique

Tsongkhapa's "disintegratedness" explanation of karma drew pointed criticism from the Sa skya scholar Gorampa and other Tibetan philosophers. They argue that, in positing disintegratedness as the mechanism of karmic efficacy, he is inappropriately claiming to find something under analysis of how things really work or exist. Gorampa's *Distinguishing the Views* (2010, pp. 211–212) first outlines Tsongkhapa's presentation of what is distinct in Candrakīrti's Prāsaṅgika-style Madhyamaka:

> Svātantrika Mādhyamikas assert that things conventionally exist by way of their own character; Prāsaṅgikas do not assert this, so how do they conventionally posit persons and phenomena? . . . *When you search for the object designated by a conventional term, you do not find it.* It is unique to this system to posit causality and so forth as simply conventional designations.

3. Samten/Garfield translation of Tsongkhapa (2006) makes it clear that arising and ceasing cannot be separated: "If at the time of arising, neither enduring nor ceasing existed, the produced would be just like space which has not arising . . . If at the moment of cessation, neither arising nor enduring existed, it would be without cessation, just like sky flower."

Within this context, Gorampa (2010, p. 212) summarizes Tsongkhapa's explanation of how karma works:

> A foundational consciousness has no place within Tsongkhapa's presentation of the conventional, but he does give an account of the effects of karma. . . . On this point, Vaibhāṣikas claim that when an action stops, "karmic non-exhaustion" arises and this generates the effect. Sautrāntikas claim that "having attained karma" arises and that it is this that generates the effect. Cittamātras say that action sets latent predispositions in the foundational consciousness and these predispositions generate the effect. But these systems all differ from Prāsaṅgika in asserting that things exist by way of their own essential nature. Refuting those views, Tsongkhapa says that a unique and critical point of this system is that there comes to be an actual thing that is the disintegration of the action and this disintegration gives rise to the karmic effect.

Gorampa has a very specific critique in mind. Each of the other schools has some special entity that it locates and uniquely posits as arising just as the action ends and doing the work of accounting for karmic effectiveness. Tsongkhapa says that they are all wrong, but then—as Gorampa sees it—he finds and posits his *own* special entity in exactly the same way and for just the same purpose. Addressing Tsongkhapa, Gorampa (2010, pp. 227–228) drives this point home:

> You just mouth the words, "the designated object is not found when one searches for it." In fact, there is something that you find upon searching because when you use reason to analyze how actions give rise to their effects, you assert that there is some thing—disintegration—that serves as the basis of karmic effects. . . . Buddhist realists assert as bases for karmic effects non-exhaustion, attainment, and a foundational consciousness. You are just as mistaken as they are in that you assert as a Prāsaṅgika view that what plays this role is some actual thing called *disintegration* (*dngos po zhig pa*).

He (2010, p. 228) brings his point home by paraphrasing Candrakīrti's own refutation of a Cittamātra foundational consciousness as a refutation of Tsongkhapa's effective disintegration.

> Since the action is not essentially stopped it can produce an effect even without actual disintegration.

This merely substitutes the words "actual disintegration" (*zhig dngos*) for Candrakīrti's word "foundation" (*kun gzhi*) in his *Introduction to the Middle Way* (VI.39). Gorampa's point is clear: Tsongkhapa has no way to explain why the arguments Candrakīrti uses against the foundational consciousness as the basis for karma effects would not equally apply to the idea of a functioning thing called disintegration.

In effect, Gorampa's argument takes us back to the mysterious bird and insists that perplexity and the acceptance of brute fact is where we should remain. Analysis can only bring us to emptiness; if it takes us to anything else, we have fallen into reification. On this view, Prāsaṅgika Madhyamaka discourse regarding what things are and how they work conventionally must remain utterly non-analytical. To go beyond this and then claim one has found something is to contradict emptiness.

According to Gorampa, then, Tsongkhapa is wrong because he thinks that he can analyze karmic efficacy, and, at the end of that analysis, explain how the process works. For Gorampa, finding anything in this way is part of the *structure* of delusion, not a solution to it. This kind of analytical delusion and fabrication (*prapañca*) is that from which Nāgārjuna sought to free us by relentlessly showing that no entity or process, however subtle, could withstand analysis. The world just appears in a certain way. It works satisfactorily when left unanalyzed; when we analyze, since all is empty, there is nothing to find. It is folly to search for, and even worse to convince yourself that you have found, entities such as foundational minds or disintegratedness that account for its inner mechanisms. Taking conventional things so seriously is precisely the problem, not part of the solution, because all of these things are illusory, merely the sort of things that appear to deluded minds, unawakened minds.

A Reply

While Gorampa's objection has some bite, it is in the end unconvincing. To see this, consider the fact that Gorampa—in the very process of making this argument—is himself already undertaking the same sort of analysis for which he derides Tsongkhapa. Gorampa does not just say, "My position is empty and so is yours, so let's just leave it at that." Instead, he seeks clarification of the best way or most useful way to state matters, and he gives reasons—based in ordinary conventional experience—for thinking his account is better that Tsongkhapa's. In doing so, he is inevitably engaging in the same sort of philosophical investigation that he faults Tsongkhapa for pursuing.

Moreover, Tsongkhapa, in adverting to disintegration, is not positing a new *entity* to explain karma and causality. Instead, he is elaborating Nāgārjuna's and

Candrakīrti's analysis of the impermanence and interdependence of conventional phenomena, explaining why they are *not* entities at the ultimate level. Disintegrations, that is, are not new *things*, and in particular not new ultimately real things. Instead, disintegration is the final stage of any momentary event. To appeal to momentariness is hardly to engage in ultimate analysis; it is merely to limn the conventional.

In Candrakīrti's Prāsaṅgika Madhyamaka, to say that all phenomena are empty is to say that every entity exists only as an imputation, a conventional designation. There is the imputed or ascribed entity and then there is its basis of imputation. When one searches among the bases of imputation, there is absolutely nothing one can find or point out that *is* the imputed entity. Each entity therefore exists only as imputation to a collection of parts, or moments, or other constituents. In the temporal dimension, this is to point out that what we take to be continuants are in fact sequences of disintegrating moments. Disintegration is hence integral to conventional existence, and hence to emptiness. Things are not reducible to their components, temporal or spatial, but depend on minds that organize fragmentary and transient perceptions so as to impute one or another entity.

Gorampa and Tsongkhapa disagree regarding whether useful analysis of entities is possible within this conventional realm. Gorampa (and some other critics of Tsongkhapa) think that even "slight analysis" collapses the conventional appearance of imputed entities into unfindability and emptiness. Tsongkhapa, on the other hand, argues that all virtue—from generosity to wisdom—arises from undistracted, analytical reflection on conventional facts.

On this view, the threshold of ultimate analysis, which reduces all things to emptiness, is reached only when one pursues questions such as, "Does this thing exist this way in reality, or does it just appear that way to my mind?" It is not reached only when one simply asks, "How is that actions give rise to karmic effects?" Short of fundamental ontological questions, all questions about what is what—which entities are to be imputed in relation to what bases—are open-ended, negotiable, and conventional. We can always refine and improve our notions of what exists and how things work so as to better support a given form of life, and the very point of philosophical reflection is to do so.

The Karma Convention and the Possibility of Morality

Recent scholarship confirms that the Buddhist tradition inherited, rather than invented, the concept of cyclic rebirth within which distinct living beings successively find themselves in situations determined by their past actions. Gombrich (2006) and Obeyesekere (2002) have shown that Buddhists (and

Jains) refined this framework by *ethicizing* older Indian notions about the power of ritual and ascetic conduct to project, postmortem, good and bad rebirths. Wright (2004) celebrates this creation of a cultural framework within which there is an unfailing relationship between our ethical choices and the kind of persons we become. Egge (2002) gives close scrutiny to a wide range of early Buddhist texts on this theme, isolating two distinct discourses. One juxtaposes outer ritual action with inner mental purification, valorizing only the latter as right practice. The other discourse is the synthetic discourse of karma, wherein the moral efficacy of action hinges largely on purity of our intentions.

Yet this "ethicization" of karma as inner intention never fully displaced older, ritual meanings (Main 2005); there has been a complex layering of ideas about karma within Buddhist texts. Awareness of this density is evident in the early attribution to the Buddha (*Aṅguttara Nikāya*, 4:77) of the statement that pondering the fruition of karma will lead to insanity. The *Aṅguttara Nikāya* and many later texts emphatically identify karma with intention or volition (*cetanā*), but the tradition also gives prominence to stories about persons who encounter karmic consequences of actions they performed, in past lives, inadvertently or even against their wills. Such narratives are routinely invoked to support claims about the efficacy of practices such as guru yoga, recitation of texts, circumambulation of religious monuments (*stūpas*), and so on. It seems that their logic derives from the very old (pre-Buddhist) strata of karmic meaning, but the living tradition nonetheless still leans on their legitimizing power.

Tsongkhapa (1985, p. 627) explains that to delineate what is conventionally existent, one starts with the broad domain of all that we can conceive of and discuss. One then excludes from this sphere anything that is discredited, or falsified, by reliable epistemic inquiry. Ultimate analysis is required to extirpate commitment to some things, such as an intrinsically existent self. But the extirpation of other commitments requires only that individuals or societies engage in persistent and repeated analysis *at the conventional level*. It might take someone years to come to an understanding of how his aggressive behavior is harmful to others. It might take centuries for societies to grow into the knowledge that holding slaves is non-virtuous. And yet such realization could never be arrived at through the ultimate analysis of whether slavery is an intrinsically existent entity. Conventional understanding of its harmfulness is all that is required; nonetheless, it *is required*, and so rigorous conventional analysis, taking conventionally reality seriously as a domain to be comprehended, cannot be forgone.

For Tsongkhapa, entities exist only in framework-specific ways, but these frameworks change and may be improved. When we investigate how karma works within such a philosophy, it is relevant to examine the received frameworks shared by traditional Buddhist philosophers. Clearly, there was received conventional wisdom about karma. And for Tsongkhapa and many other traditional Buddhist philosophers, philosophy—including even the philosophy of emptiness—is not a means to destroy our commitment to and engagement with the conventional world, but is a means to facilitate that commitment and engagement by helping us to understand it more deeply and to perfect our ways of acting in it. Morality is hence not undermined, but facilitated by conventional analysis.

We *can* do philosophy cross-culturally, but only if we are mindful that this can never be a trans-cultural project, but an actual crossing between domains. We are not all heirs to the same assumptions about birds transmitting their footprints through yogurt; we are not all heirs to the Indian and Tibetan Buddhist karma convention. A general concept of karma has become part of popular culture around the world, but karma-based cyclic rebirth is not within the sphere of everyone's tacit knowledge.

Nonetheless, we learn much about ethics, and about how to bring Buddhist insight into our own ethical discourse, by taking these unfamiliar ideas seriously. We see the long-persisting power of a philosophy that denies any objectively real, framework-independent world, yet insists that it is on that very account that what we do each day, each moment, can bring powerful help or harm. We see that, across domains, language and conceptualization run aground as we try to push out our analysis of how things work. And yet we may find deeper insight by not abandoning that analysis too early. In this case, that further insight is the reminder that our choices, our actions, can never un-happen. Ineluctably, they shape the world and make us who we are as we vanish and arise, moment by moment.

11

The Connection Between Ontology and Ethics in Madhyamaka Thought

Jan Westerhoff

Introduction

Can we reach conclusions about how people should act from premises about how things are? *Prima facie* the Madhyamaka attempts to do just this in trying to move from the factual to the normative via the theory of emptiness. Scholars in the Madhyamaka tradition argue that because persons are insubstantial (*pudgalanairātmya*) and things other than persons are insubstantial as well (*dharmanairātmya*), unwholesome mental attitudes like attachment and aversion are without bases, since ultimately there is neither craver nor craved, nor a subject feeling aversion or a thing felt aversion toward, and for that reason actions motivated by such mental attitudes should not be performed.

Paul Williams has raised the point—using the conceptual framework of the two truths—that we would still want to assume that persons and things are conventionally real (even though ultimately unreal), rather than assuming that they do not exist at all (neither conventionally nor ultimately).[1] But this leaves unexplained why an insubstantial self cannot be the subject of attachment

1. For further discussion of Williams's argument, see Chapters 6, 7, and 12 of this volume.

and aversion anymore—such attitudes do not seem to depend on holding some kind of *ātman*-like view of the self. Or, to rephrase the problem slightly: most neuroscientists nowadays agree that there is no "pearl" in the mind, neither an anatomical nor a functional locus of control in the brain, no Cartesian theater where it all comes together. Most people know that a Rolex watch is just a compound of atoms and some (depending on their interpretation of quantum mechanics) might even believe that all these atoms are ultimately mind-dependent. Yet belief in these facts is generally not deemed to be incompatible with attachment to one's own self or to one's Rolex watch.

The discussion between Williams and the Mādhyamaka thus revolves around two senses of self of different strength. The first, which we are going to refer to as the *Self*, corresponds to the idea of an *ātman* in Classical Indian philosophy.[2] It is a permanent, unitary substance transmigrating from life to life that constitutes the foundation of our personal identity. The second sense of self, we will call this the *person*, is an altogether less demanding affair.[3] It is neither permanent (though it persists for some extended period of time) nor substantial, depending on a variety of physical and mental factors for its existence. The person is, in short, what our conventional sense of self refers to, a dependent and impermanent entity, yet something that is nevertheless real. Williams argues that Śāntideva's argument is exclusively directed against the Self, not against the person. Madhyamaka reasoning, Williams claims, leaves the person untouched, something which is, after all, a good thing, since the denial of the person would have disastrous consequences for the project of a bodhisattva ethics. Yet while a person is in place, it is unclear why our familiar set of selfish attitudes supposedly directed toward the Self cannot just be redirected toward the person.

Possible Connections Between No-Self Theory and Ethics

In order to assess this argument, it is necessary to provide a closer examination of the relation between ontological and ethical thought in Madhyamaka.[4] We will focus in particular on the question whether the conventional existence of a self is a necessary pre-condition for Mahāyāna ethical practice. When

2. For a comparative discussion of Śāntideva's ethics and a Classical Indian theory that incorporates such an *ātman* (Śaṅkara's Advaita Vedānta), see Todd (2013).

3. For the sake of brevity we shall use the term *self* as shorthand for "Self or person."

4. See also Chapters 2, 7, 8, and 9 in this volume.

considering the Buddhist theory of the self and the ethics of the bodhisattva path, three different options present themselves:

(1) There is actually no close connection between the theory of selflessness and the Buddhist ethical pronouncements. The Mādhyamika does not argue for a relation of logical entailment between the two, but uses other arguments (such as those based on the karmic consequences of unwholesome mental attitudes or on the assumption that all beings were in some life one's father and mother) to argue for ethical norms.
(2) The Mādhyamika holds that there are only conventionally real persons, no Selves, and has an argument to show that this fact has ethical implications. Apart from the difficulties of determining what this argument is, this position also faces the problem that, at least for the Prāsaṅgika Mādhyamika, "phenomena that are established by way of their own character" do not even exist conventionally. So it looks as if this option is not available for the Prāsaṅgika.
(3) The Mādhyamika does not accept that persons are real even conventionally, so that there is not even a conventional object of attachment and aversion. Yet if persons are not even conventionally real, there appears to be a *prima facie* difficulty with describing different pain events as had by different subjects. But in this case a bodhisattva would have difficulties, for example, removing the greater pain of A before the smaller pain of B, since A and B are not even conventionally real.

The Close Connection Between Emptiness and Ethics

The claim that there is no close systematic connection between Madhyamaka's ontological and ethical claims is difficult to defend in the presence of numerous Madhyamaka sources that attempt to establish just such a connection between its key ontological insight (emptiness) and the foundation of ethical practice (compassion).

In verse 6 of the *Bodhisaṃbhāra*, Nāgārjuna points out that the Perfection of Wisdom is the mother of bodhisattvas. Skill in means (*upāyakauśalya*) is their father, and compassion (*karuṇā*) is their daughter.[5]

5. Lindtner (1987, p. 228).

Compassion thus appears as a consequence of the Perfection of Wisdom, which is nothing other than the insight into emptiness. Their close connection is also stressed in *Ratnāvalī* IV.96, which states that

> [t]o some others [the Buddha] preached the law beyond duality, deep, terrifying those who are afraid (of such principles); to others again the essence consisting of the two tenets of compassion and emptiness, the two means leading to enlightenment.[6]

This verse forms part of the discussion of the graded nature of the Buddha's teaching.[7] In his commentary, rGyal tshab considers this to be the highest level of teaching and glosses this section as follows:

> [T]o some trainees of highest faculties, who will achieve the unsurpassed enlightenment, they teach [a doctrine] that has an essence of emptiness—the profound mode of subsistence [of phenomena] frightening to the fearful who adhere to the true existence of things—and compassion.[8]

Nāgārjuna makes it very clear that emptiness and compassion depend on one another,[9] but he is also aware that some might perceive a tension between the two. Verse 161 of the *Bodhisaṃbhāra* states that

> [o]ne who correctly examines (*samyakparīkṣā*) all phenomena (*dharma*) [sees] that there is no ego (*aham*) and no mine (*mama*). Still he does not abandon great compassion (*mahākaruṇā*) and great kindness (*mahāmaitrī*).[10]

This point is also made in the *Vimalakīrtinirdeśasūtra* where the Buddha himself points out that a *bodhisattva* "considers selflessness yet does not abandon the great compassion toward living beings."[11]

6. *dvayāniśritam ekeṣāṃ gāmbhīraṃ bhīrubhīṣaṇaṃ | śūnyatākaruṇāgarbham ekeṣāṃ bodhisādhanaṃ* (Tucci 1936, p. 252).

7. See also Candrakīrti's quoting this passage in the *Prasannapadā* (Poussin 1903–1913, p. 360) commenting on *Mūlamadhyamakakārikā* XVIII.5.

8. Hopkins (1998, p. 91).

9. In the *Sūtrasammucaya*, Nāgārjuna points out that "[a] *bodhisattva* must not apply himself to the *gambhīradharmatā* without *upāyakauśalya*" (*byang chub sems dpa' thabs la mkhas pa dang bral bar chos nid zab mo la sbyor bar mi bya ste* [Lindtner 1987, p. 174; Shakya 1999/2000]) where *gambhīradharmatā* refers to emptiness (see Nakamura 1987, p. 199, where this term is glossed as *pratītyasamutpāda*) and *upāyakauśalya* to the compassionate action of the *bodhisattva* (compare also Bendall and Rouse 1922, pp. 98–99). Verse 2 of the *Acintyastava* states: "Just as You in Mahāyāna personally understood the selflessness of phenomena, accordingly You have, under the sway of compassion, demonstrated it to the wise [*bodhisattvas*]" (*yathā tvayā mahāyāne dharmanairātmyam ātmanā | viditaṃ deśitā tadvad dhīmadbhyaḥ karuṇāvaśāt*) Lindtner 1987, pp. 139–140]).

10. Lindtner (1987, p. 247).

11. 10.18 *nairātmyam iti ca pratyavekṣate satvamahākaruṇāṃ ca notsṛjati* (Takahashi 2006, 10.18). See also Thurman (1976, p. 89).

The Remaining Two Alternatives

The idea of the conceptual isolation between Buddhist ontological and ethical teaching does not seem to sit well with the textual evidence available. Our discussion will therefore focus on the two remaining alternatives (that persons are conventionally real and ultimately unreal, or that they are both conventionally and ultimately unreal). Both these alternatives agree that for the Mādhyamika there is a close connection between ontology and ethics. We want to find out what this connection amounts to, and in what way we are supposed to move from the one to the other. The *locus classicus* for establishing this connection is, of course, Śāntideva's *Bodhicaryāvatāra* VIII.101–103:

> 101. The continuum of consciousness, like a series, and the aggregation of constituents, like an army and such, are unreal. Since one who experiences suffering does not exist, to whom will that suffering belong?
>
> 102. All sufferings are without an owner, because they are not different. They should be warded off simply because they are suffering. Why is any restriction made in this case?
>
> 103. Why should suffering be prevented? Because everyone agrees. If it must be warded off, then all of it must be warded off; and if not, then this goes for oneself as it does for everyone else.[12]

We seem to have here an argument that starts out with a familiar piece of Buddhist ontology, the mereological reductionist's claim that Selves are unreal and are merely superimposed on a collection of psycho-physical aggregates, and that ends with a statement of the bodhisattva ethics, namely that all instances of suffering are to be prevented equally. This appears to support the claim that specific ontological theses (which in this case are not unique to Madhyamaka, though certainly shared by it) can be used to establish ethical pronouncements, that for the Madhyamaka ontology and ethics are sufficiently intertwined that correct knowledge of how the world is allows us to find out how we ought to act in it.[13]

12. *saṃtānaḥ samudāyaśca paṅktisenādivanmṛṣā* | *asya duḥkhaṃ sa nāstyasmāt kasya tat svaṃ bhaviṣyati* || *asvāmikāni duḥkhāni sarvāṇyevāviśeṣataḥ* | *duḥkhatvādeva vāryāṇi niyamastatra kiṃkṛtaḥ* || *duḥkhaṃ kasmānnivāryaṃ cet sarveṣāmavivādataḥ* | *vāryaṃ cetsarvamapyevaṃ na cedātmani sarvavat* || The translation follows Wallace and Wallace (1997, p. 102).

13. It is worth noting that an additional complication for assessing the possible ethical implications of the Madhyamaka theory of emptiness is that there is no unanimous agreement concerning what precisely this theory amounts to. Williams (1998, pp. 118–119) considers it as a metaphysical theory resulting from a soteriological agenda ("Therefore the rationale for distinguishing between wholes and parts, composites and simples, on the basis of types of existence, and the introduction of an axiological dimension through valuing one type of existence more than another—together with playing on the superficial paradox that the whole is *nothing in itself* and therefore is thought to be somehow not fully real—has its basis in the wider Buddhist spiritual context of decreasing

So has Śāntideva here accomplished the impossible and found a way to bridge the is-ought gap, or is the argument simply a *non sequitur*? The matter is certainly not straightforward.

In 1998 Williams has set out a lengthy criticism of Śāntideva's argument that can, however, be given a fairly concise summary. The criticism runs as follows. Since for the Mādhyamika everything is empty, the Self or person must be empty, too, and therefore cannot exist at the level of ultimate truth, though he might assume that there are persons that exists at the level of conventional truth only. There are thus only two possibilities: that persons are conventionally real and ultimately unreal, or that they are conventionally unreal and ultimately unreal. If the former is true, we can easily conceive of a case in which somebody has convinced himself by various arguments that he is only conventionally real, but still does not prevent all suffering that appears, but only that suffering felt by his conventionally existent person. But if this is the case, then there cannot be any *necessary* implication of the bodhisattva ethics by the no-self doctrine, since neither the truth of nor the belief in the no-self doctrine gives rise to a contradiction when coupled with the non-observance of the bodhisattva ethics.[14]

The Mādhyamika might now be tempted to switch to the second possibility and claim that persons are neither conventionally nor ultimately real.[15] But this

attachment"), while other authors, such as Siderits (2007 p. 205) who defends a semantic non-dualist interpretation of the Madhyamaka theory of emptiness would not consider it as leading to metaphysical claims at all ("It would be one thing if emptiness had some metaphysical implications, such as that everything is somehow connected to other things. Then we could imagine that realizing the emptiness of all things might undermine the boundaries we draw between ourselves and others. Perhaps that would make us less selfish as a result. We saw why this sort of interpretation seems unlikely. But it is harder to see how realizing emptiness could transform our lives if this realization only concerns the nature of truth"). He nevertheless does believe that ethical implication will also follow on his interpretation, pointing out that the claim that there is a single ultimately true theory leads to "a subtle form of self-assertion. If I insist that there is an absolutely objective way things are, I claim that the way the world is is independent of your interests and limitations—and mine as well. So my table-pounding may seem self-effacing. But I am nevertheless claiming that the truth is on my side. Such a behaviour may be an obstacle to genuine realization of non-self. This is why the Madhyamaka thinks that in addition to realizing the selflessness of persons, we must realize the essencelessness of *dharmas*. The latter realization robs us of the grounds for a notion of the ultimate truth. It thus represents, they may think, the culmination of realizing non-self." Of course, both interpretations agree that Madhyamaka does not considers Selves to ultimately real, and as the possible ethical implications of *this* position are mainly at issue in the following discussion, we can leave aside the further issue how different interpretations of Madhyamaka could entail the supposed ethical consequences.

14. Williams (1998, pp. 110–111): "In spite of the common English equivalence of 'selfless' and 'unselfish', the absence of True Self is not equivalent of, nor does it entail, unselfishness. [. . .] The 'ought' of unselfishness simply does not follow from the 'is' of '*anātaman*.'" (1998, p. 110): "there is no contradiction whatsoever in accepting as true a teaching of no Self (*anātman*)—even seeing it directly in the fullest possible way—and being selfish." (1999, p. 147): "[I]t simply does not follow that lack of *ātman* logically *entails* selflessness. It is perfectly logically possible both to hold that one lacks an *ātman* and to be selfish. People do, and are. Many modern psychologists would accept that we lack an *ātman*, but are also be [*sic*] selfish. They cannot be accused of logical contradiction."

15. As some Madhyamaka sources appear to do in a quite explicit manner. Candrakīrti's *Madhyamakāvatāra* 6.122 asserts that "[s]ince such a Self is not born, it does not exist, just like a child of a barren woman; and since it is not even the basis of grasping at I, it cannot be asserted even conventionally" (*mo gsham bu ltar skye ba dang*

reply makes it difficult to understand how we could uphold our conventional practices that do involve the existence of differences between persons. It is not a sign of great advance on the bodhisattva path, but a sign of madness if we set out to brush other people's teeth before our own, for the reason that there are so many more of them. Our ability to think coherently about ourselves and others will be undermined if we are not able to refer to persons even on the level of everyday transactions.[16]

Thus, the opponent argues, Śāntideva is faced with a dilemma: either he accepts the existence of a conventionally real person, in which case there is no logical connection between the non-self doctrine and the ethical conduct of a bodhisattva since selfish behavior is still possible, *or* he denies even the conventional existence of the person, in which case selfish behavior is no longer possible, but neither are all sorts of practices referring to an at least conventionally real notion of a person, including some that are essential for the successful conduct of a bodhisattva.[17] This is the core of Williams's criticism of Śāntideva.

The Importance of Meditative Realization

Is his criticism successful? The first question we have to ask ourselves is whether Śāntideva was actually trying to do what Williams thinks he was. Was his aim to construct an argument that leads from a set of non-normative

bral phyir / de ltar gyur ba'i bdag ni yod min zhing / 'di ni ngar 'dzin rten du'ang mi rigs la / 'di ni kun rdzob tu yang yod mi 'dod). See also Williams (1998, p. 217): "Cf. here dPa' bo gTsug lag phreng ba p. 590: 'Since there does not exist any self (Self) anywhere even conventionally, that very grasping after self and possessions is irrational, and it is necessary to abandon it' (*bdag ni kun rdzob nyid tu'ang gang na'ang yod pa min pas bdag dang bdag gir 'dzin pa de nyid mi rigs te spang dgos so*)." Williams (1998, pp. 222–223): "Cf Thub bstan chos kyi grags pa p. 532 for a clear statement of the person as a fiction on this basis: 'for there does not exist truly established as unitary the continuant and collective apart from their bases of imputation' (*gdags gzhi de dag / las gzhan pa'i rgyud dang tshogs pa gcig tu bden par grub pa med pas so*)."

16. "Śāntideva's position absolutely requires that it makes sense to talk of pains floating free from the subjects whom we normally speak of as possessing pains, and indeed that such talk is truer to reality" (Williams 1998, p. 157). "We could not locate a pain, and therefore there would be no pain, without a body-map. Pains *essentially* happen at a place, and that place is bodily and its identification and integration involves the unity provided by the self" (Williams 1998, p. 243, n. 84). "If pains cannot be identified and individuated, it would be impossible to identify and individuate a removal of a pain. Without reference to persons what is to count as the removal of a pain?" (Williams 1998, p. 164).

17. "[W]hen we emphasize the fictitious nature of the conventional self, then the danger of nihilism arises, for the opponent can object that there is no longer reason to care for the suffering of anyone. Rather than entailing altruism, Śāntideva's argument ends up providing a justification for total apathy" (Harris 2011, pp. 102–103; see also Clayton 2001, p. 85). Note also that the concept of karmic responsibility is affected if we cannot link together actions carried out in this life and effects resulting in a later life by the idea of a conventionally existent person that acts as a continuant. See Williams (1998, p. 50); Harris (2011, pp. 100–101, n. 11). See also Chapter 6 by Jenkins in this volume.

premises about the emptiness of persons via a logical deduction to a normative conclusion about how a bodhisattva should act?

This understanding does not do justice to the complex relation between Madhyamaka ontology and ethics that Śāntideva sets out to establish in the *Bodhicaryāvatāra*. In particular, it fails to account for the crucial difference between believing in the truth of some proposition on the basis on arguments, and its realization. Buddhism traditionally distinguishes between the "three trainings" that constitute the foundation of all Buddhist practice, the sequence of listening (*śruti*), thinking (*cintā*), and meditation (*bhāvanā*).[18] "Listening" subsumes receiving teachings from books or discourses, while "the goal of the second phase of that training—namely, thinking—is not merely belief (*manaḥ-parīkṣā*) in the validity of Buddhist doctrine, but inferential knowledge (*anumāna*) of the realities presented in that doctrine. The goal of the third phase of that training—namely, meditation—is perceptual knowledge (*pratyakṣa*) of those same realities."[19]

It is evident that justified belief in the selflessness of persons (i.e., a product of the second training) on its own does not preclude the existence of selfish behavior. To achieve this the third training, meditative realization of selflessness has to be added. [20]

This is because selfish behavior comes from deeply ingrained habitual tendencies that can persist independent of the propositions one believes; the realization of selflessness, however, consists in the very eradication of these barely conscious and quasi-automatic responses. The Buddhist authors would agree that the mere acceptance of reductionism about the Self as a philosophical theory does not have far-reaching ethical consequences. But this point does not generalize to "seeing it directly in the fullest possible way,"[21] perceiving it through the realization of selflessness.

But, Williams objects, if an argument is in fact invalid it will not be able to bring about inferential knowledge of its conclusion, and so the fruit of third training (direct perceptual knowledge) cannot be obtained:

18. See Lindtner (1987, p. 269).

19. Wallace (1999, p. 206).

20. "Meditation is central to Śāntideva's account, for it is through meditation that one embeds discursive knowledge into one's character" (Garfield 2015, p. 307). "There is no evidence whatsoever that Śāntideva ever intended that philosophical reflection alone should suffice to establish a moral imperative; on the contrary, Mahāyāna Buddhism teaches that perfect morality is impossible without perfect wisdom, and that perfect wisdom is impossible without meditation on perfect wisdom" (Pettit 1999, p. 134). See also Nāgārjuna's *Bodhicittavivaraṇa* 86: "Those who are strengthened by meditational development (*bhāvanā*) are frightened by the sufferings of others. [In order to support them] they even forsake the pleasures of trance (*dhyānasukha*) and even go to the Avīci hell (*avīci*)!" *(gang zhig bsgom pas brtan pa ni // gzhan gyi sdug bsngal gyis bred nas / bsam gtan bde ba dor nas kyang // mnar med pa yang 'jug par byed* [Lindtner 1987, pp. 208–209]).

21. Williams (1998, p. 110).

> If an argument does not logically follow, repeated familiarization with it in meditation does not bring it about that it logically follows, even if it might lead to psychological conviction. It is no use arguing that repeated familiarization in meditation with the idea of square circles will make the idea of square circles coherent. It might well be the case psychologically for all I know that a particular person, contemplating repeatedly that we lack an *ātman*, comes to be less selfish. But that would not be as a matter of logical implication, and there is in Śāntideva's argument no logical reason why this altruism should come about.[22]

However, this criticism overlooks that once we take into account the sequence of the three trainings, Śāntideva's argument appears a bit different from the way Williams originally presented it. Remember that his argument against the logical implication between selflessness and non-selfishness rests on the observation that there are possible (and in fact actual) cases of agents with justified belief in selflessness that still carry out selfish actions. But this argument rests on the assumption that it is mere justified belief, not realization we are talking about. Once we read the argument as claiming that there is a logical implication between the *realization* of selflessness and selfless actions, it is considerably harder to argue that there are persons endowed with the former who lack the latter. Williams argues for the compatibility of two psychological states: belief in selflessness and tendency to perform selfish actions. But, as we have just tried to point out, it makes more sense to assume that what Śāntideva was interested in was the compatibility of the *realization of selflessness* and selfish actions, and his claim is that *these two* are not compatible.

Williams might respond here that this reply is circular, for whatever putative counterexample he came up with, we could always declare that simply because this was an example of an agent engaged in selfish behavior, that agent could not have realized the emptiness of the Self. But this would presuppose that we *define* the realization of selflessness as the inability to engage in selfish behavior. Yet this is not the case; in fact, the defender of Śāntideva has some story of why the former should entail the latter (briefly put, because the realization of selflessness entails the destruction of habitual tendencies that result in selfish behavior). In order to defend the incompatibility of the realization of selflessness and selfish behavior, we cannot just examine all beings who have realized selflessness, and then check whether any of these still shows tendencies toward selfish behavior—not only because beings who have realized

22. Williams (1999, pp. 146–147).

selflessness are very difficult to find, but also because such a proof by cases would not be sufficient to establish a universal proposition. Rather, in order to demonstrate the negative thesis that the two are not compatible, we would want to explain which elements of the realization of selflessness stand in direct opposition to an inclination to act selfishly.

The Is-Is Gap

So where does that leave us with respect to the is/ought gap?[23] Has Śāntideva pulled off the seemingly impossible feat of bridging this? Clayton[24] has argued that Śāntideva would not have had to bridge this gap since the is/ought distinction "is not very applicable in Buddhist contexts."[25] She argues that it does not make sense to ask the Buddhist whether one can start from a set of factual premises and end up with a normative conclusion, since for the Buddhist there are no clearly factual premises, "all knowledge of the external world, the facts, is inevitably vested with interest, or value."[26] Yet even if that is true, that does not rule out the intelligibility of a closely related question within the Buddhist worldview, namely that concerning the relation between its ontological stance and its ethical pronouncements. Even if we reject the question "Can Śāntideva close the is/ought gap?" as not well-formed, there remains the more fundamental question of how Śāntideva (and the Mādhyamikas in general) conceptualized the relation between their core ontological account (the theory of emptiness) and their core ethical account (the bodhisattva ethics).

I would argue that constructing a deductive inference that starts exclusively from non-normative premisses and leads to a normative conclusion was not Śāntideva's objective in the first place. Properly understood, it appears, his argument does not set out to show how an "ought" is implied by an "is," but how one "is" is implied by another "is."[27] The point is not to

23. Note that for this it would be sufficient to establish that whoever does not follow the bodhisattva ethics acts irrationally (Clayton 2001, p. 91). That such an argument would still require one non-factual premise ("you should act rationally") need not concern us here.

24. Clayton (2001, pp. 88–90).

25. Clayton (2001, p. 88).

26. Clayton (2001, p. 89).

27. I thus agree with Harris's criticism of Pettit's claim that the thesis "that the 'ought' of unselfishness simply does not follow from the 'is' of *anātman* can be brought seriously into question" (1999, p. 133). As Harris rightly points out "[i]n this interpretation, Śāntideva would have derived an *is* (emotional equanimity) from an *is* (lack of self), and a further argument is needed to explain why an emotionally equanimous person *ought* to act altruistically" (2011, p. 115). I think that the first *is*, which I have referred to as the state of the realization of selflessness, involves considerably more than "emotional equanimity," but agree that providing us with a deductively valid argument for why one ought to act altruistically is not Śāntideva's point here.

provide an argument for how one should act on the basis of how the world happens to be, but to argue that one state, that of the realization of selflessness, is such that it subsumes under it another state, that in which selfish action is impossible. The former subsumes the latter because it entails a shift in the way we experience the world, a transformation of the way phenomena appear to us.[28]

But if the realization of selflessness and selfish behavior are not compatible, then it is not the case that in order to be truly selfless one has to reject the existence of a person or a Self, both at the ultimate and at the conventional level. This is good news, since the rejection of a conventionally existent person leads to a number of intractable problems, as Williams (1998) aptly points out.[29]

The Conventionally Existent Person

We would therefore want to endorse a theory that accepts the existence of a conventionally existent person, but rejects that of an ultimately existent Self. Such an approach is well supported by the Tibetan commentarial tradition:[30]

Thub bstan chos kyi grags pa notes that

> it is taught that there exists self and other conventionally, as conceptualised in dependence on the aggregates, even though there does not exist and independent self and other ... it is taught that there is the mere postulation in mutual dependence, without being established by nature, of both self and other which are the enjoyers of pleasure and pain.[31]

Alternatively, one might interpret Śāntideva's argument as going from an *ought* to another *ought* via an *is*. In this case we would read Śāntideva as starting with the premises that our own suffering ought to be prevented, and that other beings are not very different from ourselves. From this we then infer that the suffering of others should be prevented, too. (I owe this point to Charles Goodman.)

28. Garfield (1998, p. 24). It is important to note that in the context of bringing about this transformation, what originally appeared as a dilemma (too much emphasis on the conventional self leads to egoism, too little to total apathy) can be reconceptualized under the concept of *upāya* for meditative development. As Harris (2011, p. 119) notes, "one might switch between viewpoints, dependent on one's current mental state. If we feel attachment to the self arise, we remember that selves are nonexistent, and the attachment is lessened. If we feel apathetic towards helping sentient beings, then we can focus on their conventional suffering, and empathy will arise."

29. See in particular pages 153–176.

30. "The distinction I am making is indeed recognized in the dGe lugs distinction between the *ātman* and the *pudgala* (*gang zag*), where the former is denied even conventionally while the latter exists as the conventional self, the person, marked by subjectivity" (Williams 1999, p. 147).

31. Commenting on *Bodhicaryāvatāra* VIII.102 (Williams 1998, p. 238, n. 72): *rang dbang ba'i bdag dang gzhan med kyang tha snyad du phung po la brten nas btags pa'i bdag dang gzhan yod par bstan pas so // . . . bde sdug la longs spyod pa po'i bdag gzhan gnyis ngo bos grub pa med par phan tshun ltos nas bzhag pa tsam yin par bstan la.*

And commenting on *Bodhicaryāvatāra* VIII.103, he remarks:

> [Opponent] "If there does not exist the Self, which is independent (*rang dbang*), which is the experiencer of pain . . ." [Reply] Even though there does not exist a Self which is independent still, merely in conventional transaction, there exists a 'self' which is postulated in mutual dependence, and an 'other,' and the pain of those.[32]

Tsongkhapa also makes it clear that regarding the self as conventionally nonexistent is a mistaken view:

> [I]f you fail to limit the object of negation when you use reason to investigate whether the self and the aggregates are one, different, and so forth, then when you see the arguments that contradict those positions, you will think "Persons and such do not exist at all," or, "Things such as persons are non-things, empty of all function, like the horns of a rabbit and such." This is a nihilistic view. Therefore, you should be aware that this is a point where you may slip with regard to the correct view.[33]

dGe lugs commentarial literature makes clear that the notion of the selves to be rejected includes both philosophically constructed ones (such as the *ātman* defended by Indian non-Buddhist schools), as well as innate and largely unconscious conceptions that arise without the need for theoretical elaboration.[34] Yet in the same way in which it is essential to understand what exactly is meant by "conventionally existent objects" in order to understand the Madhyamaka theory of the selflessness of things, we have to get a clear idea of the nature of

32. Williams (1998, p. 238, n. 72): *sdug bsngal myong mkhan gyi rang dbang ba'i bdag med pa [. . .] rang dbang ba'i bdag med kyang tha snyad tsam du phan tshun ltos nas bzhag pa'i bdag dang gzhan dang de dag gi sdug bsngal yang yod pa'i phyir.*

33. Tsongkhapa (2002, p. 301). *'di la yang sngar bshad pa ltar du dgag bya'i tshad legs par ma zin par gcig tha dad sogs la rigs pas brtags pa na / de dag la gnod pa mthong ba'i tshe gang zag la sogs pa ni ye mi 'dug go snyam pa dang / gang zag la sogs pa'i dngos po rnams rig bong gi rwa la sogs pa ltar don byed pa thams cad kyis stong pa'i dngos po med pa'o snyam pa byung na ni chad lta chen po yin pas yang dag pa'i lta ba'i gol sar shes par bya ste* (Tsongkhapa 1985, 743:6–11).

34. In his review of Williams's argument Pettit (1999, p. 131) points out the dGe lugs distinction between "the 'rational negandum' (*rigs pa'i dgag bya*) versus the 'path negandum' (*lam gyi dgag bya*), and innate ignorance (*lhan skyes kyi ma rig pa*) versus theoretical or conceptualized ignorance (*kun brtags kyi ma rig pa = parikalpitāvidyā*). The rational negandum of Mādhyamika analysis would include the 'True Self' or ātman, which is a philosophical conception (*grub mtha'i sgro btags pa*) as well as the innate conception (*lhan skyes kyis sgro btags pa*) of self. In other words, any kind of self which is conceived to exist inherently is a rational negandum of Mādhyamika analysis, whether such conception is conscious or not. The root of saṃsāra, according to Tsongkhapa, is innate ignorance, which would consist in an innate misapprehension of a self, while the theoretical misconception of a 'True Self' would be a conceptualized ignorance which only obtains for those who uphold the philosophical systems which teach it. Thus, the innate misconception of self is the more important negandum of Mādhyamika analysis, and because it is not particularly conscious, it is more difficult to deal with."

the "valid conventional self"[35] to understand the theory of the selflessness of persons.

Some authors identify this sense of self, the person, with "conceptions [. . .] which are emotionally neutral,"[36] as something that is "not necessarily associated with conflicting or selfish emotions."[37] Understanding the conventionally existent person in this way goes directly against Williams's assumption that whenever we have any kind of conventionally existent person, the door is open for selfish behavior that this conventionally existent person supports. Yet following the argument sketched above, the realization of selflessness would be compatible with the continued existence of such a "valid conventional self" (thus serving as a basis for the distinction between self and others at the conventional level, which Williams argues is essential for the actions of a bodhisattva) while ruling out the sense of self connected with "conflicting or selfish emotions" (making selfish behavior impossible).

Conventional Selves for Prāsaṅgikas

The greatest difficulty with explicating this sense of self is its seeming conflict with the unwillingness of the dGe lug pas (*qua* their Prāsaṅgika orientation) to acknowledge the existence of any intrinsically existent objects, of anything existing *svabhāvatas*, at the level of wordly conventions.[38] So there seems to be a difficulty in reconciling a presupposition of the most plausible interpretation of Śāntideva's argument in *Bodhicaryāvatāra* VIII.101–103 (namely that persons exist at the level of day-to-day interaction, but that there are no fundamentally real Selves) and an interpretation that denies that anything exists substantially at the conventional level. The self certainly *appears* to us to exist in such a substantial manner, as something that exists independent of our body and

35. Pettit (1999, p. 132).

36. Pettit (1999, p. 133).

37. Pettit (1999, p. 132).

38. Tsongkhapa notes that "no phenomenon can, even conventionally, have a nature that is established by way of its particular character" (Tsongkhapa 2002, vol. 3, p. 225). *chos gang la'ang rang gi mtshan nyid kyis grub pa'i ngo bo tha snyad du'ang med pa* (Tsongkhapa 1985, p. 699). He also rejects the existence of things conventionally established by their intrinsic nature (*tha snyad du rang bzhin gyis grub pa*) and things conventionally established from their own side (*tha snyad du rang ngos nas grub pa*). See Tillemans (2003, p. 94). Hopkins points out that "it is suitable to give the definition of a Consequentialist as: a Proponent of the Middle Way School who does not accept, even conventionally, phenomena that are established by way of their own character. [. . .] Mind and body—the individual parts, the whole, the parts over time—are our bases of designation but are not us, and we are not them. Still, if the basis of designation does not have certain qualities such as consciousness, then it does not have the prerequisites for being called a person. These qualities make it suitable to be a basis of designation of a person, not to *be* a person. A person is posited by thought in dependence upon these" (Hopkins 1995, pp. 52–54).

psychological states, is continuous, permanent, the locus of control, and the unifier of our physical and mental life. But it seems that on a Prāsaṅgika reading we cannot even avail ourselves of this appearance, even if we agree that it is nothing more than an appearance and that at the ontological rock-bottom there are no Selves (nor is there anything else).

The problem is exacerbated by the fact that on most contemporary non-substantialist and reductionist accounts of the self, it does indeed look like something "conventionally established from its own side." The reason for this is that once a self is posited in dependence upon the aggregates, this leaves us with the question of who or what is doing the positing. "Positing" looks very much like what an intentional agent does, yet there is nothing much resembling such an agent among the five *skandhas*.

This point is brought out well by Douglas Hofstadter in a metaphor reminiscent of examples favored by Madhyamaka authors:

> [i]t dawned on me—and it has ever since seemed to me—that what we call "consciousness" was a kind of mirage. It had to be a very peculiar kind of mirage, to be sure, since it was a mirage that perceived itself, and of course it didn't believe it was perceiving a mirage, but no matter—it still was a mirage. It was almost as if this slippery phenomenon called "consciousness" lifted itself up by its own bootstraps, almost as if it made itself out of nothing, and then disintegrated back into nothing whenever one looked at it more closely.[39]

If we equate consciousness with our notion of a conventionally existent self, it seems to be that even if it is a construct, it does not appear to itself as a construct (to use a phrase of Thomas Metzinger's: its constructed nature is "transparent" to us, and therefore invisible). But if this is the case then it seems to be "conventionally established from its own side," rather than established by anything else.

It is useful at this point to take into account a familiar problem that occurs in the Madhyamaka conception of the emptiness of phenomena

39. Hofstadter (2007, p. xii). See also Dennett (1991, p. 418): "Our tales are spun, but for the most part we don't spin them; they spin us. Our human consciousness, and our narrative selfhood, is their product, not their source"; Metzinger (2010, p. 108): "The brain is like a *total flight simulator*, a self-modeling airplane that, rather than being flown by a pilot, generates a complex internal image of itself within its own internal flight simulator. The image is transparent and thus cannot be recognized as an image by the system. Operating under the condition of a naive-realistic self-misunderstanding, the system interprets the control element in this image as a nonphysical object: The 'pilot' is born into a virtual reality with no opportunity to discover this fact. The pilot is the Ego."

(*dharmanairātmya*). As one of the consequences of this theory is that everything is a conceptual construct, there cannot be any non-constructed things from which everything is constructed. It is constructs all the way down. Yet this is not a problem if we bring in the notion of beginningless ignorance (*anādyavidyā*), which entails that there have always been minds that could have constructed the previous constructional stage.

But in the case of the constructed person, the matter is more complicated. Of course we could postulate a similar infinitely descending series of narrators, each of which creates a fictive, narrative person, and is in turn created by another narrator one level down. But this would no more be a satisfactory account of how the person comes about than an infinite series of homunculi in our head would be the basis of a satisfactory account of vision.

If the person is a construct, and if it does not involve a backward infinite stack of constructors, it must come about by some kind of loop. And if that is right, "conventionally established from its own side" seems to be an apposite description of the kind of thing it is.

How Much of a Self Is Left at the Conventional Level?

In order to resolve this issue, the Prāsaṅgika has to differentiate between those properties of the person that are part of its ability to perform its function, and those that are "invalidated by a reasoning consciousness analyzing the ultimate,"[40] to use Tsongkhapa's third criterion for conventional existence.[41] This implies that there are certain functions of the self that are not rejected at the conventional level, such as its ability to act as a locus of cognitive integration, constitute a referent of names, allow the differentiation of distinct physico-psychological streams and the pain and pleasure associated with each, act as a subject of moral responsibility, and so on.[42] Others, however, such as the properties of permanence, partlessness, and independence, are shown to

40. Newland (1992, p. 84).

41. "How does one determine whether something exist conventionally? We hold that something exists conventionally (1) if it is known to a conventional consciousness; (2) if no other conventional valid cognition contradicts its being as it is thus known; and (3) if reason that accurately analyzes reality—that is, analyzes whether something intrinsically exists—does not contradict it. We hold that what fails to meet those criteria does not exist." (Tsongkhapa 2002, vol. 3, p. 178), *de la tha snyad du yod par 'dod pa dang med par 'dod pa ni ji 'dra ba zhig gi sgo nas 'jog pa yin snyam na / tha snyad pa'i shes pa la grags pa yin pa dang ji ltar grags pa'i don de la tha snyad pa'i tshad ma gzhan gyis gnod pa med pa dang/ de kho na nyid la'ang rang bzhin yod med tshul bzhin du dpyod pa'i rigs pas gnod pa mi 'bab pa zhig ni tha snyad du yod par 'dod la/ de dag las ldog pa ni med par 'dod do/* (Tsongkhapa 1985, p. 627, ll. 14–18).

42. The dGe lugs pa would consider this to be the wholly imputed "mere I" that does not have any existence other than as a conceptual construction. See Wilson (1991, p. 169).

lead to contradictions *even at the conventional level* by the familiar Madhyamaka analysis.[43]

Consider this imperfect but hopefully illuminating example. In a piece of fiction we ascribe those properties to characters in the fiction that the text clearly asserts them as possessing (such as that Dr. Watson is a medical doctor, or that he has a war wound). These properties are an essential part of what makes the story work as a story; they are the properties that allow the fictional characters to fulfill their functions. Yet there are other properties that give rise to contradictions even within the make-believe world of the story (such that Watson has a war wound in his shoulder, rather than in his leg).[44] In these cases we are reluctant to ascribe any of the contradiction-entailing properties to the fictional character. Such properties are not even real at the level of fiction.

Or consider a different example, also imperfect, though in a different way. Suppose you are a doctor in a mental asylum treating a patient who believes himself to be Napoleon.[45] In order to facilitate smooth interaction, there are some of his Napoleon-beliefs you will indulge in (that wearing a bicorne is a great fashion choice) and others that you will not (that it is a good idea to attack Russia). The reason is obviously not that the former have any greater claim to truth than the latter; neither of them have any basis in fact. But affirming the former kinds of beliefs aids smoothly running relations between you and the patient, while the latter does not.

The Prāsaṅgika will argue that the former set of conventionally kosher properties of the self are sufficient in order to resolve the kinds of difficulties that Williams mentions, such as ascribing pleasure and pains to different individuals in a sensible way. The latter, *svabhāva*-based properties (the conventionally *treif*) are not required to ensure the associated smooth functioning of the self in the world of everyday interaction, lead to inconsistencies when examined closely, and are not to be regarded as belonging to the set of conventional truths in any way. They correspond to inconsistent fictional properties, or to the more disruptive delusions of madmen.

Why can't I rebuild my selfish emotions on the sense of self with the kosher properties? It seems that the emotional response connected with self-grasping needs something that has at least some degree of independence

43. This corresponds to 'Jam dbyangs bzhad pa's interpretation in his *dBu ma chen mo*. Newland (1992, p. 141) summarizes: "[W]ater appears to be inherently existent, and is therefore a falsity, but water also appears to moisten, quench thirst, and so forth. Water is 'true' in the sense that it does not deceive a worldly consciousness about the fact of its existence or the fact of its capacity to perform its characteristic functions. The worldly perspective in which water is apprehended to exist *just as it appears* must be a wrong consciousness, but the worldly perspectives in which water is apprehended to exist and to perform its functions are conventional valid cognizers."

44. See Katz (1998, p. 13).

45. Murat (2011).

and permanence to be grasped at. Yet the aim of meditation on selflessness is to bring about the realization that the person is nothing but a conceptual fiction, and a momentary fiction at that. Not only does the person lack the necessary independence that makes us care about it in a substantial way (and it is precisely this lack of independence that explains why we do not care in the same way for fictional characters in novels, films, or computer games), it is also not even around long enough for us to become attached to it. The Prāsaṅgika "mere I" seems to be a sense of person that is strong enough to do some of the conceptual work we expect the notion of a person to do, yet insubstantial enough to avoid the inconsistencies and saṃsāric entrapments that accompany other concepts of personal identity.

As a reader enters into the would-be world of a novel, or a psychiatrist into the worldview of his patient, a bodhisattva may enter into any conceptual scheme in order to help those who are confined to this scheme. But this does not in any way presuppose that all aspects of this scheme have to be conventionally true, agreed upon by cowherds, and so on. The bodhisattva can (and has to) differentiate between those aspects of the scheme conducive to the functioning of the objects and properties that comprise the scheme and those that contravene such functioning, that are inconsistent, and that are conventionally false.

An interesting consequence of this view is that conventional truth cannot be equated in any way with majority belief. For it is likely to be true that most people (to the extent that they have reflected on this matter at all) consider it to be true that they possess some permanent, partless, and independent core of their personality, a Self, yet the Prāsaṅgika will want to deny that such beliefs are even conventionally true. As Tsongkhapa's triple criterion underlines, conventional truths have to satisfy certain evaluative standards in order to be regarded as such.

This interpretation also shows that there is no difficulty with considering Madhyamakas as "acting in accordance with what is acknowledged by the world,"[46] an epithet traditional Tibetan doxographers applied to Candrakīrti.[47] This is precisely because it does not reduce to the view that the mere acceptance of given beliefs establishes them in some way,[48] a view justly criticized by Kamalaśīla on the grounds that it is possible that "what is [generally] acknowledged is wrong."[49] Mere majority acceptance is not enough; as Tsongkhapa's three criteria show, conventional truths have to be able to withstand investigative scrutiny. And once the commonly acknowledged view of a permanent,

46. *'jig rten grags pa ltar spyod pa'i dbu ma pa.*

47. Tillemans (2011, p. 154).

48. *dam bcas pa tsam gyis grub pa, pratijñāmātreṇa siddha.*

49. *grags pa yang log par srid pa* (Tillemans 2011, p. 154).

partless, and independent person is scrutinized in such a way, it is found to lead to inconsistencies in a way that an entity that is the locus of cognitive integration, a referent of a personal name, and so forth, is not. Such an entity can provide the foundation of all the ethical practices of the bodhisattva path while being wholly consistent with the Prāsaṅgika view that a substantial self does not even exist at the conventional level.

12

Compassion and the Net of Indra

Graham Priest

Introduction: Whence Compassion?

The thought that compassion (*karuṇā*) is a central moral virtue, perhaps *the* central such virtue, of Buddhism, hardly needs argument.[1] The question that will concern us in this chapter is "why?" What is the ground for its being so?

Of course, compassion is a virtue, or at least valued, in most ethical traditions; and different answers to the question of what grounds it will be given in different traditions. A Christian might answer the question by saying that it is because God—at least, God the Son—commanded it.[2] But in Buddhism, there is no *deus*, and so no *deus ex machina*. If one is to find a ground for compassion, it has to be something *intra-machina*.

The machinery, of course, must be of a kind that is acceptable to Buddhist theory. To illustrate: Aristotle provided a justification for many virtues. He holds to a certain notion of human flourishing (*eudaimonia*). The virtues (*arete*) are those human dispositions that are conducive to such flourishing (see, e.g., Kraut 2010). Thus, temperance is a virtue: intemperance inhibits rational reflection, a

1. "Compassion" may not be the best translation of *karuṇā*, given its connotations of passiveness. "Beneficence" or "caring" may be closer to the mark; but I will stick with the standard translation here. For further discussion of *karuṇā*, see Chapters 4–7 of this volume.

2. "[Y]ou shall love the Lord your God with all your heart, and with all your soul, and with all your mind, and with all your strength . . . [and you] shall love your neighbour as yourself. There is no other commandment greater than these." Mark 12:29–31.

core part of human flourishing. But if Buddhism has a notion of flourishing, it is not Aristotle's; and in any case, compassion is not a virtue that features significantly in the Aristotelian catalogue.

The notion of a virtue does not feature at all in a Hobbesean account of morality; but his machinery does provide a framework which grounds moral notions. Why, for example, should one obey the Sovereign? Because of a compact made to establish their sovereignty (see, e.g., Lloyd and Shreedhar 2008). But the fiction of a social compact has no role in Buddhist thinking. And again, compassion is not something particularly significant in Hobbesean thought.

What kind of machinery does Buddhism have for answering our target question? Fairly obvious considerations will take us some way. The Four Noble Truths assure us that human life is one of disquietude (*duḥkha*), and that a major cause of this is an attachment to an illusory self. Compassion, the concern for the well-being of others, is a good policy for dissipating such self-centeredness. This is fine as far as it goes. But it relegates compassion to a piece of practical advice—on a par with: don't have a heavy meal before you meditate; it makes you drowsy. This has to be missing something important. And in any case, it hardly grounds the role that compassion plays in Mahāyāna thought. In this, the bodhisattva takes a vow of compassion to all sentient creatures, and it cannot be just so that this takes them further down the path of enlightenment. At a certain stage they have achieved individual enlightenment, including the dissipation of the illusion of self and the corresponding attachment. But they voluntarily refuse to take the final step in the process, entry into *parinirvāṇa*, until all sentient creatures can do so as well.

The justification of compassion is, in fact, at its most difficult and crucial in Mahāyāna traditions. In this chapter, we will be concerned with the Madhyamaka tradition in particular, and those later Buddhist traditions that have endorsed its core metaphysical notion of emptiness (*śūnyatā*) (which is most of them), a notion closely connected with conventional reality as it is conceived in these traditions, as we will see. I will argue that it is emptiness that grounds the virtue of compassion. The next section will provide enough background in metaphysical issues to make the ensuing discussion intelligible. We will then be in a position to look at the envisaged answer. Following that, we will look at an objection and some ramifications of the account.

Metaphysical Background

So let us turn to the notion of emptiness, and the claim that all things are empty. It will not be my concern, here, to try to justify this claim. I merely explain.

Let us start by backtracking for a moment to the older Abhidharma metaphysics.[3] All Buddhists agree that there is no such thing as a self; that is, something—a part of the person—that persists through their existence and defines them as one and the same person during that time. What, then, is a person? According to the Abhidharma tradition, the answer is as follows. Consider your car. This has lots of bits. They came together under certain conditions, interact with each other and with other things; some wear out and are replaced. In the end they will all fall apart. We can think of the car as a single thing, and even give it a name (like XYZ 123), but this is a purely conventional label for a relatively stable and self-contained aggregate of components. Now, a person is just like the car. The parts they are composed of (the *skandhas*) are psycho-biological; but otherwise the story is much the same.

Of course, it is not just a person who has parts. Lots of things do: chairs, trees, countries, and so on. The Abhidharmikas could see no reason to treat other partite things in any different way. They are all conceptual constructions out of their parts.

But must there then be ultimate impartite things? The answer would appear to be "yes." To have conceptual constructions, one must, it would seem, have something out of which to construct them. So, the Abhidharmika said, there are ultimate constituents of the world, *dharmas*. These have *svabhāva*, self-being. That is, they exist, and are what they are intrinsically, independently of any process of mental construction. There were different views about what, exactly, the *dharmas* were: the different Abhidharma schools disagreed about the details.[4] But all agreed that they were metaphysical atoms, the ultimate constituents of the world. Thus the picture of two realities (*satya*) emerged: an ultimate reality of the things with self-being; and a conventional reality, the *Lebenswelt* of the things conceptually constructed out of them.

Mahāyāna Buddhism subjected this metaphysical picture to a fundamental critique. In particular, it rejected the Abhidharma view that things in the world were constructed out of ultimate parts with a different ontological status. In the Madhyamaka version, this took the form of an argument that *all* things are empty of self-being: there is nothing with *svabhāva*.[5]

So, if everything has the same ontological status, and this is not some ultimate reality, in what way do things have their being? Not intrinsically, but only in relation to other things. To give an example from Western philosophy,[6]

3. For a discussion of the early Buddhist view of the self and, more generally, Abhidharma metaphysics, see Siderits (2007), esp. chapters 3 and 6.

4. Perhaps the most influential view in the end was that these were tropes (property instances) of a certain kind. See Ganeri (2001), pp. 98 ff.

5. On Madhyamaka metaphysics, see, e.g., Siderits (2007), chapters 7, 9, and Williams (2009), chapters 2, 3.

6. See Smart (1964), pp. 81–99.

consider the year 1066. According to Newton, this date refers to an objective thing, a time. The time is independent of the events in time, and would indeed have existed even had there been no such events. On the other hand, according to Leibniz, 1066 has no self-standing reality of this kind: 1066 is merely a locus in a set of events ordered by the before/after relation. Thus, 1066 is just the place in this ordering that applies to things after Caesar's invasion of Britain, before the British colonization of Australia, and so on. Had there been no events in time, there would have been no 1066; 1066 has its being only in relationship to other things.

According to Madhyamaka, everything has its being in this relational way. The partite objects of the Abhidharmikas have their being in this way. A partite object has whatever sort of being it has in relationship to, among other things, its parts. The Madhyamaka network of being-constitutive relations included this part-whole relation—though it would be wrong to think now that the parts are real in a way that the whole they compose is not. Both have exactly the same kind of reality—relational.

The web of relations that were relevant for the Mādhyamikas were wider than mereological ones, however. (Some things may have no physical parts.) Two other kinds were particularly significant for them. One is causal. Thus, you are the thing that you are (including existing) because of your relationship to your genetic inheritance (let us update the picture a bit here), the way your parents treated you, the school you went to, and so on.[7] The other is conceptual. Again, the Abhidharmikas held that an object of conventional reality is what it is, to the extent that, and only to the extent that, we conceptualize it in a certain way. This view is also subsumed in the more general Madhyamaka picture.

The upshot: nothing has ultimate reality; everything has the same conventional ontological status. To be empty is to be conventionally real, which is the only kind of reality there is.

We are not quite finished with our ontological background yet. The Madhyamaka view of emptiness was taken to its limit by the Chinese Huayan school of Buddhism.[8] If something is empty, its nature depends on *some* other things. According to the Huayan, it depends on *all* other things.[9] This does not

7. Of course, causation plays an important role in Abhidharma thinking, too. The *dharmas* enter into causal relations with each other. But just because of this, the causal relationship is not part of what determines something's being, as it is in Madhyamaka.

8. On this, see Williams (2009), chapter 6, and Liu (2007), chapter 10.

9. One does find views of this kind expressed sometimes by people in the Madhyamaka tradition. Thus, His Holiness the Dalai Lama says, "We begin to see that the whole universe we inhabit can be understood as a living organism where each cell works in balanced cooperation with every other cell to sustain the whole" (Gyatso 1999, pp. 40–41).

mean that all the relations involved are equally important. Consider a person again; for example, say, me. Arguably, the behavior of my parents toward me in my infant years is more important in making me what I am than, say, the behavior of my first girlfriend. But all of the relations have some role in the making. The matter is rather like that in classical gravitational theory. Every object exerts a gravitational influence on every other, however far apart. Thus, the net gravitational force on me is partly determined by a rock on a planet in another galaxy. Of course, since gravitation attraction falls off rapidly with distance, this will be very small, but it is there, nonetheless. So it is with the relations that constitute me.

The step that takes the Huayan from *some* to *all* is a very simple one. Consider emptiness itself—whatever, exactly, one takes that to be. (In this tradition, it is called *principle, li*: 禮).

Things get their nature, in part, by relating to it in a certain way—that is, by being empty. But emptiness is not something with self-being either. As Madhyamaka had argued, all things are empty, including emptiness itself. It, therefore, has its nature by depending on other things. What things? The things it grounds: the empty objects themselves. So if *a* and *b* are any objects, *a* depends on emptiness, and emptiness depends on *b*. By the transitivity of dependence, *a* depends on *b*.[10]

The interdependence of all things is illustrated by the beautiful metaphor of the Net of Indra. This is described by one modern commentator as follows:

> Far away in the heavenly abode of the great god Indra, there is a wonderful net which has been hung by some cunning artificer in such a manner that it stretches out indefinitely in all directions. In accordance with the extravagant tastes of deities, the artificer has hung a single glittering jewel at the net's every node, and since the net itself is infinite in all dimensions, the jewels are infinite in number. There hang the jewels, glittering like stars of the first magnitude, a wonderful sight to behold. If we now arbitrarily select one of the jewels for inspection and look closely at it, we will discover that in its polished surface there are reflected all the other jewels in the net, infinite in number. Not only that, but each of the jewels reflected in this one jewel is also reflecting all the other jewels, so that the process of reflection is infinite.[11]

10. This kind of reasoning is perfectly sound Madhyamaka reasoning, though I know of nowhere it is explicitly made in that tradition.

11. Cook (1977), p. 2. For an English translation of the description given by Fazang, probably the most influential thinker in the Huayan tradition, see Liu (1982), p. 65.

All the jewels in the net encode each other. Each one, as it were, contains the whole. In the metaphor, the jewels represent the objects of phenomenal reality; and the infinite reflections represent their mutual dependence.

Of course, it must be remembered that this is a metaphor, and has its limitations. In particular, one would naturally understand the jewels as having self-being—which is exactly what the theory of emptiness undercuts.[12]

Śāntideva's Argument

We can now come to the justification for compassion. It is common—maybe even inevitable—for ethical theories to have metaphysical underpinnings. Thus, Aristotle's virtue ethics presupposed his teleological account of nature, especially human nature; and a Hobbesean ethics presupposed a metaphysics of autonomous, independent, agents. It is natural, then, for us to look for such a justification of compassion. How might one do this?

In searching for an answer, the first place one might think to look is in arguably the greatest of all Indian Mahāyāna ethicists, Śāntideva. And in his *Bodhicaryavatāra* we do find what looks like a metaphysically based argument for compassion at VIII.90–103. What I take to be the core of it is given at verses 101–102, as follows:

> A continuum and collection,
> just like such things as a series or an army, are unreal.
> The one for whom there is suffering does not exist.
> Therefore for whom will that suffering become their own?
>
> Since all ownerless sufferings are
> without distinction,
> [they] should be alleviated just because of being suffering,
> What restriction is made in that case?[13]

The argument would seem to be this: It is clear that it is good to get rid of one's own suffering. One is inclined to think that there is an important difference between one's own pain and that of another. I can feel my own pain in a way

12. For an account of the way in which the Madhyamaka relations of dependence generate a (non-metaphorical) network, see Priest (2015).

13. The translations from Śāntideva I use are those given in Chapter 4 of this volume. How to interpret the passage from which they come is contentious. For a discussion of the various possibilities, see that chapter. It would take me far afield to argue the point here, but let me just state for the record that I find what follows to be the most plausible interpretation of the text. In Chapter 4, it is called the "*abhidharma* reading." For different views, and further discussion, see Chapters 5–8.

that I cannot feel yours. To sustain this thought, one needs to suppose that pains have possessors, like you and me. If there are no such things as people, this thought collapses. There are lots of painful *skandas* out there. If there are really no people to possess them, then a motivation to get rid of any of them is a motivation to get rid of all of them. These things must be bad independent of any bearer: there isn't one.

As a moment's reflection shows, the argument depends on a distinction between the reality of the pain-states and the reality of persons. Persons are not real, so we should not be concerned by the owners of pains. But if the pains themselves were not real, we should have no concern for these either: the ground for compassion collapses. The argument, thus, presupposes an Abhidharma metaphysics. The *dharmas* of pain are real in a way that persons are not. For a Mādhyamika, the argument will not work: persons and pains are on an equal ontological footing. Pains are real enough, though their reality is conventional; but people have exactly the same sort of reality. And the possessor of a pain *does* seem to be a relevant consideration. I have a unique relationship with my own pain, giving me a distinctive reason for getting rid of it, in a way that I do not have a relationship with yours. Nor, obviously, does it help to point out that the person has no *ultimate* reality; for neither do the painful states.[14] So if this is the argument that Śāntideva is giving, it does not work from a Madhyamaka perspective (even though Śāntideva was a Madhyamaka).

Interconnectedness

If one is looking for an acceptable Mahāyāna metaphysical justification of compassion, perhaps the most obvious place to seek it is with the notion of emptiness.[15] After all, the rise of Mahāyāna occasioned two important theoretical developments in Buddhism. The first was making emptiness the metaphysical keystone. The second was making compassion the ethical keystone. It would seem odd if these were totally independent.

To see a connection, start by coming back to a Hobbesean ethics. Hobbesean ethics makes sense because (and only because) one thinks of individuals as atomic existences, which are what they are independently of others—providing the autonomy for each to enter into a compact with others of the same kind. In other words, one has to think of each individual as

14. The point is well made by Williams (2000), chapter 5.

15. For further discussions of the connection see Chapters 3, 5, 6, 8, and 11 of this volume.

possessing *svabhāva*. This grounds the picture in which they look after their own interests, and their own interests only—indeed, of their having independent interests in the first place. From the point of view of emptiness, this is precisely not the case—much as it might sometimes appear that my being is atomic and autonomous in this way. My nature is not self-standing, but depends for what it is on other things; and one of the most important of these is the individuals with whom I interact causally. *Their* natures, in turn, are determined in exactly the same way. By the very order of things, then, there is an interconnectedness and interdependence between things, and between people in particular. Thus, I am what I am, most importantly, because of my causal interactions with others: my parents, my friends, the people I read (about), and so on—similarly for all people. Let us call this their inter-being.[16] This inter-being is what makes the Hobbesean picture illusory. It is also this which grounds compassion.

Some have held that the mere interdependence of people is sufficient to establish the claim that we should have regard for their interests—and so be compassionate. Here, for example is King (2005, p. 160):

> The basic Buddhist worldview of interdependence has two implications relevant to universal responsibility. First, because we live in a vast web of interconnectedness, "our every action, our every deed, word, and thought, no matter how slight or inconsequential it may seem, has an implication not only for ourselves, but for all others too."[17] That is, it is because of interconnectedness that our actions create a ripple effect that results in a "universal dimension of every act." Second, a corollary of interdependence is also relevant to universal responsibility: the fact that "my" interest and well-being are inseparable from the interest and well-being of others means that not only can my interests not trump "your" interest, but that no individual's interest can trump any other individual's interest. What remains is to act in the interest of all.

Unfortunately, this certainly does not seem to follow. The slave and the slave-owner are mutually dependent. The owner depends on the slave to labor for him and make him rich. Reciprocally, the slaves depend on their owner to give them food, shelter, and any other means of life he sees fit to provide. It does not follow *from this* that the owner should have any moral compunction to look after the slaves' interests at all. Without further consideration, it could

16. The term is taken from the Vietnamese Zen monk Thich Nhat Hanh, e.g., Hanh (1993).
17. She quotes here His Holiness the Dalai Lama (Gyatso 1999, p. 41).

equally be the case that they are permitted to exploit them ruthlessly until they die—especially if they can buy new slaves cheaply.

In the passage from Śāntideva just mentioned, verse 91 runs as follows:

> As the body, having many parts, divided into hands etc.
> should be protected as one.
> Just so, the world, though divided, is undivided in the
> nature of suffering and happiness.

One might take this to be hinting at something like King's argument. The parts of the body are mutually dependent, so each will look after the well-being of the others. So it should be with people.[18]

This argument is no better, though. For a start, it is not clear that this is a good analogy. The parts of the body look after each other, when they do, because they are all part of one conscious organism, which looks after its parts. This is not the case with the totality of sentient beings. Moreover, even in the bodily case, it is not true that each part will look after the well-being of each other part. The hand might cut off a foot in danger of going gangrenous. Or a person may have a ruptured spleen removed, so that the whole body does not die.

We will return to this matter in a moment when we consider Nietzsche's views. For the present, we just need to note that the argument *simply* from interconnectedness fails. From the fact that a bunch of entities are interdependent, it in no way follows that each should look after the interests of the others. There may be good reason to privilege the well-being of some over that of others.

From Emptiness to Compassion

If there is a connection between emptiness and compassion, then, there must be more to the matter. What could it be? This section will try to spell this out.[19]

Come back to the metaphor of the Net of Indra. Suppose that a mental state of being disquieted (*duḥkha*) manifests itself as a red fleck in a jewel in the net. Then any red fleck in a jewel will cause a red fleck in any other jewel. So disquiet in any jewel will be coded in any other. Of course, this is true of all jewels, those that represent normal adults and those that represent, for example, rocks, cows, or infants. So this encoding does not imply that the fleck is *experienced* as disquiet. That requires (the agent represented by) the jewel to have certain

18. For a discussion, see Wetelsen (2002).

19. The project here, note, is not one of textual exegesis. As far as I know, the following argument is not to be found in canonical texts. The aim is to answer our target question with resources that Madhyamaka has at its disposal.

cognitive abilities and attainments. In particular, a certain kind of awareness is necessary—and rocks, cows, and infants don't have it.[20]

All this is a metaphor, of course. But what it indicates is that disquiet in others occasions disquiet in other sentient creatures of sufficient awareness, such as me. In one way, we are all very familiar with this phenomenon. Negative emotions of others, even of those we simply pass in the street, tend to be communicated to us. We naturally respond to fear, hostility, anger, in a like manner. Fear in others can trigger a wave of fear in us; the hostility of another triggers a hostile response; and so on.

Of course, matters are not altogether as simple as that. We do not always seem to be troubled by others we know to be suffering. I know, for example, that poverty is rife in certain countries (and certain parts of even affluent countries); but sometimes I do not seem to be moved by this at all. However, all kinds of things can affect us unknowingly. For example, as doctors often note, one can be stressed, but may be quite unaware of this until the stress manifests as headaches, other bodily pains, and even serious illness. I take it that disquiet in others *does* affect us, even if we are not conscious of this. Deep in the unconscious, it plants the seeds of unease—if only because we know that things of the kind that have happened to others to disquiet them can equally happen to us—much as we might want to repress this thought with an act of bad faith.[21]

Is this simply special pleading? No. There is evidence from experimental psychology that this is, indeed, the case. One recent study says:

> The key suggestion is that observation or imagination of another person in a particular emotional state automatically activates a representation of that state in the observer, with its associated autonomic and somatic responses . . .
>
> These results suggest that regions associated with feelings of emotion can be activated by seeing the facial expression of the same emotion, a phenomenon described as emotional contagion.[22]

Another says:

> . . . results showed that those participants who have viewed negative news items reported significantly greater increase

20. Maybe even certain psychopaths don't have it. Then they are no more *moral* agents than infants.

21. Returning to our metaphor, the further away the source of the red fleck is, the weaker the effect. Similarly, the further one is from the sufferer (cognitively), the weaker the effect. It may not be surprising, then, that much of the effect of the suffering of others falls below my conscious cognitive horizon.

22. Singer et al. (2004), p. 1158.

> in anxiety and negative affect along with greater decrease in positive affect than those participants who viewed the combined positive and negative news items.
>
> This study . . . demonstrates that anxiety and momentary mood disturbance do not dissipate with a distraction activity.[23]

And yet a third says:

> The study . . . adds to a small but growing, number of studies indicating that television coverage of traumatic events may have significant [negative] secondary impacts on public mental health.[24]

Disquiet in others does, then, disquiet us—even if we are unaware of it.

Sometimes, of course, matters are more extreme than mere apparent indifference. We can actually enjoy the suffering of others. Thus, for example, most of us know what it is like to experience pleasure when something bad happens to someone we dislike, such as someone to whom we bear a grudge. In such cases, something is blocking or undercutting the natural "resonance." But as the example makes clear, we enjoy the suffering because we have a negative attitude to the other in the first place—such as dislike, envy, or hatred. In other words, such a thing is possible only because we are already in a state of disquiet.[25] (The jewel, as it were, is clouded by such attitudes.) If that disquiet goes, so will the pleasure in the other's disquiet.

In sum, if all this is right, it follows that the disquiet of others is very much my concern. It may be suggested that it follows only that one should be concerned with the well-being of those with whom one comes into contact: one does not need to have any concern for anyone else. This is short-sighted, however. It may be true that the immediate effects on me are from those with whom I interact personally. But they, in their turn, are affected by others, who are affected by others, and so on. And the chain of encoding is transitive. Disquiet will knock on down the line.

Indeed, many of the effects on a person are ultimately from sources entirely beyond their ken. And one does not have to have a profound understanding of the world to see that *duḥkha*—in the form of poverty, oppression, greed, distrust, hate, desire for power—generates much suffering in the world: from simple violence and theft, to war and genocide. Even when such events are

23. Szabo and Hopkins (2007), pp. 58, 61.

24. Putnam (2002), p. 310.

25. And if someone *is* truly indifferent to the disquiet of others, this, itself, is likely a sign of a troubled person; indeed, in extreme cases, it is the sign of some sort of disturbed psychopathology. See, further, Garfield (2010/2011).

at a distant location in space, their effects ricochet through international relations, concerning military actions, international aid, refugees, and so on. These events and their consequences ultimately involve us all. As John Donne put it in his poem *Devotions upon Emergent Occasions and Severall Steps in my Sickness—Meditation XVII* of 1624:

> No man is an iland, intire of it selfe; every man is a peece of the
> Continent, a part of the maine; if a clod bee washed away by
> the Sea,
> Europe is the lesse, as well as if a Promontorie were, as well as
> if a Mannor of thy friends or of thine owne were; any mans death
> diminishes
> me, because I am involved in Mankinde; And therefore never
> send to
> know for whom the bell tolls; It tolls for thee.

And if it be suggested (unrealistically) that you should just, then, take yourself off to a desert island so that you do not have to interact with others, one should remember that putting people in solitary confinement is a form of punishment. The inability to interact with others is wont to generate profound disquiet of its own.

The Import of Metaphysics

Let us be clear about the nature of the project engaged in here. This is to read off facts about moral psychology from a metaphysical picture of the world. It might be thought that there is something fundamentally misguided about such a project: inferring facts of cognitive psychology, such as disquiet, from facts about the metaphysical nature of people. I think not. Facts concerning the physical nature of people can obviously have consequences in cognitive psychology; and facts of metaphysical nature are even more fundamental. Recall, also, that some of the relations of dependence that generate the encodings in the Net of Indra are causal relations.

Nor am I the first person to engage in this kind of project. A moment ago bad faith was mentioned—the pushing to the back of the mind unpalatable thoughts. As hardly needs to be said, the notion is Sartre's. And Sartre is a master of trying to read off facts of human cognitive psychology from the metaphysical nature of people (*être pour soi*) both in his philosophical writings, such as *L'Etre et le Néant*, and in his novels, such as *La Nausée*. Sartre's metaphysics of essencelessness, and its consequence of radical freedom, are not, of course, the metaphysics of emptiness.[26] But the move from metaphysics to psychology that Sartre makes is of the same kind.

So once more back to the Net of Indra. Change the metaphor slightly. Let us suppose that the interaction between the jewels is not one of reflection; suppose instead that the interaction is one of resonance—in the way that vibrations of an object can cause similar vibrations in closely located free-standing objects. Interpret the vibrations as the "vibes" of a tranquil mind or of a disquieted mind, which we all show to others. When we are surrounded by people who are agitated, angry, and aggressive, it is much harder to be peaceful; and conversely, disquiet will normally be mitigated if we are surrounded by compassionate, peaceful people—and so on, transitively. The effect, of course, is reciprocal. There can, then, be no radical disjuncture of being between myself and others.[27]

Making Others Suffer

What has been argued is that the inter-being of people does indeed ground an important solidarity. In the end, my peace of mind cannot be divorced from that of those with whom I interact. Compassion is, indeed, the consequence of inter-being.

Of course, one may object. In this section, let us consider one well-known objection. Nietzsche is well aware that my well-being depends on others. He holds, nonetheless, that suffering may be a good. As he said, notoriously: anything that does not kill me makes me stronger.[28] Moreover, he holds that

26. Though there certainly are similarities that would be worth exploring. For example, Sartre's slogan that *hell (suffering) is other people* (from the play *Huis Clos*) could be thought of as simply the downside of the slogan that heaven (peace of mind) can be other people. As the Zen story goes: "A Soldier named Nobushige came to Hakuin, and asked: 'Is there a paradise and a hell?' 'Who are you?' inquired Hakuin. 'I am a samurai,' the warrior replied. 'You are a soldier!' exclaimed Hakuin. 'What kind of ruler would have you as a guard? Your face looks like that of a beggar.' Nobushige became so angry that he began to draw his sword, but Hakuin continued: 'So you have a sword! Your weapon is probably much too dull to cut off my head.' As Nobushige drew his sword Hakuin remarked: 'Here are the gates of hell!' At these words the samurai, perceiving the master's discipline, sheathed his sword and bowed. 'Here open the gates of paradise,' said Hakuin." (Reps and Senzaki 1971, p. 80.) For more on the connection between Buddhism and Existentialism, see Batchelor (1983).

27. To change the metaphor yet again: Jay Garfield once commented to me that Buddhist ethics is like plumbing. You have a problem with your draining and sewage system? Okay, let me show you how to fix it. I would add: and if the people in the next apartment have a problem with their drainage and sewage system, it quickly becomes yours. You should help them fix it, too.

28. *Twilight of the Idols* 1, Maxim 8.

making others suffer may be good—and compassion a corresponding weakness. Thus we have, for example:

> Let us be clear as to the logic of this form of compensation: it is strange enough. An equivalence is provided by the creditor receiving, in place of literal compensation for an injury (thus in the place of money, land, possessions of any kind), a recompense in the form of a kind of pleasure—the pleasure of being allowed to vent his power freely upon one who is powerless, the voluptuous pleasure "*de faire le mal pour le plaisir de la faire*," the enjoyment of violation. This enjoyment will be greater the lower the creditor stands in the social order, and can easily appear to him as a most delicious morsel, indeed as a foretaste of higher rank. In "punishing" the debtor, the creditor participates in the *right of the masters*: at last, he, too, may experience for once the exalted sensation of being allowed to despise and mistreat someone as "beneath him". . .[29]

and:

> [T]he essential feature of a good, healthy aristocracy is that it does *not* feel that it is a function (whether of the kingdom or of the community) but instead feels itself to be the *meaning* of highest justification (of the kingdom or the community),—and, consequently, that it accepts in good conscience the sacrifice of countless people who have to be pushed down and shrunk into incomplete human beings, into slaves, into tools, all *for the sake of the aristocracy*.[30]

Why does Nietzsche make these somewhat extraordinary claims? As best I can understand it, it is because the surviving of suffering, and its infliction on others, is an exercise of the "will to power," which characterizes the "superior person" (*übermensch*).

Now, it is true that one who survives a tragic experience, such as incarceration in a Nazi concentration camp, may well have had to develop an admirable strength of character; but it could have been better had it not had to be done in this tragic way. The self-discipline required to develop a robust peace of mind is much to be preferred. And, it must be said: for all that some people develop the strength to survive a tragic experience, such circumstances will just as often, if not more often, damage and crush people in the process—as the example of the Nazi concentration camps reminds us too clearly.

29. *On the Genealogy of Morals*, second essay, sec. 5. Translation from Nietzsche (1969), pp. 64–65.
30. *Beyond Good and Evil*, sec. 258. Translation from Nietzsche (2002), p. 152.

As for the need to valorize oneself by making others suffer, I can only regard this as a sign of a deeply troubled person. (Nietzsche, indeed, is not known for his untroubled psyche.) Why would one feel any need to do this unless one felt some deep sense of inadequacy, and the *duḥkha* that goes along with it? Indeed, such a need is a prime example of *duḥkha* and its doings. There are better ways of dealing with it than by feeding it.

Nietzsche was contemptuous for those who had the mentality of sheep, who followed the herd, and submitted passively. Whether or not he was right in this matter (he wasn't), peace of mind does not entail such passivity. Compassionate action is often not easy—it often means *not* going along with the herd—and neither is nonviolent resistance of the kind sometimes undertaken by Buddhists (see, e.g., Keown 2005, chatper 7). Indeed, compassion often requires as much strength of character as surviving suffering; and others do not come off worse as a result of it.

Implications of the Net

The preceding sections have argued for an account of compassion based on the Net of Indra. In what follows, let us look at a few of the consequences (and non-consequences) of such an account.

Buddhism is often taken to be sympathetic to environmental ethics, concerned with the flourishing of all environments/species.[31] One might well try to read from this a metaphysics of inter-being. Here is King again:

> The Dalai Lama is also an ardent environmentalist who does not see the welfare of human and non-human life as separate categories. "If an individual has a sense of responsibility for humanity, he or she will naturally take care of the environment." His Holiness promotes respect for the environment and non-human species from two perspectives. The first is pragmatic. In light of our dependence on the web of interdependent life, he writes, "the threat of nuclear weapons and the ability to damage our environment through, for example, deforestation, pollution, and ozone layer depletion, are quite alarming." His second approach is to observe that caring for other species and the environment is a natural expression of benevolence. "Compassion and altruism require not only that we

31. See, e.g., Keown (2005), chapter 3. For further references, and a critique of ways in which this is often done, see Ives (2009).

> respect human beings, but that we also respect, take care of, and refrain from interfering with other species and the environment."[32]

Clearly, there is much sense in this; but one should not get too carried away.

Compassion concerns suffering, and suffering involves sentience. Our mental states, it is true, are very dependent on our interactions with others and our environment. But it does not follow that we should respect the well-being of all species and all environments.[33] How far down the evolutionary scale sentience goes is debatable; but mosquitoes are too far down. Of course, one should eradicate the mosquitoes in Africa that cause much human suffering, and if that means draining the swampy environments in which they flourish, so be it.[34] The improvement in human living conditions, health, and well-being in history owes much to our ability to manipulate inhospitable environments and hostile species (such as those of certain bacteria and parasites) with engineering, drugs, and other bits of technology.

Of course, this is not to say that we should treat the environment and other species in a cavalier fashion. Many species other than humans are sentient. Compassion requires a regard for their well-being. And many of the things we are now doing to the environment are likely to cause significant suffering to future generations of sentient beings. Compassion requires us to stop these, and to find better ways to bring about any beneficial ends these activities are supposed to deliver.

Phronesis and Compassion

Of course, how to determine what is the best (most compassionate) action in these and similar cases may well not be obvious. If one is a doctor, should one respect the wish of a parent for his child not to be given a blood transfusion, even though one knows that without it the child is very likely to die? To take a more extreme example: Violence always causes suffering and should be avoided if possible. True—but sometimes it may be necessary so that greater suffering may be avoided. One might argue that if it had been possible to kill

32. King (2005), p. 131. The quotations come from Gyatso (1992), pp. 3, 10.

33. Nor is it to say that all sentient creatures are *equally* important. If there is a hard choice between the suffering of a person and the suffering of a cat, then, *ceteris paribus, phronesis* would dictate attending to the well-being of the person.

34. If people can be reborn as mosquitoes, this may complicate the discussion, though not, in the end, I think, alter the conclusion. In any case, I do not accept the doctrine of rebirth. Neither, I think, does Buddhism need it. See Priest (2014, chapter 14).

Hitler in 1933, this would have been the best thing to do. What should one do in such cases? What one should do is determined by compassion: certainly compassion to those who are suffering; but also to those whose actions bring about the suffering.[35] But what is that?

In any situation, what to do will depend on both the concrete details of the context in which we find ourselves, and the exact consequences of our actions. These, in turn, will depend on laws of nature, such as those concerning the environment, and laws of human (or better, sentient) psychology. Indeed, just because of the Net of Indra, situations are always complex. Any action is likely to have both good consequences and bad consequences. The determination of the best course of action will therefore require an act of judgment, or *phronesis* (practical wisdom), as Aristotle put it (*Nichomachean Ethics*, Book 6, Chapters 5, 7). This does not, of course, mean that all situations are unclear. In many situations the most important effects of a possible action will obviously be on a certain individual and those close to them. We should act in such a way as to promote their well-being. Thus, it is quite clear that if, next time I am in the pub, I pull out a gun and shoot one of those enjoying a quiet drink, this act is not going to do this. But in general, the ethics of compassion provides no simple-minded answer to hard moral questions.

What, then, of the Precepts? Buddhism has a standard set of moral guidelines: don't kill, don't lie, and so on.[36] These look like pretty universal edicts. Violating them can certainly get one kicked out of the *Saṅgha*. In the Mahāyāna traditions, it is recognized that it might be right to violate the Precepts sometimes. There are stories, for example, of the Buddha in an earlier rebirth killing someone because it was the best thing to do in the context. But nonetheless, the edicts are enforced pretty rigidly. Don't expect to get away with breaking one if you are a much lesser mortal!

As is clear from what has been said, however, rules of any kind can be at best rules of thumb, and they should never be promoted to thoughtless demands. This does not mean that the Precepts are not generally good guidelines. Most of them probably are. But the effects of an action will always be context-dependent, and this must be taken into account. In particular, it must be remembered that the Precepts were formulated at particular times and places, and might well be heavily dependent on the sociohistorical contexts in question. And rules of thumb that were pretty good at one time may not work at another. This should

35. It should be remembered that those who deliberately make others suffer are almost certainly suffering themselves. Plausibly, this is the source of their desire to hurt others. At the very least, it is very hard to see how someone at peace with herself could want to perpetrate suffering on others.

36. See Harvey (2000), chapter 2, and Keown (2005), chapter 1.

be borne in mind when interpreting what is of value in historical formulations of Buddhist ethical codes. For example, much traditional Buddhism has been down on gays and lesbians (and being patriarchal, particularly down on male homosexuality.)[37] Now it may well have been the case that being gay at various times in Indian and Chinese history was not a great strategy for leading a happy life. But in enlightened contemporary societies—or at least those parts of them that are enlightened—where sexual preference is not an issue, gay sexuality is no more (or less) problematic than straight sexuality.

Conclusion: Why Be Moral?

Let me conclude the essay with one final observation. There is a standard conundrum about morality: Why should one be moral? If, for example, one were given the Ring of Gyges, which makes its wearer invisible, why should one not behave entirely out of self-interest? There are various standard answers to the question. It suffices to point out here that the above account of ethics provides a very simple answer to the question.

For a start, why should a person behave in such a way as to develop their own inner peace? This hardly needs an answer. A troubled state of mind is not a state we feel happy being in. Of course, one would like to get rid of it. (You enjoy the headache?–OK, don't take the aspirin!) But what of others? Nagel puts the point in the following way:

> Do pleasure and pain have merely agent-relative value or do they provide neutral reasons as well? If avoidance of pain has only relative value [sc. to the agent], then people have reason to avoid their own pain, but not relieve the pain of others (unless other kinds of reasons come into play). If the relief of pain has neutral value as well, then anyone has reason to want any pain to stop, whether or not it is his. From an objective standpoint, which of these hypotheses is more plausible? Is the value of sensory pleasure and pain relative or neutral . . .?[38]

The objective standpoint is provided by the Net of Indra. From this perspective, there is no absolute duality between myself and someone else. My being encodes theirs, and theirs mine. The value, then, is not relative to an individual

37. See Harvey (2000), chapter 10, and Keown (2005), chapter 4.
38. Nagel (1989), p. 158f.

agent. As far as peace of mind goes, my relation to your interests is the same as my relation to my own—or better: we both have an interest in our common interest. Note that this is not to say that one should be compassionate simply as a matter of self-interest (as, maybe, for Hobbes).[39] The Net of Indra undercuts the very nature of the distinction between self-interest and other-interest.

39. Another answer to our question that is sometimes given by Buddhists is that you should act well because otherwise unfortunate consequences will boomerang back on you because of the laws of karma. This really does reduce moral action to self-interest.

Appendix

Bodhicaryāvatāra-pañjikā VIII.90–103 by Prajñākaramati, Commenting on Śāntideva

Translated by Mark Siderits and Charles Goodman

To the extent that one has not brought about oneness of others with the self, to that extent one has not completely fostered the thought directed toward benevolence with respect to others. This results from activity based on seeing oneself as distinct due to self-grasping. Hence, in order to abolish that,

> *parātmasamatām ādau bhāvayed evam ādarāt* |
>
> 90ab. To begin with one should thus diligently foster
> [the thought of] the sameness of others and oneself.

"To begin with," i.e., first. The state is one of inversion by putting oneself after others. "Thus," i.e., as is about to be described. "Diligently," i.e., with great determination.

This describes the precise form of that [sameness]:

> *samaduḥkhasukhāḥ sarve pālanīyā mayātmavat* ||90||
>
> 90cd. "All are equally subject to suffering and happiness,
> and should be protected just like myself."

No distinction whatsoever is thought to exist with respect to those. So just as my suffering is painful, so is that of those [others] as well. Just as my happiness is pleasant, so is that of those [others] as well. That is to say, the suffering and happiness of all living beings are alike. Therefore they should be protected, just like myself. Just as one spares oneself from suffering and the causes of suffering, so others are to be spared as well. Just as one always wants to do the pleasant, so it is the same for others as well; their welfare is to be fostered like one's own.

How then is it that the many beings of different types and distinct conditions are to be treated as one by oneself? And how is it that suffering and happiness [of all] are intrinsically non-distinct? In response he says,

hastādibhedena bahuprakāraḥ kāyo yathaikaḥ paripālanīyaḥ |
tathā jagadbhinnam abhinnaduḥkhasukhātmakaṃ sarvam idaṃ tathaiva ||91||

91. Just as the body, with its multiplicity of forms due to the
differences of hands, etc., should be protected as one whole,
in the same way all different beings, being alike with respect
to suffering and happiness, should be treated as one.

Just as a body that is characterized by a plurality of forms such as those of hands, feet, head, and so on is considered a single thing to be protected due to the avoidance of suffering and procurement of happiness, just so the totality of beings in the world should be considered as a single whole thing to be protected by the self. An "and" has been elided in "alike with respect to suffering and happiness." Thus "just like what has different hands, etc., so all" also refers to the many beings of different types and distinct conditions. This is the meaning: Just as due to repetition, a body that is not actually a single thing is considered to be one, so with respect to the many beings of different types and distinct conditions there is also no difference whatsoever.

Perhaps it will be said: If the world shares one intrinsic nature with you, then why would it be that pain in other series [i.e., other persons] does not hurt you? In response to this objection he says,

yady apy anyeṣu deheṣu madduḥkhaṃ na prabādhate |
tathāpi tadduḥkham eva mamātmasnehaduḥsaham ||92||

92. While my suffering does not harm the bodies of others, it is
indeed still suffering, which is hard to bear due to my self-love.

If my suffering does not cause hurt in other distinct bodies, still it is indeed my suffering. Why? Through self-love it is difficult to bear, i.e., intolerable. This ["through self-love"] states the reason. The meaning is that activity with respect to some does not set aside the [universal] nature of suffering. He will explain that this is also an error.[1]

1. The explanation of the erroneousness of a reason based on self-love begins in v. 96.

tathā yady apy asaṃvedyam anyad duḥkhaṃ mayātmanā |
tathāpi tasya tadduḥkham ātmasnehena duḥsaham ||93||

93. So while others' pain is not felt by me myself, still that pain is difficult to bear for the one whose pain it is, due to [that person's] self-love.

Hence having rejected the distinction between self and other, the intrinsic nature of suffering is by itself a reason for averting it. So he says:

mayānyadduḥkhaṃ hantavyaṃ duḥkhatvād ātmaduḥkhavat |

94ab. I should prevent the suffering of others, because
it is suffering, like my own suffering.

I should prevent whatever suffering occurs, just like my own suffering. That the suffering of others is suffering—this is the consequence of a reason based on intrinsic nature. It should be prevented solely due to possessing the intrinsic nature of suffering. And the reason is not unestablished, for it is proven that suffering has this intrinsic nature undifferentiatedly.[2] Nor is [the reason] inconclusive, since the proposition that one's own suffering is not to be prevented due to non-difference [from that of others] is rejected as erroneous.[3] For this reason there also can be no contrary reason [i.e., a reason for the opposite conclusion].[4]

There is this further consequence:

anugrāhyā mayānye 'pi sattvatvād ātmasattvavat ||94||

94cd. I should also be benevolent to others, because
these are beings, just as I am myself a being.

2. An unestablished reason is one that is not actually found in the locus that is the subject of dispute. For instance in the stock sample inference,

There is fire on the hill
Because there is smoke, like in the kitchen

the fault of unestablished reason would hold if there were no smoke but only fog on the hill.

3. An inconclusive reason is one that is present both where the property to be proved is present and also where it is absent. For instance in the inference,

There is smoke on the mountain
Because there is fire, as in the kitchen

the reason-property "being fire" is present both where there is smoke (as in the traditional kitchen) and where there is no smoke (as in the flame of an acetylene torch).

4. The existence of a contrary reason is the third of the three main ways in which an argument can fail. This holds when there appear to be equally good reasons both for and against the conclusion of the argument in question.

Whatever beings there are, I should show benevolence to all of them, just as I am myself a being. That all beings are also living things is a reason based on intrinsic nature as well. In the mere state of having the nature of a being is found the intrinsic nature of being an appropriate object of benevolence. And this [reason] is not unestablished, for it is established in the locus of having the nature of a being. [The reason] also could not be inconclusive, since that would lead to the absurd result that one should not help oneself. And as before, there could be no contrary reason.

[Objection:] "There is a difference between oneself and others, namely striving after [one's own] happiness. So the reason is inconclusive after all." To this he says,

yadā mama pareṣāṃ ca tulyam eva sukhaṃ priyam |
tadātmanaḥ ko viśeṣo yenātraiva sukhodyamaḥ ||95||

95. Since I and others are exactly alike in desiring happiness, what is so special about me that justifies striving after only my own happiness?

Are exactly alike, i.e., just the same, in desiring, i.e., wanting, happiness. So what distinction is there between myself and others? None at all that would justify promoting happiness just here in myself and not in others—that is the meaning.

Refuting the objection that the first reason is inconclusive, he says,

yadā mama pareṣāṃ ca bhayaṃ duḥkhaṃ ca na priyam |
tadātmanaḥ ko viśeṣo yat taṃ rakṣāmi netaram ||96||

96. Since fear and suffering are unwanted by both me and others, what is so special about me such that I protect this and not that?

"Fear," that is, connected to a cause of suffering; "and not that," i.e., not others.

This being so, if it were said, "While the nature of suffering does not differ [from one person to another], still it is understood that it is for just the person who is harmed by that suffering to prevent it, not for anyone else," he [the author] says [in response]:

tadduḥkhena na me bādhet yato yadi na rakṣyate |
nāgāmikāyaduḥkhān me bādhā tat kena rakṣyate ||97||

97. If one says that the suffering of other persons does not harm me, hence efforts need not be made to prevent it,
Then since the suffering of future bodies does not harm me, why should efforts be made to prevent it?

"No harm—i.e., injury—comes to me by means of the suffering of that other person"—if consequently for this reason I do not protect someone else, then there would be the following difficulty. "There is no harm whatsoever to this [presently] appropriated body [of mine from suffering] of a future body marked by suffering of birth in hell, etc., in a future life," since this is what is said in the world, or what follows from that. This being so, for what purpose does one protect it from that? Because with respect to what is called the body, evil is to be avoided and the good promoted.

Moreover, if it were said, "I am only one at all times, so here there is no difference between the two bodies. This is not a valid objection," to this he says,

aham eva tadāpīti mithyeyaṃ parikalpanaā|

98ab. "It will also be just me then as well" is a mistaken construction,

Because the self is to be repudiated and is refuted for the world, what will be the object of this concept of "I"? So due to the absence of any one thing that is the object of the concept of "I," this is a mistaken construction, it is attachment: "It will also be just me then as well," i.e., even in another life. This is due to grasping what are merely the illusory five appropriation skandhas.

And this is said due to the force of attachment, but once again in reality it has no object whatsoever, for it is of the nature of conceptual construction.

As for why it is said to be a mistaken conception, he says,

anya eva mṛto yasmād anya eva prajāyate ||98||

98cd. For it is one thing that dies and something else entirely that is born.

When there is no one thing like a self that goes to the next world, only the *skandhas*, then it is not at all the case that that very set of five *skandhas* that ceases to exist here arises again in the next world. Rather, something utterly new arises there upon the cessation of the old, qualified by a specific conditionality, formed by the defilements and karma, through the causal continuity of the intermediate being. Thus is the false concept of "I" produced due to the power of habitual traces left by false conceptualizations carried out over the course of beginningless rebirth.

Moreover, there is another objection; he says,

yadi yasyaiva yad duḥkhaṃ rakṣyaṃ tasyaiva tan matam |
pādaduḥkhaṃ na hastasya kasmāt tat tena rakṣyate ||99||

99. If it is thought that the suffering to be prevented is just one's own,
Pain in the foot is not that of the hand. Why should the one protect the other?

Let it be so, then by the same token prevention of impending bodily pain is not to be strived after. Here [i.e., in the present life] in a single body also, pain is distinguished according to the various limbs. So if it is not rational to prevent suffering in another, then why, seeing something falling toward hitting the foot and the like, would the hand prevent it by reaching out? For with respect to being other there is no difference [between the case of another person's suffering and the case of the hand and foot], so this would not be appropriate—that is the meaning.

Now,

ayuktam api ced etad ahaṃkārāt pravartate |
yad ayuktaṃ nivartyaṃ tat svam anyac ca yathābalam ||100||

100. If it is objected that while that [partiality with respect to one's
own suffering] is mistaken, it results from the sense of "I,"
That is wrong, and this way of thinking of oneself and the
other is to be abandoned to the best of one's ability.

The sense of "I" with respect to this body is due to conceiving of an "I" even though there is no self. Protective attention toward the foot etc. results, i.e., is produced. This [conceiving of an "I"] is not correct. Since what is mistaken does not meet with success, it is to be abandoned, i.e., removed, with respect both to oneself and to others, to the best of one's ability, i.e., to the extent that one is capable. Only because of insufficiency of power is it acceptable to overlook it. This is the meaning.

Perhaps it will be said: "While there is no self or the like, still there is a single series, and likewise the collection of many things such as hands and feet is a single body. In this case such things as warding off harm and the like as one's own will be restricted to the pair that is suitably linked in this world and the next. Hence your "for there is no difference" [between the case of another person and the case of the hand and the foot] has an unproven reason, and the previous reason ["because it is suffering"] is inconclusive." To this objection he says,

saṃtānaḥ samudāyaś ca paṅktisenādivan mṛṣā |
yasya duḥkhaṃ sa nāsty asmāt kasya tat svaṃ bhaviṣyati ||101||

101. The series and the collection, like a queue, an army and so on, are unreal.
The one who owns the suffering does not exist. Therefore, whose will it be?

The series does not exist as a single ultimately real entity. But this is just a stream-like succession of resultant moments in the relation of effect and cause, for nothing distinct from that is apprehended. Thus in order to express with a single word these moments, the buddhas create "series" as a conventional designation, for practical purposes. This is only nominally existent.

So attachment to this is not right. That is not appropriated by anything other than a self. The collection is likewise not some one ultimately real thing over and above the things that are collected, for it is not apprehended apart from them. But the mistaken concept with respect to this is understood by means of the analysis of the partite, which is not laid out here. And so this is also just conventionally real, like the former [the series]. He then says there are numerous examples of both—the queue, the army, etc. The series is like a queue, the collection is like the army and the like. Due to the term "and the like," such similes as that of the necklace and so on are grasped. Just as, apart from the form of ants arranged one after another, there is no queue resembling a single continuous thread, and as apart from assembled elephants, horses, footsoldiers, and so on there is no other single thing whatsoever to be an army, the collection is so as well. And [since] this is analyzed extensively elsewhere, it is not analyzed here. Thus since it lacks an ultimately real object, the thought is mistaken. Alternatively this means that it does not hold up under analysis. Hence, since there is nothing whatsoever like a self that could be an owner, there is nothing to which suffering is connected. Hence "whose will this suffering be that is thought to be one's own?" The meaning is that there is no one at all.

Now [it may be asked], if such things as the self do not exist, how will there be an example such as "like the self" and "like the reality of the self"? This is true. But this is not furnished out of addiction to proof, but rather for the purpose of blocking the opponent's attachment to the concept of a self. For if the opponent's attachment to the concept of self had been given up, then there would be no point at all in the use of an inference. Since it has not been given up, with just that intention a convincing proof and example are stated [for the opponent who] distinguishes between self and other. It is not the case that there is non-establishment of an example for everyday use [i.e., in an inference meant to establish some positive result for a general audience]. Once it has been agreed that this is just the five appropriation skandhas, the example disappears, and there is no fault at all, for the word "self" is only furnished here [in this context].

Coming to the main point, he now says,

asvāmikāni duḥkhāni sarvāṇy evāviśeṣataḥ |
duḥkhatvād eva vāryāṇi niyamas tatra kiṃ kṛtaḥ ||102||

102. All sufferings are ownerless because all are devoid
of distinction [between "mine" and "other"].

Because it is suffering, it is to be prevented; how can any limitation be imposed? The analysis [of "ownerless"] is that owners do not exist for those [sufferings] under discussion; the meaning is that those [sufferings] that are not "mine" are utterly lacking in a counterpositive.[5] Why? Not for any? No, all are indeed ownerless, for there is no difference. There is no such thing as being an owner of anything on the part of anyone, for there is no difference. Having obtained the non-distinction between self and other, they are to be prevented, i.e., to be warded off, just because they are suffering. There is here no other ground, mineness and the like. How can this limitation be imposed—in virtue of what difference is it imposed—by which sufferings of one's own are to be prevented

5. The opponent sought to justify his bias in favor of preventing his own suffering on the grounds that the suffering of others has the property of being "non-mine." This is a negative property, which is understood as the absence of the positive property of being mine. But it is generally agreed that in order for an absence to itself be real, it must be the absence of some real entity (its counter-positive): there can be the absence of a pot on the ground in front of me because pots do exist elsewhere. So the argument here is that since there is nothing that could make something be "mine," it follows that no occurrence of suffering could have the property of being "non-mine."

and not sufferings of others? Thus it is determined that the reason "because it is suffering" is not inconclusive.

"Now if there is no one whatsoever who bears suffering in *saṃsāra,* then surely suffering itself would not be something to be prevented, because of the complete absence of anyone full of compassion [and] of any bearer of suffering," anticipating this objection he says,

> *duḥkhaṃ kasmān nivāryaṃ cet sarveṣām avivādataḥ* |
> *vāryaṃ cet sarvam apy evaṃ na ced ātmāpi sarvavat* ||103||

> 103. Why then is suffering to be prevented? Because it is
> agreed upon without exception by all [that it is].
> Thus if it is to be prevented, then indeed all of it is to be prevented.
> If not, then one's own case is just like that of other persons.

If you think that it is not at all to be prevented just because of the lack of a self, then this is not right. Why? Because it is agreed upon, not disputed, by all. Even for the Cārvāka there is the practice of avoiding one's own pain. And for them this is no fallacy, even though they do not acknowledge the existence of a self, due to non-apprehension of its intrinsic nature. And the existence of that is not established merely by means of acknowledgment, for there is absence of a reliable cognitive instrument for the proof of that, and there is designation of the logical difficulty of having many forms. This being so, if suffering should be prevented, then all of it should be prevented; if it is not the case that all of it should be prevented, then this applies to one's own as well. The suffering that is the intrinsic nature of the five appropriation *skandhas* is not to be prevented, since they lack distinction, like all others—this is the summation.

References

Ackrill, J. L. (1980). "Aristotle on *Eudaimonia*," in A. O. Rorty (ed.), *Essays on Aristotle's Ethics*. Berkeley: University of California Press, pp. 15–34.

Anderson, E. (1999). "What Is the Point of Equality?" *Ethics* 109: 287–337.

Annas, J. (1992). "Ancient Ethics and Modern Morality." *Philosophical Perspectives* 6: 119–136.

Āryadeva and rGyal tshab. (2007). *bZhi brga pa'i rnam bshad legs bshad snying po*. Sarnath: Gelugpa Student Welfare Committee.

Āryadeva. *Treatise of Four Hundred Verses* (*Bstan bcos bzhi brgya pa zhes bya ba'i tshig le'ur byas pa / Catuḥśatakaśastrakārikā*). Translated into Tibetan by Sūkṣmajāna and Patsab nyima grags. Toh. 3846. bStan 'gyur, sDe dge edition. dBu ma Vol. Tsha 1b–18a.

Asaṅga. *Compendium of Higher Knowledge* (*mNgon pa kun btus/ Abhidharma-sammuccaya*). Translated into Tibetan by Jinamitra, Śīlendrabodhi, and Ye shes sde. Toh. 4049. sDe dge edition. Sems tsam, Ri 1b1–77a7; 44b1–120a7.

Barnhart, M. (2012). "Theory and Comparison in the Discussion of Buddhist Ethics." *Philosophy East & West* 62, no. 1: 16–43.

Batchelor, S. (1983). *Alone with Others: An Existential Approach to Buddhism*. New York: Grove Press.

Bendall, C., and W. H. D. Rouse. (1922). *Śikṣā Samuccaya: A Compendium of Buddhist Doctrine*. London: John Murray. Reprint, Delhi: Motilal Banarsidass, 1971.

Boyd, R. (1988). "How to Be a Moral Realist." First appeared in Geoffrey Sayre-McCord (ed.), *Essays on Moral Realism*. Reprinted in Darwall,

Gibbard, and Railton (eds.), *Moral Discourse and Practice: Some Philosophical Approaches*. Oxford: Oxford University Press, 1997, pp. 105–135.

Braarvig, J. (1993). *Akṣayamatinirdeśa Sūtra: The Tradition of Imperishability in Buddhist Thought*. Vol. II. Oslo: Solum Forlag.

Candrakīrti. *Clear Words: Commentary on the Fundamental Verses of the Middle Way (dBu ma rtsa ba'i 'grel ba tshig gsal ba zhes bya ba/Mūlamadhyamakavṛtti-Prasannapadā)*. Translated into Tibetan by Kanakavarma and Patsab nyima grags. Toh. 3860. bStan 'gyur, sDe dge edition. dBu ma Vol. 'a, 1b–200a.

Candrakīrti. *Commentary on Four Hundred Verses on the Bodhisattva's Yogic Deeds (Byang chub semse dpa'i rnam 'byor spyod pa bzhi brgya pa'i rgya cher 'grel pa/ Bodhisattvayogācāra-Catuḥṣatakaṭika)*. Translated by Sūkṣmajāna and Patshab nyima grags. Toh. 3865. bStan 'gyur, sDe dge editon. dBu ma Vol. Ya, 30b–239a.

Candrakīrti. *Commentary on Introduction of the Middle Way (dBu ma la 'jug pa'i bshad pa/Madhyamakāvatāra-bhāṣya)*. Translated by Tilakakalaśa and Patsab nyima grags. Revised by Karnakavarma and Patsab nyima grags. Toh. 3862. bStan 'gyur, sDe dge edition. dBu ma Vol. 'a, 220b–348a.

Candrakīrti. *Commentary on the Seventy Verses of Emptiness (Stong pa nyid bdun cu pa'i 'grel pa/Śūnyatāsaptativṛtti)*. Translated by Abhayākara and Dharma grags. Toh. 3867. bStan 'gyur, sDe dge edition. dBu ma Vol. Ya, 267a–336b.

Candrakīrti. *Commentary on the Sixty Verses on Reasoning (Rigs pa drug cu pa'i 'grel pa/Yuk tiṣaṣṭhikavṛtii)*. Translated by Jinamitra, Dānaśīla, Śīlendrabodhi, and Yeshes sde. Toh. 3864. bStan 'gyur, sDe dge edition. dBu ma Vol. ya 1b–30b.

Candrakīrti. *Introduction of the Middle Way (dBu ma la 'jug pa zhes bya ba/ Madhyamakāvatāra)*. Translated by Tilakakalaśa and Patsab nyima grags. Revised by Karnakavarma and Patsab nyima grags. Toh. 3861. bStan 'gyur, sDe dge edition. dBu ma Vol. 'a, 201b–219a.

Candrakīrti. (1960). *Prasannapadā (Madhyamakavṛtti*, ed. P. L. Vaidya. Darbhanga: The Mithila Institute of Post-Graduate Studies and Research in Sanskrit Learning.

Candrakīrti. (1970). *Prasannapadā Madhyamakavṛtti, ed. Louis de la Vallée Poussin (LVP). Mūlamadhyamakakārikā (Mādhyamikasūtras) de Nāgārjuna, avec la Prasannapadā commentaire de Candrakīrti*. St. Petersburg: Bibliotheca Buddhica IV, 1903–1913. Reprint, Osnabrück: Biblio.

Carpenter, A. (2012). "Faith Without God in Nāgārjuna," in A. P. Co and P. A. Bolaños (eds.), *Thomism and Asian Cultures*. Manila: University of Santo Tomas Publishing House.

Chakrabarti, A. (1983). "Is Liberation (Mokṣa) Pleasant?" *Philosophy East & West* 33: 167–182.

Chang, G., ed. (1983). *A Treasury of Mahāyāna Sūtras*. London; University Park: Penn State University Press.

Chodron, T. (2001). *Working with Anger*. Ithaca, NY: Snow Lion.

Clayton, B. (2001). "Compassion as a Matter of Fact: The Argument from No-self to Selflessness in Śāntideva's Śikṣāsamuccaya." *Contemporary Buddhism* 2, no. 1: 83–97.

Clayton, B. (2006). *Moral Theory in Śāntideva's Śikṣāsamuccaya: Cultivating the Fruits of Virtue*. New York: Routledge.

Cleary, Thomas, trans. (1993). *Book Ten in The Flower Ornament Scripture: A Translation of the Avatamsaka Sutra*. Boston: Shambhala.

Co, A., and P. Bolaños, eds. (2012). *Thomism and Asian Cultures*. Manila: University of Sannto Tomas Publishing House.

Collins, S. (1982). *Selfless Persons*. Cambridge: Cambridge University Press.

Conze, E., trans. (1973). *The Perfection of Wisdom in Eight Thousand Lines*. Bolinas, CA: Four Seasons.

Cook, F. (1977). *Hua-yen Buddhism: The Jewel Net of Indra*. University Park: Pennsylvania University Press.

Cowherds. (2011). *Moonshadows: Conventional Truth in Buddhist Philosophy*. New York: Oxford University Press.

Cozort, D. (1998). *Unique Tenets of the Middle Way Consequence School*. Ithaca, NY: Snow Lion.

Crosby, K., and A. Skilton, trans. (1996). *The Bodhicaryāvatāra*. Śāntideva. New York: Oxford University Press.

Dalai Lama XIV. (1992). *Worlds in Harmony*. Berkeley, CA: Parallax Press.

Dalai Lama XIV. (1999). *Ethics for a New Milenium*. New York: Riverhead Books.

Dalai Lama XIV. (2012). *From Here to Enlightenment: An Introduction to Tsong-kha-pa's Classic Text, The Great Treatise on the Stages of the Path to Enlightenment*. Ithaca, NY: Snow Lion.

Dancy, J. (2006). *Ethics Without Principles*. Oxford: Clarendon Press.

Davidson, R. (1990). "An Introduction to the Standards of Scriptural Authenticity in Indian Buddhism," in Robert Buswell (ed.), *Chinese Buddhist Apocrypha*. Honolulu: University Hawaii, pp. 291–325.

Dennett, D. (1991). *Consciousness Explained*. London: Penguin.

Discourse on the Saṁsāric Migration (Ārya-bhavasaṃkrānti-nāma-mahāyāna-sūtra//'phags pa srid pa 'pho ba zhes bya ba theg pa chen po'i mdo). Translated into Tibetan by Jinamitra, Dānaśīla, and Ye shes sde. bka' 'gyur, sNar thang edition: (N 211) mDo sDe, Vol. Tsa, 279b6–282b2 (vol. 63).

Dreyfus, G. (1995). "Meditation as Ethical Activity." *Journal of Buddhist Ethics* 2. http://blogs.dickinson.edu/buddhistethics/category/volume-02-1995/.

Eckel, M. D. (1987). *Jñānagarbha's Commentary on the Distinction Between the Two Truths*. Albany: State University of New York Press.

Eckel, M. D. (2003). "The Satisfaction of No Analysis," in George Dreyfus and Sarah McClintock (eds.), *The Svātantrika Prāsaṅgika Distinction: What Difference Does a Difference Make*. Boston: Wisdom, pp. 173–203.

Egge, J. R. (2002). *Religious Giving and Invention of Karma*. Richmond, VA: Curzon Press.

Eimer, H. (1977). *Bericthe uber das Leben des Atisa (Dipamkaraasrijnana): Eine Untersuchung der Quellen (Asiastische Forschungen)*. Berlin: Harassoowitz.

Finnigan, B. (2011). "Buddhist Metaethics." *Journal of the International Association of Buddhist Studies* 33, no. 1: 267–298.

Finnigan, B. (2015). "Meta-ethics for Madhyamaka: Investigating the Justificatory Grounds of Moral Judgments." *Philosophy East & West* 65, no. 3.

Finnigan, B., and K. Tanaka. (2011). "Ethics for Mādhyamikas," in Cowherds (2011) pp. 221–231.

Foot, P. (2001). *Natural Goodness*. Oxford: Oxford University Press.

Frege, G. (1980). "Frege to Russell," in G. Gabriel, H. Hermes, F. Kambartel, C. Thiel and A. Veraart (eds.), *Philosophical and Mathematical Correspondence*, English translations edited by B. McGuinness and translated by H. Kaal. Chicago: University of Chicago Press.

Ganeri, J. (2001). *Philosophy in Classical India*. London: Routledge.

Garfield, Jay. (1995). *The Fundamental Wisdom of the Middle Way: Nāgārjuna's Mūlamadhyamakakārikā*. New York: Oxford University Press.

Garfield, J. (1996). "Emptiness and Positionlessness: Do the Mādhyamika Relinquish All Views?" *Journal of Indian Philosophy and Religion* 1, no. 1: 1–34.

Garfield, J. (2010/2011). "What Is It Like to Be a Bodhisattva: Moral Phenomenology in Śāntideva's *Bodhicaryāvatāra*." *Journal of the International Association of Buddhist Studies* 33, no.1: 333–358.

Garfield, J. (2012). "Mindfulness and Morality," in German as "Achtsamkeit als Grundlage für ethisches Verhalten," in M. Zimmermann, C. Spitz, and S. Schmidtt (eds.), *Achtsamkeit*. Stuttgart: Hans Huber, pp. 227–250.Also published in *Thai International Journal of Buddhist Studies* 3: 1–24 (2012).

Garfield, J. (2015). *Engaging Buddhism: Why It Matters to Philosophy*. New York: Oxford University Press.

Gethin, R. (1998). *The Foundations of Buddhism*. Oxford: Oxfored University Press.

Gombrich, R. (1975). "Buddhist Karma and Social Control." *Comparative Studies in Society and History* 17, no. 2: 212–220.

Gombrich, R. (2006). *How Buddhism Began: The Conditioned Genesis of the Early Teachings*. New York: Routledge.

Gómez, L. (1973). "Emptiness and Moral Perfection." *Philosophy East & West* 23: 361–373.

Goodman, C. (2002). "Resentment and Reality: Buddhism on Moral Responsibility." *American Philosophical Quarterly* 39, no. 4: 359–372.

Goodman, C. (2009). *Consequences of Compassion: An Interpretation and Defense of Buddhist Ethics*. New York: Oxford University Press.

Gorampa. (2010). *Distinguishing the Views: Moonlight for the Critical Points of the Supreme Vehicle (lta ba'i shen 'byed theg mchog gnad kyi zla zer) in Zab mo lta ba'i khyad par bshad pa*, edited by Thupten Jinpa. New Delhi: Institute of Tibetan Classics.

Griffiths, P. (1994). *On Being Buddha*. Albany: State University of New York Press.

Griffiths, Paul. (1999). *Religious Reading: The Place of Reading in the Practice of Religion*. New York: Oxford University Press.

rGyal tshab darma rinchen. (1999). *Byang chub sems pa'i byod pa la 'jugs pa'i rnam bshad rgyal sras 'jug ngogs*. Sarnath: Gelugpa Student Welfare Committee.

Gyatso, T. (1992). *Worlds in Harmony*. Berkeley, CA: Parallax Press.

Gyatso, T. (1999). *Ethics for a New Millennium*. New York: Riverhead Books.

Hallisey, C. (1996). "Ethical Particularism in Theravāda Buddhism." *Journal of Buddhist Ethics* 3.

Hanh, T. N. (1993). *Interbeing: Fourteen Guidelines for Engaged Buddhism* (revised edition). Berkeley, CA: Parallax Press.

Harris, S. (2011). "Does Anātman Rationally Entail Altruism? On *Bodhicaryāvatāra* 8:101–103." *Journal of Buddhist Ethics* 18: 92–123.

Harrison, Paul. (2007). "The Case of the Vanishing Poet: New Light on Śāntideva and the Śikṣā-samuccaya," in Konrad Klaus and Jens-Uwe Hartmann (eds.), *Indica et Tibetica: Festschrift für Michael Hahn,* Zum 65. Vienna: Arbeitskreis für tibetische und buddhistische Studien Universität Wien, pp. 215–248.

Harvey, P. (2000). *Buddhist Ethics.* Cambridge: Cambridge University Press.

Heim, M. (2013). *The Foerrunner of All Things: Buddhaghosa on Mind, Intention and Agency.* New York: Oxford University Press.

Hilbert, D. (1902). *Grundlagen der Geometrie,* English translation: *The Foundations of Geometry,* E. J. Townsend (trans.). La Salle: Open Court Publishing, 1965.

Hofstadter. D. (2007). *I Am a Strange Loop.* New York: Basic Books.

Hopkins, J. (1995). *Emptiness Yoga: The Tibetan Middle Way.* Ithaca, NY: Snow Lion.

Hopkins, J. (1998). *Buddhist Advice for Living and Liberation. Nāgārjuna's Precious Garland.* Ithaca, NY: Snow Lion.

Hume, D. "Of Suicide." Two Essays: Of Suicide and Of the Immortality of the Soul. London, 1777. www.davidhume.org/texts/suis.html.

Huntington, C. W., Jr., and Geshe Namgyal Wangchen. (1989). *The Emptiness of Emptiness.* Honolulu: University Hawaii Press.

Hursthouse, R. (1999). *On Virtue Ethics.* Oxford: Oxford University Press.

Ishida, Chiko. (2010). "Relocation of the Verses on 'The Equality of Self and Others' in the *Bodhicaryāvatāra.*" *Hokke-Bunka Kenkyujo* (*Journal of Institute for the Comprehensive Study of Lotus Sūtra*) 36 (March 2010): 1–16.

Ives, C., (2009). "In Search of a Green Dharma: Philosophical Issues in Buddhist Environmental Ethics," in John Powers and Charles S. Prebish (eds.), *Destroying Māra Forever.* Ithaca, NY: Snow Lion, pp. 165–185.

Jaini, P. S., ed. (1959). *Abhidharmadīpa with Vibhāshāprabhāvṛitti* [*sic*]. Tibetan Sanskrit Works Series, Volume IV. Patna: Jayaswal Research Institute.

Jenkins, S. (1998). *The Circle of Compassion: An Interpretive Study of Karuṇā in Indian Buddhist Literature.* PhD diss., Harvard University.

Jenkins, S. (2010/2011). "On the Auspiciousness of Compassionate Violence." *Journal of the International Association of Buddhist Studies* 33, no. 1–2: 299–331.

Jha, G., trans. (1986). *The Tattvasaṁgraha of Śāntarakṣita with the Commentary of Kamalaśīla.* Delhi: Motilal Barnasidass.

Joshi, Lal Mani, and Bhikṣu Prāsādika, ed. and trans. (1981). *Vimalakīrtinirdeśa-sūtra: Tibetan Version, Sanskrit Restoration, and Hindi Translation,* Bibliotheca Indo-Tibetica V. Sarnath: Central Institute of Higher Tibetan Studies.

Kagan, S. (1997). *Normative Ethics.* New York: Westview.

Kamalaśīla. *Commentary on the Difficult Points of the Verses on Compendium of Reality (De kho na nyid bsdus pa'i dka' 'grel/Tattvasaṁgraha-Pañjikā)*. Translated by Devendrabhadra and Grags 'byor shes rab. Toh. 4267. bStan 'gyur, sDe dge edition. Tshad ma Vol. Ze, 133b–363a.

Kamalaśīla. *Commentary on the Difficult Points of the Verses on Compendium of Reality (De kho na nyid bsdus pa'i dka' 'grel/Tattvasaṁgraha-Pañjikā)*. Translated by Devendrabhadra and Grags 'byor shes rab. Toh. 4267. bStan 'gyur, sDe dge edition. Tshad ma Vol. Ze, 133b–363a.

Katz, J. (1998). *Realistic Rationalism*. Cambridge, MA: MIT Press.

Keown, D. (2001). *The Nature of Buddhist Ethics*. New York: Palgrave.

Keown, D. (2005). *Buddhist Ethics: A Very Short Introduction*. Oxford: Oxford University Press.

Kher, V. Chitrarekha, (1992). *Buddhism as Presented by Brahmanical Systems*, Bibliotheca Indo-Buddhic Series No. 92. Delhi: Sri Satgugur Publications.

King, S. (2005). *Being Benevolence*. Honolulu: University of Hawai'i Press.

Kraut, R. (2010). "Aristotle's Ethics." *Stanford Encyclopedia of Philosophy*, http://plato.stanford.edu/entries/aristotle-ethics/ (Accessed February 21, 2012).

Lamotte, E. trans. (1976). *The Teaching of Vimalakīrti*. Translated by Sara Boin. London: Pali Text Society.

Lamrim Chenmo Translation Committee, trans. (2002). *Tsong kha pa. The Great Treatise on the Stages of the Path to Enlightenment*. Ithaca, NY: Snow Lion.

Lang, K. (1986). *Āryadeva's Catuḥśataka: On the Bodhisattva's Cultivation of Merit and Knowledge*. Copenhagen: Akademisk Forlag.

Lang, K. (2003). *Four Illusions: Candrakīrti's Advice for Travelers on the Bodhisattva Path*. Oxford: Oxford University Press.

Liland, F. (2009). *The Transmission of the Bodhicaryāvatāra: The History, Diffusion, and Influence of a Mahāyāna Buddhist Text*. PhD diss., University of Oslo.

Lindtner, C. (1987). *Nagarjuniana: Studies in the Writings and Philosophy of Nāgārjuna*. Delhi: Motilal Banarsidass.

Liu, J.-L. (2007). *An Introduction to Chinese Philosophy*. Oxford: Blackwell.

Liu, M.-W. (1982). "The Harmonious Universe of Fa-tsang and Leibniz: A comparative Study." *Philosophy East & West* 32: 61–76.

Lloyd, S., and S. Shreedhar. (2008). "Hobbes' Moral and Political Philosophy." *Stanford Encyclopedia of Philosophy*, http://plato.stanford.edu/entries/hobbes-moral/ (Accessed February 21, 2012).

Main, J. (2005). "The Karma of Others: Stories from the *Milindapañha and the Petavatthu-atthakathā*." *Journal of Buddhist Ethics* 12.

McClintock, S. (2000). "Knowing All Through Knowing One." *Journal of the International Association of Buddhist Studies* 23: 225–244.

McClintock, S. (2010). *Omniscience and the Rhetoric of Reason*. Boston: Wisdom Publications.

McKeon, R., ed. (1941/reprinted 2001). *The Basic Works of Aristotle*. New York: Modern Library.

Metzinger, T. (2010). *The Ego Tunnel: The Science of the Mind and the Myth of the Self.* New York: Basic Books.

Mitra, R., ed. (1988). *Aṣṭasāhasrikā.* Calcutta: Asiatic Society of Bengal.

Murat, L. (2011). *L'homme qui se prenait pour Napoléon: Pour une histoire politique de la folie.* Paris: Gallimard.

Myers, K. (2010). *Freedom and Self-Control: Freedom in South Asian Buddhism.* PhD diss., University of Chicago.

Nāgārjuna. *A Detailed Commentary on the Verses on Rice Seedling* (*Śālistambakavistarākh yāṭīkā/'phags pa sā lu ljang pa zhes bya ba theg pa chen po'i mDo'i rgya cher bshad pa*). Translated into Tibetan by Dharmaśrībhadra, Legs pa'i blo gros and Jñānakumāra. Revised by Dpal brtsegs. Toh. 3986. bStan 'gyur, sDe dge edition. mDo 'grel, Vol. Ngi, 20b4–55b3.

Nāgārjuna. *Fundamental Verses of the Middle Way* (*dBu ma rtsa ba'i tshig le'ur byas pa shes rab ces bya ba/Prajñā-nama-mūlamadhyamakakārikā*). Translated by Jñānagarbha and Cog ro klu'i Rgyal mtshan. Revised by Hasumati Kaśmīra, Pa tshab nyi ma grags. Rerevised by Kanaka and Pa tshab Nyi ma grags. Toh. 3824. bStan 'gyur, sDe dge edition. dBu ma Vol. Tsa, 1b–19a.

Nāgārjuna. *Verse on Rice Seedling* (*Śālistambaka-kārikā//sā lu ljang pa'i tshig le'ur byas pa*). Translated into Tibetan by Dharmaśrībhadra, Legs pa'i blogros, and Jñānkumāra. Revised by Dpal brtsegs. Toh. 3985. bStan 'gyur, Sde dge edition. mDo 'grel, Vol. Ngi, 18a3–20b4.

Nagel, T. (1989). *The View from Nowhere.* Oxford: Oxford University Press.

Nakamura, H. (1987). *Indian Buddhism: A Survey with Bibliographical Notes.* Delhi: Motilal Banarsidass.

Ñānamoli and Bodhi, trans. (1995). *The Middle Length Discourses of the Buddha: A New Translation of the Majjhima Nikāya.* Boston: Wisdom Publications.

Newland, G. (1984). *Compassion: A Tibetan Analysis.* London: Wisdom.

Newland, G. (1992). *The Two Truths in the Mādhyamika Philosophy of the Ge-luk-ba Order of Tibetan Buddhism.* Ithaca, NY: Snow Lion.

Nietzsche, F. (1969). *On the Genealogy of Morals and Ecce Homo*, trans. W. Kaufmann. New York: Vintage Books.

Nietzsche, F. (2002). *Beyond Good and Evil*, eds. R.-P. Horstmann and J. Norman (trans.). Cambridge: Cambridge University Press.

Nyanamoli, Bhikku, trans. (1976). *The Path of Purification: Visuddhimagga.* Berkeley, CA: Shambala.

Obeyesekere, G. (2002). *Imagining Karma: Ethical Transformation in Amerindian, Buddhist and Greek Rebirth.* Berkeley: University of California Press.

Oldmeadow, P. R. (1994). *A Study of the Wisdom Chapter (Prajñāpāramitā pariccheda) of the Bodhicaryāvatārapañjikā of Prajñākaramati.* PhD. diss., Australian National University.

Pagel, U, trans. (1995). *The Bodhisattvapiṭaka, Buddhica Britannica* V. Tring, UK: Institute of Buddhist Studies.

Pettit, J. (1999). "Review of *Altruism and Reality.*" *Journal of Buddhist Ethics* 6: 120–137.

Pinker, Steven. (2002). *The Blank Slate: The Modern Denial of Human Nature.* New York: Penguin.

Poussin, L, ed. (1903–1913). *Mūlamadhyamakakārikās de Nāgārjuna avec la Prasannapadā de Candrakīrti.* St. Petersburg: Academy of Sciences.

Poussin, L, ed. (1907–1912). *Madhyamakāvatāra par Candrakīrti*, Bibliotheca Buddhica 9. St. Petersburg: Academy of Sciences. Reprint, Osnabruck: Biblio Verlag, 1970.

Poussin, L, trans. (1990). *Abhidharmakośabhāṣyam.* Translated by Leo Pruden. Berkeley: Asian Humanities Press.

Powers, J., and C. S. Prebish. (2009). *Destroying Mara Forever: Buddhist Ethics Essays in Honour of Dameon Keown.* Ithaca, NY: Snow Lion Publications.

Pradhan, P., ed. (1975). *Abhidharmakośa of Vasubandhu.* Revised second edition. Edited by Aruna Haldar. Patna: K. P. Jayaswal Research Institute.

Prajñākaramati. *Bodhicaryāvatārapañjikā.* sDe dge edition.

Priest, G. (2014). *One: Being an Investigation into the Unity of Reality and of its Parts, Including the Singular Object which is Nothingness.* Oxford: Oxford University Press.

Priest, G. (2015). "The Net of Indra," in K. Tanaka, Y. Deguchi, J. Garfield and G. Priest (eds.), *The Moon Points Back.* New York: Oxford University Press.

Putnam, F. W. (2002). "Televised Trauma and Viewer PTSD: Implications for Prevention." *Psychiatry* 65: 310–312.

Red Pine, trans. (2001). *The Diamond Sutra: The Perfection of Wisdom.* Washington, DC: Counterpoint.

Reps, P., and N. Senzaki (eds.). (1971). *Zen Flesh, Zen Bones.* London: Penguin Books.

Rice Seedling Sutra. *Śālistambasūtra: Arya-sālistamba-nāma-mahāyāna-sūtra. 'Phags pa sā lu'i ljang ba shes bya ba theg pa chen po'i mdo.* D. T. Suzuki (ed.), 1995–1961. The Tibetan Tripitaka, Peking Edition. P876, vol. 34.

Rosenblum, B., and F. Kuttner. (2006). *Quantum Enigma: Physics Encounters Consiousness.* New York: Oxford University Press.

Rotman, A. (2008). *Divine Stories: Divyavadana, Part I.* New York: Columbia University Press.

Russell, B. (1904). "Russell to Frege 12.12," in G. Gabriel, H. Hermes, F. Kambartel, C. Thiel and A. Verrart (eds.), *Philosophical and Mathematical Correspondence*, English translations edited by B. McGuinness and translated by H. Kaal. Chicago: University of Chicago Press, 1980, pp. 166–170.

Saitō, Akira. (1993). "A Study of Akṣayamati (=Śāntideva)'s *Bodhisattvacaryāvatāra* as Found in the Tibetan Manuscripts from Tun-huang," Grant-in-Aid for Scientific Research (C). Mie 1993.

Saitō, Akira. (1996). "Śāntideva in the History of Mādhyamika Philosophy," in Kalpakam Sankarnarayan, Motohiro Yoritomi, and Shubhada Joshi (eds.), *Buddhism in India and Abroad: An Integrating Influence in Vedic and Post-Vedic Perspective.* Mumbai: Somaiya Publications, pp. 257–264.

Saitō, A. (2006). "Śāntideva's Critique of 'I' or Self in the Early and Later Recensions of the *Bodhi(sattva)caryāvatāra.*" *Studies in Indian Philosophy and Buddhism* 13: 35–43.

Saitō, A. (2010). "An Inquiry into the Relationship Between the Śikṣāsamuccaya and the *Bodhi(sattva)caryāvatāra*." *Studies in Indian Philosophy and Buddhism* 17: 17–24.

Śāntarakṣita. *Verses on Compendium of Reality* (*De kho na nyid bsdus pa'i tshig le'ur byas pa / Tattvasaṁgrahakārikā*). Translated by Guṇākaraśrībhadra and Lha bla ma zhi ba hod. Toh. 4266. bStan 'gyur, sDe dge edition. Tshad ma Vol. Ze, 1b–133a.

Śāntideva. (1988). *Bodhicaryāvatāra of Śāntideva with the Commentary Pañjikā of Prajñākaramati*. Buddhist Sanskrit Texts # 12. Second edition. Edited by S. Tripathi. Darbhanga: Mithila.

Śāntideva and rGyal tshab. (1999). *Byang chub sems pa'i spyod pa la 'jug pa'i rnam bshad rgyal sras 'jugs nogs*. Sarnath: Gelugpa Student Welfare Committee.

Śāntideva. (1996). *The Bodhicaryāvatāra*. Translated by Kate Crosby and Andrew Skilton. New York: Oxford.

Śāntideva. (1997). *A Guide to the Bodhisattva Way of Life*. Translated by Vesna A. Wallace and B. Allen Wallace. Ithaca, NY: Snow Lion.

Schopen, G. (2005). *Figments and Fragments of Mahāyāna Buddhism in India*. Honolulu: University of Hawai'i Press.

Schulman, D. (2012). *More than Real: A History of the Imagination in South India*. Camgridge, MA: Harvard University Press.

Shakya, M. B. (1999/2000). "Nāgārjuna on Relative Bodhicitta." *Buddhist Himalaya* 10: 1–2.

Siderits, M. (1989). "Thinking on Empty: Madhyamaka Anti-Realism and Canons of Rationality," in S. Biderman and B.A. Scharfstein (eds.), *Rationality in Question*. Leiden: E. J. Brill, pp. 231–249.

Siderits, M. (2006). "Buddhist Reductionism and the Structure of Buddhist Ethics," in P. Bilimoria, J. Prabhu, and R. Sharma (eds.), *Indian Ethics: Classical and Contemporary Challenges*. Aldershot, UK: Ashgate, pp. 283–295.

Siderits, M. (2007). *Buddhism as Philosophy*. Aldershot, UK: Ashgate.

Siderits, M. (2011). "Is Everything Connected to Everything Else? What the Gopīs Know," in Cowherds (2011), pp. 167–180.

Singer, P. (1972). "Famine, Affluence, and Morality." *Philosophy and Public Affairs* 1, no. 3: 229–243.

Singer, T., B. Seymour, J. O'Doherty, H. Kaube, R. J. Dolan, and C. Frith. (2004). "Empathy for Pain Involves the Affective but not Sensory Components of Pain," *Science* 303: 1157–1162.

Smart, J. J. C., ed. (1964). *Problems of Space and Time*. London: Macmillan.

Spiro, M. (1971). *Buddhism and Society: A Great Tradition and Its Burmese Vicissitudes*. New York: Harper and Row.

Sprung, M, trans. (1979). *Lucid Exposition of the Middle Way*. Boulder, CO: Prajñā.

Swanton. C. (2003). *Virtue Ethics: A Pluralistic View*. Oxford: Clarendon Press.

Szabo, A., and Hopkinson, K. L. (2007). "Negative Psychological Effects of Watching the News in the Television: Relaxation or Another Intervention May be Needed to Buffer Them." *International Journal of Behavioral Medicine* 14: 57–62.

Takahashi, H. (2006). *Vimalakīrtinirdeśa: A Sanskrit Edition Based upon the Manuscript Newly Found at the Potala Palace*. Tokyo: Tokya Taisho University Press.

Tanaka, K. (2014). "In Search of the Semantics of Emptiness," in J.-L. Liu and D. Berger (eds.), *Nothingness in Asian Philosophy*. London: Routledge, pp. 55–63.

Tatz, M., trans. (1986). "Asanga's Chapter on Ethics with the Commentary of Tsong-Kha-Pa." *Studies in Asian Thought and Religion*, vol. 4. Lewiston/Queenston: Edwin Mellen Press.

Tessman, L. (2005). *Burdened Virtus: Virtue Ethics for Liberatory Struggles*. New York: Oxford University Press.

Thakchöe, S. (2011). "Prāsaṅgika Epistemology in Context," in Cowherds (2011), pp. 39–56.

Thakchöe, S. (2012). "Through the Looking-Glass of the Buddha-mind: Strategies of Cognition in Indo-Tibetan Buddhism." *Octa Orientalia Vilnensia* 11, no. 1: 93–115.

Thakchöe, S. (2013). "A Reply to sTak tsang's Charge Against Tsongkhapa's uses of Pramāṇa in Candrakīrti's Philosophy," *Journal of Indian Philosophy* 41: 535–561.

Thurman, R. (1976). *The Holy Teachings of Vimalakīrti*. State College: Penn State University Press.

Tillemans, T. (2003). "Metaphysics for Mādhyamikas," in Georges Dreyfus and Sara McClintock (eds.), *The Svātantrika-Prāsaṅgika Distinction*. Boston: Wisdom, pp. 93–123.

Tillemans, Tom J. F. (2010). "Madhyamaka Buddhist Ethics." *Journal of the International Association of Buddhist Studies* 33, no. 1–2: 359–378.

Tillemans, T. (2011). "How Far Can a Mādhyamika Buddhist Reform Conventional Truth? Dismal Relativism, Fictionalism, Easy-Easy Truth, and the Alternatives," in Cowherds (2011), pp. 151–165.

Todd, W. (2013). *The Ethics of Śaṅkara and Śāntideva: A Selfless Response to an Illusory World*. Farnham, UK: Ashgate.

Tripathi, S., ed. (1998). *Bodhicaryāvatāra of Śāntideva with the Commentary Pañjikā of Prajñākaramati*. Buddhist Sanskrit Texts # 12, second edition. Darbhanga: Mithila.

Tsongkhapa. (1985). *Lam rim chen mo, Tso Ngön*. Qinghai: People's Press.

Tsongkhapa. (1987). *Rigs pa'i rgya mtsho*. Sarnath: Pleasure of Elegant Sayings.

Tsongkhapa. (1999). *Lam gyi gtso bo rnam gsum gyi rtsa ba in The Three Principal Aspects of the Path: An Oral Teaching by Gehse Sonam Rinchen*. Ithaca, NY: Snow Lion.

Tsongkhapa. (2002). *The Great Treatise on the Stages of the Path to Enlightenment*. Ithaca, NY: Snow Lion.

Tsongkhapa. (2004). *dBu ma la 'jug pa'i rgya cher bshad pa dgongs pa rab tu gsal ba (Illumination of Thought: A Detailed Commentary on [Candrakīrti's] Introduction to Madhyamaka)*. Sarnath: Gelugpa Students' Welfare Committee.

Tsongkhapa. (2006). *Ocean of Reasoning: A Great Commentary on Nāgārjuna's Mūlamadhyamakakārikā* Translated by N. Samten and J. Garfield. New York: Oxford University Press.

Tsongkhapa. (2010). *Rtsa shes dka' gnad chen po brgyad kyi brjed byang In Zab mo lta ba'i khyad par bshad pa*. Edited by Thupten Jinpa. New Delhi: Institute of Tibetan Classics.

Tucci, G. (1934). "The *Ratnāvalī* of Nāgārjuna." *Journal of the Royal Asiatic Society of Great Britain and Ireland* 307–325.

Tucci, G. (1936). "The Ratnāvalī of Nāgārjuna." *Journal of the Royal Asiatic Society of Great Britain and Ireland* 237–252, 423–435.

Vaidya, P. L., ed. (1961). *Śikṣāsamuccaya of Śāntideva*, Buddhist Sanskrit Texts 11. Darbhanga: Mithila Institute.

Vaidya, P. L. (1988). *Bodhicaryāvatāra of Śāntideva with the Commentary Pāñjikā of Prajñākaramati.* 2nd edition. Edited by Sridhar Tripathi. Darbhanga: Mithila Institute.

Vaidya, P. L. (1999). *Śikṣā-samuccaya of Śāntideva.* Darbhanga: Mithila Institute.

Vasiliou, I. (2011). *Aiming at Virtue.* Cambridge: Cambridge University Press.

Vasubandhu. *Commentary on the Treasury of Knowledge* (*Chos mngon pa'i mdzod kyi bzhad pa/Abhidharmakośabhāṣya*). Translated by Jinamitra and Dpal brtsegs rakṣita. Toh. 4090. BStan 'gyur, sDe dge edition. Mngon pa Vol. Ku, 26b–258a.

Vasubandhu. *Treasury of Knowledge* (*Chos mngon pa'i mdzod kyi tshig le'ur byas pa / Abhidharmakośakārikā*). Translated by Jinamitra and Dpal brtsegs rakṣita. Toh. 4089. BStan 'gyur, sDe dge edition. Mngon pa Vol. Ku, 1b–25a.

Vasubandhu and Yaśomitra. (1932–1936). *Sphutārthā: Abhidharmakośavyākhyā* by Yaśomitra, edited by Unrai Wogihara. Tokyo: Publishing Association of Abhidharmakośavyākhyā, [reprinted 1971], Part 2.

Vasubandhu. (2008). *Abhidharmakośa & Bhāṣya of Ācārya Vasubandhu with Sphutārthā Commentary of Ācārya Yaśomitra*, edited by Dwārikā Dās Śāstri, Swāmī. Vols. 1 & 2. Varanasi: Bauddha Bharati.

Vetter. T. (1992). "On the Authenticity of the *Ratnāvalī*." *Asiatische Studien* 46: 492–506.

Waldron, J. (2010). *Torture, Terror, and Trade-Offs: Philosophy for the White House.* Oxford: Oxford University Press.

Walker, M. U. (2007). *Moral Understandings: A Feminist Study in Ethics*, 2nd edition. Oxford: Oxford University Press.

Wallace B. A. (1999). "The Dialectic Between Religious Belief and Contemplative Knowledge in Tibetan Buddhism," in John Makransky & Roger Jackson (eds.), *Buddhist Theology: Critical Reflections of Contemporary Buddhist Scholars.* London: Curzon Press, pp. 203–214.

Wallace, V., and B. A. Wallace. (1997). *A Guide to the Bodhisattva's Way of Life by Śāntideva.* Ithaca, NY: Snow Lion.

Walser, J. (2002). "Nāgārjuna and the *Ratnāvalī*: New Ways to Date an Old Philosopher." *Journal of the International Association of Buddhist Studies* 25: 209–262.

Walser, J. (2005). *Nāgārjuna in Context.* New York: Columbia University Press.

Warren, H., ed. (1950). *Visuddhimagga of Buddhaghosācariya*, Harvard Oriental Series 41. Edited and revised by Dharmananda Kosambi. Cambridge, MA: Harvard University Press.

Westerhoff, J. (2009). *Nāgārjuna's Madhyamaka: A Philosophical Analysis.* Oxford: Oxford University Press.

Wetelsen, J. (2002). "Did Śāntideva Destroy the Bodhisattva Path?" *Journal of Buddhist Ethics* 9: 412–424.

Williams, P. (1998). *Altruism and Reality: Studies in the Philosophy of the Bodhicaryāvatāra.* London: Curzon Press.

Williams, P. (1999). "Response to John Pettit." *Journal of Buddhist Ethics* 6: 138–153.

Williams, P. (2000). *Studies in the Philosophy of the Bodhicaryāvatāra.* Delhi: Motilal Banarsidass.

Williams, P. (2009). *Mahāyāna Buddhism: The Doctrinal Foundations* (2nd ed.). London: Routledge.

Wilson, J. (1991). "Pudgalavāda in Tibet? Assertions of Substantially Existent Selves in the Writings of Tsong-kha-pa and His Follower." *Journal of the International Association of Buddhist Studies* 14, no. 1: 155–180.

Wogihara, U., ed. (1932–1936). *Sphutārthā: Abhidharmakośavyākhyā by Yaśomitra.* Tokyo: Publishing Association of Abhidharmakośavyākhyā.

Wright, D. S. (2004). "Critical Questions Toward a Naturalized Theory of Karma in Buddhism." *Journal of Buddhist Ethics* 11: 77–93.

Index

Printed in Great Britain
by Amazon

50320521R00173